AMERICAN EDUCATION

AN INTRODUCTION

Courtesy, Eastern Illinois University

AMERICAN EDUCATION

AN INTRODUCTION

REVISED EDITION

EMMA REINHARDT

HEAD, DEPARTMENT OF EDUCATION AND PSYCHOLOGY
EASTERN ILLINOIS UNIVERSITY

HARPER & BROTHERS, PUBLISHERS
NEW YORK

CONTENTS

Courtesy, Standard Oil Company (N.J.)

PART FOUR. ADMINISTRATION AND FINANCE

EDITOR'S FOREWORD
TO THE FIRST EDITION

Today public education is even more than usual the object of appraisal, reappraisal, and often heated attack. Whatever else this lively concern may indicate, it is certainly an index of the value and importance attributed to education. That it is—next to parenthood—the most important business of our country is a proposition that receives more lip service than the kind of material support commensurate with its importance.

Because of the cultural lag inherent in our dynamic society, many erroneously see education as a luxury, indulgence in which has got out of hand by way of "fads and frills." They suffer from "The Old Oaken Bucket" delusion, nostalgically affirming "How dear to my heart are the scenes of my childhood." They are oblivious to the demonstrated need and economic as well as social value of an education geared to the kind of society and world in which we now live. It is not too much to say that survival of our society, its values and way of life depend very largely upon the impact that education, broadly conceived, will have upon our citizenry. It is, in a most fundamental sense, the "bastion of democracy."

Education valid for citizens of a democracy must "see life steadily and see it whole" and must implement democratic values. Judged by each of these standards Dr. Reinhardt has written a superior book. Moreover, for one reader at least, she has injected more of human warmth than is often found in similar works. That a course in an introduction to education can be largely a dreary recital of names, dates, places, and events is attested by regretful memory of such a course. The present volume is happily in pleasant contrast. It has warmth without sacrifice of scholarship and without failure to face reality.

While Dr. Reinhardt gives the usual historical development of education in this country, she also introduces highly relevant material that in too many teacher training programs has been slighted. Notable here is the inclusion of cultural anthropological concepts. Teachers need to understand our culture and subcultures in all their complex variations if they are to teach all the children of all the people. And such understanding does not come simply from living in a culture, any more than living in a given economy makes one an economist.

The book too is written by a teacher—students are challenged. Problems and methods of solving them are well provided but pat answers are not. The appendices of selected references and audiovisual materials arranged by chapters, a list of books on teachers (autobiography, biography, and fiction), the Code of Ethics of the National Education Association of the United States, and, finally, "Then and Now," sketching our educational progress since about 1920—all of these will provide enrichment for the student and welcome aids to the teacher.

I close with a quotation from Dr. Reinhardt's text: "Whether or not we have 'tomorrows that sing' depends, finally, not upon soldiers or other wartime heroes, but upon citizens prepared to carry on peacetime activities with the same skill and devotion that our fighting men display. Whether or not we have such citizens depends in no small measure upon the work of teachers, the sculptors of new citizens."

H. H. REMMERS

EDITOR'S FOREWORD
TO THE REVISED EDITION

In this revision Dr. Reinhardt has somewhat restructured and extensively rewritten the first edition of *American Education: An Introduction*. The basic themes, however, have been retained. In evaluating its substantive content I should essentially be repeating what I said in the Foreword to the First Edition. The present edition has been brought up to date and has improved the already excellent first edition by making the present volume an even better teaching tool. Dr. Reinhardt's fine prose style "distills to the sweet substance of pellucid thought" the many aspects and complexities of American education.

Even more than a half dozen years ago, education has come to be perceived as a crucial issue of concern to our survival as an open, democratic society. Among the concrete evidences of this are the actions of the Eighty-third Congress in passing Public Law 531, authorizing the Coöperative Research Program and that of the Eighty-fifth Congress in passing the National Education Defense Act with its extensive provisions for the preparation of teaching materials, of counselors, teachers of foreign languages, science and mathematics, and the like and for evaluation of the projects to be developed in these programs.

This book again will appeal not only to those concerned with teacher preparation but to any lay citizen thoughtfully concerned with its problems.

H. H. REMMERS

PREFACE
TO THE FIRST EDITION

American Education: An Introduction is written especially for students who are preparing to teach. They are likely to be enrolled in their first course in education—a course that may well be their most significant. If it is challenging and stimulating, they may gain respect for education as an area of study that will be reflected in their subsequent professional work. They may develop pride in teaching as a calling that will lead them to recognize it as a career deserving of the talents of our most gifted people.

For several decades authors have been writing textbooks intended to give an introductory view of the broad field of education. The earliest books were often encyclopedic in scope. They touched sketchily upon a vast array of topics. Although some still follow this plan, the trend is toward the inclusion of a limited number of topics with fairly comprehensive yet not exhaustive treatment.

This volume presents an overview of education in the United States and information concerning opportunities in and requirements for teaching. Major topics chosen for consideration are the individual and the culture; educative agencies in the community; the role of the school in a democracy; the development, administration, and financial support of schools in the United States; modern elementary and secondary schools; characteristics of good teachers; certain aspects of preparation for teaching; and teaching as an occupation.

Although designed primarily for prospective teachers, this book is also useful for students not specializing in education who desire an understanding of the school in the modern social order, for teachers in service who wish to keep abreast of the times, and for public spirited laymen who seek to be informed about education in general.

The author is indebted to many writers, editors, and publishers who have generously granted permission for the use of excerpts and illustrations from their works. Specific acknowledgments are made in appropriate places throughout the book. However, her obligation to these persons is also gratefully acknowledged here.

The author wishes also to express her gratitude to the many colleagues at Eastern Illinois State College who have given valuable suggestions and assistance. Among them are Dr. Elizabeth K. Lawson, Dean of Women, who read the entire manuscript, and Dr. Arthur F. Byrnes, Director of the Audio-Visual Education Center, who prepared the list of audio-visual material.

EMMA REINHARDT

December, 1953

PREFACE
TO THE REVISED EDITION

In this revised edition of *American Education: An Introduction* the basic purposes of the original volume have been retained. However, more than half of the material has been rewritten and the general structure has been changed. To facilitate use of the unit plan of instruction, topics have been organized around four major units.

The author is indebted to many writers, editors, and publishers who have generously granted permission for the use of excerpts from their works, and to many individuals who have graciously supplied photographs. Specific acknowledgments are made at appropriate places throughout the book. However, her obligation to these persons is also gratefully acknowledged here.

The author wishes to express her gratitude to the many colleagues at Eastern Illinois University who have given valuable suggestions and assistance. Among them are Dr. Curtis Ray Garner, Associate Professor of Education, who read the entire manuscript, and Dr. Verne Allen Stockman, Associate Professor of Education and Director of the Audio-Visual Center, who prepared the list of audio-visual material.

EMMA REINHARDT

February, 1960

PART ONE

TEACHING AS A PROFESSION

Courtesy, *Look Magazine*

Courtesy, Duluth (Minnesota) Public Schools

Teaching is an art and like all arts it can be learned with varying degrees of proficiency. Some are so gifted by nature that they can perform as good teachers without learning the arts of teaching, just as some singers can have brilliant musical careers without studying voice culture. On the other hand, there are some individuals who are naturally so handicapped for a teaching career that instruction in the teaching arts can do as little for them as musical study for the tone deaf. Most teachers fall between these two extremes. It is a crime against students to permit individuals of the second kind to enter the ordinary classroom as teachers, no matter how great their gifts may be in other respects or in other fields. Whatever teaching is, it should at least not be an obstruction to learning. But it is certainly no crime, it is not even a hardship, to require of naturally gifted teachers—those who are to the teaching manner born—that they learn the formal rudiments of the art of teaching. They can always improve their skills. An enormous amount of time can be saved by familiarizing oneself with teaching devices and techniques even if one already possesses the educator's insight and an adequate educational philosophy. No one who has not actually attempted to teach the details of a curriculum can properly appreciate the great difference that mastery of specific ways and means can make in motivating interest, facilitating communication and starting a train of thought in students which runs its course to the click of understanding. There are some things that are best learned not on the job. And although we can rely on any teacher to learn by trial and error experience, why should the students pay the price for that experience?

Sidney Hook, EDUCATION FOR MODERN MAN

Part One, Teaching as a Profession, is designed to help students measure realistically the rewards in teaching with what they desire in life. It is intended to assist them in assessing the qualities that contribute to a great teacher and in realizing the kind of preparation that the calling requires. It gives a glimpse of what lies ahead when the long-awaited day of seeking employment arrives.

CHAPTER I

What Makes a Great Teacher

John Erskine once observed: "A good teacher is so rare that the rumor of him spreads with the speed of scandal." Exaggerated though this statement may be, it contains more than a grain of truth. The number of eminent teachers is never legion.

What is a teacher? What makes him great? In light as well as in serious vein, we find a multitude of answers.

In a gay mood someone contributed a fanciful answer:

To a child thrust into a strange world, a good teacher is the best thing that can possibly happen.

A teacher is Courage with Kleenex in its pocket, Sympathy struggling with a snow suit, and Patience with papers to grade.

Teachers spend 12 hours a day searching for truth and the other 12 hours searching for error.

They are incorruptible, indispensable, infallible, invincible, and nearly inexhaustible.

A teacher does not really mind sniffles, squirmings, stomach aches, spills, sloth, and sauciness. Neither does she disintegrate before tears, trifles, fights, futility, excuses, parents who spout, little boys who shout, and little girls who pout.

Most of all, a teacher is somebody who *likes* somebody else's children —and still has strength enough left to go to the PTA meeting.[1]

In a thoughtful tone another paid the teacher this tribute:

The teacher is a prophet;
    He lays the foundations of tomorrow.

[1] "What Is a Teacher?" *Journal of the National Education Association,* October, 1952, p. 450.

The teacher is an artist;
   He works with the precious clay of unfolding personality.
The teacher is a friend;
   His heart responds to the faith and devotion of his students.
The teacher is a citizen;
   He is selected and licensed for the improvement of society.
The teacher is an interpreter;
   Out of his maturer and wider life he seeks to guide the young.
The teacher is a builder;
   He works with the higher and finer values of civilization.
The teacher is a culture-bearer;
   He leads the way toward worthier tastes, saner attitudes, more gracious manners, higher intelligence.
The teacher is a planner;
   He sees the young lives before him as a part of a great system which shall grow stronger in the light of truth.
The teacher is a pioneer;
   He is always attempting the impossible and winning out.
The teacher is a reformer;
   He seeks to remove the handicaps that weaken and destroy life.
The teacher is a believer;
   He has abiding faith in the improvability of the race.[2]

Yes, a teacher is all of these things—and more. He is an actor, a psychologist, a nurse, a counselor, a foster parent, a janitor—all wrapped up into one. He is "the fount of all knowledge, the funnel for the wisdom and experience of the ages. . . ."

But what makes a teacher great? What distinguishes the memorable from the mediocre?

The concept of what a fine teacher is really like takes on new meanings continuously in different times and places. So gradual is the change, however, that a casual observer may not recognize it.

Often the teacher of an earlier day is ridiculed or criticized without taking into account the period in which he lived. The unflattering stereotype that some people have of teachers usually includes characteristics that were once approved or demanded. While we may resent the stereotype that makes the teacher a "brisk wielder of the birch and rule" or a prudish, dowdy "old maid," we must

[2] Joy Elmer Morgan, "A Tribute to the Teacher," *Educational Forum*, May, 1955, p. 416.

remember that in years not too far distant a premium was placed on stern discipline, circumspect behavior, drab, conservative attire, and (for women teachers) freedom from marital ties.

How slowly changes even in the way a teacher dresses win approval is amusingly illustrated in Virginia Church's verse entitled "Almost Human":

> The other day
> Our lady Vice-Principal
> Got onto the street car.
> She was wearing a brand-new dress.
> I heard a woman in the seat back of me
> Remark to her friend:
> "Ain't it awful the way these women dress?
> You can't tell school teachers from ladies now-a-days."[3]

APPROACHES TO THE PROBLEM OF WHAT CONSTITUTES A GOOD TEACHER

In spite of agreement that the teacher we desire for our schools is different in some respects from his predecessor, we still want to determine what constitutes a first-rate teacher. Deliberative consideration has resulted in a wealth of material concerning the characteristics of a good teacher. In recent years several hundred research studies have attempted to throw new light on the problem of measuring teaching ability and efficiency. Four approaches to the problem have been used:

1. Evaluation of *performance*. This is usually done thru observation of behavior in various types of learning-teaching situations.
2. Evaluation of *personal qualities*. Such evaluations may be inferred from studies of behavior or from paper and pencil tests.
3. Evaluation of the *mental prerequisites* of teaching efficiency—the knowledge, skills, interests, attitudes, and ideals that seem to lie back of and to control performances.
4. Evaluation of pupil *growth and achievement*. Studies of the teacher factor can usually be made concurrently with studies of the effects of other factors upon pupil growth and achievement.[4]

[3] Virginia Church, *Teachers Are People*, Wallace Hebberd, 1945, p. 26.

[4] A. S. Barr, "The Measurement of Teaching Efficiency," *Growing Points in Educational Research*, American Educational Research Association, 1949, p. 251.

Each of these methods of approach has both its strengths and its weaknesses. If pupil growth and achievement could be measured accurately, this approach would seem the most defensible. But these outcomes are difficult to measure and factors other than teacher effectiveness that influence growth and achievement are difficult, if not impossible, to control.

Observation of performance, what the teacher does, also has merit. Yet what is good in one situation may not be in another. Acts are good or bad only in relation to a specific situation and in relation to certain values. Besides there are different acceptable ways of teaching. No one procedure can be singled out as "best."

Studies of personal qualities are concerned with the kind of teachers we desire. They presuppose that we know the traits needed, can measure them, and know in what degree and combination they should exist. Such knowledge, of course, is lacking.

Attempts to relate measures of the mental prerequisites to teaching success have not proved statistically significant. However, the findings do not warrant the hasty conclusion that it matters little whether a teacher possesses low or high mental ability. Findings may conceivably show that the term teaching success has been poorly defined and that a constellation of irrelevant factors has been studied.

At present the trend is to use all four approaches. Results secured from one method are checked with those obtained from other approaches.

THREE ASPECTS OF TEACHING EFFICIENCY

An analysis of careful opinions and of research studies reveals that three aspects of teaching efficiency—personal and social traits, knowledge of subject matter, and professional preparation—have received a large amount of attention. We shall discuss them as they apply to teachers in the mid-twentieth century.

Personal and Social Traits

The prominent place given to personal and social traits both in scientific studies and in popular thinking is not surprising since much of a teacher's value comes from his personal influence. Melvin expresses the idea in these words: "Every teacher who helps human beings helps them according to his own strength. The teacher is not merely a master of incidental knowledge that can be picked up for a pittance of hours in a closet with a book. He is not merely the trickster who knows a few techniques and manipulates them in teaching. On the contrary, his every glance is a carrier of knowledge, his touch, his word, his judgment make teaching thin and mean or rich and meaningful. To teach greatly, the teacher must himself be great. . . . The teacher himself is education."

Innumerable lists of traits assumed to be determinants of teaching adequacy have been compiled. Some embody opinions of pupils. Letters submitted in the "Best Teacher" contest conducted formerly by the sponsor of the Quiz Kids program reveal children's ideas concerning "The Teacher Who Helped Me Most." After reading 90,000 entries during five years, Paul Witty of Northwestern University, originator and judge of the contest, has reported that the teachers most admired are those with a "coöperative, democratic attitude." Pupils prefer a teacher who is well adjusted and genuinely responsive in human relations. They mentioned most frequently 12 qualities of a good teacher:

1) A friendly attitude ("Miss X's class is just like one big happy family; I am not afraid of school any more"); 2) consideration for the individual ("She doesn't make a monkey out of you before everybody"); 3) patience ("She never gives up until you are able to do it"); 4) wide interests ("She brings in outside ideas and helps us to apply what we learn in our everyday lives"); 5) good manners ("There was something about his voice and his smile that made me feel good clear down to my stomach"); 6) fairness ("She gives you exactly what you deserve"); 7) sense of humor ("She puts some fun into each day so school does not seem so monotonous"); 8) good disposition ("I'm sure she must have a temper, as most people do, but I have never seen an example of it"); 9) interest in the individual ("She has helped me over a period of self-consciousness, and my improvement is due to her making me feel at ease"); 10) flexibility ("When she found she was wrong she said so, and tried something else"); 11) generosity ("Miss X acted as though she didn't know I was dumb and so I decided she'd

never find out. That's the first good report card I ever got"); 12) skill ("Suddenly I could read out of my reader. She taught me and I didn't know it").

The children had another way of describing the good teacher. They told what the good teacher doesn't do:

"She doesn't yell, holler, scream, shout; get angry, mad, furious; fly off the handle; pound the desk; fuss; fly in a rage; bite your head off."

"She doesn't have pets."

"She never makes fun of any pupil before the class."

"She doesn't wear the same dress all the time."

"He doesn't use big words."

"She doesn't talk all the time."[5]

Other lists mirror the opinions of adults. One of the most pretentious investigations of teachers' traits was made by Charters and Waples in connection with the Commonwealth Teacher-Training Study. They sought the opinions of many persons—pupils, school administrators, teachers, parents, and professors of education. From their findings, Charters and Waples compiled a list of 23 essential traits.

Perhaps the fact that compilations often include many more than 23 traits may be explained by the common practice of enumerating characteristics that belong to many outstanding teachers rather than to one teacher. Thus we may fall into the error of seeking a multitude of virtues that no one individual could reasonably be expected to possess. Anyone who realistically examines the pious pronouncements must agree with Mabel Louise Culkin: "I cannot think without pain of the morbidly industrious and highly imaginative work done by collectors of character traits for the ideal teacher. The list of virtues thus catalogued should be properly applied to angels."

In an effort to telescope and organize the overwhelming wealth of terms descriptive of a successful teacher, Barr proposed a list of 12 qualities, as follows:

1. *Resourcefulness*
   Originality, creativeness, initiative, versatility, imagination, adventurousness, progressiveness.

[5] "The Good Teacher," *Time*, August 21, 1950, p. 44.

2. *Intelligence*
   Foresight, judgment, intellectual acuity, understanding, mental ability, intellectual capacity, common sense.

3. *Emotional Stability*
   Poise, self-control, steadfastness, sobriety, reserve, dignity, non-neuroticism, emotional maturity, adjustment, constancy, loyalty, easy-going realism in facing life, not excitable, stable integrated character.

4. *Considerateness*
   Appreciativeness, kindliness, friendliness, courteousness, sympathy, tact, good-naturedness, helpfulness, patience, politeness, thoughtfulness, tolerance.

5. *Buoyancy*
   Optimism, enthusiasm, cheerfulness, gregariousness, fluency, talkativeness, sense of humor, pleasantness, carefreeness, vivaciousness, alertness, animation, idealism, articulativeness, expressiveness, wit.

6. *Objectivity*
   Fairness, impartiality, open-mindedness, freedom from prejudice, sense of evidence.

7. *Drive*
   Physical vigor, energy, perseverance, ambition, industry, endurance, motivation, purposefulness, speediness, zealousness, quickness.

8. *Dominance*
   Self-confidence, forcefulness, decisiveness, courageousness, independence, insensitiveness to social approval, self-sufficiency, determination, thick-skinnedness, self-reliance, self-assertiveness.

9. *Attractiveness*
   Dress, physique, freedom from physical defects, personal magnetism, neatness, cleanliness, posture, personal charm, appearance.

10. *Refinement*
    Good taste, modesty, morality, conventionality, culture, polish, well-readness.

11. *Cooperativeness*
    Friendliness, easy-goingness, geniality, generosity, adaptability, flexibility, responsiveness, trustfulness, warm-heartedness, unselfishness, charitableness.

12. *Reliability*
    Accuracy, dependability, honesty, punctuality, responsibility, conscientiousness, painstakingness, trustworthiness, consistency, sincerity.[6]

[6] A. S. Barr, "Characteristics of Successful Teachers," *Phi Delta Kappan*, March, 1958, pp. 282–283.

In addition to attempting to formulate a usable list of qualities, Barr also tried to define them in terms of behavior. His approach is illustrated by the definition of buoyancy.

BUOYANCY

General Definition: Resilience of spirit; ability to emerge from or elude depression: ability to stay on top in difficult situations.

RELATED CONCEPTS	DESCRIPTIVE PHRASES
Vivaciousness	Looks and acts with alertness
Enthusiasm	Makes an optimistic approach to life
Cheerfulness	Shows happy attitude
Optimism	Displays feeling that life is good
Sprightliness	Moves easily, rapidly
Gregariousness	Loves and enjoys other people
Sense of humor	Does not treat all things with dead seriousness
Animation	Alive, alert

ILLUSTRATIVE BEHAVIOR

1. The children on this particular day were depressed because the rain kept them from play. The teacher met the situation by explaining that we all like rain. It makes for brighter and fresher trees and flowers. It helps the crops, and builds a good underground water supply so we can have water to drink and irrigate with.
2. A geography teacher began her geography class enthusiastically with the comment: "Isn't this a good day for the races!" A curious student said, "What races? I don't know of any races." Teacher: "Oh, I wasn't thinking about the dog races. I was thinking of the human race." John: "What's the human race? How many races are there? Why do they call them races?"
3. It was the day after vacation. The teacher greets the class with a friendly, cheerful, "Good morning. Have you had a pleasant vacation?"
4. The teacher remembers everyone and has a good word for all. For example, she comments on Susie's new shoes and commends the poor crippled boy for the excellence of his pencil sketch of his dog.
5. To a boy who had attempted to demonstrate a complicated skill but failed, the teacher says: "Well this is not our day. We can't succeed all the time. I'm certain you will do that next time."[7]

Attempts to ascertain the relationship between the presence or

[7] *Ibid.,* p. 283.

absence of given traits and successful teaching have not been encouraging. Apparently a given trait derives significance from the total personality setting. Weakness in one trait may be compensated for by strength in another. Lack of fluency, for example, may be overlooked if one is master of his subject. This is well illustrated in the case of Louis Agassiz, who had rare ability to interest students in science but was far from fluent. "His command of English never became perfect. He always had a strong accent and frequently he had to pause and grope for the proper word. These imperfections were more than balanced by his clarity, simplicity and enthusiasm, and only endeared him further to the public." Some deficiencies, however, such as lack of honesty or dislike of children, are not offset by desirable qualities.

Emphasis on total personality rather than discrete traits should help us avoid the error of trying to cast teachers in a standard mold. Each teacher, like every other individual, is unique. We must not expect a uniform product. As Scates reminds us, "There is no particular single pattern in the form of a standardized profile which represents a good teacher. There are many combinations of traits possible which would make persons entirely acceptable to most situations. Further, special profiles will be called for by numerous special teaching conditions. An ideal balance for a school is to be looked for more in terms of the group of teachers than in any one person."

In his stimulating book, *Teacher in America*, Barzun also observes that all sorts of people may be successful teachers.

Remember you need lecturers and discussers and tutors. They can differ in endless, unpredictable ways. You can take the halt, the lame, the blind; men with speech defects or men who cannot be heard above a whisper; gross and repulsive men (at first) like my blessed mathematics instructor; men who are lazy and slow, who are bright and unstable, or incorrigible *enfants terribles*; you can even risk some who are deficient in learning, and join them to form an admirable as well as an induplicable faculty. This is possible because the students also display a variety of human traits and cannot all be reached and moved by the same spells.[8]

[8] Jacques Barzun, *Teacher in America*, Little, Brown and Company, 1945, p. 187.

A report of the National Education Association likewise points out that teachers cannot be put into one type.

There is the attractive, quickly sympathetic, alert young teacher who is always surrounded by a group of pupils who are coming back for the special response and help that the teacher is sure to give. There is the older teacher, rich in understanding and skill, to whom pupils and parents alike constantly go for counsel and information. There is the scholar-citizen who combines the best of general education and pedagogical skill with the whole-hearted devotion to the building of a better society—in local community, state, nation, and the world. There will be more and more teachers . . . of these truly professional types as the public provides conditions under which greatness of spirit and service can develop.[9]

Knowledge of Subject Matter

Although many laymen think that teachers succeed mainly because of their personal qualities, even the most ardent believer in the idea that "teachers are born and not made" usually admits that a pleasing personality alone is insufficient. To plead for personality without other qualifications is what Robert Maynard Hutchins terms "the formula for educational futilitarianism." Knowledge of subject matter is indispensable. Every teacher should have a broad cultural education in order to live a rich, meaningful personal life and contribute to the improvement of society. Like all responsible people, he must have competence in managing his own affairs and participating in social groups.

Besides a broad general education, every teacher needs mastery in the major areas in which he will teach and acquaintance with closely allied fields of learning. He must be able to draw upon a wealth of knowledge in order to teach effectively and to inspire genuine love for learning.

Professional Preparation

While academic education is basic, it is only one part of the preparation essential for a teacher. Along with it must go profes-

[9] National Education Association, *Our Children, Annual Report of the Profession to the Public*, 1946, p. 14.

sional education. The idea that "anyone who knows his subject can teach it" yields ground slowly. The knowledge and skill that old-time teachers gained through experience, often at the expense of their pupils, can be acquired in preservice preparation. That absence of professional preparation is a drawback is attested to by a successful superintendent of schools, Paul J. Misner of Glencoe, Illinois. After his graduation from high school Mr. Misner took a six-weeks' course at a nearby teachers college. This, plus his native ingenuity, was his total preparation for his teaching post in the fall. He remembers his first year of teaching as the hardest. "I learned more about the job of teaching that year than I ever did before or since. But I don't recommend starting out that way. It's too hard on the pupils." He would agree with Sidney Hook that "there are some things that are best learned *not* on the job."

The kind of academic and professional education needed by modern teachers is discussed in Chapter III.

FOUR DESCRIPTIONS OF SUCCESSFUL TEACHERS

Let us summarize by giving four descriptions of successful teachers.

A Composite Picture

The first is a composite picture based on generalizations formulated by Francis V. Rummell, formerly of the Office of Education, who interviewed a number of successful teachers. He found that all these teachers see teaching as a way to make life rich, even though they barely earn a living. They are concerned about improving the standards of their profession. They are enthusiastic about their community and have nothing whatever to say about taboos and personal liberty. Perhaps most significant of all is the following generalization:

All the teachers shared to a remarkable degree one specific quality— artistry in human relations. . . .
These teachers have a zest for the dozen-and-one times every day that they have to be quick on the intellectual trigger to keep up with the mischievous, the creative, the contradictory, the nimblewitted.

They are emotionally alive to catch the overtones of social behavior—so important with the baffled, the insecure, the hypersensitive, and the frustrated. They are zealously democratic in their methods, if we consider that true democracy is respect for the individual. Finally, they are humanitarian, or they would not care particularly about children's needs.

These teachers have a high degree of sensitivity to children's emotional problems. Again, aside from achievements in their own fields of scholarship and in varying degrees, they have something of the actor, the master of ceremonies, the lovelorn columnist, the humorist, the crusader, the public-relations expert. In all phases of their work they take the avenue marked "human relations."

Consequently they do not talk about teaching "methods" but of understanding the child and about the urgency of teaching him, by example and by precept, the principles of democratic living.[10]

Portrait of Rose Murphy

Our second description gives a picture not of a group but of an individual. Although Rummell probably did not interview Rose Murphy, an alumna of Indiana State Teachers College, she may be cited as an excellent teacher who exhibits artistry in human relations. Her portrait, sketched by Dean Grinnell, deserves a place in our gallery.

I saw Rose Murphy this noon. We chatted on Main Street for a few minutes and then sat together over a cup of coffee for another half hour. I came back to work with a lighter step and a firmer faith in my profession. What to put in this editorial had been bothering me before I left on my vacation. In fact, the imp of Unperformed Duty nagged me all around Europe. I had thought to write it before I went away, but it was still unwritten. Yet the edges of my idea had showed themselves often. In a general way I knew. Seeing Rose brought the idea to flower. She had been the subject all the time, only I had been seeing her in generalities, as the qualities of a teacher, of any good teacher. If this sounds more like a eulogy than an editorial, I'll not care. Every teacher should approve a eulogy written while the subject is alive to enjoy it. Moreover, Rose, like Hamlet, is touched with universality. . . . But to my subject.

She is as stout as ever. I wouldn't say fat. And though she has three

[10] Francis V. Rummell, "What Are Good Teachers Like?" *Education Digest*, November, 1948, p. 5.

grown daughters, she is as young looking as when I saw her first too many years ago. Her eyes sparkle with good humor and belief in people and life. Maybe that has kept her young. Certainly it wasn't laziness that did it. She has always been as willing and as tireless as a donkey engine, but she never "puts-puts" about how much work she is doing. The good life is a simple formula for her and when she tells me about it, it seems as natural and beautiful as roses and plum blossoms. Here it is: she loves children and she finds joy in helping them grow up. They are all as much her children as the three she nursed when her husband was alive and she wasn't teaching—more than a generation ago.

Exactly what subject is assigned to her is not important. When I first knew her, it was science in junior high school. Later she ran a home economics department. She kept on studying in extension classes and summer schools. She has her Master's degree now and teaches English. Her teaching reminds me of Jonathan Swift's writing and good drinking water. It accomplishes its purpose without calling attention to itself. It sneaks up on one. Her method is so closely interwoven with her knowledge of the children and of her subject that it is almost unnoticed in the pattern of learning.

But I wouldn't be writing about her for my editorial if she were only an excellent classroom teacher. That isn't why the old grads look her up when they come back to the home town; that isn't why she looks little older than her daughters and why the high school youngsters are glad to have her as a chaperone—or hiking companion; that isn't why the town has come to depend on her in so many of its youth projects; that isn't why I felt taller after I had talked with her.

Rose teaches mostly by being. I found myself repeating what Matthew Arnold said of teachers:

> ". . . souls tempered with fire,
> Fervent, heroic, and good,
> Helpers and friends of mankind."

If she ever suffered from too much ego, the tears and laughter of children took it out of her long ago. In the years I have known her, she has wept and rejoiced in hundreds of young personalities. By a wonderful paradox, though she has given kindness, fair play, honesty, ardor, faith to the formation of more than a generation of young men and women, she has more to give today than when she was a slim, almost-too-lively girl on her first job.

Emerson rebuked the world for mischoosing its heroes. We place our adulation on many who have done nothing finer than to accumulate dollars or to get elected to office. I insist that the home town has no nobler citizen than Rose Murphy. She will laugh merrily when she reads that statement and then she will be serious, wishing she could be what I say she is. She is the good teacher, and the good teacher calls home the heart to the best there is in life.

That is why Rose Murphy is the subject of this editorial.[11]

Flossie Wiley: An Unforgettable Teacher

Our third sketch is the tribute of a former student to Flossie Wiley of Champaign, Illinois, whom he singles out as an unforgettable teacher.

My first notice of Miss Wiley was a school-yard warning after I started first grade at Leal, "Better not do that or you'll be sent up to see Miss Wiley." Later, in my room, I saw her for the first time, as she stepped down from her principal's office to greet the new students. She spoke in a friendly way, but I was frightened by her. I had heard about that paddle in Miss Wiley's office, and that firm mouth spoke to me as it did to even the biggest boys in the school: This was a woman who was not to be pushed around.

Thus Miss Wiley was not a teacher who won instant popularity among her school-children. Instead, full appreciation came slowly— but lastingly.

First, then, you were a bit awed by her. Later, particularly after you were exposed to her capable teaching methods, you grew to respect and like her. (I, for one, consciously leaned on the knowledge gained in her sixth grade history class—both in high school and college.) And, as time went on and you and your family were touched by the great warmth that burned within this woman, you came to accord to her that admiration which now is being reflected in honors that flow from the heart of an appreciative community.

For there is something more about Miss Wiley that you must understand. In commenting on her retirement this spring, a school board official said: "Whenever there was a catastrophe in a family of one of her pupils, Miss Wiley was the first one there with her apron on. She made herself a part of the lives of all her children and their families, always serving beyond what was her duty as a principal or teacher."

Miss Wiley, you see, is of a vanishing breed. She had been told, during her school training, that the ideal teacher puts aside all thought of her private life and, instead, devotes her life to the community. This concept, she acknowledges, is an old-fashioned idea and, perhaps,

[11] J. E. Grinnell, "Rose Murphy," *Indiana Teachers College Journal*, October, 1948, p. 1.

much too demanding on the individual teacher. But it has been a way of life for her.

And just as she always helped the neighbor in trouble, Miss Wiley also gave special love and attention to the children who needed it: those from homes where there was little guidance or affection.

A home-spun philosophy, received from her grandparents, also motivated Miss Wiley through the years. "They told me," she says, "that you can't be strong for yourself unless you are strong for other people." And in thus giving to others, she has made her own life very full.

While Miss Wiley has been flexible enough to change her methods with the years (no more paddle, of course!), and while she says that teaching today is vastly improved over a generation ago, she still believes that teachers could give a little more of their lives to the community than they do.

For instance, she is sympathetic to the remark made by a student to her mother: "Mother, it made me feel so bad to see my teacher sitting in the drug store smoking and talking so loudly."

She feels that although communities should not make undue inroads into the private lives of teachers, there still remains an obligation on the part of the teacher to set a very special example in the community.

Miss Wiley has set a wonderful example in this community. And a grateful city has answered: "Well done, exceedingly well done."[12]

Miriam Sander of Webster Groves, Missouri

We present our fourth sketch in the words of Clarissa Start, columnist for the *St. Louis Post-Dispatch*, who chooses her son's first-grade teacher as her own "teacher of the year."

What makes a good teacher? First of all, she has not only the acquired skills but the knack of teaching. In an earlier column, I wrote of our delight and that of other parents at the way our children were learning to read, not just the familiar words by sight but unfamiliar words by phonics.

During the winter months when we "played school" at night, we learned much about Miss Sander through imitation as her pupil demonstrated how you could make one word from another, or explained an arithmetic competition in which the champion met the challengers. Often I marveled at how she could instill such enthusiasm year after year, class after class.

[12] Godfrey Sperling, Jr., "Flossie Wiley: An Unforgettable Teacher," *Christian Science Monitor*, June 5, 1956, p. 18.

Also, Miss Sander is a perfectionist. Sloppy work does not merit the coveted red penciled "C." We tried to soothe disappointment one night by explaining that one wrong problem out of 10 wasn't so bad, this was 90 per cent and in college 90 per cent is A, and so on. We were told sternly, "In Miss Sander's class, one mistake means the whole page is wrong." And then I recalled Miss Sander saying in an early conference, "It's important that the children develop good work habits in first grade. If we let them slip through now, they'll be poor students in high school."

Miss Sander is a strict disciplinarian and hooray for that. There is no bedlam, no unruliness in her room on any occasion and once at a public meeting where behavior was appalling, I noticed you could single out her pupils in contrast. Some may think this is robbing the little dears of their traditional right to be demons. I think it's civilizing.

But most important, she teaches idealism. Sophisticates might smile at such admonitions as, "We try, don't cry"; "Good citizens are kind and thoughtful"; "God has given us a beautiful earth to live on and we should try to make our world better"; "We all have equal shares of time. Our happiness and success depend on how we use our time"; "Useful children are happy children." But to the first grader, or to any of us, these are great truths by which to live.[13]

A SELF-SURVEY

Now that you have read about the characteristics of good teachers, try to appraise your own aptitude for teaching. Use the following self-rating scale prepared by the Central Washington College of Education. Ask a mature person to help you judge the accuracy of your rating. After you have taken the self-examination, ask yourself these questions:

1. To what extent do I possess the qualities necessary for success in teaching?
2. In what qualities do I rank low?
3. How will my low rating in these qualities affect my probable success as a teacher?
4. What plan shall I follow to overcome my deficiencies?
5. Do I need try-out experiences to aid me in deciding whether or not I should choose teaching as a career?

[13] Clarissa Start, "Naming Her Own 'Teacher of the Year,'" *St. Louis Post-Dispatch*, May 23, 1958, Part Six, p. 2.

A Self-Rating Scale for Determining Fitness for Teaching[14]

	Never	Seldom	Sometimes	Often	Always
I. LEADERSHIP ABILITY					
1. Have you served as leader in student groups; i.e., have you held an office, taken part in programs, or led discussions?					
2. Do your fellow students respect your opinions?					
3. Do they regard you as a leader?					
4. Do your fellow students ask you for help and advice?					
5. Do you sense how others feel; i.e., whether they approve certain proposals, or like or dislike certain persons?					
6. Do you try to make others happy by listening to what they say, and by being courteous, friendly, and helpful?					
7. Do you succeed in getting others to follow your suggestions without creating friction or ill will?					
II. HEALTH AND PHYSICAL FITNESS					
1. Do you have good health?					
2. Do you have lots of vitality? Can you stand to do hard physical tasks or nerve-racking work?					
3. Can you engage in activities which others in your group customarily do?					
4. Do you give others the impression that you are physically fit, well-groomed, and attractive in personal appearance?					
5. Do you keep cheerful and even-tempered even when tired or ill?					

[14] Reprinted from *You'd Like Teaching*, 1946 College Bulletin, College of Education, Central Washington College, Ellensburg, pp. 31–35.

	Never	Seldom	Sometimes	Often	Always
III. GOOD SCHOLARSHIP					
1. Have you maintained a better-than-average record in high school?					
2. Are you interested in the subjects you have taken or are taking in high school?					
3. Do you enjoy studying and find it easy to concentrate when you do study?					
4. Do you express your ideas well before a class or public group?					
5. Is it easy for you to explain things so that others understand and can follow your directions?					
IV. INTELLECTUAL TRAITS AND ABILITIES					
1. Are school subjects easy for you?					
2. Do you spend time finding out more about a topic discussed in class or covered in an assignment?					
3. Do you read books or magazine articles on current topics?					
4. Do you like to work out ideas "on your own"?					
5. Do you suggest new ideas or plans which can be carried out by school groups?					
V. EMOTIONAL STABILITY					
1. Are you an even-tempered, cheerful, happy sort of person?					
2. Can you "take it" without getting angry or upset?					
3. Do you keep from worrying and feeling depressed?					
4. Are you naturally patient with and tolerant of others?					

A SELF-RATING SCALE FOR DETERMINING
FITNESS FOR TEACHING (*Continued*)

	Never	Seldom	Sometimes	Often	Always
5. Are you objectively critical of yourself?					
6. Do you see the humorous side of everyday happenings even when you yourself are involved?					
VI. SOCIAL ASPIRATIONS					
1. Are you interested in the problems other people meet and do you want to help them solve them?					
2. Are you interested in finding ways by which you can help improve human living?					
3. Do you like people—especially children?					
4. Do you set high social standards for yourself and seek to reach and maintain these standards?					
5. Do you coöperate readily with other people in socially desirable activities?					
6. Are you willing to make sacrifices and to endure inconveniences to reach a goal you consider worthy?					

SUMMARY

Investigators have sought through research to ascertain the characteristics of a good teacher. Four major approaches to the problem have been employed: evaluation of performance, evaluation of personal qualities, evaluation of mental prerequisites, and evaluation of pupil growth and achievement. Each of these methods has certain limitations as well as strengths. The present trend is toward using all of them and checking the results obtained from one method with those derived from other approaches. Three aspects of teaching efficiency—personal and social traits, knowledge of subject matter, and professional preparation—have received special attention. Consideration of personal traits should emphasize total personality rather than separate traits. Many combinations of traits are entirely acceptable. Teachers should be good representatives of our social order, but they should not be expected to conform to a uniform pattern. In addition to possessing suitable personal and social qualities, teachers need academic and professional education. Word portraits of certain teachers who rank high in desirable characteristics are presented. In order that students may appraise their own aptitudes for teaching, a self-rating scale is included.

QUESTIONS AND EXERCISES

1. After you have checked the self-rating scale in this chapter, decide upon a trait that you wish to improve. Map out a plan for improvement and follow it for six weeks. Write a report of your progress.
2. Summarize the main ideas in the article, "How Do We Know a Good Teacher?" by Barbara Biber and Agnes Snyder, *Childhood Education*, February, 1948, pages 281–285.
3. Have a forum discussion on the question: Should the conduct and character of teachers be above the average of other responsible people in the community?
4. Write an essay on the subject, "The Teacher Who Has Helped Me Most."
5. Are there significant differences in desirable personal traits for elementary, secondary, and college teachers?
6. Read the life story of a successful teacher. Select the personal traits that contributed to his distinction. *Great Teachers*, edited by Houston Peterson, contains vivid sketches from biographies of stimulating teachers.
7. Invite a superintendent of schools to talk to your class on "The Kind of Teachers We Need."
8. Select a motion picture, a radio program, and a television program that portray a teacher. Is the portrayal such as to encourage young people to choose teaching as a career?

SELECTED REFERENCES

Barr, A. S., *et al.*, "The Measurement and Prediction of Teaching Efficiency: A Summary of Investigations," *Journal of Experimental Education*, June, 1948, pp. 1 ff.

Barzun, Jacques, *Teacher in America*, Little, Brown and Company, 1945.

Biber, Barbara, and Snyder, Agnes, "How Do We Know a Good Teacher?" *Childhood Education*, February, 1948, pp. 281–285.

Charles, Don C., "The Stereotype of the Teacher in American Literature," *Educational Forum*, March, 1950, pp. 299 ff.

Commission on Teacher Education, *Teachers for Our Times*, American Council on Education, 1944.

Corey, Fay L., *Values of Future Teachers*, Bureau of Publications, Teachers College, Columbia University, 1955.

Jersild, Arthur T., *When Teachers Face Themselves*, Bureau of Publications, Teachers College, Columbia University, 1955.

John Dewey Society, *Teachers for Democracy*, Fourth Yearbook, Appleton-Century-Crofts, Inc., 1940.

John Dewey Society, *The Teacher and Society*, First Yearbook, Appleton-Century-Crofts, Inc., 1937.

Jordan, Hoover H., "The 'C' Student as a Teacher," *Educational Forum*, November, 1949, pp. 69 ff.

Peterson, Houston (ed.), *Great Teachers*, Rutgers University Press, 1946.

Riley, John W., Jr., Ryan, Bryce F., and Lifshitz, Marcia, *The Student Looks at His Teacher*, Rutgers University Press, 1950.

Rummell, Francis V., "What Are Good Teachers Like?" *School Life*, June, 1948, pp. 4 ff.; and July, 1948, pp. 7 ff.

Wilson, Louise Ada, "Do Children Know the Best Teachers?" *Educational Forum*, November, 1948, pp. 63 ff.

AUDIO-VISUAL MATERIALS

Films

Teaching (11 minutes, Sound, B & W, Mahnke Productions). Discusses contributions of teachers to American democracy, traits of a good teacher, attractions in teaching, educational requirements, and various types of positions.

Who Will Teach Your Child? (24 minutes, Sound, B & W, McGraw-Hill Book Company, Inc.). Raises three important questions: (1) How can we attract people of superior ability to teaching? (2) How should these people be trained? (3) Once trained, how can they be persuaded to stay in the profession?

Recordings

Characteristics of a Good Teacher (30 minutes, 33⅓ rpm, Educational Recording Services). A. S. Barr of the University of Wisconsin describes the personal qualities and competencies of a good teacher and some of the difficulties involved in rating teachers.

Teachers Are People Too (15 minutes, Tape, Indiana University). Portrays teachers as sincere human beings who have spent years in preparation for their calling.

CHAPTER II
Invitation to Teaching

IMPORTANCE OF CHOICE OF LIFEWORK

Choosing a lifework is probably the most momentous single decision that any person has to make. On it depends the pattern of his day-by-day living. Within limits it determines his associates, his home surroundings, his hobbies, his community activities, and his pride and satisfaction in his work. A wise choice determines whether or not he will live eagerly and purposefully, enthusiastically facing the demands of each new day.

Yet, in spite of the significance of the choice, many people embark blindly on their lifework. They seem as naïve as the boy who wanted to be a retired businessman or the girl who aspired to be the widow of a banker. Some base their selection on the glamour that surrounds certain callings. The crisp white uniform of a nurse, the beauty of an airline hostess, the luxurious office of a business executive, the plaudits of the multitude for an athlete all have tremendous appeal. Some people are swayed by talking with a person who, happy in his own work, feels impelled to convert all who come his way. Others are influenced by their admiration for an acquaintance, whether he be a teacher, lawyer, physician, bricklayer, or farmer. Still others are lured by advertisements in newspapers or magazines or by announcements on radio or television. Propaganda to win recruits for certain callings, such as aviation and nursing, is often persuasive. And still other people are led into work by mere propinquity or by force of economic necessity.

Once a person has entered a field he may be bound by chains

forged by his lack of foresight. Especially in semiprofessional and professional occupations he can ill afford to waste the time and money invested in his preparation. The exercise of care and wisdom in his selection may spare him vain pining for what might have been.

Preparatory to making a choice, a young person should endeavor to study all pertinent factors. First, he should acquire an understanding of his aptitudes, abilities, and interests. Second, he should seek a clear knowledge of the nature of the work itself, its requirements, advantages and disadvantages, opportunities, and rewards. He should then strive to reason soundly, basing his thinking on the relations of these groups of facts.

This chapter is intended to assist the student who is contemplating teaching as a career. It attempts to stimulate him in his process of self-discovery, and to aid him in his quest for information about teaching.

APTITUDES, PERSONAL ABILITIES, AND INTERESTS

In scrutinizing his aptitudes, abilities, and interests the student may well refer to Chapter I, where the personal qualities basic for teachers were discussed. He should decide as fairly and as objectively as possible to what extent he now possesses these qualities or can probably cultivate them.

To be sure, no teacher has all these characteristics in exactly the right proportion. Strength along certain lines may offset or balance weakness in others. A person may not have perfect health; yet, by sensibly conserving his strength, he may stand the strain of teaching better than a more robust person who expends his energy unwisely.

The student should not convince himself too easily that his deficiencies in some traits are counterbalanced by his excellence in others. If he ranks uniformly low, and if he thinks it unimportant or impossible to remedy his shortcomings, he should turn to fields where personal characteristics are less significant than in teaching.

In sizing up his competence for teaching, the student is not limited to his own opinions or the personal judgment of a coun-selor. Doubtless he has taken tests administered by the personnel staff of his college—tests of intelligence, achievement, emotional stability, aptitudes, interests, and physical fitness. For interpreta-tion of his scores, he must rely on his counselor. Although such tests are not infallible, they should not be dismissed lightly.

Although a student may be interested in something for which he has little or no aptitude, his likes and dislikes are one of the best indicators of possible success in an occupation. Of course, interests are flexible. Work that once seemed dull and boring may become engrossing and challenging. In general, however, a student who views teaching with distaste should choose another calling.

Personal likes and dislikes probably partially account for the dis-agreements about teaching revealed by the National Education Association in 1944. Out of 3731 urban and 692 rural teachers, 12 percent in each group regarded teaching as "the most adventurous, the most exciting, the most thrilling of all professions." By way of contrast, 1 percent of the urban and 2 percent of the rural teachers in the group checked "I seldom enjoy teaching." In a study con-ducted in 1956 by the National Education Association, out of 5602 teachers 48 percent stated that if they could go back to their college days and start over again, they would certainly become teachers, and 25 percent would probably become teachers. Only 4.8 percent said that they certainly would not become teachers.

It may be largely a matter of interests that causes one person, on reaching the retirement age, to look back on his life as one of drudgery whereas another says, "It has been a good life. I would not change if I had to live it all over."

Fortunately, students may have had some experience in working with children. They may have had the informal experience of teaching a younger brother or sister a game or a story, or the somewhat more formal experience of teaching a Sunday-school class or assisting with such groups as Girl Scouts, Boy Scouts, Camp Fire Girls, Junior Red Cross, or 4-H Clubs.

Miss America of 1947, then Barbara Jo Walker and a student at

Memphis (Tennessee) State College, found her interest in teaching through church work. She wrote: "While in my teens I taught in the primary department of our church school. Working with those small children was a revelation. To my surprise, I could hold their attention. I loved them, and they returned my love. Like my mother, who taught many years, I discovered real enjoyment in teaching."

Some high schools offer seniors who aspire to teaching an opportunity to explore their interests. In the high school at Decatur, Illinois, a course called Vocational Exploration in Group Work with Children gives last-semester seniors a chance to see if they like a vocation that involves group work with children. Students may elect a five-hour course which takes them into an elementary school classroom one hour each day to observe and to participate in work under the direction of competent personnel. They are furnished enriching experiences, not simply clerical and routine tasks. To acquaint them with different age groups they are assigned to a new grade level every six weeks. Their principal activities are:

1. Locating, securing, arranging materials for
   a. bulletin boards
   b. reference reading
   c. supplementary reading
   d. audio-visual equipment
2. Learning how to operate and use
   a. duplicating machines
   b. audio-visual equipment
3. Assisting in the administration and checking of tests
   a. group mental
   b. group achievement
4. Carrying on remedial work with individual students following the teacher's diagnosis and recommendations in
   a. spelling
   b. arithmetic
   c. reading
   d. written composition

5. Working with groups of children in
    a. directing games
    b. telling stories
    c. directing social studies
    d. directing dramatic play

As a basis for evaluation, the following rating scale was devised at Decatur:

VOCATIONAL EXPLORATION IN GROUP WORK WITH CHILDREN

Evaluation of High School Student's Work

Name of Student ....
School ....Grade ....Subject Matter........

I. *Personal Appearance*

C	B	A ....
Clean, not always careful about clothing. Not always appropriate.	Clean, usually careful about clothing. Usually suitable for the occasion.	Neat, well groomed. Appropriately dressed at all times.

II. *Punctuality*

C	B	A ....
Sometimes arrives after the class has started and sometimes has to hurry to "beat the bell."	Usually on time. Has a few finishing touches to put on the plans for the day. Busy arranging materials for the class.	Always on time. Ready for the day. Interested and attentive to the children.

III. *Performance of Assigned Task*

C	B	A ....
Sometimes has to have further directions and does not always complete attempted task.	Usually follows the directions well and completes the attempted task. Occasionally suggests ways for working procedure.	Follows directions quickly and often devises ways of working more effectively and efficiently.

EVALUATION OF HIGH SCHOOL STUDENT'S WORK (*Continued*)

IV. *Initiative*

C	B	A ....
Active. Does what is required. Sometimes senses what is needed and goes ahead without waiting to be told what to do.	Does what is required very well. Offers suggestions rather frequently. Often senses what is needed and goes ahead without waiting to be told what to do.	Energetic. Does more than is required. Originates new plans and carries them to completion. Usually senses what is needed and does it without being told.

V. *Ability to Work with Children*

C	B	A ....
Accepted by most of the children. They do not seek his help.	The children understand his explanations and appreciate his help.	Welcomed by the children. Often share their findings and questions with him.

VI. *Ability to Work with Adults*

C	B	A ....
Is liked by others. Accepts suggestions. Makes a reasonable effort to put suggestions into effect. Does not encourage suggestions.	Works well as a member of a group. Usually accepts opinion of the majority. Carries a fair share of the load.	Always welcomed by others. Encourages suggestions. No annoying mannerisms. Does not ask for special favors.

VII. *Use of Language and Voice*

C	B	A ....
Usually chooses words which are sufficiently discriminating to convey differences in meaning. Sentence structure is usually correct. Expression is neither stimulating nor tiresome. Voice usually carries to the back of the room and is understood by the children.	Words are often colorful and descriptive. Sentences are usually accurate and forceful but do not reflect a high degree of originality. There is variety in expression but there is need for a greater feeling of freedom and relaxation. Voice clear and easily understood.	Words are colorful and descriptive. Sentences are always accurate and forceful. There is variety of expression. Animation and stimulation. Voice pleasant and easily understood.

SUMMARY

What contributions has the Helping Student made to the class and
the room?
What is the average grade of the student? C .... B .... A ....
Attendance ....
Days absent ....

FACTORS PERTAINING TO TEACHING

Besides appraising his abilities and interests, the student should
weigh factors pertaining to teaching itself. He may be confused by
contradictory information. On the one hand he finds the drab
features of teaching magnified. Even some of his teachers say,
"Whatever you do, don't teach." On the other hand he finds only
the enticing aspects accented. He meets people who regard teaching as "such easy work." Theirs is the attitude reflected in an
unknown author's verses entitled "Teachin'":

Jest a settin' in a school room in a great big easy chair,
And keepin' things a movin' with a lordly sort of air;
Not a thing to do but askin' lot of questions from a book,
Spectin' kids to know the answers though they're not allowed to look,
That's teachin'!
Jest a drawin' great big money an' a livin' like a lord,
Jest a makin' folks pay taxes from their hard earned stored up hoard,
Keeps them buyin' books and fixin's that they noways really need,
Snap, I'll say so, Gosh Almighty, easiest livin' ever seed,
That's teachin'!

Certification

One of the first factors in teaching that the student should consider is whether he is willing to undertake a long and specific professional education. Furthermore, he should realize that the time
required for preparation is increasing.

Certification demands have changed drastically since colonial
days when determination of qualifications for teachers rested almost exclusively in the hands of local school boards. Oral examinations, frequently based on questions entirely irrelevant to ability
to teach successfully, were given.

The experience of a candidate who presented himself to the school committee in Champaign County, Illinois, in the early part of the nineteenth century, was not unusual:

"I understand that it is necessary to get a certificate from you," said the candidate.

"Yes," replied the commissioner, "you can't get nothing fer teachin' 'thout a certificate from me. Come in and set down. Do you see that there show bill up on the wall?"

"Yes."

"What is that thar long word in the middle of the show bill?"

"That is 'Phantasmagoria.' "

"Is that so? Well, anybody that kin pernounce that word kin tech school in this deestrict. I've been tryin' to pernounce it fer some time, but couldn't make it. I'll give you a certificate."

A certificate issued in Marion County, Illinois, in 1848 to Middleton Bradley is typical of the times. On the certificate the following was written in longhand: "I, J. R. Ryman School Commissioner of Marion Co. Ill. having examined, Middleton Bradley; certify that he is moderately qualified To teach Orthography, Reading; Writing, and Arithmetic in part. Trustees of schools please, satisfy themselves of his moral character, and certify it; as I do not know what it is. Given under my hand this 8th day of Sept. A.D. 1848 J. R. Ryman S.C.M.C."

Even a quarter of a century ago many teachers had no special training. In 1931–1932 in Illinois, 126 teachers had no training above the elementary school, and 842 had less schooling than required for graduation from a four-year high school. Of 9873 teachers in one-room country schools, 2919 had not gone beyond the four-year high school. Only 309 in the one-room schools were college or university graduates, and 308 more were within one year of graduation.

But low as the standards were in Illinois, they were probably lower in many other states. In commenting on the situation, the State Superintendent of Public Instruction in Illinois wrote: "Unfortunately we have no comparable data from the other states . . . but we feel sure that such comparison in most states of the Union would be favorable to Illinois."

Today the period required for preparation is relatively long and certification requirements are fairly high. Issuance of certificates is no longer a prerogative of local, district, or county boards, but it is instead a state function. Few teachers secure their certificates by examination; most of their certificates are based upon college credits.

The would-be teacher should acquaint himself with special certification requirements in the field and in the state in which he expects to work. Although he is permitted to teach if he meets legal requirements, they represent only minimal standards. The best positions ordinarily demand much higher qualifications than those required for certification. At present, 48 states require at least four years of college to teach in high school (two states require five years of college). Thirty-nine states require four years of college for elementary teachers.[1]

Cost of Preparation

With the rigorous years of preparation for teaching inevitably goes cost. Obviously expenses are not the same in all institutions. Usually they are found to be lowest in tax-supported schools. Tuition fees in private colleges and universities are often high. At present, expenses for a year in most teacher-education institutions are likely to range from $1000 to $1500 or more. A student can obtain precise information about a specific college by consulting the catalogue or by writing to the registrar.

Scholarships and loan funds enable some students to continue in school. Part-time employment is frequently available. Students may even complete their formal education after they begin to teach.

Outlook for Employment

Before embarking on his professional education, a prospective teacher will wish to know about the outlook for securing employ-

[1] National Commission on Teacher Education and Professional Standards, National Education Association, A Manual on Certification Requirements for School Personnel in the United States, 1957 edition, p. 19.

ment. He is concerned not only about current conditions but also about the long-range outlook. He may want information, too, about opportunities in different parts of the country and in different communities.

It goes without saying that teaching is an essential line of work. Although the number of positions fluctuates slightly during booms and depressions, teachers are less likely to be unemployed in slack times than are workers in luxury lines.

Furthermore, teaching is the largest of the occupations which require college training and professional or semiprofessional skill. It engages the services of over 1,300,000 persons.

For the foreseeable future the chances of securing employment are good. The rise in birth rate in recent years has created an unprecedented demand for teachers. In 1956, the United States Public Health Service reported 4,220,000 live births. This was nearly 390,000 more than in 1951. By 1958, total elementary and secondary school enrollment had reached an all-time high of over 34 million—an increase of 41.5 percent over 1948–1949. Over this ten-year period the total instructional staff increased an average of 4 percent a year.

New teachers are required to care for increased enrollments, to replace emergency teachers, to reduce class size, to add necessary services, and to replace those who leave the profession. There will be positions open for 125,000 to 150,000 newly qualified public elementary and secondary teachers each year through 1965.

The number of college students currently finishing courses entitling them to certification under the laws of their respective states is too small to meet the demands for teachers. In 1959, only 125,-710 college graduates were qualified for teaching. Of this number nearly one-fourth did not accept teaching positions. Because of higher salaries many seniors, particularly foreign language, mathematics, and science majors, went into private industry. Of the 125,710 qualified members of the class of 1959, 78,220 were potential high school teachers. This represented a serious imbalance between the number needed for elementary and high school teaching positions. There are some 809,196 elementary and 482,733 high school teaching positions in the public schools and the ratio is likely to remain the same. Moreover, the replacement requirements of elementary school teachers are much higher than those of secondary school teachers. Hence, the colleges should be producing at least five new elementary for every three new high school teachers rather than the reverse as is now the trend.

An imbalance also exists within the group prepared for high school teaching as to distribution of the new teachers among the high school teaching fields. In some cases, such as art and men's physical education, the potential new supply outnumbers the positions filled by new teachers. In other cases, such as mathematics and English, the newly employed teachers outnumber the emerging college graduates.

So many factors affect the relationship between demand and supply, however, that the need for teachers cannot be accurately predicted. Comparison of the number of positions to be filled with the number of teachers certificated annually tells only part of the story. Some who are certificated never teach and others teach only a few years. Both groups constitute a potential teacher reserve.

Opportunities for Advancement

Ambitious young people are interested not only in the outlook for employment but also in chances for advancement. They look forward to securing eventually a better type of position than their first.

For successful teachers who have had suitable preparation and demonstrate continued professional growth, teaching is not a blind-alley job. Advancement is more than likely to come to those who prove their worth.

The avenues to better positions are legion. A teacher may begin in a small school system and then, from time to time, take more desirable positions in other communities. Or he may stay in the same school system and through merit and effort receive promotions within the system. Often he is transferred to an administrative or supervisory position. Unfortunately, a topnotch teacher is all too frequently rewarded with such an appointment rather than with a position that will utilize his teaching skill fully. An outstanding teacher who prefers to remain in the classroom should be given the same recognition and salary that would be his in an administrative or supervisory post.

Working and Living Conditions

Physical Surroundings and Health Conditions. A teacher has a right to ask about the physical surroundings in which he will work and live. The school plants in progressive communities are cheerful and well designed, with up-to-date equipment and high standards for heating, lighting, ventilation, and cleanliness. However, the shocking neglect of school buildings in many districts bears witness to the truth of this charge:

"We are still in the era of inadequate and dirty toilets, inadequate facilities for food and rest. It is physically possible to do effective teaching in an uncomfortable environment, but the chances are against it. Industry, unlike many boards of education, is not laughing about complaints of monotony, drabness, and dirt."[2]

Living conditions, like the immediate school surroundings, tend to vary inversely with the size of the community. They are dependent, too, on the amount that a teacher can afford to pay. Even before the housing shortage became acute, a teacher often had difficulty in finding homelike quarters. Now the problem is even more baffling. For a single teacher a bleak spare bedroom rented by a reluctant householder must often suffice. In small communities the lack of inviting eating places is even more of a drawback than substandard housing.

Despite the fact that the physical surroundings in which a teacher works and lives are often far from utopian, teaching has a favorable place among the professions and white-collar occupations with respect to physical and health hazards. Many school boards

[2] Dorothy McCuskey, "Teacher-Community Cooperation," *Journal of the National Education Association*, December, 1948, p. 596.

provide for periodic health examinations for their employees. Teachers are considered good risks for all types of insurance.

Apparently, teachers as a group consider themselves healthy. In a study made by the National Education Association in 1944, nearly five thousand teachers were asked to give an estimate of the general condition of their health—excellent, good, fair, or poor. "Only a microscopic fraction reported poor health; less than 10 percent of any group reported merely fair health. Fifty-four percent of the urban and 48 percent of the rural teachers reported excellent health."

However, teaching is a sedentary occupation which entails considerable nervous tension. Accordingly teachers need recreation and outside activities that differ from those connected with school work.

Teaching Load, Hours of Work, Vacations. Just how exhausting is the nervous strain in teaching is contingent in part upon the teaching load. Not only for its influence on a teacher's general health and morale but for its bearing upon his efficiency, the load is a matter of the utmost concern. Myriad factors are involved in computing a teacher's load: total pupil hours, size of classes, number of classes per day, hours of preparation, length of school day, demands of the community outside of school, number of problem children, assignment of classes in various fields, and extracurricular responsibilities. In the last analysis the teacher himself is the one who can best tell how much of a load he can carry, because teachers, pupils, and situations differ.

Although an enrollment of not more than 25 to 30 pupils per teacher in the elementary school is ordinarily deemed desirable, many classes far exceed these numbers. According to a report of the Research Division of the National Education Association in 1957–1958, in the 411,601 elementary-school classes the most frequently found size—30 pupils—was reported for 32,688 classrooms. At one extreme were nearly 4000 classes with no more than 15 children in each class. At the other extreme were 1000 classes with 50 to 55 pupils, and 400 classes with 56 or more children in each.

Three of the items in Raleigh Schorling's "An Evolving Bill of Rights for Teachers" relate to teacher load:

1. The right to teach classes that are not too large—in general, from ten to twenty pupils.
2. The right to have time in the school day for planning.
3. The right to a 45-hour week.

Perhaps to laymen a plea for a 45-hour week seems superfluous, for to anyone who has never taught school a teacher's hours seem short. School is in session only six hours a day five days a week. But untold hours must be spent on tasks related to school work. A study published in 1951 by the Research Division of the National Education Association revealed that the actual instruction of pupils takes little more than half of the average teacher's working time. Nearly as many hours go into correcting papers, preparing lessons, performing study hall and monitor duties, making reports, and sponsoring activities. These and other duties—attending conferences; participating in community activities; supervising playgrounds; making collections for milk money, charitable drives, etc.; taking care of lunchroom duties; helping pupils make up work; and conferring with parents—give teachers grounds for feeling that their work is never done.

To many teachers a five-day week and liberal vacations are alluring features. Often, however, they use the summer for attending summer school, traveling, or working, sometimes in lines related to school, such as summer camps.

The disadvantage of receiving no salary during long vacations is offset by the practice in some school systems of employing teachers on a 12-month basis. Where teachers are employed on this basis, the board of education may require them either to render some service, such as assisting in developing curriculum materials or directing educational and recreational activities, or to pursue in-service education by participating in workshops, attending summer school, or traveling.

Social and Professional Associates. The depressing working and living conditions that a teacher may encounter are to some extent compensated for by stimulating social and professional associates. He may engage in numberless forms of community activities. Usually he is invited to affiliate with representative civic, service, fraternal, and religious groups. He meets cultured and respected people. If he is willing to assume his share of responsibility for the welfare of the community, he has an open sesame to a position of leadership that is socially satisfying.

Among his colleagues a teacher finds congenial friends. From mutually shared interests in intellectual pursuits he derives inspiration and pleasure. In professional organizations he broadens his horizons. Local, state, and national associations bring him and other teachers together in pleasant and helpful relationships.

Best of all, a teacher is in daily contact with youth. Loula Grace Erdman, a teacher and prize-winning novelist, gives this as a reason for her decision to stick to teaching. She points out that "a teacher has the great privilege of constantly being able to renew her youth. It is impossible to be around young people without absorbing their eager spirit and searching point of view." From their buoyancy, their ambition, and their confidence a teacher gains refreshment and vigor. Even though he cannot stay the passing years, he can remain eternally young in spirit.

Restrictions on Personal Freedom. Since a teacher holds a place of responsibility and distinction in the community, people may meddle in his affairs and attempt to supervise his conduct. This is usually not true in large cities, but in small towns they often try to dictate the details of a teacher's personal life. They concern themselves with a host of matters—dress, church attendance, political affiliation, choice of recreation, smoking, staying out late at night, and leaving town on week ends.

Not many years ago teachers' contracts were studded with specific requirements for conduct. Stipulations against smoking, drinking, dancing, and "going out" on school nights were not at all uncommon. One teacher's contract exacted these pledges:

I promise to take a vital interest in all phases of Sunday-school work, donating of my time, service, and money without stint for the uplift and benefit of the community. I promise to abstain from all dancing, immodest dressing, and any other conduct unbecoming a teacher and a lady. I promise not to go out with any young men except in so far as it may be necessary to stimulate Sunday-school work. I promise not to fall in love, to become engaged or secretly marry. . . . I promise to sleep at least eight hours a night, to eat carefully, and to take every precaution to keep in the best of health and spirits in order that I may be better able to render efficient service to my pupils.[3]

Happily, the situation is improving. Two paragraphs in the *Handbook for Teachers* of Tulsa, Oklahoma, attest a tolerance not confined to any one city:

You will find the attitude of citizens towards teachers to be one of friendly acceptance, a person-to-person relationship. Teachers here are not a breed set apart, looked down upon, looked up to, nor expected to live restricted lives. Of course, any teacher who comes to Tulsa will wish to lead an exemplary life because he is an outstanding person. Otherwise, he would not be invited to teach in Tulsa. . . .

He is expected to lead a normal life, participating in community activities the same as any other citizen. He is expected to rear his family and be a good citizen of the city, the state, the nation. These things he will do, not merely because he is a teacher, but because he is an honest, loyal, upright person.

Nevertheless, there are still communities where a teacher's behavior is so circumscribed by petty regulations that some of the best young people reject teaching as a career. Understandably, they want a chance to lead normal lives, to mingle freely, and to enjoy pleasures that other adults accept as a matter of course.

A glaring restriction still found in many contracts is a prohibition against marriage for women teachers. Not only do many communities refuse to employ married women but they specify that the contract of a woman who marries during the school term shall be canceled. Their opposition to women teachers being married can be traced to a combination of reasons: belief that a woman's place is in the home, fear of divided interests that will lead to neglect of school work, and possible interruption of service for maternity leave.

[3] Quoted by E. W. Knight, *Education in the United States,* Ginn and Company, 3rd ed., 1951, pp. 360–361.

There is no reliable evidence to prove that a teacher's efficiency hinges upon her marital status. Several studies show that women who were competent teachers before marriage continue to do good work after marriage, and that those who were incompetent remain incompetent.

Some authorities advance cogent arguments in favor of married women teachers. They believe that these teachers have a better understanding of children, better-rounded personalities, and greater emotional stability than unmarried women. A study by the National Education Association in 1944 showed more married than unmarried women in the high-morale group.

The removal of the ban on married women is likely to have a salutary effect on the profession itself. Gifted young women who are deterred by the stigma they think attaches to the "old-maid school teacher" may decide to cast their lot with teaching. Furthermore, the teaching population may gain stability that will make the saying, "Teachers are a mob of mobile maidens meditating matrimony," outmoded.

Security

Salary. Although economic reward alone should not tip the scales in favor of an occupation, anyone would be unrealistic not to take it into account. A teacher wants to be certain that his calling will provide an income commensurate with his preparation, ability, and service. He wants to be able to maintain a comfortable standard of living without undue worry over financial affairs.

A person who is concerned primarily with amassing wealth should not look to teaching as a career. In general, financial returns are greater in business and industry and in other professions than in teaching. However, in spite of the fact that the monetary rewards are not so great as those of some other groups, teaching is not, as Henry Van Dyke contends, "the worst paid . . . of all the vocations."

To offset their modest salaries teachers have steady employment on a yearly basis with little risk. Ordinarily they receive their pay checks regularly. During a depression businessmen who in times of prosperity look a trifle condescendingly upon teachers regard them with a tinge of envy. A not unique point of view was expressed in the 1930's by a prosperous businessman: "Teachers are always complaining about low salaries. They forget that they are not taking the chances of businessmen or facing their uncertainties. They get their checks regularly, and they know in advance how much they are going to get."

Then, too, teachers are spared the expense of purchasing the costly equipment and furnishing the expensive offices that are often necessary for people in other lines of work. They do not have to undergo a "starving period" as lawyers or doctors sometimes do while building up a practice. They work in buildings provided and equipped by others, and at once receive steady compensation.

Many factors affect the size of a teacher's salary. First, men are likely to receive higher salaries than women with equivalent qualifications, even in positions of equal difficulty and importance. However, a study of salary schedules in 1950–1951 by the Research Division of the National Education Association showed that salary differentials based on sex alone are on the decline. Only 20 percent of the school systems reported that men teachers were paid more than women.

Second, the school level at which the teacher is employed has a bearing on his salary. In 1948–1949 the Research Division of the National Education Association reported that in 27 states high school teachers received an average of $500 more per year than teachers in elementary schools. Such differences are disappearing as more and more systems adopt a single salary schedule based on equivalent preparation and experience rather than on grade level. By 1957–1958, the average salary of elementary school teachers had increased to 89.4 percent of the salary for secondary school teachers. A further narrowing of the difference may be expected as long as shortage of elementary school teachers remains more acute than that of secondary school teachers, and as long as the level of preparation demanded for elementary school teachers increases.

Third, salaries vary among the states and sections of the United States. Naturally, economic conditions in a state and region influence salaries. Highest salaries are paid in the Far West and lowest in the Southeast, with the difference, in 1958–1959, of $2110 in average salaries in these regions. In 1958–1959, the average annual salaries for classroom teachers only ranged from $3070 in the lowest state, Mississippi, to $6400 in the highest state, Alaska. (See Chapter XIV, Table 8.) The average for the United States was $4775.

Salaries also differ among communities. Usually, the highest salaries are paid in large cities, and the lowest ones in rural areas. Table 1 shows the median salaries paid in 1956–1957 to educational workers of different types in 2493 cities classified according to population.

According to the Research Division of the National Education Association, which has been conducting biennial surveys of salaries paid in urban school districts since 1922–1923, the median salaries for 1956–1957 were the highest reported to date. For example, for all regular classroom teachers (kindergarten, elementary, junior high, and high school teachers) median salaries in 1956–1957 for urban school districts were: Group I, $5834; Group II, $4574; Group III, $4682; Group IV, $4489; Group V, $4240; and Group VI, $4077. These medians were from 212 to 128 percent higher than the similar medians in 1930–1931.

In terms of purchasing power, however, the increase was not so great as might appear at first glance. For example, the 1956–1957 median for Group III classroom teachers, $4682, gave a purchasing power in 1947–1949 dollars of only $3938.

Furthermore, the federal income tax has nearly wiped out the teachers' increases in purchasing power. Prior to 1939 the tax did not apply to public school teachers and it was still at low rates in 1940–1941. At 1956 rates, a single teacher with one dependent, at a salary of $4682, paid $622. The remaining $4060 was worth only $3494 in 1947–1949 dollars. State income taxes, much increased in recent years, take a further bite in many states.

A heartening sign that points to improvement in salaries is the growing public awareness of the need for adequate compensation for teachers. The Advertising Council, National Citizens Council

TABLE 1. Median Salaries Paid Employees in School Systems During 1956–1957

Type of School Employee	Population Groups					
	Group I: Over 500,000	Group II: 100,000 to 500,000	Group III: 30,000 to 100,000	Group IV: 10,000 to 30,000	Group V: 5,000 to 10,000	Group VI: 2,500 to 5,000
Classroom teachers						
Elementary school	$ 5,579	$ 4,442	$ 4,454	$ 4,317	$4,086	$3,946
Junior high school	5,565	4,522	4,783	4,540	4,282	3,875
High school	6,326	5,028	5,135	4,866	4,496	4,297
Junior college	6,503	6,286	5,918	5,528	4,500	—
Principals						
Elementary school						
Teaching	—	4,905	5,174	4,927	4,590	4,395
Supervising	9,101	7,007	6,538	6,185	5,851	5,500
Junior high school (total)	9,439	7,481	7,198	6,538	5,724	4,919
High school (total)	10,788	8,232	7,958	7,109	6,243	5,700
Junior college	13,750	9,833	9,500	8,063	7,100	—
Administrative and supervisory staff						
Superintendents of schools	22,000	16,000	12,700	10,056	8,493	7,524

SOURCE: Adapted from National Education Association, Research Division, *Salaries and Salary Schedules of Urban School Employees, 1956–57*, Research Bulletin, April, 1957, pp. 72–78.

for Better Schools, United States Chamber of Commerce, press, influential civic leaders, radio artists, and movie stars are lending their support to a campaign to drive home to the public the importance of reasonable professional remuneration for teachers.

Pension and Retirement Allowances. Understandably enough, to a youth on the threshold of his career the prospect of a pension may not constitute a lure. It is reassuring to know, however, that state retirement laws are in effect in every state except South Dakota. In addition there are about 25 local or county school pension and retirement plans. Most school systems require 30 or 35 years of service or a minimum age of 60 as a basis of eligibility for retirement. Usually retirement is compulsory at 68 or 70. The allowance is ordinarily related to length of service, a larger benefit being paid for a longer period of service.

There are two types of provisions for aged and incapacitated teachers: pension plans and joint-contributory retirement systems. In a pension plan, the state or city government pays the entire cost. In a joint-contributory plan, money is contributed by the members and by the state or city. A joint-contributory plan is more reliable than a pensionary plan. There is no assurance that the latter type will continue from year to year. Since a pension is a gift which the government gives out of its goodwill, it may withdraw the gratuity at any time even from those on retirement who have been receiving the benefits. Under a joint-contributory plan the teacher is not a mere recipient but is a member of a system. The plan is in the nature of a contract between the member and the government and so long as the member contributes, the government has certain obligations toward him. After he retires, the government cannot legally stop his allowance.

The trend is toward basing joint-contributory retirement systems on actuarial science. Two-thirds of the present retirement laws require actuarial evaluations and, to some extent at least, meet actuarial standards. Delaware and New Mexico are the only states that still have noncontributory retirement systems.

All state retirement systems, except one, have special provisions for disability retirement allowances. Usually retirement for disability is limited to permanent disability. Minimum qualifications are usually 10 to 15 years of membership service. If the disability is clearly temporary, the member's account is on an inactive status until his return to teaching.

One of the current problems is to arrange for reciprocity between states. The laws should be changed so that teachers who move across state lines can receive credit for out-of-state service.

Another problem is to protect and improve retirement systems. Benefits under the federal Social Security Act have increased to such an extent that some public school retirement systems suffer by comparison. A number of states have provided for social security coverage either in addition to or by coördination with the retirement benefits. South Dakota has social security only.

Leaves of Absence. Quite as indispensable to security as arrangements for retirement are safeguards for teachers who are temporarily incapacitated. The welfare of the teacher as well as of the school is served if teachers are given financial support when absent because of illness. Sick leave is mentioned in the laws of 23 states and in most city school districts.

Although practices are not uniform, the majority of school systems grant a week or two of sick leave annually with full pay. In many cases the number of years of service determines the amount of sick leave. Some systems have a cumulative plan under which from 20 to 25 days of unused sick leave may accumulate.

Leaves of absence for reasons other than illness are permitted in many systems. Usually teachers may be absent for several days without loss of pay for justifiable reasons like illness or death in the family. More extended leaves of absence for travel or professional improvement are granted, usually without pay, by most systems. Teachers are guaranteed, however, that their positions will be held for them.

Tenure. Other measures for security are meaningless unless there is assurance of tenure. A teacher should be certain that once he has obtained a position and proved his ability to fill it satisfactorily, he will be protected against unjust dismissal.

Ordinarily teachers are employed under three types of agreement. Under the first, they are engaged for a definite period of time, usually for one year. More than half of the rural and small-town schools employ teachers for one year at a time.

Under the second, teachers receive continuing contracts. They are retained for an indefinite term, but the school board may terminate their employment at will.

Under the third, teachers are given permanent tenure after a probationary period. During probation they may be dismissed at the will of the board, but after the trial period they may continue in the same position for an indefinite term, subject to their services being efficient. They may be dismissed only for good cause and after a public hearing. Immoral or unprofessional conduct or incompetence may be cause for dismissal.

Thirty-five states and the District of Columbia have some type of legislation providing legal safeguards for employment security. Sixty-eight percent of the teachers in the United States are employed in districts having tenure legislation. In return for protection against dismissal through partisan, factional, selfish, commercial, or political interference, teachers should fulfill their contractual obligations as fully as they expect a board of education to honor its part of the contract. They should give reasonable notice if they do not desire to remain in their positions. They should manifest willingness to continue their professional growth. They should be as ready to sanction the removal of an inefficient teacher as to prevent the dismissal of an efficient teacher.

It is important to note the meaning of the term tenure law. "A tenure law is one which requires notice, statement of reasons, and a hearing before a teacher can be legally dismissed *at any time* after acquiring tenure status." The provisions of a law not its title determine whether it is actually a tenure law. Some so-called continuing contract laws or "fair dismissal laws" may embody all the provisions of a tenure law. Some so-called tenure laws may be only a spring-notification requirement. Only tenure provisions guarantee due process *at all times*, that is during a school year and at the close of a school year.

It should be stressed that all tenure laws do not give the same rights. Teachers may be misled in thinking they have tenure rights that do not exist under their legislation.

Tenure laws may be contract-type laws or laws merely stating legislative policy. A contract-type law affords real protection because a legislature cannot legally impair the obligations of its contracts, since the Constitution of the United States guarantees the sanctity of contractual relations. A law merely stating legislative policy may be modified in such a way that teachers cease to have tenure status because one legislature cannot tie the hands of future legislatures.

Since the courts in many states have not yet been called upon to decide whether the status of tenure teachers is contractual or legislative only, the effectiveness of many tenure laws remains in doubt. Only in Indiana has a contract-type law been so classified by the courts. In California, Illinois, New Jersey, New York, Oregon, and Wisconsin tenure laws have been classified as statements of legislative policy only, subject to modification by legislative amendment which can result in terminating the tenure status of tenure teachers.

Intangible Rewards

In recent years there has been emphasis, and properly so, on the material rewards of teaching. However, for a real teacher the most gratifying rewards are intangible and immaterial. Teaching is a service occupation that demands the everlasting and unceasing gift of self. Beyond a certain point mere increase in salary will not bring to teaching the kind of people most needed. George Herbert Palmer of Harvard once wrote:

The idea, sometimes advanced, that the professions might be ennobled by paying them powerfully, is fantastic. Their great attraction is their removal from sordid aims. More money should certainly be spent on several of them. Their members should be better protected against want, anxiety, neglect, and bad conditions of labor. To do his best work one needs not merely to live, but to live well. Yet in that increase of salaries which is urgently needed, care should be used not to allow the attention of the professional man to be diverted from what is important—the outgo of his work—and become fixed on what is merely incidental—his income. . . . Professional men are not so silly as to despise money; but after all, it is interest in their work, and not the thought of salary, which predominantly holds them.[4]

Among the intangible rewards of teaching are the opportunity to do creative work, the prestige of the calling, and the opportunity for service.

Opportunity for Creative Work. A young person who seeks challenging creative work may well consider teaching. Here is no factory-line job of dry-as-dust routine. Here is a creative task with unlimited incentives for exercising judgment, initiative, and originality. Each school day brings the promise of new and stirring adventure. Each day brings the privilege of teaching in a manner that John Mason Brown characterizes as "eye-opening, ear-quickening, vista-exploring, and exciting."

The creative aspect of teaching is accentuated in an excerpt from an address to a group of women teachers:

Have you ever stopped to analyze the teaching act and compare it with other types of work? Study the teacher at work with 30, 40, or 50 boys and girls. She remembers all she has heard about individual differences. She is plagued by the fact that there are three in her class who have IQ's above 140 and must be helped to live up to their capacities. For five and one-half hours she pours out herself, now lifting the group to heights of interest, enthusiasm, initiative, now pulling them along to diligence and perseverance, appealing to the slow learner and to the swift, the willing and the reluctant. Many days hers is as exhaustive and creative a role as that of a Marian Anderson singing to 5,000 people or a Judith Anderson carrying audiences night after night through the agonies of the Medea. She is Marie Curie in search of radium, Bette Davis at the end of a day before a camera, Edna St. Vincent Millay writing "Finis" to "The Buck in the Snow." She is the surgeon at the end of an operation, the judge who has decided on the custody of children in a divorce case.

Creativity leaves one, whatever her art, be it music, drama, or teaching, with a fatigue that is good. Stop your friends when they begin to commiserate with you and say, "Of course I'm tired. I've had a won-

[4] George Herbert Palmer, *The Ideal Teacher*, Houghton Mifflin Company, 1910, pp. 6–7.

derful day." And then tell them all you have accomplished with your pupils.[5]

Prestige. The esteem in which the public holds a calling may have considerable weight in influencing vocational choice. Unstinted social recognition is necessary if teaching is to appeal to capable recruits. Some years ago Hartmann ranked, according to prestige, 25 occupations in the judgment of 100 representatives of other occupations. He found that no kind of teaching was listed below ninth place.

> The public school teacher stands lowest among the accepted professional groups, but definitely above the great body of business, industrial, and commercial pursuits. If the public school teacher lacks caste, it must be only with the numerically small professional groups who stand above her; certainly this does not hold for the great body of citizens who fall below her in "status." If "average" social status is represented by the mean positions of such diverse vocations as salesman, nurse, bookkeeper, farmer, and carpenter, then there is not the slightest doubt that teachers as a class stand above these in "repute." In the eyes of the well-established professions, the school teacher may well suffer that uncertain appraisal which has historically been the fate of every semi-profession during its transitional stages but in the eyes of the larger body of nonprofessional claimants she stands definitely among the elect.[6]

In 1950, according to a nation-wide survey conducted by Elmo Roper, teachers were considered the most useful members of a community. Ten percent voted for lawyers as the most important people in a community, 13 percent for merchants, 20 percent for the mayor or some other top public official, and 27 percent for the clergy. Teachers led with a vote of 31 percent.

Young people who hesitate to enter teaching because they think that it is devoid of prestige may be unaware of reasons for the layman's attitude. First of all there are innumerable misconceptions deeply ingrained in popular opinion. Participants in the Kalamazoo Conference sponsored in 1952 by the National Commission on

---

[5] Maud R. Hardman, "We Women Teachers," *Delta Kappa Gamma Bulletin*, Fall, 1948, p. 12.

[6] George W. Hartmann, "The Prestige of Occupations," *Personnel Journal*, October, 1934, p. 151.

Teacher Education and Professional Standards took cognizance of the situation in a section report. "Many shibboleths, catch phrases, slogans, and fallacious beliefs have grown up about teachers and their work. These should be challenged for accuracy and validity. Acquiescence toward repeated folklores serves only to encourage the reiteration." The report singled out 16 points for refutation. Among them were the validity of analogies between teaching and the medical and legal professions, always to the disparagement of teaching, and the accuracy of the old saws, "Any teacher can teach anything" and "Anyone can teach."

A second source of the profession's shaky social standing has its origin in the traditionally low economic status of teachers. In our society with its predilection for measuring values with a price tag, "the poorly paid custodian of the gateway to 'culture,'" to borrow Mead's words, does not command as much adulation as a tycoon of industry. How well this question, from a letter published in the "People's Forum" in a daily newspaper, crystallizes a common sentiment: "If you [teachers] are so smart, why aren't you rich?"

A third reason for grudging recognition stems from the teachers' own belittling of their calling. Since they are prone to say apologetically, "I'm just a school teacher," others take them at their word and treat them as second-class citizens. They could profitably heed the sound advice of Edwin A. Lahey, a columnist for the Chicago *Daily News:* "It's about time that the school teacher realized his importance and acted the part. In the 'American way of life' we talk about, there is nothing quite as essential as the system of free public education, controlled by local government. And the essence of that system is in the school teacher."

Opportunity for Service.   Foremost among the appeals of teaching is the knowledge that one is rendering genuine service to humanity and to civilization.

A teacher sees, and knows, and fosters the growth and development of children. To them he becomes

> the living world
> The library of a dead past,
> And the encouragement of a mighty future.

Since no two children are alike, he is ever alert to individual needs. "He quickens the indolent, encourages the eager, and steadies the unstable." Truly "the excitement of teaching comes from the fact that one is teaching a subject one loves to individuals who are worth more than all the money in the world."

Sometimes pupils express their gratitude for a teacher's help and understanding. They bring "red apples" in their comments: "I always feel that I can talk things over with you" and "I enjoyed the lesson today." They are represented by the little boy who asked the editor of a Texas newspaper to print a kiss for his teacher because, as he said, "She's my teacher, and I love her most of anything."

Sometimes appreciation of pupils is unspoken. Sometimes it is long delayed. But it is none the less certain.

Every teacher, "sower of unseen harvests," can sympathize with a Christmas letter that an editor of a newspaper in a small town wrote some years ago to a beloved primary teacher who spent 42 years in the schools of that town. Here is part of the letter:

Dear Miss Merrill:

I wonder if you remember me. It has been just thirty-two years (nearly a third of a century) since I went to school to you, down in the old East building, and tracked in mud and snow and dirt and a belligerent disposition on my brass-toed shoes. It is a long time ago. But I am a boy again, because I have been out riding with Tots and Max and a lot of their little friends in a bob-sled, in the first snow of the season.

Yes, it is a long time ago. It has been five whole years since you were Tots' teacher and three years since you taught Max. I wonder why I had to wait until I lived over again in Tots and Max before I came to appreciate the wonderful beneficence of your life.

With the dawn of Christmas Day almost here, I wonder if you can even slightly comprehend how loving hearts from all over this wide world are going out to you in a spirit of gratitude and thanks because of your influence upon their lives.

I wonder if, in all the world, there lives another human being who has come to know the soul and structure of the child heart as you.

I wonder if, in all the world, there lives another who has with divine patience answered so many baby questions—and smiled.

I wonder if, in all the world, there lives another who has healed so many hurts of children, hurts of soul and flesh.

You have never stopped, I know, to reckon how many folks there are, in all the various avenues of earth who have never seen anything save a smile of love from your lips.

Tell me, Miss Merrill, how many miles your tired fingers have traveled behind a pair of scissors, cutting "pretty things" for baby eyes to see.

Tell me, Miss Merrill, how many bits of bright paper you have folded for them, and how many pairs of child eyes have looked up to you in full appreciation.

Tell me, Miss Merrill, how many stories you have woven around the birth of the baby Jesus in the manger at Bethlehem, how many stories of Washington, of Lincoln, of the Flag, how many stories of the birds, the flowers, the clouds, the rainbow.

Tell me, Miss Merrill, how many prayers you have taught, real prayers that went straight to the Throne, because they were prayers of innocence and sublime faith. I remember when Max came home one evening, her brown eyes all sober, and told how you had taught them to pray for Constance, who had gone on. It broke up the whole family.

I wonder if you realize, Miss Merrill, that among all the hundreds of people, who started first in school to you, those now in the fullness of their years—I wonder if you DO realize that thousands of times they have been made better, tenderer, richer, because when they lifted the veil that sometimes hides the treasures of the past—Miss Merrill was standing there—in the old first room. . . .

You are to be envied above all others that I know, but there lives no one who would take from you even one kind thought.[7]

Not only is there the endless delight of watching and guiding the growth and development of children, but there is also the priceless satisfaction of knowing that one is serving his country and helping build a better world.

During World War II we thrilled to the heroism of such men as Gabriel Peri, a French official, who, before he was shot by the Nazis, wrote: "I should like my fellow country-men to know that I am dying that France may live. I have made a last examination of conscience and am satisfied. If I had to begin over again I

---

[7] Written by Burr Swan, editor of *The Pike County Republican*, Pittsfield, Illinois.

would travel the same road. In a few minutes I am going to prepare the tomorrows that sing."

But whether or not we have "tomorrows that sing" depends,
finally, not upon soldiers or other wartime heroes, but upon citizens prepared to carry on peacetime activities with the same skill
and devotion that our fighting men display. Whether or not we
have such citizens depends in no small measure upon the work of
teachers, the sculptors of new citizens.

Little wonder that a man of vision like James Hilton declared:

"If I had a child who wanted to be a teacher I would bid him
Godspeed as if he were going to a war. For indeed the war against
prejudice, greed, and ignorance is eternal, and those who dedicate
themselves to it give their lives no less because they may live to see
some fraction of the battle won. They are the commandoes of the
peace, if peace is to be more than a short armistice. As in a relay
race, our armed men have handed victory to those who dare not
stand still to admire it, but must run with it for very life to a
further and larger goal."

SUMMARY

In choosing his lifework, a student should take into account
his aptitudes, abilities, and interests, as well as the nature of the
work itself, its requirements, advantages and disadvantages, opportunities and rewards. He should try to determine as objectively as
possible the extent to which he possesses or can cultivate basic
qualities deemed essential for teachers. He should decide whether
or not he is genuinely interested in becoming a teacher. Through
informal experiences in working with children he may test his
interest and aptitude.

Teaching requires an extended period of preparation as is shown
by a study of requirements for obtaining a teacher's certificate.
The cost of attending a teacher-education institution for a year
is likely to range from $1000 to $1500 or more. Outlook for employment for the foreseeable future is excellent and opportunities
for advancement are satisfactory for teachers who prove their
worth.

Although not always ideal, the physical surroundings in which a teacher works and lives are reasonably satisfactory. Teaching load and hours of work are·sometimes burdensome. A five-day week and liberal vacations, however, somewhat compensate for a heavy load. Usually social and professional associates are stimulating and congenial. Restrictions upon a teacher's personal life are tending to disappear.

Provisions for security and welfare as represented by salary, pension and retirement allowances, leaves of absence, and tenure are improving. Although economic rewards in teaching are ordinarily less than in business and industry and professions such as medicine and law, teachers have steady employment and receive their pay checks regularly. State retirement laws are in effect in every state except South Dakota. A number of states have social security coverage in addition to or in coördination with retirement benefits. The majority of school systems grant leaves of absence for illness and for other justifiable reasons. Legal safeguards for employment security protect 68 percent of the teachers in the United States.

Some of the most satisfying rewards of teaching are intangible. They include opportunity for creative work, prestige, and opportunity for service.

QUESTIONS AND EXERCISES

1. In what ways do a teacher's influence and opportunities for service affect your attitude toward teaching?
2. Why are statistics on teachers' salaries often misleading?
3. Consult the school law of your state to ascertain provisions on these matters: certification, tenure, retirement, and pension.
4. Hold a panel discussion on these topics: (a) Should high-school teachers receive more salary than elementary teachers with equal ability, preparation, and experience? (b) Should men and women teachers receive equal pay for equal work, if they have the same ability, preparation, and experience? (c) Should married women be employed as teachers?
5. How will consolidation of schools affect the demand for teachers?
6. Investigate the supply of teachers in your state. In what fields does it equal or exceed the demand? Consult reports of your col-

lege placement bureau to ascertain probable chances of securing a position in your major field.

7. In what ways do teachers sometimes manifest a "martyr complex"?

8. "Would you choose teaching again?" was the question asked a sampling of New York City teachers in 1950. Fifty-six percent answered "No." Mention reasons that may have prompted their reply.

9. From *Unseen Harvests*, edited by Fuess and Basford, choose a selection that shows convincingly the personal satisfactions derived from teaching.

10. Write a short paper on the topic, "Why I Have Decided to Teach."

SELECTED REFERENCES

Anderson, Earl W., *Teaching as a Career*, U.S. Department of Health, Education, and Welfare, Office of Education, Bulletin No. 2, 1955.

Armstrong, W. Earl, and Stinnett, T. M., *A Manual on Certification Requirements for School Personnel in the United States*, National Commission on Teacher Education and Professional Standards, National Education Association, 1957 ed.

Commission on Teacher Education, *Teachers for Our Times*, American Council on Education, 1944.

Elsbree, Willard S., *The American Teacher*, American Book Company, 1939.

Holman, Mary V., *How It Feels to Be a Teacher*, Bureau of Publications, Teachers College, Columbia University, 1950.

Houle, Cyril O., *Teaching as a Career*, The American Job Series of Occupational Monographs, No. 5, Science Research Associates, 1944.

Huggett, Albert J., and Stinnett, T. M., *Professional Problems of Teachers*, The Macmillan Company, 1956.

Lieberman, Myron, *Education as a Profession*, Prentice-Hall, Inc., 1956.

National Education Association, Committee on Tenure and Academic Freedom, *Analysis of Teacher Tenure Provisions: State and Local*, June, 1954.

National Education Association, Committee on Tenure and Academic Freedom, *Teacher Tenure Manual*, May, 1950.

National Education Association, Research Division:
    Public School Retirement at the Half Century, Research Bulletin, December, 1950.

Salaries and Salary Schedules of Urban School Employees, 1956–57, Research Bulletin, April, 1957.

Teacher Personnel Practices, 1950–51: *Appointment and Termination of Service,* Research Bulletin, February, 1952.

Teacher Personnel Procedures, 1950–51: *Employment Conditions in Service,* Research Bulletin, April, 1952.

Teachers in the Public Schools, Research Bulletin, December, 1949.

Teaching Load in 1950, Research Bulletin, February, 1951.

The Legal Status of the Public-School Teacher, Research Bulletin, April, 1947.

The Status of the American Public-School Teacher, Research Bulletin, February, 1957.

Stroh, M. Margaret, *Find Your Own Frontier,* Delta Kappa Gamma Society, 1948.

Woellner, Robert C., and Wood, M. Aurilla, *Requirements for Certification of Teachers, Counselors, Librarians, Administrators for Elementary Schools, Secondary Schools, Junior Colleges,* University of Chicago Press, 1958 (revised annually).

Teachers—Autobiography, Biography, and Fiction

Boyce, Burke, *Miss Mallett,* Harper & Brothers, 1949.

Breasted, Charles, *Pioneer to the Past,* Charles Scribner's Sons, 1943.

Chase, Mary Ellen, *A Goodly Fellowship,* The Macmillan Company, 1939.

Church, Virginia, *Teachers Are People,* Wallace Hebberd, 1945.

Crabtree, J. W., *What Counted Most,* University Publishing Company, 1935.

Devel, Leo (ed.), *The Teacher's Treasure Chest,* Prentice-Hall, Inc., 1956.

Erskine, John, *My Life as a Teacher,* J. B. Lippincott Company, 1948.

Flexner, Abraham, *I Remember,* Simon and Schuster, Inc., 1940.

Foff, Arthur, and Grambs, Jean D. (eds.), *Readings in Education,* Harper & Brothers, 1956.

Fuess, Claude M., and Basford, Emory S. (eds.), *Unseen Harvests,* The Macmillan Company, 1947.

Hilton, James, *Goodbye, Mr. Chips,* Little, Brown and Company, 1934.

Holt, Rackham, *George Washington Carver,* Doubleday, Doran and Company, 1943.

James, Henry, *Charles W. Eliot,* Houghton Mifflin Company, 1930.

Johnson, Henry, *The Other Side of Main Street,* Columbia University Press, 1943.

Lutes, Della, *Country School Ma'am*, Little, Brown and Company, 1941.

McCuskey, Dorothy, *Bronson Alcott, Teacher*, The Macmillan Company, 1940.

McKinney, Isabel, *Mr. Lord; the Life and Words of Livingston C. Lord*, University of Illinois Press, 1937.

Palmer, George H., *Autobiography of a Philosopher*, Houghton Mifflin Company, 1930.

Palmer, George H., *Life of Alice Freeman Palmer*, Houghton Mifflin Company, 1924.

Patton, Frances, *Good Morning, Miss Dove*, Dodd, Mead & Company, Inc., 1954.

Perry, Bliss, *And Gladly Teach*, Houghton Mifflin Company, 1935.

Peterson, Houston (ed.), *Great Teachers*, Rutgers University Press, 1946.

Phelps, William Lyon, *Autobiography*, Oxford University Press, 1939.

Sharp, D. Louise (ed.), *Why Teach?* Henry Holt and Company, 1957.

Shepard, Odell, *Pedlar's Progress: The Life of Bronson Alcott*, Little, Brown and Company, 1937.

Stroh, M. Margaret, *Eyes to See*, Delta Kappa Gamma Society, 1947.

Stuart, Jesse, *The Thread That Runs So True*, Charles Scribner's Sons, 1950.

Tharp, Louise Hall, *The Peabody Sisters of Salem*, Little, Brown and Company, 1950.

Tharp, Louise Hall, *Until Victory: Horace Mann and Mary Peabody*, Little, Brown and Company, 1953.

Weber, Julia, *My Country School Diary*, Harper & Brothers, 1946.

Williams, Edward Irwin Franklin, *Horace Mann: Educational Statesman*, The Macmillan Company, 1937.

AUDIO-VISUAL MATERIALS

Films

Planning for Personal and Professional Growth (18 minutes, Sound, B & W, McGraw-Hill Book Company, Inc.). A case study of personalities and careers of four teachers, this film illustrates the importance of planning for personal and professional growth.

What Greater Gift? (30 minutes, Sound, B & W, or C, National Education Association). Dramatizes the teacher as a professional person. A high school senior with her heart set on teaching learns through interviews with a veteran teacher and through work with children at the Play Center why teaching is a satisfying and important career.

Filmstrips

Let's Take a Look at Teaching (50 frames, Silent, B & W, Wayne University). An overview of the teaching profession. Summary of a typical teacher's day.

Teaching as a Career (47 frames, Silent, B & W, National Film Board of Canada). Presents the advantages and disadvantages of teaching as a career. Covers such points as educational requirements, personal aptitudes, specialized preparation, salary, and opportunities for advancement.

Recordings

Teacher Salary Schedule (15 minutes, Tape, Minnesota State Department of Education). School boards will seek to establish a salary structure that will induce the right type of teachers to gravitate toward their schools. The cost of education rests on society as a whole.

Teacher Tenure (Fair Dismissal) (15 minutes, Tape, Minnesota State Department of Education). Avoiding the fear that results when cheap politics invades the classroom.

CHAPTER III

Good Teachers Don't Just Happen

Teachers of the kind society needs don't just happen. They don't spring full-blown into being. They represent a happy combination of native endowment and education. They are available only insofar as capable young people choose teaching as a career and prepare properly for it. This chapter deals with some aspects of the problem of securing and educating able teachers.

TEACHER RECRUITMENT

How to spur the interest of competent young people in preparing for teaching is a pressing problem. The surplus of teachers that existed before World War II has been succeeded by a shortage that may be more than temporary.

The source of supply of teachers is less dependable than formerly. Until a couple of decades ago thousands of young people from lower-middle-income families turned to teaching as almost the only socially acceptable calling open to them. Since little if any special training was required for certification, teaching became a convenient steppingstone occupation. Men often taught for a few years to finance their study for a profession such as law or medicine, and many women taught only long enough to secure money for a trousseau. For women who did not marry, teaching was a "genteel" way of earning a living. It was better than remaining dependent upon parents or other relatives for food and clothing.

Today the standards for entrance into teaching have generally been raised enough to lessen its lure as a stopgap calling. Besides, a practically unlimited choice of remunerative and socially acceptable occupations is open to middle-income groups. Hence, unless a concerted effort is made, many potentially acceptable teachers will not even consider teaching as a possible career.

The continuous process of trying to guide desirable candidates into teacher education is, for lack of a better word, often called recruitment. The process is not merely a matter of increasing the number of teachers. Rather it is a means of obtaining capable young people from whom to select candidates.

Responsibility for recruitment rests with teachers and their professional organizations, teacher-preparing institutions, and the lay public.

Teachers at all levels are in a strategic position to carry on recruitment. If they are "living witnesses" of a calling that yields deep satisfactions, they can exercise a positive influence. The process may start as early as the elementary school. A librarian at Illinois State Normal University permits pupils in the upper grades to tell stories to the children in the lower grades as a means of arousing interest in teaching. Teachers of fifth- and sixth-grade girls at the Sarah J. Rawson School in Hartford, Connecticut, have students who are interested in work with younger children leave their classrooms for a certain period each day to participate in some of the kindergarten program. Many of these junior aides who are now in high school have signified their intention of becoming teachers.

For high school students varied opportunities of working with younger children are provided; the plan in Decatur, Illinois, is described in Chapter II. Certainly, evidence of potential capabilities may be discovered in junior and senior high school. Direct occupational study and guidance should be provided as early as the junior high school. Counselors with a clear perception and deep appreciation of the unlimited possibilities open to teachers can guide some outstanding young people into the profession.

Not only as individuals but also as members of professional organizations can teachers be instrumental in interesting young people in teaching. Such groups as Phi Delta Kappa and Delta

Kappa Gamma are sponsoring fruitful recruitment programs. Delta Kappa Gamma holds many conferences with high school girls and provides several scholarships for prospective teachers.

The Future Teachers of America and the Student National Education Association, affiliates of the National Education Association, have workable programs for selective recruitment and pre-professional experience. FTA clubs are organized in high schools and Student NEA chapters in colleges. The former are vocational and exploratory in nature. They present to topnotch high school students the unlimited opportunities that teaching offers. Student NEA chapters in colleges offer personal experience working with local, state, and national education associations. They seek to develop a mature program based on the assumption that prospective teachers should prepare for responsibilities they must assume upon becoming practitioners. In 1958 FTA had 4000 clubs with a total membership of 118,000, and Student NEA had 700 chapters with a total membership of 44,000.

The high standards set by FTA chapters are indicated by the Future Teacher's Pledge:

The Good Teacher Requires:

PHYSICAL VITALITY. I will try to keep my body well and strong.

MENTAL VIGOR. I will study daily to keep my mind active and alert.

MORAL DISCRIMINATION. I will seek to know the right and to live by it.

WHOLESOME PERSONALITY. I will cultivate in myself goodwill, friendliness, poise, upright bearing, and careful speech.

HELPFULNESS. I will learn the art of helping others by doing helpful things daily in school and home.

KNOWLEDGE. I will fill my mind with worthy thoughts by observing all that is beautiful in the world around me, by reading the best books, and by association with the best companions.

LEADERSHIP. I will make my influence count on the side of right, avoiding habits that weaken and destroy.

These things will I do now that I may be worthy of the high office of teacher.

State teachers' associations as well as the National Education Association try actively to recruit teachers. Some conduct essay contests in an effort to interest outstanding high school seniors in entering teaching. Others make printed material available to acquaint high school pupils with the profession.

The Iowa State Education Association's pamphlet, *You Can Take It With You*, bases its appeal along the following lines: "If you can choose teaching as a career, your interests can be your career. Teaching is a way of living as well as a way of making a living. Your training as a teacher is an investment in yourself. If you have certain qualities, you will find happiness in teaching."

Teachers' organizations aid recruitment in many ways other than disseminating information about teaching. Perhaps their most practicable contribution is their endeavor to create conditions that make teaching alluring. Students are unlikely to enter or remain in a calling if the conditions surrounding their work are unsatisfactory. Accordingly, teachers in service are striving to bring about improvement in working and living conditions, salary, tenure, retirement, supervision, and leadership.

Teacher-preparing institutions take seriously their share of responsibility for acquainting both high school and college students about the possibilities in teaching. Some activities intended to foster good public relations affect recruitment indirectly. For example, prospective students become interested in college through publications—annual catalogues, summer bulletins, college newspapers, and student yearbooks—which may be distributed to high schools, libraries, and newspapers. They are influenced by publicity about a college disseminated through slides, films, radio programs, newspaper releases, and high school assembly programs presented by college forensic, dramatic, and musical organizations. Other activities are intended to encourage recruitment directly. Among them are guidance conferences in which members of the college staff and occasionally representatives of the student body participate. Conferences may be conducted on college campuses or at high schools. Campus visiting days are often planned for high school seniors.

Once students are enrolled in college, the recruitment cause can be furthered by guided observation in elementary and secondary school classrooms, contacts with children through such groups as Girl Scouts and Boy Scouts, personal interviews, courses giving information on opportunities in teaching, and better programs for future teachers. Some suggestions for improving programs are given in this chapter.

The lay public as well as teachers and teacher-education institutions has a role in recruiting teachers. The esteem in which the public holds teaching carries tremendous weight. Young people are reluctant to enter a field that does not rank high in community regard. The opinions of parents are particularly significant. Unless fathers and mothers are willing for their sons and daughters to teach, the calling cannot draw the young people it deserves.

The public helps determine the caliber of tomorrow's teachers through the kind of teaching staff and the quality of the local school program it provides. Pupils form their ideas of teachers and teaching from their own school experiences. Overworked, underpaid, uninspiring teachers leave an imprint that exhortations about importance of teaching cannot smooth away. In many respects the local school system is in a key position in helping pupils decide for or against teaching as a career.

PRESERVICE TEACHER SELECTION AND GUIDANCE

Preservice selection of teachers is inevitably linked with recruitment and guidance. Selection must be made from candidates who intend to become teachers. Unless a sufficiently large number of the right kind of people are available, selection fails to serve its real purpose. While the current teacher shortage may make any consideration of selection seem impractical, raising the standards high enough to command respect will in the long run increase the number of people attracted to teaching.

Any plan of preservice selection assumes that we can tell about a person's chances to succeed in teaching at some future date. The accuracy of prediction depends on the ability (1) to define what constitutes successful teaching, (2) to identify traits that contribute to it, (3) to measure or identify these traits in individuals, (4) to change or develop trait patterns and to forecast changes.

On all these points we admit frankly that research has not supplied a scientific basis for selection. Lack of agreement as to which teachers in service are successful puzzles researchers. A teacher who is rated superior by one supervisor may be judged unsatisfactory by another. Typical college measures of success show low correlation with those used by employers. With this variation in judgment as to competent and incompetent teachers who are actually employed we can expect difficulty in distinguishing traits which contribute to effective and ineffective teaching.

In the absence of scientific evidence we must trust largely to judgments made by such groups as school officials and leaders in education. For generations schoolmen have used subjective estimates as their chief guide in choosing teachers. Although they have made mistakes of judgment, their opinions are doubtless preferable to mere chance selection and throw valuable light on the preservice prediction of teaching ability.

Methods of identifying and measuring traits in individuals are still unsatisfactory. Some procedures are highly subjective; others are relatively objective. By combining such techniques and sources of information as interviews, letters of recommendation, principal's rating, standard tests, and physical examinations, data are secured concerning scholastic achievement, physical fitness, personality, character, special aptitudes, attitude toward teaching, general interests, experience with youth groups, work experience, and socioeconomic status.

In view of the difficulties inherent in the task, thoughtful investigators are modest in their claims to success in predicting teaching ability. They are likely to be as cautious in their statements as Morse of the University of Michigan is when he writes:

Does this mean that there is no place for certain of the present practices in teacher selection? Obviously the profession is interested in obtaining not only the passable candidates but in obtaining those who are best fitted. Thus, if one does no more than a rough screening to eliminate the ill-equipped or obviously misplaced and provide encouragement to the optimum group he will have performed a significant service. On the factual side, we can appraise such things as the student's content knowledge in his field; on the skills side, his facility in reading, use of English, and objective thinking. Here we can require a given degree of competency as well as a set number of subject hours. We can appraise his interest in teaching, his personality characteristics and his basic motivational patterns. With due allowances for inaccuracies of such measures, the scores can be the basis of arbitrary elimination of the less adequate, used by the staff for guidance and therapy in some instances and by the student in self-appraisal in all instances. These items are not considered as predictors of teaching success; they can only form the basis for obtaining a potentially superior group upon which to graft the desired professional training. Until the newer methods of teacher selection are perfected and validated, programs must be content to claim only that they are dealing with minimum background essentials rather than selection in the true sense.[1]

When and How Selection Takes Place

Some colleges have a procedure for selection prior to admission to the institution. Under this plan students must meet certain standards before they are permitted to enroll. The nature of the standards depends on a number of factors. Among them are the attitude of the college toward the urgency of getting students of high quality for teaching, the opinion of advisers as to whether or not through remedial instruction the college can help a candidate overcome certain deficiencies, the facilities of the college, and the supply of and demand for teachers.

In state-supported institutions state legislation has a bearing on selective admission. In some states the laws make selective admission difficult; in others, they make it mandatory. For example, state universities in Ohio and Nebraska must accept nearly all applicants who are graduates of accredited high schools, but the candidates are not necessarily permitted to enter the school of education. By way of contrast, the enrollment of students in state teachers' colleges in New York and New Jersey is regulated by the state department of education on the basis of qualification of students and size of college.

Once students are enrolled in college the process of selection

---

[1] William C. Morse, "Some Problems of Pre-Service Teacher Selection," *University of Michigan School of Education Bulletin*, April, 1948, p. 100.

operates at various times. It may take place on the freshman level; it may be deferred until the junior year. In the latter case, additional data upon which to base a decision are available. Moreover, juniors are more mature and can profit better from vocational counseling than can freshmen.

Whatever the plan employed, the selective process should be continuous. The evidence available when a student enters college is insufficient for wise judgment. Furthermore, changes in personal qualifications occur after admittance. Some students overcome initial deficiencies, while others develop undesirable traits or fail to make the expected growth. Accordingly, elimination and redirection of a student should be possible at any time.

Responsibility for guidance should rest not with the personnel department alone, but with the entire staff. All teachers should collect pertinent data about students, and all should share in the guidance program.

Moreover, students should have a voice in making decisions concerning themselves. If they understand what is required for success in teaching and can consider evidence bearing on their own competence or promise, they are likely to take responsibility for deciding how to proceed.

The Commission on Teacher Education attaches considerable weight to practice in self-analysis and self-education for a prospective teacher. The Commission believes that "it develops his ability to understand his own motivations and work out plans for satisfying them in ways consistent with professional success; it promotes his skill in the identification of problems and the location and use of resources relevant to the solution thereof; and it predisposes him to treat his own students, later on, with the same respect that he has enjoyed. Initiative and self-reliance, rather than docility and dependence, are fostered."

If selection is to accomplish its purpose, teachers and public alike should support leaders who are endeavoring to establish and enforce high standards. A timely effort in this direction is being made by the National Education Association through its Commission on Teacher Education and Professional Standards. Eventually we may succeed in spreading the idea that admission to a teacher-preparing institution is a privilege, not a right. Consideration of the welfare of pupils rather than the candidates' desire for teacher education must be paramount.

TEACHER PREPARATION

Teacher-education colleges have a responsibility for providing programs designed to develop the academic, professional, and social competences deemed essential for teachers. Both curricular and extracurricular experiences may contribute to these outcomes.

We shall consider first some aspects of programs which are planned to contribute to academic and professional rather than to social competences. However, since no hard and fast line separates these competences, the same experiences often contribute to more than one outcome.

Programs ordinarily include (1) academic courses to provide broad cultural contacts with various fields of learning, (2) academic courses to provide specialization in specific subjects or fields or in work at specific levels such as the primary grades, (3) professional courses including professional laboratory experience, and (4) experiences to promote satisfactory personal growth.

Academic Education

Since every teacher should have sound scholarship and broad, general culture, his education should acquaint him with the major fields of human interest and knowledge. He should be a truly educated person who can imbue others with a love of learning. As Henry Suzzallo once wrote: "In the best modern and democratic sense the new type of teacher must be a thoroughgoing humanist regardless of his special field of scholarship. . . . He will need to be a civilized person if he is to bring all the resources of civilization to bear upon the youth, which is to say that he will be liberally educated. There are too many academic specialists in our public schools who know very much about a field of study and nothing much about the wide ranges which make up the rest of life."

Traditionally teacher-education institutions have included some provision for liberal education in their curriculums. The term liberal has a wide connotation. Chapman and Counts explain it in this way:

Since the college is only incidentally a place of preparation for vocational efficiency, it must be judged mainly by the extent to which those who engage in its activities are being liberalized. For many reasons there is need at the present time to stress those values which are inherent in the very name of the institution—the college of liberal arts. The word "liberal" in its most obvious meaning, as applied to education, has a wide connotation. It signifies a generous and plentiful training, a training that frees from ignorance, superstition, dogmatism and narrowness in ideas, doctrines, or sympathies. To be liberal is to be free, to be liberated, to believe in the extension of freedom in educational, political, social, religious, and other institutions. It is something dependent upon knowledge, yet of a different order. Knowledge is but one element in the making of a "free-man." An individual is liberated not by information and by great learning, but rather by an attitude toward life. To be able to see two sides of a question, to realize ignorance, to appreciate expert service, to feel an abiding obligation to study and direct the course of social life, to be public spirited, to recognize the claims of national and international obligations, these are the hall-marks of the man whose education has made him free. Only as our colleges submit their students to broad, generous, and humane learning, calculated to foster these virtues, can they hope to send forth free citizens. Only as men and women of this temper take their places in the Great Society with a fixed determination to cleave to that which is good and to shun that which is evil, can any hope be held out for a more secure and humane world.[2]

That every person needs a liberal education because he is a human being was well stated in a radio address by Dr. Stringfellow Barr, formerly president of St. John's College, Annapolis.

Not every citizen's occupation requires advanced training in a vocational school. It may require only experience and the power to think well about that experience. But every citizen requires a liberal education in order that he may think well—not merely that he may think well about the occupation which he, but not all men, follows, but that he may think well about the common problems which confront all

[2] J. Crosby Chapman and George S. Counts, *Principles of Education*, Houghton Mifflin Company, 1924, pp. 486–487.

citizens of a free society, whether in war or in peace. No slave should receive a liberal education, whether he be a serf, a chattel slave, a wage slave, or the subject of a totalitarian state. Slaves should be given vocational training, for slaves are not men in the full sense, but tools of other men. In a slave society, only the masters should be liberally educated. But in a free society education in the liberal arts is the right and the necessity of every citizen. . . . In war, as in peace, we cannot afford a stupid citizenry.

During the past third of a century traditional provisions for liberal education have been modified in some colleges by the general education movement. Gaining a foothold in universities like Harvard and Minnesota, the general education idea spread to other schools, including teachers' colleges.

The Harvard Report defines general education as "that part of a student's whole education which looks first of all to his life as a responsible human being and citizen." It stresses common understandings and skills required in effective living. It contributes to his abundant living regardless of his special role in economic and social life.

Since prospective teachers have personal and social problems not unlike those of other people, their general education should be essentially the same as that of all other college students. For a teacher, general education serves the twofold purpose of developing him as a "worthy member of society" and as a "worthy deputy of society." It should "equip him to improve the professional situation in which he works, to take his place as a citizen of democracy, to exemplify the personal virtues he advocates, and to contribute to the advancement of the work of his professional guild toward the general social welfare."

The pattern of courses has varied from campus to campus. In some institutions the courses have followed traditional curricular divisions with one or more offerings in the humanities, the social sciences, and the natural sciences. Other schools have pioneered in cutting across departmental boundaries and built courses around some central problem of man or nature.

Perhaps concern as to whether the label should be "liberal" or "general" education is beginning to diminish. As Woodring points

out: "The word 'general' in general education means not specialized in the sense of preparing for a single trade or vocation. All
good general education, like all sound liberal education, is designed to develop complete human beings, free of the limitations
of ignorance, prejudice, and provincialism, who are capable of
taking their full part in a free society. General education, in the
best sense, and liberal education, in the best sense, have identical
aims."[3] And, he adds, "Whether we call it 'liberal' or 'general' is
of little moment; this is the education teachers need."[4]

If four years of college are allotted to teacher education, the
authors of the National Survey of the Education of Teachers in
1933 recommend that at least 25 percent of the time should be
spent on general education. The final report of the Commission
on Teacher Education recommended that at least three-eighths of
the college experience for prospective teachers should be general
in content. Since this agrees with the recommendation of the
Harvard Committee, it seems to indicate agreement that the time
devoted to general education should be the same for prospective
teachers as for other students. One of the groups at the Second
Bowling Green Conference in 1958 proposed that the total program for the bachelor's degree for teachers should include approximately 45–50 percent general education, 25 percent subject-matter
field or fields, 15–20 percent professional areas, and 10 percent free
electives.

Specialized Education. All teacher-education colleges agree on
the necessity for comprehensive specialization in the teaching field
or fields. However, the nature and scope of this specialization are
not uniform. For prospective high school teachers specialization
in particular subjects or fields is obligatory; from 24 to 36 semester
hours are usually stipulated in a given subject or field. In some
colleges prospective secondary teachers are expected to have only
one major field, but in others they may have two major fields, or
a major and a minor, or a major and two minors.

[3] Paul Woodring, A *Fourth of a Nation*, McGraw-Hill Book Company,
Inc., 1957, p. 231.
[4] *Ibid.*, p. 232.

Programs quite unlike those ordinarily prescribed for secondary-school teachers are urged by leaders concerned with modifying the existing high school programs. Preparation in broad fields corresponding to the major areas taught in secondary schools is recommended.

The breadth of preparation necessary for a core teacher is indicated by a list of competences drawn up by the John Dewey Society.

1. The core teacher should be able to sense and help solve the problems faced by individual boys and girls.
2. The core teacher should be able to relate the more common problems and concerns of youth to the larger social setting with its values, problems, and achievements.
3. The core teacher should be able to function as a group leader working with his students.
4. The core teacher should be able to relate community conditions and resources to the education of youth.
5. The core teacher should be able to draw upon and use effectively major general resources of scholarship needed to understand and deal with the more common and persistent personal-social problems and concerns of youth.
6. The core teacher should be able to guide youth in the selection of educational activities which foster continuous all-round development.
7. The core teacher should be able to guide youth in the wise selection of an occupation.[5]

Although an elementary teacher cannot specialize in all the fields in which he is called upon to help children develop insights, he should develop depth in some area of subject matter. Such specialization gives vitality to his teaching and enhances his own sense of achievement.

The best type of specialized preparation for elementary teachers is an open question. According to Gray of the University of Chicago, "In many cases 'elementary education' is adopted as the field of concentration which may or may not include specific academic

---

[5] Hollis L. Caswell (ed.), *The American High School: Its Responsibility and Opportunity*, Eighth Yearbook of the John Dewey Society, Harper & Brothers, 1946, pp. 189–195.

courses. In probably a majority of the cases a sequence of profes-
sionalized subject matter is required paralleling a sequence of general courses in education. In still other cases a major, a major and
a minor, or two minors are required in academic fields. A final
plan involves a careful selection of courses which extend general
or liberal education into specific areas of greatest value to elementary school teachers, such as United States history as an extension of the social science area."

The major difficulty in planning a program for preparing elementary teachers stems from the fact that school officials frequently
expect and want the impossible. They expect an elementary
teacher to be prepared in every basic and special subject of the
elementary curriculum and to be competent in areas of child
growth and development and in human relations to an extent that
would require training equal to that of a psychologist, a psychia-
trist, a social worker, and a trained nurse.

Ashbaugh has given timely warning that we should call a halt
to ever-increasing demands for more and more varied knowledge
and more and more varied skills and abilities on the part of elementary teachers.

The present demands of scholastic competency in almost all fields
of knowledge, the insistence upon practical efficiency in such varied
areas as psychology, social welfare, health, nutrition, nursing, etc., all
sum up to a manifest impossibility of the attainment of a product of
which we have a right to be proud. That our present graduates of
teacher training institutions have a bit of acquaintance in a great
variety of fields, that they are as emotionally stable, as socially adap-
table, as willing to undertake the task as they are is a great compliment
to the young people themselves and to the efforts of the teacher training institutions. I question seriously as to whether it is any compliment
to those who develop the philosophy of education which calls for such
an extensive program of both knowledge and skill.[6]

Ashbaugh advises that we furnish to elementary teachers the
supplementary services of welfare workers, physicians, psychologists, psychiatrists, nurses, and nutritionists. He believes that

[6] E. J. Ashbaugh, "A Growing Problem in Elementary Education," *Educational Forum*, May, 1947, pp. 416, 427.

unless such provision is made, "we are headed for an ever-increasing dearth of good elementary teachers because the most intelligent young people will not undertake the impossible task which is demanded of them."[7]

Professional Preparation

A third element in the preparation of teachers is education to develop professional competence. This includes both professional knowledge and professional skills. Critics of teacher education who clamor for little or no professional work differ from professional educators in their conception of the purposes of American public education and of the teaching-learning process that gives most promise of fulfilling these purposes. Stephen M. Corey, Dean, Teachers College, Columbia University, has pointed up the differences in this way:

If you are disposed to believe that the primary, if not the exclusive, aim of public education is to teach a limited number of important skills or a predetermined body of important subject matter; that those who are hard to teach this material to should not go to school very long; that the boys and girls who do not learn the skills and the subject matter as fast as adults believe they should are somehow bad and that teachers shouldn't have to contend with them; and that discipline is best engendered in children by imposing on them somewhat fixed and presumably high standards—if you hold these beliefs or others like them, your conclusions about teacher education are almost inevitable. You will conclude that teaching, as such, is not too difficult or too complicated, and that almost anyone can do it commendably *if* he is reasonably bright, is a college graduate, knows enough about what he's trying to teach, and can make children behave. . . .

When you believe these things, and, as I have said, many sincere and respectable people do, it is quite reasonable to contend that knowing what is to be taught is by all odds the major responsibility of the teacher and that professors of psychology or history or philosophy or sociology in liberal arts colleges can teach an additional course or can give their current courses a twist that will throw some light on educational questions. Believing these things, it is quite natural to urge that the amount of time being given to professional education might well be reduced so that, as President Griswold recently put it, we can

[7] *Ibid.*, p. 427.

provide for a "massive infusion of the Liberal Arts" into the education of secondary school teachers. Believing these things, it is easy to contend that the tricks of the teacher's trade can best be picked up on the job by the new teacher working hand in hand with the experienced teacher who has himself learned these tricks.

You and I, it seems to me, find it impossible to accept this view of teacher education because we hold different convictions about what American public education should be, about the young people for whom it should be provided, and about the kind of teachers who are needed to facilitate it. Most of us believe that the tremendous variations among boys and girls, variations in their backgrounds, their motivation, and their needs, require that the curriculum be flexible rather than predetermined. Most of us believe that all American boys and girls should have experiences, at least in the elementary and secondary schools, that are maximally meaningful to them at the time and that their judgments are necessary if we are to know what is meaningful. Most of us believe that discipline is a consequence of practice in planning and decision making and of experience with their effects. Most of us believe that good citizenship and health are proper and important educational goals and that these goals are not achieved merely by learning information *about* citizenship or health.

Because of these beliefs most of us take the view that good teaching is exceedingly difficult and complex and dynamic and exacting. Good teaching is of a different order from keeping school. We are certain, too, that the attitudes and feelings and concepts and practices that distinguish the fine teacher have been learned and can, to a substantial degree, be taught. This conviction almost inevitably leads us to the conclusion that the preservice as well as the in-service education of teachers cannot be casual or incidental and that it cannot be turned over to people with quite different assigned duties. The professional education of teachers must be someone's central concern.[8]

Acquiring professional competences calls for extended preparation. The Commission on Teacher Education recommends that "strictly professional elements should be allocated from one-eighth to one-sixth of the time available in a four- or five-year program of teacher preparation. It is to be recognized that there will be doubt as to whether some important elements should be classified as general or professional education and that acceptable

[8] Stephen M. Corey, "Controversy in Teacher Education: the Central Issue," *The Future Challenges Teacher Education*, American Association of Colleges for Teacher Education, Eleventh Yearbook, 1958, pp. 31–32.

integrations may be worked out that cause the professional block
to appear to exceed or to fall short of this proportion."

Usually from 15 to 20 semester hours of professional courses
including special methods and student teaching are required for
high school teachers, and from 20 to 30 semester hours for elementary teachers. Schools differ, however, in the specific content
and organization of professional courses.

A current trend is to group significant topics of professional
education into three or four large areas. This integration not only
furnishes continuity of experience but also gives increased flexibility and variety. Woodring proposes organizing all undergraduate
courses into two large blocks of time. One would include all essential material about the child and the learning process; the other
would deal with the philosophical problems which underlie all
education. One group at the Second Bowling Green Conference
identified these four areas of professional education that should be
required of all teachers: (1) an understanding of the nature of
the individual—human growth and development; (2) nature of the
teaching-learning process—psychology of learning; (3) purposes
and functions of the school in society—social and historical foundations of education; and (4) the practicum—student teaching.

Another trend is toward student participation in planning
courses. This has a twofold advantage for future teachers. First,
the students come to grips with democracy in action. They learn
realistically how group processes operate. Since they are likely to
teach as they have been taught rather than as they are taught to
teach, they are likely to allow their own pupils to share in planning
educational experiences. Second, they gain insight into the whole
process of institutional planning; therefore, they are ready to
coöperate in the affairs of their school when they begin their professional career.

The best time for professional education is a troublesome question. In some colleges it is scheduled after two years of general
education; in others it is introduced at the beginning of college
work and parallels it throughout. At its national meeting in 1949,
the American Association of Colleges for Teacher Education voted

for the inclusion of professional education as an integral part of each of the four years of college.

Professional Laboratory Experiences. Professional laboratory experiences represent a type of professional work that may profitably be incorporated into each of the four years of college. As defined by the American Association of Colleges for Teacher Education, the term refers to "all those contacts with children, youth, and adults which make a direct contribution to an understanding of individuals and their guidance in the teaching-learning process." Such experiences may be offered not only in professional but in academic courses. They should contribute to the clarification of concepts taught in various courses as well as to the personal growth of the student. They should include observations based on individual or class assignments or a combination of both. They should also afford participation in a wealth of activities with children in both school and community situations.

Students in a first-term sophomore course in education at the North Texas State College in Denton shared in 17 kinds of experiences:[9]

1. Taking part of first-grade children to walk while the room teacher gave a test to the others.
2. Accompanying first-grade children to the playground for free play.
3. Helping individual children with reading.
4. Assisting children with their Junior Red Cross boxes.
5. Helping to re-arrange the schoolroom.
6. Checking the children's workbooks.
7. Helping a child to write his class report for the school newspaper.
8. Preparing materials (papers, filing pictures, indexing books, etc.) for use in the schoolroom.
9. Typing report of test scores.
10. Helping to score standardized tests.
11. Taking materials to and visiting the Negro school.
12. Taking children on a "Field Trip" or walk.
13. Checking *Weekly Reader* "tests" and discussing them with the teacher.
14. Telling stories to the second-grade children.

[9] Nellie L. Griffiths, "Some Pre-Student-Teaching Experiences," *Educational Administration and Supervision*, December, 1949, p. 492.

15. Hectographing some poems for the fifth grade.
16. Helping to give some tests.
17. Checking arithmetic papers.

The climax of professional laboratory experiences is student teaching. This term is used to designate "a period of guided teaching when the student takes increasing responsibility for guiding the school experiences of a given group of learners over a period of consecutive weeks."

In many respects student teaching is the most vital part of a teacher's education. It has somewhat the same place as interning does in preparing for the medical profession. Only through supervised full-time work with pupils over a period of time can a student gain a sense of the many-sided parts of the teacher's total task.

The amount of time spent on student teaching is not uniform. The American Association of Colleges for Teacher Education recommends that full-time student teaching be given over a period long enough "to permit the student teacher to understand the growth of learners resulting from the guidance given. There is need for each student to stay with at least one laboratory situation for a period sufficiently long to see how activities develop and how learnings are extended and horizons widened. The student should stay with a laboratory situation long enough to see the growth emerge from coöperative efforts of teachers and learners so that he may know the satisfactions of teaching, know his strengths and weaknesses in guiding teaching-learning situations, and attain a functional understanding of the learning process."

A student teacher should take part in the major activities of a teacher both in and out of the classroom. He should learn the overall organization of the school; attend faculty meetings, parent-teacher meetings, school functions, clubs, athletic events, and dramatic productions; assist with extracurricular activities and playground supervision; and enter into community life in general.

The plan implies scheduling programs so that a student will be free to teach for a number of weeks without interruption. The exact length of time and when it is called for depend on the college, the kind of laboratory experiences prior to student teaching, and the needs and individuality of the student himself.

Ordinarily student teaching comes near the close of preparation, usually in the senior year. However, since readiness is an individual matter, the particular assignment to teaching should be made when it best fits the students' needs. To determine readiness, some schools impose special conditions for admission to student teaching. In an investigation of 216 teacher-preparing institutions, McGrath found that some have no special standards but others have as many as fifteen. He suggests the following seven criteria for selection that could be used as a starting point in nearly all teacher-education colleges:

1. Successful report on a physical health examination.
2. Successful ratings on a battery of tests.
3. Written recommendations of at least three faculty members.
4. Satisfactory speech and hearing test.
5. Successful record of participatory experiences with youth groups.
6. Satisfactory grade point average, and meeting the graduation and certification requirements.
7. Committee action to consider all factors.

Student teaching may be carried on in schools on or off the campus. The campus school, the most common, should be an integral part of the college and should serve as a coördinating center of all its work. J. E. Windrow, Director of the Division of Public Services of George Peabody College for Teachers, aptly sets forth the relation that should exist between the college and a campus school:

If the teachers college would keep its own integrity, it should be able to say to the world at all times, "Come, this is my school, the professional center of all my efforts: (1) *Understand* its philosophy and ways of working; (2) *study* its curriculum, based on the vital interests and needs of its children; (3) *observe* its teachers, who are the best classroom artists the nation affords; (4) *consider* its organization and administration, whose success is measured in results, not machinery; whose schedules are designed to serve, not control; whose faith in democratic human relations is real, not verbal; (5) *meet its parents*, who have a vital interest in the contemporary world and the building of a better society; (6) *see* its program of guidance, which is concerned with helping children discover their needs, develop their life purposes, formulate plans of action, and proceed to their realization; (7) *view* its physical environment, which is both pleasing and comfortable, made so through the intelligent effort and coöperative planning of its faculty, students, parents, and community; (8) *appreciate* this miniature democracy, wherein pupils, teachers, and parents work together to solve their common problems; where learning activities literally teem with opportunities for critical thinking; where children are required to face facts and do what they do in the face of facts; where decisions are made and responsibilities assumed; where fundamental honesty and social concern are the guiding principles of daily living; where the whole community provides a laboratory for learning; where children and teachers are led out into the stream of life and find the security which comes with an awareness and understanding of the things around them."[10]

The trend, however, is toward using public schools as well as campus schools. An advantage of the off-campus school is that it provides lifelike teaching situations that the student will encounter when he is teaching in the public schools. A disadvantage is that it often represents mediocrity—a situation that a teachers' college should neither endorse nor perpetuate.

Discriminating selection of off-campus schools for student teaching is of the essence. The school should be willing to coöperate whole-heartedly with the off-campus program. It should have master teachers with sympathetic attitudes toward preservice education for teachers and a willingness to learn the skills and techniques needed in supervising student teachers. It should have an adequate curriculum adapted to pupil and community needs.

Although many colleges which prepare teachers offer no professional laboratory experiences beyond student teaching, there is growing recognition of their practicality. The American Association of Colleges for Teacher Education states three purposes that can be served by these experiences: "(a) to permit students to do more intensive work in areas of special interest or competence; (b) to

[10] J. E. Windrow, "The Function and Future of the Laboratory School," *Professional Laboratory Experiences*, Twenty-Seventh Yearbook, Association for Student Teaching, 1948, pp. 88–89.

make it possible to strengthen shortage areas; and (c) to help students gain a new over-view of the larger school situation and to study the interrelationships of its various parts."

The Association believes that the nature and extent of the laboratory work that follows student teaching should be decided on the basis of individual needs. "For some the work will be largely observation, for others direct teaching; for some there will be many short contacts, for others an extended period of work in a single situation; for some the experiences will be largely within the school situation, for others chiefly in the community. For some such laboratory contacts will be extensive; for others they will be a resource to be used occasionally."

A valuable form of professional laboratory experience after student teaching is internship. The term refers to a period of teaching carried on with the approval and close supervision of a teacher-education institution. During this period the intern assumes the activities of responsible teaching, with frequent counsel from the college staff and from supervisors and teachers of the school system in which he is interning. Although internship is often limited to students who are seeking an advanced degree, it is sometimes available for undergraduate students.

Development of Social Competences

Social competences cannot be neatly separated from the academic and professional. All must be interlaced in a meaningful way. Shaped by the sum total of a person's experiences, social development goes on continuously and inevitably. Primarily from liberal or general education a student derives productive ideas, sets of beliefs, ethical views, and spiritual values which become part of his inner life and mold his personality. The plans mentioned at this point, however, contribute not so much to deep inner meanings as to external or social behavior.

For promoting social growth, colleges have programs whose form depends on community and college facilities and the policies of the personnel staff. Some colleges provide curricular offerings in the form of special courses in social adjustment or of units in fields like home economics and physical education. Illinois State Normal University has experimented with a two-hour credit course that gives both men and women practice in sending invitations, planning and giving teas, receptions, and dinners, and acting as hosts and hostesses.

Other colleges capitalize on extracurricular activities for developing social competence. Campus organizations have projects to aid students in their personal growth. For example, a freshman handbook with information on dress and behavior may be issued by upperclassmen. Talks on phases of social adjustment are given to small discussion groups or the entire student body.

Organizations do more, though, than supply information about behavior. They sponsor activities—dances, teas, games, concerts, dramatic productions, and lecture programs—which contribute to social growth. The importance of engaging in these activities can scarcely be overemphasized. "Social development usually does not result from a series of lectures on the subject, but rather from an interplay of students and faculty members in a social environment." Fraternities and sororities pay special attention to social training for their members. In the close daily contacts of group living, members of properly supervised fraternal organizations have a natural setting for perfecting social graces.

If a college has dormitories, their directors may outline programs for social training. The plan at the Illinois State Normal University, described by the dean of women, is illustrative.

In our two dormitories, a planned program of social training is provided throughout the year. A mature householder for the men's dormitory supplements the personal attention of the Dean of Men, developing approved social habits through group living, dining room experience, and more elaborate social events such as teas, receptions, open house, and parties formal and informal. In the women's dormitory, reserved for freshmen, 19 junior and senior women are invited by faculty committee to become "Honor Residents". . . .

These older students, chosen for social maturity and interest in counseling, are leaders in the Hall, under the guidance of the Director of the Hall, who is also the Assistant Dean of Women, and is especially trained in personnel work. Honor Residents do not room with freshmen, but are located in every corridor, with responsibility for the fresh-men in their corridors. An upper-class woman sits at each table with a group of freshmen (table combinations are changed at intervals). At least once a day, service of plates by a hostess at each table is practiced, the Honor Resident serving the first week in the fall, and a different freshman serving each day thereafter. Dressing for more formal dinners on Wednesday evenings and Sunday noons is regular practice, and inviting guests is encouraged by providing a special menu for these occasions. House meetings, Honor Resident meetings with the Director of the Hall, and corridor meetings of Honor Residents and the Director supplement group guidance.[11]

Graduate Programs

The acquisition of the competences that teachers need calls for extended college preparation. Although four years are now regarded as a minimum, the trend is toward five years. In the not too distant future, some specialized positions may call for six or seven years.

Changes are recommended in graduate programs in order to help teachers carry on their tasks in the modern school. The prevailing requirements for graduate degrees should be modified to accent preparation not for research but for better teaching. Broad education rather than highly specialized technical training, and study of subject content as well as professional education, are desirable.

The National Council for Accreditation of Teacher Education recommends that the five-year curriculum should be broken into two parts, each with its separate focus. The two parts should be planned as a whole, however, with the understanding that the curriculum will not be completed until the fifth year has been taken. The first part should be four years in length and should prepare the teacher to begin to teach. The second part should be one year in length and should be given after one or more years of teaching experience. Although the fifth year should include some additional general or liberal education, emphasis should be in the field of subject matter concentration and further professional education.

[11] Anna R. Keaton, "Training in Social Competence," *Teachers College Journal*, March, 1948, p. 105.

Engendering Professional Attitudes

The National Council for Accreditation of Teacher Education points out that on the first day of school the new teacher becomes a member of a school faculty and a member of the teaching profession. Accordingly the preservice curriculum should help the prospective teacher understand his functions in working with a faculty group and his responsibilities as a member of the teaching profession. He needs to know the characteristics of a profession and to appreciate the significance of professional ethics. He should have a knowledge of professional organizations to which he may belong, their goals, and their services.

Every student who expects to teach should catch a glimpse of teaching as a growing profession. It has many characteristics that distinguish a profession from a trade or business, such as these:

1. It involves primarily intellectual activities.
2. It has a body of specialized and technical knowledge and requires a mastery of corresponding skill in practice.
3. It requires fairly high standards for entrance to the field.
4. It has professional standards for the regulation of its group.
5. It has associations that are indicative of a feeling of group consciousness among teachers.
6. It offers opportunity for a lifework.
7. It places service above personal gains.

Several of these characteristics are discussed in other chapters. Here we shall consider only professional ethics and organizations for teachers.

Professional Ethics

Members of a profession formulate in a code of ethics the standards that will govern their relation to the public and to other members of the profession. Codes of ethics for teachers date back to 1896 when the first official state code was adopted by the state teachers' association of Georgia. Since then 46 other state associations and Puerto Rico have adopted similar codes. Moreover, numerous guiding principles have been prepared by individuals and by local groups of teachers. In an effort to secure a uniform code, the National Education Association appointed a committee on ethics in 1924. The code drawn up by the committee was officially approved in 1929 and has since undergone four revisions. The revision adopted by the Representative Assembly at Detroit in 1952 follows.

We, the members of the National Education Association of the United States, hold these truths to be self-evident—

—that the primary purpose of education in the United States is to develop citizens who will safeguard, strengthen, and improve the democracy obtained thru a representative government;

—that the achievement of effective democracy in all aspects of American life and the maintenance of our national ideals depend upon making acceptable educational opportunities available to all;

—that the quality of education reflects the ideals, motives, preparation, and conduct of the members of the teaching profession;

—that whoever chooses teaching as a career assumes the obligation to conduct himself in accordance with the ideals of the profession.

As a guide for the teaching profession, the members of the National Education Association have adopted this code of professional ethics. Since all teachers should be members of a united profession, the basic principles herein enumerated apply to all persons engaged in the professional aspects of education—elementary, secondary, and collegiate.

FIRST PRINCIPLE: *The primary obligation of the teaching profession is to guide children, youth, and adults in the pursuit of knowledge and skills, to prepare them in the ways of democracy, and to help them to become happy, useful, self-supporting citizens. The ultimate strength of the nation lies in the social responsibility, economic competence, and moral strength of the individual American.*

In fulfilling the obligations of this first principle the teacher will—

1. Deal justly and impartially with students regardless of their physical, mental, emotional, political, economic, social, racial, or religious characteristics.
2. Recognize the differences among students and seek to meet their individual needs.
3. Encourage students to formulate and work for high individual goals in the development of their physical, intellectual, creative, and spiritual endowments.
4. Aid students to develop an understanding and appreciation not

only of the opportunities and benefits of American democracy but also of their obligations to it.

5. Respect the right of every student to have confidential information about himself withheld except when its release is to authorized agencies or is required by law.
6. Accept no remuneration for tutoring except in accordance with approved policies of the governing board.

SECOND PRINCIPLE: *The members of the teaching profession share with parents the task of shaping each student's purposes and acts toward socially acceptable ends. The effectiveness of many methods of teaching is dependent upon cooperative relationships with the home.*

In fulfilling the obligations of this second principle the teacher will—

1. Respect the basic responsibility of parents for their children.
2. Seek to establish friendly and cooperative relationships with the home.
3. Help to increase the student's confidence in his own home and avoid disparaging remarks which might undermine that confidence.
4. Provide parents with information that will serve the best interests of their children, and be discreet with information received from parents.
5. Keep parents informed about the progress of their children as interpreted in terms of the purposes of the school.

THIRD PRINCIPLE: *The teaching profession occupies a position of public trust involving not only the individual teacher's personal conduct, but also the interaction of the school and the community. Education is most effective when these many relationships operate in a friendly, cooperative, and constructive manner.*

In fulfilling the obligations of this third principle the teacher will—

1. Adhere to any reasonable pattern of behavior accepted by the community for professional persons.
2. Perform the duties of citizenship, and participate in community activities with due consideration for his obligations to his students, his family, and himself.
3. Discuss controversial issues from an objective point of view, thereby keeping his class free from partisan opinions.
4. Recognize that the public schools belong to the people of the community, encourage lay participation in shaping the purposes of the school, and strive to keep the public informed of the educational program which is being provided.

5. Respect the community in which he is employed and be loyal to the school system, community, state, and nation.
6. Work to improve education in the community and to strengthen the community's moral, spiritual, and intellectual life.

FOURTH PRINCIPLE: *The members of the teaching profession have inescapable obligations with respect to employment. These obligations are nearly always shared employer-employee responsibilities based upon mutual respect and good faith.*

In fulfilling the obligations of this fourth principle the teacher will—

1. Conduct professional business thru the proper channels.
2. Refrain from discussing confidential and official information with unauthorized persons.
3. Apply for employment on the basis of competence only, and avoid asking for a specific position known to be filled by another teacher.
4. Seek employment in a professional manner, avoiding such practices as the indiscriminate distribution of applications.
5. Refuse to accept a position when the vacancy has been created through unprofessional activity or pending controversy over professional policy or the application of unjust personnel practices and procedures.
6. Adhere to the conditions of a contract until service thereunder has been performed, the contract has been terminated by mutual consent, or the contract has otherwise been legally terminated.
7. Give and expect due notice before a change of position is to be made.
8. Be fair in all recommendations that are given concerning the work of other teachers.
9. Accept no compensation from producers of instructional supplies when one's recommendations affect the local purchase or use of such teaching aids.
10. Engage in no gainful employment, outside of his contract, where the employment affects adversely his professional status or impairs his standing with students, associates, and the community.
11. Cooperate in the development of school policies and assume one's professional obligations thereby incurred.
12. Accept one's obligation to the employing board for maintaining a professional level of service.

FIFTH PRINCIPLE: *The teaching profession is distinguished from many other occupations by the uniqueness and quality of the profes-*

sional relationships among all teachers. Community support and respect are influenced by the standards of teachers and their attitudes toward teaching and other teachers.

In fulfilling the obligations of this fifth principle the teacher will—

1. Deal with other members of the profession in the same manner as he himself wishes to be treated.
2. Stand by other teachers who have acted on his behalf and at his request.
3. Speak constructively of other teachers, but report honestly to responsible persons in matters involving the welfare of students, the school system, and the profession.
4. Maintain active membership in professional organizations and, thru participation, strive to attain the objectives that justify such organized groups.
5. Seek to make professional growth continuous by such procedures as study, research, travel, conferences, and attendance at professional meetings.
6. Make the teaching profession so attractive in ideals and practices that sincere and able young people will want to enter it.

Organizations for Teachers

Members of a profession have organizations that give evidence of a feeling of group solidarity. Teachers' organizations have had an enviable role in professionalizing teaching. Innumerable groups with large memberships are now in existence. Some are open to every teacher, whereas others are restricted to special groups. Some are local in scope; others embrace county, district, state, or nation. The *Educational Directory*, published annually by the Office of Education, lists about five hundred national and regional associations and more than one hundred state organizations. Local associations have become so numerous that the directory does not include them.

National Organizations. There are many national organizations for teachers, such as the National Society for the Study of Education; national associations for teachers of academic subjects; the American Federation of Teachers, which is affiliated with the American Federation of Labor; the National Teachers Division of the United Public Workers of America, CIO; and the National Education Association.

The American Federation of Teachers, founded in 1916, is controlled entirely by classroom teachers. The governing body is its convention held annually. The interim governing and administrative body is The Executive Council of 16 vice-presidents and the president who is a full-time officer. The president and vice-president are subject to election every two years. Dues in each local are determined by the local, and include local, state, and national affiliation. The official publication is *The American Teacher*.

The National Education Association, the largest society of its kind in the world, came into being as the National Teachers' Association on August 26, 1857, in Philadelphia. Its purpose was "to elevate the character and advance the interests of the teaching profession and to promote the cause of education throughout the country."

In 1870 the National Association of School Superintendents and the American Normal School Association joined the National Teachers' Association and the name was changed to the National Education Association. In 1906, under a special act of Congress, the organization was incorporated as the National Education Association of the United States.

The National Education Association coördinates efforts of teachers in solving professional problems. It is instrumental in raising standards for teachers, in promoting teacher welfare, and in securing educational legislation. Membership is open to anyone interested in education who pays annual dues of $10 or a life membership fee of $225. About 47 percent of the teachers in the United States are enrolled in the organization.

In addition to meeting the general needs of teachers, the National Education Association through its departmental structure also serves special needs. Since the first departments were created in 1870, additional ones have been established from time to time until in 1958 there were 30. (See Figure 1.)

State Organizations. The first state teachers' association was organized in 1840 in Alabama. Today there is such an association in every state in the Union and in Puerto Rico. Their membership in 1959 totaled 90 percent of the country's teachers. Most of them

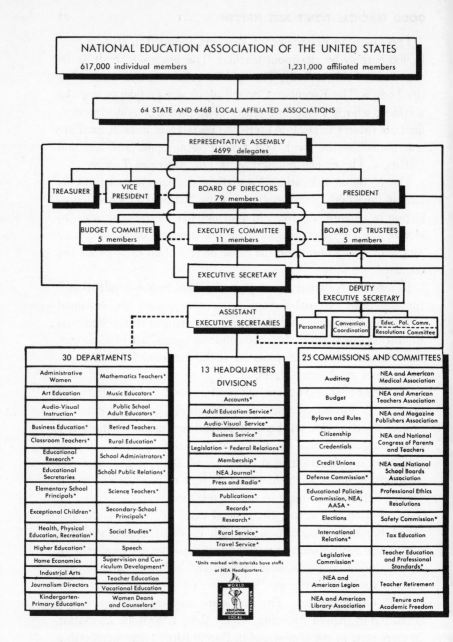

FIGURE 1. Organization of the National Education Association.

employ full-time secretaries and own their own headquarters building. Each association publishes a journal with news of the group's activities and articles of professional interest.

Local Associations. Local associations are the oldest teachers' organizations in the United States. One of the first was organized in New York City in 1794.

In addition to being the oldest, local associations are also the most numerous. In 1959, more than 6400 local associations were affiliated with the National Education Association.

Activities of the local associations deal with:

1. Improving the professional services of members.
2. Building *esprit de corps* in the teaching staff.
3. Improving teaching conditions and economic status—efforts at the local level.
4. Improving teaching conditions and economic status—efforts at state and national levels.
5. Rendering community and civic services.
6. Interpreting the association and the profession.

International Organizations. The twentieth century has witnessed the founding of six international organizations of teachers. The most recent, the World Confederation of Organizations of the Teaching Profession, came into existence in Copenhagen, Denmark, in 1952, through the union of three international teachers' associations. The Confederation has its headquarters in the National Education Association building.

Purposes of the Confederation are to foster a conception of education directed toward promoting international understanding, to improve preparation of teachers so as to equip them better to serve the interests of youth, to defend the rights and interests of the teaching profession, and to promote closer relationships among teachers in different countries.

Each year a different theme is chosen on which national associations prepare reports as the basis of discussion by the delegates. After the conference, the reports are published in English and French for world-wide distribution.

SUMMARY

Recruitment to secure competent young people for teaching is a responsibility of teachers · and their professional organizations, teacher-education institutions, and the lay public. Linked with recruitment is preservice selection to obtain persons who are most likely to succeed as teachers. Selection may take place prior to admission to the institution or at various times after the student is enrolled in college. Teacher-education programs should seek to develop the academic, professional, and social competences deemed essential for teachers. Both curricular and extracurricular experiences may contribute to these outcomes. Preparation should include academic courses designed to contribute to sound scholarship and general culture, academic courses to furnish specialization in specific subjects or fields, professional courses including laboratory experiences, and experiences to promote satisfactory social growth. During the preparatory period students should envisage teaching as a growing profession whose members are interested in professional ethics and organizations.

QUESTIONS AND EXERCISES

1. What is the relation between improved preparation for teaching and respect for the calling?
2. How may the public attitude toward teachers' colleges affect the kind and number of young people who choose teaching as a career?
3. State arguments for and against the conversion of teachers' colleges into state colleges.
4. Should preparation of teachers be largely at state expense?
5. How have professional organizations of teachers influenced American education?
6. Hold a round-table discussion on the question, Should teachers affiliate with labor unions?
7. Should general education be the same for teachers as for other people?
8. List criteria that you think should be used in determining whether or not a student should be accepted as a candidate for teacher preparation.

9. Distinguish between the purposes of liberal arts and teachers' colleges.
10. If a teacher knows his subject well, does he need professional education?
11. Examine and characterize ten professional education magazines.
12. Examine yearbooks of five professional organizations that your instructor specifies.
13. Secure information concerning dues, official publication, time and place of meeting, and work of your state teachers'-association. If possible, attend a meeting of it.
14. Show how this statement by Faunce may apply to the in-service preparation of teachers: "The world is held back chiefly, not by bad men and women, but by good ones who have stopped growing." Outline a plan for in-service education that you could follow during your first five years of teaching.

SELECTED REFERENCES

Andrews, Leonard Otwell, "School Exploratory Experience for Prospective Teachers," *Educational Research Bulletin*, September, 1950, pp. 147 ff.
Association for Student Teaching:
   Audio-Visual Aids in Teacher Education, Evaluating Programs of Student Teaching, Twenty-Sixth Yearbook, State Teachers College, Lock Haven, Pa., 1947.
   Evaluation of Student Teaching, Twenty-Eighth Yearbook, State Teachers College, Lock Haven, Pa., 1949.
   Improving Instruction in Professional Education, Thirty-Seventh Yearbook, State Teachers College, Lock Haven, Pa., 1958.
   Practicing Democracy in Teacher Education, Twenty-Fifth Yearbook, State Teachers College, Lock Haven, Pa., 1945–1946.
   Professional Laboratory Experiences, Twenty-Seventh Yearbook, State Teachers College, Lock Haven, Pa., 1948.
Bigelow, Karl W., "How Should America's Teachers Be Educated?" *Teachers College Record*, October, 1954, pp. 20–24.
Commission on Teacher Education, *The Improvement of Teacher Education*, American Council on Education, 1946.
Harvard University Committee on the Objectives of a General Education in a Free Society, *General Education in a Free Society*, Harvard University Press, 1945.
Huggett, Albert J., and Stinnett, T. M., *Professional Problems of Teachers*, The Macmillan Company, 1956.

National Education Association, Department of Higher Education, *Current Trends in Higher Education* (published annually).

National Education Association and American Association of School Administrators, Educational Policies Commission, *Professional Organizations in American Education*, 1957.

Second Bowling Green Conference Report, *The Education of Teachers: New Perspectives*, National Commission on Teacher Education and Professional Standards, National Education Association, 1958.

"Teacher Personnel," *Review of Educational Research*, June, 1958 (entire issue).

Witty, Paul Andrew, "An Analysis of the Personality Traits of the Effective Teacher," *Journal of Educational Research*, May, 1947, pp. 662 ff.

Woodring, Paul, *A Fourth of a Nation*, McGraw-Hill Book Company, Inc., 1957.

Woodring, Paul, *New Directions in Teacher Education*, The Fund for the Advancement of Education, 1957.

AUDIO-VISUAL MATERIALS

Films

Assignment: Tomorrow (32 minutes, Sound, B & W, National Education Association). Stresses the importance of teachers and schools in preserving the American way of life. Explains the program of the National Education Association.

Introduction to Student Teaching (20 minutes, Sound, B & W, Indiana University). Shows how three student teachers get acquainted with school personnel and policies, become accustomed to handling routine classroom matters, become familiar with a variety of instructional materials, and learn as much as they can about the pupils.

No Teacher Alone (20 minutes, Sound, B & W, National Education Association). Designed to help teachers better understand the National Education Association and how it works with state and local associations to make gains for the teaching profession and the schools.

Not By Chance (28 minutes, Sound, B & W, or C, National Education Association). Depicts a prospective teacher of high school science in a teacher-education program where she acquires the knowledge, the understanding of children, and the special skills that will make her a good teacher.

Preparation of Teachers (20 minutes, Sound, B & W, United World). Pictures phases of the teacher-education program at Ball State

Teachers College. Highlights the importance of understanding children, providing for individual differences, and developing desirable personality traits in teachers.

Recordings

A *Forward Look for the Teaching Profession* (30 minutes, 33⅓ rpm, Educational Recording Services). W. S. Elsbree, Columbia University, compares teaching with other professions and enumerates professional aims of successful teachers.

I *Do Not Walk Alone* (15 minutes, Tape, Minnesota State Department of Education). The value of membership in the Minnesota Education Association.

CHAPTER IV

Looking Toward Employment

An important goal of a prospective teacher is to secure employment. To be effective and ethical in his quest for a position, he needs to be acquainted with acceptable procedures for locating positions and for making applications. He should know the essentials of a contract and the ethical considerations involved in terminating a contract and in notifying proper authorities of a change in position. Once he has accepted a position, he has the responsibility of ascertaining how the school and community assist in orienting new teachers, and of mapping out a plan for growth in service.

LOCATING A POSITION

Most beginning teachers, as well as some experienced ones, secure their positions through the placement bureaus of the colleges and universities where they received their preparation. The majority of teacher-education institutions have such bureaus to assist their graduates. Registration is usually free. If a fee is charged, it is only nominal.

Registrants can increase their opportunities to obtain desirable positions by keeping their files up-to-date and by notifying placement officers promptly of any change in position. In spite of repeated admonitions, many registrants disregard these two vital points. Yet they expect the bureau to give them prompt service and to inform them of openings.

College officers are limited by the number of calls they receive for teachers. However, they can often render excellent service because they are in a position to know each candidate's qualifications and the characteristics of the schools that are seeking teachers. Thus they can help locate the right person in the right position. Since the success of a beginning teacher is related to the character of the school where he teaches, he should heed the advice of the college placement office.

A few beginners turn to commercial teachers' agencies. Approximately eighty such agencies maintain placement services. In 1957, 64 of these agencies were members of the National Association of Teachers' Agencies, whose purpose is "the clarifying, standardization and improving of teacher-placement procedure in the interest of education." Candidates usually pay a small registration fee. If placed through an agency, they pay a commission, usually 5 percent of the first year's salary. To avoid misunderstandings they should thoroughly read contracts with commercial agencies. Candidates should also investigate the success of the various agencies in placing teachers in the localities where they prefer to work.

Besides registering with placement bureaus or agencies, teachers usually try to locate vacancies through their own efforts. They employ such means as these: inquiries directed to superintendents or to other employing officials, information secured from friends and acquaintances in various school systems, contacts with school officials at educational meetings, announcement services by educational periodicals, and information from state supervisors of vocational subjects and other personnel who travel and hence are in touch with many school systems.

In light of the foregoing discussion, it is interesting to learn how 2600 first-year teachers in 1955 actually secured their first teaching jobs. A study conducted by the National Education Association disclosed that nine in every ten respondents got their first teaching positions either through applying on their own or through help given by a college or university placement office—presumably, the placement office of the college or university where they were educated. Even when students applied on their own, they probably requested that credentials be sent by their placement bureau.

Less than two in 100 found it necessary to pay a commercial employment agency for assistance in locating their first jobs. The smaller the district in which they worked, the more likely it was that they relied upon this source. The larger the school system, the more likely it was that they got their first job without assistance from anyone; the smaller the school system, the more likely they received aid.

Because of the greater shortage of elementary school teachers, a smaller percent of them than of secondary school teachers needed help in locating their first jobs. The percent of elementary school teachers getting jobs through commercial employment agencies was only one-third that of secondary school teachers, and the proportion getting assistance from a college or university placement office was significantly less for elementary than for secondary school teachers. Fifty-nine percent of the elementary school teachers got their first jobs on their own personal applications, while the corresponding figure for secondary teachers was only 48 percent.

ETHICAL CONSIDERATION IN SECURING A POSITION

A teacher should know the recognized, acceptable ways of seeking a position so that he may keep his search ethical in every respect. By adhering to legitimate practices, he will improve his chances of success and will avoid bringing discredit upon himself as well as upon teachers as a group. (See Code of Ethics of the National Education Association, Fourth Principle, page 89.)

An ethical applicant conducts business through professional channels. Since boards of education usually delegate to the superintendent of schools the task of recommending qualified candidates, an applicant for a position in a village or city school ordinarily interviews only the superintendent. If it is necessary to contact board members, the superintendent will inform the applicant. In rural districts with no superintendent of schools, a teacher applies directly to the board.

In the best school systems teachers are selected solely on the basis of merit. Such extraneous matters as residence in a community, relationship to a board member or a school official, or acquaintance with influential persons in the community play no part in the choice.

A candidate should refrain from asking for a specific position known to be filled by another teacher. If he wishes to teach in a given system or if he hears rumors of a vacancy, he may send a letter of inquiry to ascertain whether or not an opening exists.

A candidate should also avoid indiscriminate distribution of applications and use of "to-whom-it-may-concern" letters of recommendation. An employer desires confidential information about an applicant's qualifications for a specific position rather than an open letter filled with glittering generalities.

APPLYING FOR A POSITION

As has already been pointed out, a teacher ordinarily presents his application to the superintendent of schools.

In urban districts, as well as in many other districts, teachers usually have to fill out a formal application blank available from the school district. Some of the blanks call for routine information only, such as academic and professional preparation, teaching and nonteaching experience, personal information (sex, age, marital status, health, etc.), and a list of references. Others seek additional information of various kinds. For example, the application form for Champaign (Illinois) Community Schools includes these questions under the section on personal preparation and qualifications:

1. Professional books read in last two years aside from those used in connection with professional courses from which you have received credit.
2. For what magazines do you subscribe?
3. What current reading do you do?
4. What professional conferences or associations have you attended in the last two years?
5. Are you willing to use your abilities in extra-class activities?
6. What extra-class activities do you prefer to sponsor?
7. What specific preparation and experience have you had for this work?

8. Are you familiar with the "Home Room" system as followed in a departmentalized program?
9. State two or more standards by which you would be satisfied to have your teaching judged.
10. What do you consider the chief difficulties which you have encountered in your work?
11. What certificate have you now in force? By whom issued? When granted?
12. Have you had any experience in debate? Oratory? Dramatics?
13. What traveling have you done?
14. In your opinion, how often should a teacher take additional training in summer school?
15. What is the minimum annual salary you would accept here?
16. If elected and conditions prove satisfactory, have you any plans which would prevent your teaching here at least three years?

Letters of Application

Besides filling out a formal application blank a teacher usually writes a letter of application.

There are three types of letters written by candidates for teaching positions: (1) letters of application, (2) letters of inquiry, and (3) various types of follow-up letters.

Since letters of application may win or lose a position, teachers should learn how to write them convincingly. The Placement Bureau of Eastern Illinois University offers its registrants detailed suggestions about letters.[1]

LETTERS OF APPLICATION

In general a letter of application briefly tells of being informed of a vacancy and indicates a desire to be considered for a position. Perhaps a few salient facts pertaining to your background should be mentioned, especially as these relate to the vacancy in question. You may mention that the Placement Office is sending your credentials and offer to come for a personal interview at the convenience of the superintendent. There may be occasions when you will be called upon to enclose a data sheet—a sample may be secured in the Office.

It is ethical to write a letter of application *only for a specific position known to be vacant.* Since most school officials require letters of

[1] The suggestions were prepared by Dr. William H. Zeigel, Associate Dean, Teacher Education and Placement, Eastern Illinois University, Charleston, Illinois.

application before giving any consideration, such letters should be sent as soon as possible after it is known that a vacancy exists. In some cases the system requests the applicant to fill out its own application forms.

Mechanics of letters of application: Letters of application should be written on white paper, 8½″ × 11″ and on one side only. Most school officials prefer that letters be typewritten. They should be mailed in white envelopes (#10) long enough to hold the letter with two horizontal folds. You should not use tinted, social, or soiled stationery. Watch for misspelled words, grammatical or punctuation errors, poor paragraphing, poor penmanship, erasures, blots, irregular margins, crooked lines, and careless typing. A poor letter of application can cause you to be dismissed from consideration!

Contents of the letter of application: If you are particularly interested in a given position, it is probably well to attach a recent photograph with the application letter. This may later serve to associate you with the credentials or the personal interview. Make certain that your name and address are written legibly on the back of the picture.

The letter should tell how you learned of the vacancy.

The letter should briefly give your educational qualifications which will fit you for the vacant position. You should not refer to courses by number since these mean nothing to persons in the field; you should be specific and tell how your training fits you for the work. The certificate which you will have upon graduation should be named.

You should briefly indicate the nature of your extra-curricular and church or community experiences which might enable you to serve better in the school system where you are making application. You should be accurate and honest in indicating the amount of participation and whether you feel competent to direct various activities. School officials are interested in persons who have worked with the Scouts, FFA, 4-H, and like organizations. While school law prevents officials from asking about your church affiliation, it may possibly be to your advantage to list church, lodge, and fraternal affiliations particularly if you have assumed leadership responsibilities in this work.

Give complete information regarding teaching experience with regard to places, grades or subjects taught, and dates of service.

If you have a special reason for wishing to have a particular position, state it in a straightforward professional manner. Do not seek the position on a charitable basis.

Do not mention salary unless to state that you will be willing to accept the customary salary or salary according to the schedule.

Indicate a willingness to furnish further information and to come for a personal interview at the convenience of the school officials.

You may furnish the name and address of any reference in addition to references which will be furnished in the credentials. For example: If applying in Decatur, you may wish to add the name of a well-known Decatur person.

LETTERS OF INQUIRY

If you desire to teach in a certain school system or geographical area or have heard rumors of a vacancy for which you are qualified, it is ethical to write a letter of inquiry before making application.

As much care should be devoted to this letter as to the letter of application. It might briefly state the reason for your interest in the particular school system and you should make inquiry concerning a definite position.

For example: "Have you a vacancy in your sixth or seventh grade?" Nothing else need be said except to request an application blank and possibly information concerning the vacancy if one exists.

FOLLOW-UP LETTERS

It is frequently advisable to write a follow-up letter. Since the purpose of such a letter is to keep your qualifications uppermost in the mind of the employing official, perhaps one of the best times to write such a letter is shortly after having a personal interview but before any final action is taken. It always pays to be courteous with reference to any favors or kindnesses shown, and a letter of thanks may strike a responsive chord in the mind of the prospective employer. Possible reasons for such a letter might be:

1. To supply additional information after applying.
2. To thank for consideration and for any personal favors during the interview such as lunch, transportation, housing, etc.
3. To thank following your election to a position.

It is important, as always, to pay attention to mechanical features. Such letters should be brief, courteous, and dignified.

Personal Applications

Another way in which officials appraise candidates is through a personal interview. Although the task is sometimes delegated to assistants, superintendents usually conduct the interviews.

The chief purposes of a personal interview are to afford:

1. A general appraisal of the candidate's personality.

2. Opportunity to gain some insight into candidate's educational philosophy and professional outlook.
3. Opportunity to evaluate candidate's voice and personal characteristics.
4. Opportunity to learn of candidate's ambitions and plans for the future.
5. Opportunity to get information on the candidate's education and experience.[2]

The Placement Bureau of Eastern Illinois University gives specific suggestions for making a personal application.[3]

THE PERSONAL INTERVIEW

Preparing for an interview: There are certain things which can be done ahead of time in order to insure that the interview runs smoothly:

1. Learn what you can of the school and community so that you will understand the situation, can ask intelligent questions and have a basis for conversation. For example, it might be well to know college students from the town, teachers who teach there, outstanding citizens, industries, and school achievements. It also might be well to know in advance about any new building program, why the previous teacher left and what the community expects of its teachers in a social way and in community service. The Placement Office may have printed material about the school system—ask at the reception desk.
2. Prepare for a good personal appearance; give careful attention to clothing, shoes, hair, finger nails, avoidance of odors, teeth and breath—do *not* over-dress.
3. Prepare in advance a list of questions you hope to have answered during the interview.
4. Take along a data sheet or an official transcript of your college record. A copy of the transcript may be secured from the Registrar's Office for $1.00 if you have used your two free copies. These should be requested at least a week in advance.
5. Appear for the interview alone. Mother and Father cannot help your chances for employment.
6. Since some interviews will be conducted in the Placement Offices

[2] National Education Association, Research Division, *Teacher Personnel Practices, 1950–51: Appointment and Termination of Service,* Research Bulletin, February, 1952, p. 15.

[3] Zeigel, *op. cit.*

with little or no advance warning, you should dress during the spring in a way that you will not feel reluctant to come in and meet a possible employer.

The interview itself: The following points should be kept in mind:

1. Greet the employer by name, shake hands firmly if he extends his hand in greeting, and remain standing until offered a seat.
2. Let the superintendent initiate and direct the conversation, at least during the initial stages of the interview. Ask your prepared questions as the discussion moves along.
3. Be natural, look directly at the interviewer, be interested, and avoid personal mannerisms which may detract.
4. Be friendly and smile on occasion, but discuss the position earnestly to reveal a sincere interest. Do not beg for the job.
5. Let the superintendent open up the discussion of salary. The Placement Office will try to inform you of what the school's salary schedule calls for and current salary trends.
6. Don't be too aggressive—even in times of teacher shortage, it doesn't build good will.
7. The superintendent should terminate the interview and you can offer to take further steps as indicated. Express appreciation and leave promptly. You may ask when the board may take action.

The follow-up: Remember the appointment usually comes after the interview—sometimes days later. These things may be done:

1. While in the community you may wish to investigate housing, stores, recreation, etc. If you know people in the community, you may wish to meet them. Be ethical and tactful in what you say regarding the town and school system.
2. Visit other school personnel if requested.
3. Write a letter of appreciation as described in this brochure under "Follow-Up Letters."
4. Do not attempt to bring pressure of others in getting the position.
5. If offered the position:
    a. try to consider carefully its advantages and disadvantages—not letting the beginning salary weigh too heavily.
    b. notify the school as promptly as possible of your *acceptance or rejection of the offer*.
6. If not offered the position, remember that there were other capable candidates and that there will be other notifications. The superintendent has seen you and may be able to use you some other year.

Other Procedures for Appraisal of Candidates

Besides asking applicants to fill out application blanks and appear for personal interviews, superintendents use other procedures for evaluating their qualifications. Among these are collecting information and opinions from the persons named as references, observing the applicant's classroom work, requiring him to take a physical examination, requesting him to submit transcripts of credit, and asking him to take written examinations. Written examinations are not used extensively, however, except in large cities. A few cities use the National Teacher Examinations, prepared and administered by the Educational Testing Service of Princeton, New Jersey, and others give their own tests. One advantage of using the National Teacher Examinations is that they are given periodically in several hundred widely scattered cities.

Superintendents, especially in large cities, often assemble an orderly array of factors to be considered in choosing candidates. This listing of qualifications forms the basis for establishing an eligibility list. A superintendent may draw up an unranked list of approved candidates, or a rated list made by combining numerical ratings on measures of ability such as written examination, education, experience, and personal characteristics. Weightings used in making rated lists vary markedly. For example, some superintendents attach great importance to education and experience, whereas others give them little weight.

In certain cities the best-qualified candidates are put on List A; all others go on List B. Vacancies are filled by choosing any qualified teacher from List A. No selection may be made from List B until List A has been exhausted.

TEACHERS' CONTRACTS

When a candidate secures a position, he should receive a contract that defines his rights and duties as well as those of the board of education.

Most states have laws governing teachers' contracts. Some require a written contract. Several prescribe a uniform contract for all school systems. Although oral contracts are valid in certain states, it is advisable for a teacher to have a written contract.

The Committee on Tenure of the National Education Association proposes six minimum essentials for a teacher's contract:

1. Definite statement as to length of school term.
2. Definite statement as to amount of salary.
3. Phraseology which is legally enforceable.
4. Specific legal requirements, such as kind of certificate, and any special provisions of state law that apply.
5. Definite date for notification of reëlection (at least 30 days before termination and preferably 60 or 90 days).
6. Provision for equal protection to employer and employee.[4]

The staff of the Michigan Education Association has prepared the contract which appears on p. 109 as an example of a good contract.[5]

The Michigan Education Association staff gives these reasons why this contract or a similar one should be used:

1. It is simple. It does not include clauses, terms, and phrases that are unnecessary.
2. The length of the school year and the opening date are clearly stated.
3. The salary and method of payment are clearly stated.
4. The services as a teacher are stated.
5. The rights of the school board or superintendent relative to assignment or transfer are definitely stated.
6. The sick-leave plan is stated clearly.
7. It provides for signatures by authorized officers of the school district and the teacher.
8. It does not contain a detailed list of teaching duties.
9. It does not contain a fifteen-day, thirty-day, or some other cancellation clause.
10. It does not include a list of causes for dismissal. These are usually hard to define and difficult to enforce. The courts will uphold any just and reasonable cause for dismissal.[6]

[4] *Teacher Personnel Practices, op. cit.*, pp. 21–22.
[5] Wesley E. Thomas, "Good Contract Recommended," *Michigan Education Journal*, March 1, 1955 (Reprint, p. 1).
[6] *Ibid.*, pp. 1–2.

Once a position has been secured, a teacher should adhere faithfully to the conditions of a contract until service thereunder has been performed, the contract has been terminated by mutual consent, or the contract has otherwise been legally terminated. Violation of a contract by a teacher may make him liable for damages

---

This Is a Good Contract

THIS CONTRACT, made the..day of.. 19........
(Insert Legal Name of School District)

BETWEEN .... of
.... County, State of Michigan, hereinafter called the School District,
and .... of ....hereinafter called the Teacher.

WITNESSETH: Said Teacher being certified to teach in the Public Schools in said County and State hereby contracts with said School District for the school year of...months commencing the
.... day of ....19........and said School District hereby contracts to hire said Teacher to teach as herein set forth, in consideration for which said School District will pay to said Teacher the sum of.. Dollars
payable in ....equal installments as follows: (1)..
....

The services of the Teacher shall consist of teaching in the Public School of said School District; the Teacher shall not be required to perform any other services not connected with the Public Schools.

(2)..

The Teacher is subject to assignment and transfer at the discretion of the Superintendent of Schools or the Board of Education.

IN WITNESS WHEREOF the parties hereto have hereunto set their hands and seals this day and year above written.

(Legal Name of School District)

By.. By..
    (Name)   (Official Position)   (Name)   (Official Position)

By..
    (Name)   (Official Position)   (Signature of Teacher)

---

assessed against him and may lead to revocation of his teaching certificate. In Illinois the School Code reads as follows:

No teacher who has entered upon contractual continued service may terminate such service during the part of the school year when school is in session nor for a period of sixty days just previous to the beginning of the school term except by agreement of the board and the teacher. No teacher entered upon contractual continued service shall be permitted to terminate it during any other part of the school year except by service upon the secretary of the board of written notice of the termination. Any teacher terminating said service not in accordance with this section is guilty of unprofessional conduct and liable to suspension of certificate, as provided under the law relating to the certification of teachers, for a period not to exceed one year.

Not only should conditions of a contract be fulfilled, but due notice should be given when change of position is contemplated. According to the Code of Ethics of the National Education Association, a teacher should "give and expect due notice before a change of position is to be made." In some states failure to give such notice may result in suspension of a teacher's certificate.

INDUCTION OF NEW TEACHERS

Many school systems have special plans for helping new teachers get started. Five practices are common:

1. Helping new teachers locate living quarters.
2. Holding conferences soon after school opens, at which their special problems are discussed.
3. Providing new teachers with personal copies of rules and regulations governing the school system.
4. Assigning an experienced teacher to give counsel to each new teacher.
5. Asking new teachers to report several days earlier than other teachers for special meetings and discussion.[7]

A commendable undertaking of the New York State Teachers Association is mailing an attractively printed message to all new teachers in the state each September. Here is the message:

WE WELCOME YOU—

a newcomer into a profession that is both old and honorable. It has traditions and ideals and great names which deserve your respect. It will remain honorable if you treat it with honor.

Its duties are often heavy and you will sometimes know weariness, anxiety, and discouragement. It will require all your tact, patience, tolerance, and courage.

Its rewards are intangible but satisfying. They come from the friendship of children and youths, from the respect of the community, from the pleasant companionship of fellow teachers. They come from the opportunities you will have to help those who need help and to light the able and ambitious on their way. They come from the realization that you are helping in the shaping of our society and of tomorrow's world.

[7] *Teacher Personnel Practices, op. cit.*, p. 23.

To this high calling, you bring the enthusiasm and vigor of youth, and the knowledge, the skills, and the understanding of children which are fruits of your years of preparation. To you, we who have served a little longer pledge our coöperation and support as we welcome you into the fellowship of teachers.

Many school systems issue handbooks for new teachers. Tulsa, Oklahoma, has a 40-page booklet crammed with pertinent information about the city and its schools.

The Ohio Education Association has an informative and interesting handbook, *Professional Pointers for Teachers*, that covers all sorts of problems, ranging from preparation for the first day to what organizations to join. An excerpt from the preface gives a taste of the style:

Pull up a chair equipped with cushions and crackers, and visit with us for one evening. As you read, we surround you and waft gentle thoughts into your pet day-dreams. Soon you will be as wise as the principal is, and as arrayed for the battle against ignorance as the oldest war horse in your building! Sh-h!!! Their secrets are all in this book.

Lay groups often share in the process of welcoming teachers. In Portland, Oregon, the American Association of University Women coöperates with the board of education in orienting new teachers. Sponsorship means an invitation to a member's home and two other contacts including a personal invitation to the A.A.U.W. tea for new members.

IN-SERVICE EDUCATION

A teacher's preparation should not end when a contract is signed or when a college degree is conferred upon him. That education should be a continuous process is as true for teachers as for pupils. The profession has no place for the George Apleys who wish that there were not quite so many new ideas. Advances in knowledge and changes in curriculum and social conditions make growth on the job imperative. "Who dares to teach must never cease to learn."

Although in-service education is not an innovation, the meaning of the term is changing. Until a few years ago it described the individual efforts of teachers to further their education. Since many teachers did not have a Bachelor's degree, they were concerned primarily with securing credits for a degree. If they were not pursuing a degree, they were frequently securing credits in order to raise their place in the salary schedule. They engaged in a variety of activities—summer study, summer work experiences, extension and home study, school visitations, travel, professional and cultural reading, attendance at professional meetings, and participation in community affairs.

Today in-service education is coming to be regarded as a coöperative endeavor. It centers around individual and group attempts to reach solutions of problems that grow out of actual teaching situations. It contributes not only to personal growth but also to a sense of group responsibility for the entire school.

The best programs of in-service education utilize genuine coöperative staff activity. According to the Commission on Teacher Education, "Democratic group methods provide the procedure to be employed. Through the development of policies councils, planning committees, study group conferences, and workshops teachers are enabled to share in educational planning and doing. Thus the teacher gains respect—his own, and that of others. Thus the power that resides in the ideas possessed by all teachers has an opportunity to express itself fully for the advantage of the schools. Able to help form policies and encouraged to act responsibly and freely in the implementation thereof, teachers find a new satisfaction in their profession. They learn by doing. And the educational program improves."

Democratic coöperation can take place only in a situation which stimulates free discussion and free inquiry. Administrators and teachers have to learn to work together in an atmosphere characterized by mutual understanding and respect. Teachers should arrive at decisions without being bound by predetermined ideas of the administration. From their administrators they should receive encouragement, sympathetic support, and intelligent leadership.

Programs of in-service study should be mapped out by staff members. Since it is usually not feasible for all the teachers to concentrate on a single project, there must be provision for more than one activity. Among areas often selected for study are child growth and development, the local community, curriculum and instructional problems, teacher welfare, school and community relations, and teacher-pupil relations.

Although groups may delve into different problems, there must eventually be coördination and integration. Once a solution has been reached it should be coöperatively evaluated and, if necessary, modified.

Since persons besides the teaching staff are concerned with the school, in-service education programs may enlist the coöperation of many segments of the community. The nonteaching staff, parents, and the public should all have a share in such programs.

In view of the fact that a coöperative study of group problems demands a vast amount of time, it cannot be regarded as a kind of extracurricular undertaking. The countless hours consumed by conferences and meetings of policy councils, planning committees, and study groups should not be added to an already crowded day. Specially scheduled time for in-service study should be allotted during the school day and school year, and suitable adjustment should be made in teachers' programs. The practice of employing teachers for the full twelve months of the year may be the ultimate solution. Under this plan teachers spend part of their summer on projects that enhance their personal and professional growth. For example, for six weeks during the summer teachers at Glencoe, Illinois, engage in activities that have been coöperatively determined. Certain teachers travel or attend colleges for advanced study, and others remain in Glencoe to take part in locally organized community programs. Each teacher may change his type of summer activity from year to year.

SUMMARY

Most beginning teachers secure their positions through their own efforts or through the placement bureaus of their colleges or universities. Some register with commercial teachers' agencies. A teacher should be ethical in seeking a position. He should conduct business through professional channels; seek employment on the basis of his qualifications only; apply for a specific position only when a vacancy is known to exist; avoid indiscriminate distribution of applications and use of "to-whom-it-may-concern" letters of recommendation. Candidates are usually asked to fill out formal application blanks and to write letters of application. Ordinarily a personal interview is required. When a candidate accepts a position, he should be given a written contract that defines his responsibilities as well as those of the school board. He should adhere to the conditions of the contract until the service called for has been performed or until the contract has been legally terminated. Due notice should be given when a change of position is contemplated. After he has accepted a position, he has an obligation to familiarize himself with procedures employed by the school and community in orienting new teachers, and to plan for his professional improvement through in-service education.

QUESTIONS AND EXERCISES

1. Invite the director of your college placement bureau to talk with your class about the services rendered to its registrants.
2. Secure sample contracts from the superintendent of schools in your home town. How do they compare with the contract recommended by the Michigan Education Association?
3. Invite a superintendent of schools to talk with your class about ways in which he thinks candidates can improve the effectiveness of their written and personal applications.
4. How does the school system in your community induct its new teachers?
5. Ask the superintendent of schools in your home community for a copy of the teachers' handbook. What types of information does it contain? Does it omit essential information that a new teacher would need?
6. Arrange a sociodrama for an interview.
7. Is it ever ethical to request a release from a contract? If so, what are some valid reasons for asking for a release?
8. What can a teacher do ethically if a school board refuses to release him from a contract?

9. Is a teacher ever justified in asking for an open letter of recommendation? Explain.
10. Should application blanks for prospective teachers call for information on religion and/or church affiliation, political party, and race?

SELECTED REFERENCES

Armstrong, Earl W., "Suggestions for Securing Teaching Positions," Federal Security Agency, Office of Education, Division of Higher Education, Circular No. 224, 9th rev., March, 1950.

Eye, Glen G., and Lane, Willard R., *The New Teacher Comes to School*, Harper & Brothers, 1956.

Lawson, Elizabeth K., and Reinhardt, Emma, "New Teachers Tell Their Story," *The Clearing House*, April, 1958, pp. 492–494.

National Education Association, Research Division, *Locating a Teaching Position*, Special Memo, February, 1957.

National Society for the Study of Education, *In-Service Education*, Fifty-Sixth Yearbook, 1957, Part I.

The Newly Appointed Teacher, published for Metropolitan School Study Council by Bureau of Publications, Teachers College, Columbia University, 1950.

Yauch, Wilbur A., Bartels, Martin H., and Morris, Emmet. *The Beginning Teacher*, Henry Holt and Company, 1955.

PART TWO

CULTURE AND EDUCATION

Courtesy, Standard Oil Company (N.J.)

It would seem to be unnecessary to emphasize the fact that education is a social process; the principle is axiomatic and applies as much to informal as to formal education. And yet there are still educationists who believe that education is autonomous, self-contained, and subject only to its own laws of development.

. . . .

At the other extreme stand those who believe that the school can go ahead of society and help to build a new social order. Both theories rest on the idea that the school is a self-determining agency, and both fail to realize that formal education is provided by society—ranging from the most primitive to the most advanced—to produce certain ends through the training of its younger generation to become members in it.

The statement that education is a social process implies that the individual is the creature of the group culture in general. In so far as he can learn from experience, he is the product of all the experiences that come to him in his cultural environment.

I. L. Kandel, *Education and Social Forces*,
EDUCATIONAL FORUM

Part Two, Culture and Education, presents a background for viewing education as a social process. It seeks to help students gain insight into the nature of culture as a basis for understanding the nature of education. It introduces them to the part various agencies of education play in molding the developing child. Special attention is given to the function of the school in preserving and promoting the democratic way of life.

CHAPTER V

Growing Up in American Culture

The infant whom Wordsworth envisions as coming

> Not in entire forgetfulness,
> And not in utter nakedness,
> But trailing clouds of glory . . .

has the same physical characteristics whether born in Timbuctoo or the United States. "Mewling and puking in the nurse's arms," he gives slight promise of his potentialities of development. Only familiarity with the course of human maturation enables us to envision the growth of a squirming, helpless body into "the whining school-boy, with his satchel and shining morning face, creeping like snail unwillingly to school."

The human infant, unlike the young of lower animals, does not have his patterns of future behavior clearly established at birth. Instead he has a highly plastic neuro-muscular-glandular system. At first he makes undifferentiated, diffuse, random movements. He cries, coos, gurgles, wiggles, grimaces, opens and closes his hands, and slashes with his arms and legs. He responds indiscriminately to various forms of stimulation. Sooner or later, in a way that we cannot discern precisely, from his aimless movements emerge coördinated actions and specialized forms of behavior.

Contrasted with subhumans, which have greater development at the time of birth, the human infant is immature and helpless. Table 2 gives illuminating information about the number of accomplishments of a monkey and a baby. The monkey with its early acquisition of skills appears precocious, but its illusory superiority is secured at the expense of little talent for learning. The range of its attainments is severely circumscribed, and the peak of its ability quickly reached. The baby, unlike the monkey, is off to a slow start. His apparent initial handicap, however, turns out to be an asset. He is endowed by original nature with a small repertory of specific skills but with an untold capacity for learning. During his prolonged infancy he lays the foundation for adaptation to a complex environment and, in the course of time, forges far ahead of the monkey.

TABLE 2. Chronological Table Comparing the Ontogenetic Ages of Similar Developmental Items in *Macacus rhesus* and in Man

Developmental Items	Age of Appearance in Macaque	Age of Appearance in Man
Crying, sneezing, suckling, winking	1 day	1 day
Response to sound (unadaptive)	2 days	1 day
Head and eyes turn to follow object	3 days	2–3 mos.
Grasp at object seen (visual stimulus)	5 days	5–6 mos.
Recognitive responses to sound	11 days	5–6 mos.
First attempts to walk	12 days	12 mos.
Solid food first eaten	4 weeks	6–12 mos.
Scoops objects with palmar prehension	3 weeks	6 mos.
Opposes thumb and fingers	5 weeks	7–10 mos.
Sustains weight by reflex clasping	0–3 days	0–3 weeks
Plucks pellet (or grain of corn) opposing thumb and fingers	6 weeks	10 mos.
Attempts to draw mother into play	5 weeks	10–18 mos.
Holds head up steadily and gazes about	5 days	3–4 mos.
Follows moving hand with eyes	6 days	3–4 mos.
Attempts to crawl	12 days	9 mos.
Runs (trots)	14 days	18–24 mos.
Weaned	7 weeks	6–12 mos.
Crumpling explorative play with paper	8 weeks	6–9 mos.
Attains virtually all adult vocalizations	9 weeks	12–24 mos.

SOURCE: A. Gesell, *Infancy and Human Growth*, The Macmillan Company, 1928, p. 345. Reprinted by permission of the author.

An experiment by Kellogg and Kellogg throws further light on comparative accomplishments of an ape and a child and on the limits set by heredity. In 1931 they took a female chimpanzee, Gua, aged 7½ months, and for nine months reared her with their son Donald, who was two and a half months older. They treated the chimpanzee and the child as nearly alike as possible, and tried to provide an identical psychological and physiological environment. Careful tests, experiments, and comparisons were made throughout the period. In the early part of the experiment the chimpanzee was equal and, in some respects, superior to the child. Gua had greater muscular strength, superior muscular coördination, quicker and more accurate movements, greater accuracy in localization of sound, superior memory, and faster rate of learning in all fields such as skipping, opening doors, eating with spoon and drinking from a glass, and bladder and bowel training. She was more coöperative, was quicker to obey, showed a tendency to kiss for forgiveness, and evinced more frequent sly behavior. She was also sensitive to weak stimuli such as faint noises and raindrops. Her faster rate of learning was probably due to a more rapid rate of maturation. However, toward the end of the nine-month period, Donald progressed more rapidly in acquiring verbal and manual skills. Up to the age of about a year, the ape was superior to the child, but after that the child began advancing at a more rapid rate. At the close of the experiment the child's abilities were expressed by an index of 68, as compared with the ape's 58. While at first the ape outdistanced the child, she was handicapped eventually by limits set by inheritance.

INTERRELATION OF HEREDITY AND ENVIRONMENT

Man is molded by heredity and environment. So inextricably are they intertwined that we do not know which counts more heavily. Both are ever present and mutually dependent. From the moment of conception environment constantly influences hereditary factors. Given original nature, environment can modify it in a most significant manner.

Basically man is an animal. He is a biological organism with certain physiological needs; he must drink, eat, breathe, and eliminate waste substances. The lengths to which he will go to satisfy a basic need may be demonstrated by his efforts to secure food if he is starving. A person who would ordinarily abhor crime may, like Jean Valjean, steal a loaf of bread to satisfy hunger. A parent who would usually teach his children to be law-abiding citizens may become the person described in the headline " 'Fagin' Father Given Year on Penal Farm." An unemployed father in this instance ordered his 14-year-old son to steal chickens and loot automobiles in order that the family might have food. When need is imperative, things not ordinarily used for food may be consumed. In *The Good Earth* Pearl Buck tells of pitiful attempts to sustain life during famine in China. "The cobs of corn they had dried and eaten, and they stripped the bark from trees, and all over the countryside people were eating what grass they could find upon the wintry hills. There was not an animal anywhere. A man might walk for a handful of days and see not an ox nor an ass nor any kind of beast or fowl."[1] A little earth was stirred up and given to the children. "This earth they had been eating in water for some days—goddess of mercy earth, it was called, because it had some slight nutritious quality in it, although in the end it could not sustain life. But made into a gruel it allayed the children's craving for a time and put something into their distended, empty bellies."[2]

As a physical organism man has certain capacities or structures that mark him off from other animals and limit his accomplishments. He cannot breathe oxygen from water like a perch; he cannot run with the speed and grace of a gazelle; he cannot soar high in the sky like an eagle.

But man is more than a biological organism. He is a social animal. He is dependent upon others not only for survival but also for human qualities. The traits that make him distinctively human seem to rest on society and culture. Although he could not acquire these qualities without native structures that mark him off from other animals, still the human characteristics are apparently learned, not native. Human nature is the product of social experience and interaction. Left to himself, man is a brutish being.

[1] Pearl Buck, *The Good Earth*, The John Day Company, 1931, p. 76.
[2] *Ibid.*, p. 83.

In this respect, man and lower animals differ strikingly. Lower animals develop their distinctive qualities even though they have no contact with others of the species. As Benedict puts it:

There are societies where Nature perpetuates the slightest mode of behaviour by biological mechanisms, but these are societies not of men but of the social insects. The queen ant, removed to a solitary nest, will reproduce each trait of sex behaviour, each detail of the nest. The social insects represent Nature in a mood when she was taking no chances. The pattern of the entire social structure she committed to the ant's instinctive behaviour. There is no greater chance that the social classes of an ant society, or its patterns of agriculture, will be lost by an ant's isolation from its group than that the ant will fail to reproduce the shape of its antennae or the structure of its abdomen.[3]

MEANING OF CULTURE

The traits manifested by human beings depend largely upon their social heritage, or, as anthropologists prefer to call it, their culture. At birth a child begins to acquire the practices of the group. Knowingly or unknowingly he takes on types of actions and forms of belief of the culture. Through these socially inherited ways of living his behavior and personality are shaped.

To the lay reader the word culture may be a trifle confusing since for anthropologists it does not have the popular connotation of "refinement," "manners," "etiquette," or "the best." Culture is not the possession of a "privileged class," a "select" few. It is the sum total of different kinds of behaviors and objects found in the group. It includes the entire man-made environment of the group. Ralph Linton, an anthropologist, defines culture as "the sum total of behavior patterns, attitudes, and values, shared and transmitted by the members of a given society."

Culture has a twofold division: material and nonmaterial. Material culture is tangible and concrete. It includes all kinds of implements and objects whether raw materials or manufactured products—diverse items such as knives and forks, spears, machine guns, adobe huts, skyscrapers, telephones, television sets, tractors,

[3] Ruth Benedict, *Patterns of Culture*, Houghton Mifflin Company, 1934, p. 11.

sarongs, mink coats, fountain pens, helicopters, foodstuffs, books, and pictures. Nonmaterial culture is intangible. It comprises types of behavior and kinds of knowledge—customs, beliefs, habits, morals, folkways, political ideas, prejudices, and religious faiths.

Through countless ages the culture, a vast complex of social practices fashioned to fit the exigencies of new experiences, has evolved. Certain ways of life have become characteristic of a given group of people. They are the social inheritance of every individual who grows up in that society.

So powerful and inescapable is this social heritage that to say we have inherited it gives a false emphasis. According to Levy, "*It has inherited us*. We are delivered up to it at birth and it moulds us and shapes us. To an extent we fear to realize, we are its creatures. We have its taboos, its religions, its politics, its language. It has words we cannot utter, thoughts we must not think, criticisms we dare not voice, and organs of the body we examine only in private. It has habits and decencies, cruelties and crudities, we assimilate so naturally as to be unaware of them. If they are pointed out to us we cannot, we dare not, see them."

Because of social inheritance, man is in a very real sense the heir of the ages. Through mutual aid and through oral and written language he is able to profit from earlier experiences of the race. Each generation adds its bit to the sum total of human knowledge and passes on the accumulated mass to succeeding generations.

Without the process of social inheritance man in the short span of a single life could not acquire the equipment needed to cope with the complex physical and social world. What would happen if social inheritance were interrupted has been depicted by Graham Wallas:

If the earth were struck by one of Mr. Wells's comets, and if, in consequence, every human being now alive were to lose all the knowledge and habits which he had acquired from preceding generations (though retaining unchanged all his own powers of invention, and memory, and habituation) nine-tenths of the inhabitants of London or New York would be dead in a month, and 99 per cent of the remaining tenth would be dead in six months. They would have no language to express their thoughts, and no thoughts but vague reverie. They could not read notices, or drive motors or horses. They would wander about, led by the inarticulate cries of a few naturally dominant individuals, drowning themselves, as thirst came on, in hundreds at the riverside landing places, looting those shops where the smell of decaying food attracted them, and perhaps at the end stumbling on the expedient of cannibalism. Even in the country districts, men could not invent, in time to preserve their lives, methods of growing food, or taming animals, or making fire, or so clothing themselves as to endure a northern winter. An attack of constipation or measles would be invariably fatal. After a few years mankind would almost certainly disappear from the northern and temperate zones. The white races would probably become extinct everywhere. A few primitive races might live on fruit and small animals in those fertile tropical regions where the human species was originally evolved, until they had slowly accumulated a new social heritage. After some thousands of generations they would probably possess something which we should recognize as a language, and perhaps some art of taming animals and cultivating land. They might or might not have created what we should call a religion, or a few of our simpler mechanical inventions and political expedients. They probably would not have re-created such general ideas as "Law" or "Liberty"; though they might have created other general ideas which would be new to us.[4]

UNIVERSALS OF CULTURE

An examination of culture patterns reveals that certain things are considered important in all cultures. The underlying framework is the same for Americans as for Africans.

As a result of their study of primitive peoples anthropologists have attempted to sketch the universal pattern of human culture. Clark Wissler classifies the facts of culture under nine heads:

1. Speech
     Languages, writing systems, etc.
2. Material traits
     a. Food habits
     b. Shelter
     c. Transportation and travel
     d. Dress
     e. Utensils, tools, etc.

[4] Graham Wallas, *Our Social Heritage*, Yale University Press, 1921, pp. 16–17.

        f. Weapons

        g. Occupations and industries

    3. Art, carving, painting, drawing, music, etc.

    4. Mythology and scientific knowledge

    5. Religious practices

        a. Ritualistic forms

        b. Treatment of the sick

        c. Treatment of the dead

    6. Family and social systems

        a. The forms of marriage

        b. Methods of reckoning relationship

        c. Inheritance

        d. Social control

        e. Sports and games

    7. Property

        a. Real and personal

        b. Standards of value and exchange

        c. Trade

    8. Government

        a. Political forms

        b. Judicial and legal procedures

    9. War[5]

The elements of culture listed by Wissler do not necessarily represent all the forms that may eventually come into being. Cultural patterns are not static, but dynamic. They change constantly, sometimes slowly, sometimes fairly rapidly. As new forms emerge, old ones disappear. The culture of today is a product of the past; the culture of tomorrow will be in part a creation of the present.

CULTURAL VARIATIONS

Although uniformities exist within cultural patterns, there are also wide variations. We shall mention some of the variations in national, regional, class, and family cultures with special reference to the American culture.

National Characteristics

Every nation has its own cultural patterns. Its design for living furnishes the standpoint from which it criticizes the ways of any

---

[5] Clark Wissler, *Man and Culture*, Thomas Y. Crowell Company, 1923, p. 74.

other cultural group. Orientals think that Americans confuse bigness, mere physical size, with greatness, and rapid change with
progress.

Young observes that "when two such contrasting cultures come
into contact with each other, conflict is very likely to ensue if one
group tries to impose its will upon the other."

To pick out the dominant attitudes and beliefs that make up
national characteristics is a baffling undertaking. Yet it is ever
interesting because, as Ralph Barton Perry has said, "almost anybody can have an opinion without impertinence" and "there are
no experts who have the answers."

Definition of national characteristics depends on the point of
view of the observer. Nations, like individuals, often do not see
themselves as others see them. Americans are surprised when
foreigners regard "Uncle Sam" as "Uncle Shylock" or as an "im-
perialist."

In an All-India radio talk G. L. Mehta, former envoy of India,
explains our "common man" to his people.

The common men and women of America are informal, hospitable
and, above all, generous. They are extroverts, not shy and reserved.
They are cheerful, optimistic, confident.

Ask an American when you meet him how he is. He will not say,
"Getting along" or "Not yet dead"; he will tell you, "Fine, very fine;
never better in my life!"

Americans look forward to the future, they do not hanker after the
past; indeed, they have not too much of a past to look to!

The American mind is essentially an engineering mind; Americans
are at their best in adapting discoveries and inventions; in making improvements and innovations; in producing and reproducing things on
a mass scale.

And let us recognize that the United States has acquired unparalleled strength, wealth and productivity in a very short time and that
the American "standard of living" is the highest in the world today—
whether we approve or not of all its manifestations.

But because of these high levels of income and productivity, we
should not imagine the common American living on the forty-fifth
floor of the Hotel Waldorf-Astoria in New York, working on the fifty-
fourth floor of Empire State building, and driving at furious speeds on
superhighways.

Americans are also "domesticated," fond of their families and homes and communities in which they live and, above all, they work hard. They are continuously searching for labor saving devices, because a man is more expensive than a machine in their country. But this does not evidently seem to save much of their labor, as they feel almost guilty when they have nothing to do.

Brought up on a religion of work, output and productivity—in which they are ironically at one with the Communists—most Americans, including the well to do, cannot and do not expect rough work to be done by others. Since domestic servants are rare and are prohibitively expensive, the American man and his wife (as also their children) have to do almost all the domestic work themselves. Dignity of labor is not a phrase but a daily necessity.

There is a deeper reason, however, for this common attitude toward work. Americans firmly believe that, given equal opportunity, a "fair field and no favor," they can rise to the highest rungs of the ladder in business, industry, professions and public life.

Although Americans do exert themselves to the utmost to make money and live well, curiously enough, they do not believe in amassing wealth. It has been incisively observed by a British sociologist that the acquisition of money is important in America but its retention relatively unimportant.

Perhaps in no other country do people give so easily and freely almost without counting the cost. This is not because of a superabundance of wealth, for people are known to contribute even at a personal sacrifice.

It is true that material success is a primary objective of Americans and such success is measured in terms of dollars. But with this goes spontaneous and genuine good will for common people everywhere, a fellow feeling, a positive manifestation of a humane spirit.

The American Constitution is perhaps the only one in the world which declares "the pursuit of happiness" as an inalienable right of citizens along with life and liberty. From the cradle to the grave, Americans seek to translate this injunction in their lives and activities and organizations.

The people of America are gregarious. They like to meet people and they like others to meet them and they like to be liked. They are very fond of meetings and conventions, large banquets and fabulous parties.

They also change their habitations without sentimental attachment to a locality. They go from one profession or trade to another, they migrate from one city to another and settle down in completely strange surroundings. The fact that the United States is one vast country and has one law, one culture, one language, no customs barriers and plenty of economic opportunities enables them to do all this.

Like common people everywhere, Americans want to live in peace. They believe, in Abraham Lincoln's words, that their Declaration of Independence gives "liberty, not alone to the people of this country but hope to the world for all future time."[6]

Now we shall view American culture through the eyes of an American sociologist. Kimball Young suggests six characteristic features:

(1) belief in individual material success and general national progress; (2) an amazing faith in universal literacy and education to solve our social and personal problems; (3) belief in the virtue of sheer size or bigness, witnessed in our eternal building of ever-larger skyscrapers, larger industrial plants, bigger corporations, and larger school plants; (4) rapid movement through space, seen in increased mobility of our population and enhanced means of communication and transportation; (5) novelty or constant change to something new and more exciting, as in sensational news, exciting drama, speed racing, crazes, and fads; and (6) sense of power or the craving for domination, especially in terms of physical bigness—the booster and the "bigger and better" spirit in almost every important feature of our public life.[7]

The list of characteristics might be extended indefinitely. Other students of the American scene include such items as cockiness, resourcefulness, versatility, genius for technological developments, generosity, enthusiasm, the cult of the average man, interest in sports, faith in hard work and thrift, and interest in joining organizations.

As we attempt to select characteristics, we are struck by the fact that our statements are often paradoxical because our traits are frequently contradictory. Furthermore, as Ralph Barton Perry reminds us, "There is no American characteristic which is not exemplified elsewhere, or which some Americans do not lack. All that one can possibly claim is that there is among the people of

[6] G. L. Mehta, "Busy, Talkative, Generous Americans," quoted in *St. Louis Post-Dispatch*, August 10, 1958, p. 2 (8F).

[7] Kimball Young, *Sociology*, American Book Company, 2nd ed., 1949, pp. 37–38.

this half-continent taken as a whole, a characteristic blend of characteristics."

Whatever other features are mentioned, however, one characteristic is especially outstanding: belief in the principles of democracy. Americans believe in the infinite worth of every human being. They are devoted to freedom and are determined to maintain it for themselves and for others. They think that this is the greatest country in the world and will do whatever is necessary to preserve its rights. They are peace-loving in principle but warlike in practice. They have rarely had as long a period as a generation without a fight with someone. Although traditionally isolationist, they have engaged in two world wars. Yet, even in the midst of war, they are interested in bringing about a durable peace in the world.

Regional Characteristics

Striking variations in culture are found in different regions of the world. For instance, in the United States a husband is prohibited by law from having more than one wife at a time. In Nigeria he is permitted to have many wives. The Oba of Benin, Akenzua II, ruler of Nigeria, has eight wives. "My father had one hundred wives," he explains, "but I must be guided by the economic situation. I must limit my household." Each of the Oba's eight wives has her own suite in the harem—the part of the palace reserved for women. All eight are such good friends that they frequently invite one another to dinner. Daily they meet and chat in the common courtyard in the center of the palace.

In the United States, as William Allen White has phrased it, geographical regions are "not merely colored places on the map. They present different views of life." Both material and nonmaterial traits of their culture vary. Folsom illustrates the differences:

Culture is not a mere abstraction. It becomes vividly real when we study it geographically. It is distributed about the earth like flora and fauna. We can plot areas of culture on a map as we plot areas of heavy rainfall, of mountainous country, of forest or desert. On an automobile trip we discover that red barns, consolidated farmhouses, "overshoot" barns, women's sunbonnets, brick sidewalks, village greens, and other peculiarities occur within definite geographic limits, as surely as do white pine trees, mocking birds, natural lakes, and mosquitoes. We find, for example, that the large red barn, located at considerable distance from the veranda-adorned farmhouse, is characteristic of an area extending westward from New York and New Jersey. In northern New England the barn is seldom red; it is very close to the porchless house, and some of the outbuildings are nearly always consolidated with the house itself. In the South a still different farm architecture prevails. We discover also that the region of the red barn and the veranda is approximately the region where people pronounce their "r's," and where the Presbyterian is the dominant church. In New England "ah" means "r," and the white frame church at the head of the village green is Congregational. In Virginia, "ah" means long "i," and the quiet-looking brick church, at a less conspicuous corner, is apt to be Episcopal.[8]

A person who migrates from one region to another becomes aware of his dissimilarity from people who have spent years in the other region. The differences may be minor or fundamental. They may range from use of a colloquialism like "tote," a peculiarity in pronunciation like "boid," a preference for "grits," or a dislike of firecrackers at Yuletide, to differences in attitudes toward classes or minority groups and in ways of earning a living.

Children whose parents move from one region to another encounter the reality of regional behavior patterns. Imagine the plight of a child from a rural home deep in the heart of the Ozarks who is suddenly transplanted to a crowded area on Chicago's South Side. He will be painfully aware of the significance of regional culture. To avoid disagreeable tensions and to win approval of his peers, he must adapt to ways patterned by the cultural milieu.

Class Characteristics

While certain rudimentary societies have no class structure, some kind of class system is found among nearly all peoples, even the nonliterate. In North America the Kwakiutl Indians, the Plains Indians, and the Pueblos all have a class organization. In

[8] Joseph K. Folsom, *Social Psychology*, Harper & Brothers, 1931, p. 478.

such lands as Polynesia and New Zealand, many parts of Africa and Asia, and in Europe class structure is common.

In the United States for many years an open-class system prevailed. Membership in a class depended not upon birth but upon individual initiative and effort. In other words, attained status overshadowed ascribed status due to birth and lineage. Frontier conditions with abundant free land, rich natural resources, practically unlimited possibilities for expanding business, and political freedom with emphasis on democratic ideals all fostered the open-class pattern. An individual's social position and his degree of social mobility were determined by his personal qualities, achievements, self-obtained possessions, authority, and power.

But with the passing of the frontier and the coming of modern industrialism social stratification has taken place. Reared in the democratic tradition, people in the United States are loath to admit the existence of class. They cherish the idea that "all men are created equal." Yet by their actions they belie their affirmations. Hollingshead, who studied the class system in Elmtown, a town of 6200 inhabitants in the middle-western corn belt, graphically puts the matter in this way:

> Elmtowners in general are inconsistent in the way they talk and act with reference to the idea of classes. If they are asked bluntly, "Do you believe there are 'classes' in the community?" they are very likely to say "No." Yet, they will tell you the Binghams are "a leading family here" or the "Sweitzers are like the Binghams, Woodsons, McDermotts, and Jennings. These families are different from the rest of us; they are very exclusive. I guess you'd call them our aristocracy." During the course of the conversation, the same speaker will say that there are several different "types of families" in the community and, justifying his judgment by describing the "way they live," place them in different categories. The democratic tradition that there are no classes in American society is the reason for this type of behavior. Therefore, Elmtowners deny the existence of class directly but act as if classes exist.[9]

There have been numerous reports on the class system in the

[9] This and other quotations reprinted with permission from A. B. Hollingshead, *Elmtown's Youth*, 1949, John Wiley & Sons, Inc.

United States. We shall include as illustrative Yankee City, Brasstown, and Old City.

One of the most detailed pieces of research on class was a pioneer study by W. Lloyd Warner and associates in Yankee City. Warner defines a social class system as "two or more orders of people who are believed to be, and are accordingly ranked by members of the community, in socially superior or inferior positions." In his method of determining class, people are ranked by members of the community themselves on the basis of such factors as source of income, occupation, place of residence, length of residence, home ownership, family descent, and clique membership. The members of a given class have common attributes and interests. They tend to associate with their own class, and to share marital, economic, and other opportunities with one another.

In Yankee City, a New England city of 17,000 population, Warner and Lunt identify six classes. They divide the commonly recognized upper, middle, and lower classes into their respective upper and lower sections. This division yields upper-upper, lower-upper, upper-middle, lower-middle, upper-lower, and lower-lower classes.

The upper-upper group consist of "old families" who pride themselves on their aristocratic lineage. They live in highly restricted residential areas in large expensive houses with well-kept grounds. Their furnishings are antiques that have been handed down over the years. They tend to think that birth and breeding are the true marks of social standing. They are either professional people or proprietors of the larger business and industrial enterprises. They make up about 1.4 percent of the population of Yankee City.

The lower-upper group also reside in the same kind of neighborhood, but their houses have been purchased recently and their antiques are "boughten." They are socially new and not completely accepted by those who "really count." They imitate closely the behavior of the upper uppers. Vocationally they occupy the top brackets. In Yankee City they comprise 1.6 percent of the population.

The upper-middle class are good and respectable people, but they are not fully admitted to the "inner circle" of the upper class. They live in smaller houses in new neighborhoods. They are active in community work and are often voted to positions of leadership. They include 10 percent of the people in Yankee City.

The lower middles are the top crust of the lower half of society and are so regarded by "those beneath them, by those above them and by themselves." The upper groups usually speak of them as "good, substantial people, eager to get ahead." They live in small houses. They are often employed in retail stores and in factories. They are often members of fraternal and auxiliary organizations. They account for 28.4 percent of the people in Yankee City.

The upper-lower group have small houses. They are semiskilled workers. They are trying to break into the middle group. They make up about one-third of the population of Yankee City.

The lower-lower group are at the bottom of the social scale. They live in poor houses, often tar-paper shacks "on the other side of the tracks." They are unskilled workers. They have more children than the other groups. The lower lowers constitute 26 percent of the population of Yankee City.

Another exploration of class was made by Stendler in Brasstown, an industrial town of 15,000 inhabitants, most of whom make their living in the factories.

Stendler describes Brasstown as a place in which the class system is "tacitly accepted but never openly acknowledged by its residents." She identifies four classes. We present her word pictures of families thought by Brasstowners to be typical of each class.

The Rockwells typify the small, exclusive upper class.

They were "old family"; in their day they had given much to the town. A bridge, the town hall, the public library, all were memorials to members of Brasstown's first family. Renoirs in the Rockwells' possession were loaned to the Metropolitan Museum in New York upon occasion. They were not the richest family in the town, but they were able to maintain a residence in Brasstown and one in quiet, secluded Long Acres, whose upper class claimed them as members. The Rockwells and others like them had little communication with

Brasstown society; their wives held themselves aloof from the women's clubs, and their children did not attend the public schools.[10]

For the middle class, descriptions of two groups of families are given. The first group represents the upper-middle class which includes a professional, managerial, or large business group.

The McDowells were described as good, comfortable, salt-of-the-earth kind of people, staunch church members. He was president of the local bank, but the family lived simply and unassumingly, although in the best section of town. The Pebles and the Loomises, on the other hand, were considered to be "flashy." Each had started a little plant or business of his own on a shoestring in the twenties and exemplified the typical American success story of moving up the ladder, making good through cheap labor and poor working conditions. These were the people who built the big houses, who had the big cars with license plates spelling out their initials, whose socially ambitious wives were the clubwomen of the town. Then there were the Campbells, men with doctorate degrees in chemistry, who were in high managerial positions in the local factories. These men were comparative newcomers in town, but by adopting the symbols of the upper-middle class they were able to assume their places in it.[11]

The lower-middle class is made up of the white-collar group— clerks, school teachers, small proprietors, and skilled craftsmen. They are generally thought of as "good, self-respecting, honest Americans who recognize the importance of trying to get ahead. 'Like the Barnetts; they're a good example. A nice little family. She was a Rogers from Rockville before she was married—studied music. He's a steamfitter up at Eastern Foundry, belongs to the Elks. They have a nice little home up on Pine Street Extension.' "[12]

The working class is made up mainly of operators on conveyors, foreigners, and any large group of industrial workers recently imported from other communities. They are "all right" but "ordinary." The Strieskis are typical. "They're dull, stolid, thrifty Poles

---

[10] Celia Burns Stendler, *Children of Brasstown*, University of Illinois Press, 1949, p. 21.
[11] *Ibid.*, pp. 21–22.
[12] *Ibid.*, p. 22.

who've saved enough to buy a little house up on Grosvenor Street. They're ordinary people—they both work on conveyors down in the Brass shop—both rather ignorant, but they want their kids to get along, and they're raising them to be good Americans."[13]

The working class has a "lower fringe":

Some of its members were "queer" couples who lived on the outskirts of town in unions which had failed to be blessed by church or state, raising broods of "queer" children. Moral or cultural reasons also helped to decide membership. If one drank too much and was also poor, had a dirty home and no "standards" one was in "the lower fringe." If one "ran around with the niggers" or was a recently arrived "Porkchop" (Portuguese), chances were one would be assigned a place at the bottom of the scale. "Take the O'Shaughnesseys, for example. They live in the Clusters—a rough, tough, and hard-boiled lot. Father works down at the Chemical plant—makes about $50 a week with overtime, but drinks it all up. He was arrested a couple of times for being a Peeping Tom.[14]

An investigation carried on in the South gives insight into the class society of whites in a southern town.

As one becomes acquainted with the white people of Old City, he soon realizes that they are continually classifying themselves and others. There are "Negroes" and "whites"—the caste groups—a relatively simple dichotomy. There are also "leading families," "fine old families," "the four hundred," "the society crowd," "plain people," "nice, respectable people," "good people, but nobody," "po' whites," "red necks," etc.—all terms used to refer to different groups within the white caste. Not only do the whites frequently refer to these subdivisions within their own caste group, but they do so in such a manner as to indicate that they think in terms of a social hierarchy with some people at the "top," some at the "bottom"; with some people "equal" to themselves, and others "above" or "below" them. There are recurrent expressions such as: "He isn't our social equal," "She isn't our kind," "They are just nobody," "Those folks are the way-high-ups," "They're nothing but white trash!," "Oh, they're plain people like us." These expressions refer not only to individuals but also to groups, so that one may speak of superordinate and subordinate groups within the white society. And, most important of all, people

[13] *Ibid.*, p. 22.
[14] *Ibid.*, p. 22.

tend to act in conformity with these conceptions of their "place" and the social position of others in the society.

When the individuals and groups so designated are studied, striking differences between them with regard to family relations, recreational behavior, standards of living, occupation and income, education, and other traits are immediately apparent. On the basis of these differences, it is possible to define the social classes within the white society and to describe them in detail. It was soon evident that people at all levels were thinking in terms of, and often referring to, three broad social classes—"upper," "middle," and "lower"—although, when designating particular individuals, there were divergences of opinion as to their social position. There was some difference of opinion, too, as to the things that made one upper, middle, or lower; but an analysis of the relative social positions of the informants showed that these variations in conceptions of class status were, themselves, related to the social position of the informant. Thus, a "po' white," as defined by persons of the higher classes, conceived of the total structure in a somewhat different manner from an upper-class planter. In other words, the social perspective varied with the social position of the individual. People in the same social positions agreed, in the main, however, on the traits which characterized the classes, although the class traits did not apply to everyone within a class in absolute fashion. Thus, a member of a group defined by consensus as "superior" might have a few characteristics in common with a person of an "inferior" group; but when each group was considered as a whole, the differences were large and significant. Thus, "the society crowd," as a group, owns more property than the "po' whites," although some "society folks" own none at all; the "poor, but respectable" people, in the aggregate, are more church-minded than "trash," though some are not affiliated with churches.[15]

The various studies indicate that in the United States class affects all aspects of the lives of the people. It determines associates, living quarters, club memberships, churchgoing habits, movies, reading material. Hollingshead believes that "this class system is far more vital as a social force in our society than the American Creed."[16] He considers it so significant that he gives this admonition: "Those aspects of the culture which foster and

[15] Allison Davis, Burleigh B. Gardner, and Mary R. Gardner, *Deep South*, University of Chicago Press, 1941. Copyright, 1941, by the University of Chicago.

[16] Hollingshead, *op. cit.*, p. 452.

perpetuate the class system over against the ideals of official America, embodied in the Declaration of Independence and the Constitution, will have to be changed, if there has to be change, before Americans will face in practice the ideals they profess in theory."[17]

Class touches the lives of children as well as those of adults. When children enter school, they not only join a formal organization, but they also become involved in an informal order, an order relatively independent of the formal organization. In the interpersonal relationships within the school their status is determined largely by their past history. They are tagged by their family name and status.

The importance of the informal order may vary in the elementary school and in the high school. Evidence on this point is somewhat contradictory. Some studies indicate that children prefer others of their own status level or a higher level, with the exception of the low-status children, while others reveal no relationship between economic class or parental occupation and friendship patterns. In the study of Brasstown, Stendler reached these conclusions:

In-school and out-of-school choice of friends differs, with in-school choices being more democratic. In their in-school choices first-grade children evince the least class bias; fourth and sixth graders have a growing tendency to stay within their own social class; among eighth graders this tendency falls off slightly. In out-of-school choices, first graders are most limited to their own social class; fourth graders are the most democratic; sixth and eighth graders revert to the first-grade pattern and choose chiefly from their own social class; working-class children are rejected as the ones with whom the chooser would not care to associate.

In order to discriminate according to social class, children must know or become aware of class symbols. Stendler's study indicates a gradual growth of awareness of such symbols. While first graders manifest little awareness of symbols of class, fourth graders are more discerning in their ratings, and eighth graders are very much

[17] *Ibid.*, p. 453.

like adults in their ratings. Children recognize the position of themselves and their acquaintances on the social scale. They pattern their behavior and beliefs after the behavior and beliefs of members of their own social class. Their choice of friends and their leisure-time activities reveal class differences.

In *Children of Brasstown* Stendler shows how children's awareness of social class position is reflected in their choice of friends. Marshall, for example, has little part in the social life of his peers because his family is beyond the pale. To quote:

The lower-class child who epitomizes lower-classness does not always stand out to the casual observer. There was Marshall in the first grade; he was an attractive little towhead, dressed neatly in coveralls and sport shirt, looking no different from the rest of his schoolmates, yet he was frequently named as one whose clothes needed mending. His teacher considered him gentle and mild-mannered, yet his peers chose him as the child who did the most fighting and swearing, and who did not have very nice manners. He was not one of the brightest children in the room, but neither was he the dullest. He lived in Hopeville, but so did several other children, and only one first grader knew this was a poor section of town. From all reports, he had no serious personality maladjustment. Then why Marshall? There were certain things about his family that were uncovered in the course of this study: they lived on a farm, something that was undesirable in many Brasstowners' eyes; they didn't have much income; and they had too many children coming too closely, by Brasstown's standards. Marshall didn't "act right" when he first came to school; his lunch box was different and so were his table manners. He was branded early in his school career, and he will continue to be branded unless something is done to help.[18]

At the high school level nearly all the studies point to a significant relationship between the social behavior of students and the socioeconomic status of parents. Cliques, composed of students who plan "going places and doing things" together consume most of the interest, time, and activities of the adolescents.

In an analysis of the social system of the 576 students of Wabash, a suburban high school in a midwestern metropolitan community, Gordon found that the clique was a source of prestige

[18] Stendler, *op. cit.*, pp. 96–97.

and a means of social mobility. Members and nonmembers had different perspectives.

A member of the "Dirty Dozen" viewed the clique as a source of prestige.

The clique you belong to has a definite bearing on your prestige. If you belong to a fast moving athletic clique, you are usually the same and this tends to build up your prestige outside of school and in dating more than with the other organizations of the school. A person who belongs to a clique usually has his share of money and is usually out for a good time.

The girls, as far as dating is concerned, like the boys who are a lot of fun and can take them to nice places. The cliques are divided in about two categories. There is the kind close to school, participating in school clubs, clique. Then there is the away from school, participating in sports, clique. The latter is the most popular in my estimation.[19]

A nonclique member saw the crucial role of the group in relation to the struggle for position.

In the fifth grade at Central, all the girls seemed able to play with each other very well, but by the sixth, seventh, and eighth grades, the girls were beginning to form cliques and get this feeling of being superior. In the seventh and eighth grade there was this group of girls who shut themselves off from the rest. They never spoke to the rest of us kids, but were always discussing our clothes and various other personal appearances.

If some new girl came into school that had a new dress for every day in the week, seemed to attract the boys and was able to throw parties where they could sneak a little beer and smoke a bit, then they would all come together and vote on whether she could run around with them or not.

If one of us would begin to pull ourselves up a bit and would get a little of the attention they thought they should be getting, they would start some rumor around about us and run us back down to where they could again feel like our superior.

I know at least a dozen girls who have simply hated school and dreaded each day as they came to it because of this particular group. I was one of the girls who was put down in my place and it really hurt, too. I still to this day have a certain inner hatred towards these girls even though I have come to know several of them fairly well and they

[19] C. Wayne Gordon, *The Social System of the High School*, The Free Press, p. 106.

can really be a lot of fun. I think this is the reason Wabash High has the reputation of being the snob school.[20]

At school, in matters other than choice of friends, social stratification has many ramifications. School board members and teachers are drawn chiefly from the middle class. Consciously or unconsciously schools, under middle-class leadership, tend to foster middle-class values.

Children from middle-class homes with values similar to those stressed at school are likely to get along with less friction than children of the lower class. Middle-class children have manners, habits, and attitudes that teachers share and try to inculcate. Lower-class children encounter a conflict of values. Behavior that wins approval at school brings disapproval at home.

In *Father of the Man*, case studies of the two Washington children portray the clash in values. Mary, who is quiet and anxious to please, wins praise from her middle-class teachers, and criticism from her lower-class family who regard her as a schemer and an apple polisher. On the other hand, Paulette, who is aggressive and inclined to "tell people off" and let them "like it or lump it," is admired by her family for her "honesty."

Reëvaluation of our teaching of values may result in a program that stands a chance of acceptance by lower-class children. Havighurst and Taba recommended that "they [boys and girls] should learn to make distinctions between the lesser mores of eating, drinking, amusement, clothing, and marriage customs, which differ from one social group to another, and the more basic moral qualities, such as honesty, loyalty, kindness, and courage, which are very nearly universal." At present the lesser mores often receive greater emphasis than the basic qualities.

In a variety of ways schools may show unconscious bias toward lower-class children. Intelligence tests contain items that are readily recognizable by children of the upper classes but are unknown to children of the lower class. Davis found that 81 percent of the children in the upper socioeconomic groups and only 52 percent of the lower socioeconomic children answered this question correctly: A

[20] *Ibid.*, pp. 109–110.

symphony is to a composer as a book is to what? ( ) paper
( ) sculptor ( ) author ( ) musician ( ) man.

When the question was changed to read: A baker goes with
bread, the same way that a carpenter goes with what? ( ) a saw
( ) a house ( ) a spoon ( ) a nail ( ) a man, 50 percent of
both groups answered correctly. Bread and homes are part of the
common life of both groups, whereas symphonies and books are
not part of the poorer child's life.

The curriculum, particularly in the lower grades, probably favors
children of the upper classes. It is highly verbalistic and deals with
ideas and experiences often remote from the lives of lower-class
children. Possibly the same criticism holds throughout the school
system. It may help account for the fact that children from the
upper groups often receive better grades than those from the lower
groups. In *Elmtown's Youth* Hollingshead states that ". . . it is
clear that, on the average, the higher an adolescent's class position,
the better his chances are to receive high grades. Conversely, the
lower one's position in the prestige structure, the more likely the
adolescent is to receive low grades."[21]

Teachers occasionally show bias in their treatment of children.
They may identify children with the social level of their parents
and treat them accordingly. Some take a superior attitude toward
lower-class families, while others have a sneering attitude toward
wealthy and socially prominent families. In discipline some teachers favor children from middle- and upper-class homes. A startling
account of how a superintendent of schools and a high school
principal excuse upper-class youngsters who evade staying after
school for being late but punish a lower-class student is contained
in *Elmtown's Youth.*

When school was out that afternoon, the Superintendent stood in
the hall near the side exit, Mr. White, a teacher, watched the front
door, while the principal patrolled the building. Mr. Gardner, another
teacher, was in the detention room. After the building was cleared of
students and most of the teachers had gone home, the Superintendent
walked back to his office, but the principal stood outside the front
door. Suddenly the door was thrown open from the outside, and angry

[21] Hollingshead, *op. cit.*, p. 173.

voices were heard. The Superintendent rushed out of his office and stood at the head of the stairs. The principal pushed and shoved "Boney" up the stairs as he repeated, "You can't get away with that stuff." As they neared the top, "Boney" broke from his grasp and started down the hall toward the side door. The Superintendent blocked his path, and "Boney" ran upstairs. The principal leaped and grabbed him by the coat collar with his left hand. "Boney" turned and started to fight. The principal spun him around, seized the visor of his cap with his right hand and yanked it down over his eyes. While "Boney" was fighting to get the cap off his face, the principal hit him three times with the heel of his hand on the back of the neck near the base of the skull. "Boney" cursed, struggled, and hit in all directions. Soon he broke free and ran toward the Superintendent, who shook and slapped him three or four times. Both men then grabbed him by the arms and shook him vigorously. The Superintendent angrily screeched, "You're going out of this building. You're never coming back until you bring your father and we talk this over." By this time, the three had reached the front door. "Boney" was shoved outside. He stood there, cursing and threatening both men with violence. In a few minutes he composed himself, straightened his clothes, and walked away, muttering to himself.[22]

In guidance, teachers have a tendency to direct the lower-class child into a vocational curriculum. Thus, either knowingly or unknowingly, teachers decide which children are not socially mobile and advise them with regard to selection of curriculum in such a way that social mobility is difficult if not impossible.

That students sense a prestige bias in different courses is brought out by this statement of a senior girl in *Elmtown's Youth:*

If you take a college preparatory course, you're better than those who take a general course. Those who take a general course are neither here nor there. If you take a commercial course, you don't rate. It's a funny thing, those who take college preparatory set themselves up as better than the other kids. Those that take the college preparatory course run the place. I remember when I was a freshman, mother wanted me to take home economics, but I didn't want to. I knew I couldn't rate. You could take typing and shorthand and still rate, but if you took a straight commercial course, you couldn't rate. You see, you're rated by the teachers according to the course you take. They rate you in the first 6 weeks. The teachers type you in a small school

[22] *Ibid.*, pp. 190–191.

and you're made in classes before you get there. College preparatory
kids get good grades and the others take what's left. The teachers get
together and talk, and if you are not in college preparatory you haven't
got a chance.[23]

Class is related to whether or not a child continues in school.
According to Howard M. Bell, "The strongest single factor in
determining how far a youth goes in his school is the occupation of
his father." Among 13,528 young people in Maryland, only one
out of every 13 children of fathers engaged in the professions
failed to go beyond the eighth grade, but two out of three whose
fathers were unskilled laborers and seven out of eight whose fathers
were farm laborers failed to exceed the same level.

Similar findings were disclosed from a study of the records of
5677 boys in Pennsylvania. At the ninth and twelfth grade levels,
the father's status had less influence than intelligence or educational opportunity; but at the college level the situation was sharply
reversed. While the most intelligent boys had only a 4-to-1 advantage over the less intelligent, the sons of men in the highest
occupational category enjoyed an advantage of more than 10-to-1
over those from the lowest occupational level.

For children from families in the lower-income groups the cost
of attending secondary school is prohibitive. During the depression
of the 1930's, when a fourth of all American families had incomes
ranging from zero to $750 per year, and when more than an
additional third had incomes ranging no higher than $1500 per
year, the average cost, per pupil, of attending high school, ex-
cluding food, clothing, shelter, and transportation, was $125 per
year.

There is a striking relationship between family income and educational opportunity. For example, a study of 1023 students with
IQ's of 117 or above who graduated from Milwaukee high schools
in 1937 and 1938 found that in families with an income of $8000
or above 100 percent of these students went to college, while in
families with incomes under $500 only one in five of these students
went to college.

[23] *Ibid.*, pp. 169–170.

Aside from the economic factor, class contributes in other ways to high drop-out among children from lower-class homes. In the first place, pupils find their studies uninteresting. School and society lack *real rewards* to offer the underprivileged groups. As Davis points out, the lower-class children see that those who work hard at school usually have families that already have the occupations, homes, and social acceptance that the school holds up as the rewards of education. "The underprivileged workers can see also that the chances of their getting enough education to make their attainment of these rewards in the future at all probable is slight. Since they can win the rewards of prestige and social acceptance in their own slum groups without education, they do not take very seriously the motivation taught by the school." Because the children cannot relate their studies to their life needs, they often do unsatisfactory work and choose to leave a situation in which they meet failure rather than success.

In the second place, children from lower-class families often have little opportunity to take part in extracurricular activities. In 13 Illinois high schools with enrollments ranging from 81 to 2683, well-to-do pupils participated in proportions one-third in excess of their relative number in the student body population. Poorer children participated in proportions about 40 percent smaller than their relative numbers indicate should have been the case. Furthermore, positions of leadership were held by pupils from families with greater incomes.

Lack of participation by children from lower socioeconomic families may be explained in a variety of ways. First, they do not have the money necessary for engaging in activities. Second, they may have part-time employment that conflicts with the activity schedule. Third, they may not be accepted by their peers. Warner points out that pupils "learn to like being with people of their own class or higher and to dislike being with people of lower classes especially if the social distance is great." As one lower-class girl of Elmtown said, "Well, why go? We're made to feel out of place and that's the way it is."

Similarly, among youth in Corinth, Mississippi, discrimination

against lower-class children was indicated in the extraclass life of
the school.

Corinth's social lines, always drawn tightly between a small nucleus
of "good families—mostly with money and position"—and a larger
group of store and mill workers (with farm people forming their own
group outside of town), have eased considerably since the war. "A
few years ago you couldn't have got a job on the school paper if you
came from the wrong lineage," one teacher said. And while children
of the town's leading families, the "North Enders," are still elected
to "as many school jobs as they want" because the voting, taken by a
public show of hands in the auditorium, makes other boys and girls
fearful of supporting someone else ("You may not want those kids
to be elected, but you don't want to be seen voting against them
either"), the girl who runs the Dramatic Club is a newcomer to town,
the associate editor of the school paper lives out on the main high-
way.[24]

In the third place, children from lower-class families often drop
out because their parents do not expect or encourage them to
continue in school. Actually, many parents urge their children to
leave school as soon as possible and get a job. Havighurst estimates
that "at least half of the children of lower- and lower-middle-class
families who have the ability to succeed in college do not have
the desire or the motivation to go to college."

Family Characteristics

Through his family a child is born into a certain geographical,
racial, ethnic, religious, and socioeconomic group. The pattern of
family life, which is part of the larger culture system of society,
differs markedly in these various groups. For a child of a head-
hunter in Borneo and a child of a first family among "The Proper
Bostonians," the cultural patterns are very unlike.

Almost as dissimilar as the culture of two nations is the culture
of children of different classes in the United States. The child of
a New York socialite learns patterns of conduct and thought foreign to a child of Okies.

[24] "Profile of Youth: Maxine Wallace," *Ladies' Home Journal*, January,
1950, p. 122.

In the home a young child is rapidly subjected to standards and values that hold sway in his group.

He meets American law first in the warning note of his mother's voice: "Stop digging, here comes a cop." He meets American economics when he finds his mother unimpressed by his offer to buy another copy of the wedding gift he has just smashed: "At the 5 and 10 cent store, can't we?" His first encounter with puritan standards may come through his mother's "If you don't eat your vegetables you can't have any dessert." He learns the paramount importance of distinguishing between vice and virtue; that it is only a matter of which comes first, the pleasure or the pain. All his great lessons come through his mother's voice, through his father's laughter, or the tilt of his father's cigar when a business deal goes right. Just as one way of understanding a machine is to understand how it is made, so one way of understanding the typical character structure of a culture is to follow step by step the way in which it is built into the growing child.[25]

For children in various social classes methods of child training differ. Ericson found significant differences in child-rearing practices in middle-class and lower-class families. Forty-eight mothers in the middle-class group were interviewed. There were 107 children in this sample. In the lower-class group, 52 mothers were interviewed. There were 167 children in this group. The general areas explored by Ericson were weaning, thumbsucking, cleanliness, training, environmental exploration and control, and age and sex roles. She summarized her findings as follows:

In the middle-class families there is more emphasis on the early achievement of learnings in the crucial areas, although the data show that even though the training is begun earlier, it is not necessarily achieved any earlier. Middle-class children are probably subjected to more frustrations in the process of achieving these learnings and are probably more anxious as a result of these pressures than are the lower-class children. Lower-class families tend to be more permissive than the middle-class families in the training of their children in all areas.

Children in the middle-class families are taught to assume responsibility early. Middle-class children are more carefully supervised in their

[25] Margaret Mead, *And Keep Your Powder Dry*, William Morrow & Co., Inc., 1943, p. 38.

activities than are the lower-class children. Middle-class children have many fewer unsupervised play activities and less free time than do the lower-class children. Middle-class life is in general more demanding with reference to all learning areas. The children are taught to respond to the demands of the social group in which they live. The early assumption of responsibility on the part of the middle-class children was not what we had expected; we had anticipated that lower-class parents would expect the early achievement for their children in assuming responsibility in the home. Apparently the middle-class children are taught this task by the parents relatively early while the lower-class children are not taught this task until the learning is relatively easy for them.

Middle-class children are taught ways of living that will prepare them to become financially independent, to assume positions of responsibility in the home and community, and to become responsible citizens of the culture in which they live.

The lower-class children are reared in families in which life is less strictly organized, and fewer demands are made upon them. They probably do not meet as many frustrations as do the middle-class children. The demands of the social group in lower-class life are not as exacting as they are in middle-class life.

From the standpoint of sociology, this investigation bears out the general theory that membership in a social class is an important influence on personality development and that there are numerous significant differences in social class groups with reference to child-rearing practices.[26]

Demands of the culture vary not only for children in different social classes, but also for rural and city children. Lois Barclay Murphy presents vividly some "hazards of civilization for children." While country children are allowed to grow up as naturally as lambs and wheat, city children are watched carefully for motor development, vocabulary, and other indices of growth or indications of superiority. Individual differences may be taken for granted in a rural family, but in more sophisticated groups a child is expected to be "well adjusted" to a variety of groups and situations. A rural child has opportunity for free play, whereas a city child

[26] Martha C. Ericson, "Social Status and Child-Rearing Practices," in Theodore M. Newcomb, et al. (eds.), Readings in Social Psychology, Henry Holt and Company, 1947, pp. 500–501.

may be kept longer in his play pen. "The rural child usually may dig tunnels, fill holes with water if he likes, make mud pies and fill his wagon with junk, rocks, dirt, or leaves, perhaps even really helping in the fall or spring; whereas the city child and many suburban children whose families cherish a House Beautiful atmosphere may have no place where they can dig and explore and just mess around."[27] A small-town child may have a gang of three or four in his own neighborhood with whom he becomes acquainted gradually. A city child may have no playmates until he encounters a confusing group of ten to twenty children in nursery school. A country child learns self-control from his own observation and experience. He can see for himself that because he leaves the gate open his pet turkey wanders onto the road and gets run over. A city child is confronted by numerous admonitions of "No" and "Don't touch" which seem to him unreasonable.

"For the city child who has been greatly stimulated by parents who greet each new evidence of motor achievement—sitting up, standing up, and finally walking—with cheers, restrictions on the use of the abilities which have received so much appreciation are unexpectedly frustrating. It is no wonder that the stimulated-frustrated child suddenly becomes a brat after his first year and a half of cherubic smiles."[28]

Through his family a child not only learns a pattern of living but also acquires a place in the larger cultural configuration. He receives a name and a social position. His family name may be an asset or a handicap. If it is a handicap, he sometimes resorts to the courts to secure a new name. Amory relates how persons have attempted to take names of leading Boston families.

In view of all their privileges it is not surprising that Boston's First Families have, on occasion, been forced to do battle for their birthright. There have been instances in which this struggle has been carried to court—when ordinary Bostonians have seen fit to become Proper Bostonians by the simple procedure of having their names changed,

[27] Lois Barclay Murphy, "Hazards of Civilization for Children," *Journal of the American Association of University Women*, Spring, 1949, p. 144.
[28] *Ibid.*, p. 145.

and have faced not only a judge but the irate Family itself. In contrast to trust cases, however, which seem to have been concluded with monotonous regularity in favor of First Families, court decisions in these name cases have gone both ways. A man who wanted to become an Amory was refused permission when a sizeable proportion of the members of that small but gamely vigilant Family appeared in court to register protest. In another case, five members of a family named Hogan—one of whom, a stenographer, gave as her reason that she was "in pursuit of happiness"—were unsuccessful in asking to have their name changed to a hyphenated name ending with Homans. They had found, arrayed in court against them, not only Boston Homanses but also a representative of the Society for the Preservation of New England Antiquities.

Surprisingly enough, the reverse decisions—those allowing name changes—seem to be on the record against the most prominent Boston Families of all, including Adamses, Appletons, and even Cabots. One Cabot case stands out above others as a classic of Boston Society. In this the judge allowed the plaintiff, a man named Kabotznick, to assume the honored name, apparently not foreseeing that his decision was also going to work a hardship on the Lowells. He was shortly reminded of this fact by an anonymous newspaper poet. Re-wording Boston's social folk song, the poet wrote:

> And this is good old Boston,
>   The home of the bean and the cod,
> Where the Lowells have no one to talk to,
>   'Cause the Cabots talk Yiddish, by God![29]

SUMMARY

In comparison with the young of other animals, a newborn infant is immature and helpless. However, his capacity for learning enables him eventually to outstrip lower animals. Since man is a biological organism, his achievements and behavior depend not only upon his native abilities and structures but also upon his environment. If he is to survive, his physiological needs must be met. If he is to acquire distinctively human traits, he must associate with other human beings. Differences in behavior and per-

[29] Cleveland Amory, *The Proper Bostonians*, E. P. Dutton & Co., Inc., 1947, pp. 34–35.

sonality result largely from environmental factors. Through social inheritance or culture the individual takes on the ways of his group. Although certain things are considered important in every culture, variations in national, regional, class, and family cultures exert their influence on the individual.

QUESTIONS AND EXERCISES

1. Evaluate Barzun's statement: "The reason teaching has to go on is that children are not born human; they are made so."
2. Explain outstanding features of American culture to a native of Japan.
3. Mention a contemporary social problem which has arisen because of differences in regional cultures in the United States.
4. List ways in which differences in class culture affected students in the high school which you attended.
5. How do differences in cultures lead to misunderstandings among nations? How can these sources of conflict be minimized?
6. Why is it difficult to distinguish between learned and unlearned tendencies? Is it easier to carry on experiments to ascertain which tendencies are unlearned in lower animals than to carry on such experiments with human beings?
7. Are differences between savage and civilized man due mainly to differences in original nature?
8. Prepare a list of a dozen or more characteristic ways in which the culture of your community is expressed. Underline those which appear rather generally throughout the country.
9. Cite several examples of subculture within our culture. Do these examples appear to be growing or diminishing in uniqueness?
10. Give some attention to changes in culture which you have observed. Consider, for example, a minor change, such as that in dress of high school students from the time you attended high school to the present.
11. Read at least one account of a culture which is greatly different from our own. Point out the differences.

SELECTED REFERENCES

Adams, James Truslow, *The American*, Charles Scribner's Sons, 1943.
Centers, R., *The Psychology of Social Classes*, Princeton University Press, 1949.

Dahlke, H. Otto, *Values in Culture and Classroom*, Harper & Brothers, 1958.

Davis, Allison, *Social-Class Influences upon Learning*, Harvard University Press, 1948.

Davis, Allison, and Dollard, John, *Children of Bondage*, American Council on Education, 1940.

Davis, Allison, Gardner, Burleigh B., and Gardner, Mary R., *Deep South*, University of Chicago Press, 1941.

Gordon, C. Wayne, *The Social System of the High School*, The Free Press, Glencoe, Illinois, 1957.

Gunther, John, *Inside U.S.A.*, Harper & Brothers, 1947.

Hollingshead, A. B., *Elmtown's Youth*, John Wiley & Sons, Inc., 1949.

Kahl, Joseph, *The American Class Structure*, Rinehart & Company, Inc., 1957.

Lynd, Robert S., and Lynd, Helen M., *Middletown*, Harcourt, Brace and Company, Inc., 1929.

Lynd, Robert S., and Lynd, Helen M., *Middletown in Transition*, Harcourt, Brace and Company, Inc., 1937.

Meltzer, Bernard N., Doby, Harry R., and Smith, Philip M., *Education in Society: Readings*, Thomas Y. Crowell Company, 1958.

Mercer, Blaine E., and Carr, Edwin R. (eds.), *Education and the Social Order*, Rinehart & Company, Inc., 1957.

Odum, Howard W., and Moore, Harry Estill, *American Regionalism: A Cultural Historical Approach to National Integration*, Henry Holt and Company, 1938.

Perry, Ralph Barton, *Characteristically American*, Alfred A. Knopf, Inc., 1949.

Stendler, Celia Burns, *Children of Brasstown*, University of Illinois Press, 1949.

Warner, W. Lloyd, Havighurst, Robert J., and Loeb, Martin B., *Who Shall Be Educated?* Harper & Brothers, 1944.

Warner, W. Lloyd, Meeker, M., and Eells, K., *Social Classes in America*, Science Research Associates, 1949.

AUDIO-VISUAL MATERIALS

Films

And So They Live (25 minutes, Sound, B & W, New York University and University of Kentucky). Portrays the tragic economic and social conditions among families in the Southern mountains, and the failure of the school program to meet local needs.

Social Class in America (16 minutes, Sound, B & W, McGraw-Hill Book Company, Inc.). Some significant contrasts in the lives of three boys from three different social classes.

Recording

You Are Not Alone—Ways of Mankind (30 minutes, 33⅓ rpm, National Association of Educational Broadcasters). A study of groups and their influence upon the individual.

CHAPTER VI

Agencies of Education

Education in some form is probably as old as the world. Some authors think that it may even antedate Homo sapiens. Be that as it may, every group deems its patterns of conduct for regulating and organizing its life so important that it has an educational process to insure their inculcation.

Methods of inducting the young into their cultural heritage differ. "In undeveloped social groups," says Dewey, "we find little formal teaching and training." Children learn informally from imitating their elders. Their playthings are likenesses of implements and their games are imitations of activities of adult life.

As children grow older, they share in the occupation of adults, thus serving a kind of apprenticeship. Probably the offspring of paleolithic man learned to hunt and fish, to fashion roughly shaped flints, to manipulate bow and arrow, and to use fire. Such learning came not from intentional training but from the overriding necessity of participating in essential pursuits.

Eventually primitive man began with forethought to pass on to his offspring certain ways of propitiating the invisible powers that controlled the world. Becoming aware of surrounding forces, such as lightning, darkness, and disease, that not only interfered with his happiness but also baffled his understanding, he attributed to these inanimate things and forces a soul or "double" similar to his own. For him every object possessed a spiritual life that played a peculiar role in his mystic world and had a meaning quite different from what it has for modern man.

This mystic belief stimulated the first deliberate efforts to educate the tribal young. Adults tried to indoctrinate them in the best ways of placating spirits through incantations, prayers, and offerings that had been reported successful by earlier generations. To keep these ceremonial traditions alive was the major purpose of formal primitive education.

So important was this phase of education that dealt with the occult that only the old men, wizards, shamans, and others who were especially versed in these matters, were allowed to direct it. Finally such teaching was entrusted to a special class which determined what the people should be taught. Since the experts could not always be available to instruct, and the youth could not always be ready to be instructed, the practice of having special ceremonial occasions for transmitting mythology, tribal taboos, and secrets arose. Thus originated the initiatory ceremonies which often included not only instruction but also ordeals and periods of testing.

An idea of the significance of initiatory ceremonies may be gained from a description of certain of them among the Arunta, a primitive Australian group with culture essentially that of the Old Stone Age.

Every native must pass through elaborate ceremonies before becoming a full-fledged member of a tribe. Though they vary as to details the rites have much in common and serve similar purposes. Among the Arunta there are four great ceremonials, beginning about ten or twelve and extending, in some cases, until the mature age of thirty years. The first is called *Alkira-kiwuma* or "throwing up to the sky"; the second, *Lartna* or circumcision; the third, *Arilta* or subincision; and the fourth, *Engwura*, a ceremonial ordeal of fire. Before the first ceremony the boy is called *Ambaquerka*; after it he is named *Ulpmerka*. During *Lartna* the initiate is known as *Wurtja*; after it he is *Arakurta*. When the next ceremony, *Arilta*, has been performed he becomes *Atua-kurka*; this he remains till after the fourth, *Engwura*, when he is recognized as *Urliara*.

The *Engwura*, the last of the initiatory rites, is made up of "series of ceremonies concerned with the totems," involving "tests both moral and physical," intended to strengthen and give "courage, wisdom, endurance and self-restraint" to those who go through them and make them more kindly and "less apt to quarrel." Naturally the rites have the effect also of causing the youth to look with greater awe and reverence upon the old men who are able to tell them so much and whom they are compelled to obey. The *Engwura* rituals vary considerably in the different totem groups which practice them. Some require only a day or two; another, the *Achilpa*, or wild-cat totem, demands four months. Spencer and Gillen report that every day of the four months was given over to a new ceremony or several of them, but that it was possible to recognize five distinct stages in the entire *Engwura*: the first, the dispatch of messengers, assembling of the people, and "dancing corroborees" participated in by men and women; the second, marked by the separation of men and women, and a performance of sacred ceremonies by the men on the specially laid-out *Engwura* ground, after which the initiates were known as *Illpong-worra*; third, the continuance of religious rites, during which the young men were forbidden to speak to certain of the elders; the fourth phase, marked by the ordeal of fire, after which initiates were given the name *Urliara*; and the fifth, in which men and women joined, when the initiates made an offering of meat to those with whom they had previously been forbidden to speak, the ban of silence was removed in a special ceremony, and the young men were recognized as full-fledged members of the tribe.[1]

ESTABLISHMENT OF SCHOOLS

Except in connection with initiation ceremonies, primitive groups had no special devices or institutions for teaching. As Dewey observes, "To savages it would seem preposterous to seek out a place where nothing but learning was going on in order that one might learn."

As a matter of direct observation and experience, children learned from adult members of the group. What the mothers and fathers had learned about satisfying human wants was passed on to their children. The few skills necessary for providing food, shelter, and clothing were learned as a part of everyday living.

But with the advance of civilization social life became more complex and the stock of skills and ideas multiplied. New techniques for gaining protection from enemies and for tilling the soil and tending the flocks accumulated. Sometimes parents found that they did not have time to teach their offspring and so they called upon others. Sometimes they singled out an individual with special

[1] Thomas Woody, *Life and Education in Early Societies*, 1949, p. 16. By permission of The Macmillan Company.

abilities who instructed not only his own children but also those of his kinsman. Often older men and women who could not otherwise contribute to the group gave the instruction. Eventually, with specialization, younger people took over the task.

The invention of writing stimulated formal education. Since the arts of reading and writing are not acquired easily or entirely incidentally, society was obliged to make special provisions for instruction. At first only a few specialists learned to read and write. Even as late as the days when knighthood was in flower, aside from churchmen, statesmen, and the few in the learned professions, most men were illiterate. In one of Sir Walter Scott's poems Douglas boasted that none of his sons save the one who had entered the priesthood "could pen a line." Consequently the school was devised and a separate group of persons entrusted with the task of teaching.

Schools are designed to help an individual in the brief space of a single lifetime acquire skills and knowledge that the race has accumulated through eons of time. They are expected to bring pupils in touch with a system of culture and to make them acceptable members of society. Not only must schools help preserve the values of the past but they must also encourage the inventiveness and initiative vital for developing new ideas for the improvement of society.

EDUCATIONAL AGENCIES OTHER THAN THE SCHOOL

Despite the fact that the school has been devised as the intentional agency, it is by no means the only educative influence. Indeed it is an open question where a child receives the most education. All his experiences are grist for his mill of learning. William Allen White stated that he learned from home, barn, river, and school. After all, a child is at school only a relatively small proportion of his entire time. If he attends school 200 days a year for six hours a day, he is in school 1200 hours a year, or 13.6 percent of the time. If ten hours are allowed for sleep, he is in school only 23.5 percent of his waking hours. Hence, the home or some other agency has the child 76.5 percent of the time he is awake.

Among the many influences other than the school that affect children and youth, we shall discuss home, church, and media of mass communication—press, motion pictures, radio, and television.

HOME

The home deserves a top place among educative agencies. Here, if his surroundings are favorable and his parents sensible and understanding, a child lays a sound foundation for progress toward emotional and social maturity. He learns to direct his emotional energies into socially acceptable channels. He gains skill in living harmoniously with himself and others. Through tasks appropriate to his age he acquires independence and resourcefulness. He attends to his personal toilet, feeds himself, and takes care of his toys and other possessions. He has a host of first-hand experiences with articles of clothing, kitchen utensils, plants, animals, and myriad other things that make up home and community life. He learns to speak his native tongue. By the time he enters school his vocabulary consists of somewhere between 2000 and 2500 words. From moral and religious training he begins to set up principles of right and wrong and to formulate never-to-be-forgotten attitudes and ideals.

In the home the virtues of good citizenship are discovered. Children learn to live and work together in harmony and affection. They learn to apply democratic principles. Annie Laurie Peters graphically presented this idea in a radio broadcast of Town Meeting of the Air.

When you married, you and John established a unit of government of which you were the self-constituted rulers. Your daughter and son, Nancy and Jack, became members by reason of birth; and since Americans can only thrive in a democracy, your home must be one.

Children in such a home say "our car," "our home," "our family," and unconsciously that unit expands to include "our school," "our town," and later still, "our state" and "our nation."

Possession entails responsibility, and joint possession develops fair-sharing, not only of luxuries, but of work, and of privations. Money may be the root of evil, but its intelligent sharing is the basis of peaceful family living. Nancy and Jack are small now to understand budget restrictions, but if they buy their ice cream with "our money" instead of "Dad's money," you will have poured some solid cement in the foundation of building a strong family.

Understanding of all situations is necessary. If John's salary is cut, tell the entire family about it, and explain how it may alter their scheme of living. The acceptance of responsibility develops the receiver. Lack of funds can be replaced or supplemented always by more generous giving by parents of their time—their talents.[2]

In pioneer days when the home was filled with "honest laborers and burdened with children" a youngster was "rich in lore of fields and brooks" and well versed in farm chores and household arts. He had experiences similar to those related by the distinguished scientist, Robert A. Millikan:

My father and mother brought up a family of six, three boys and three girls, on the small-town preacher's salary of $1300 a year. We wore one-piece suits of blue jeans and no shoes from the close of school at the end of May until its beginning about September 10. Our yard contained about an acre of ground in which we raised potatoes, corn, melons, and all manner of garden truck, and in the winter we three boys sawed ten sticks of four-foot wood a day so long as our ten cords lasted. In vacation we were required to work in the garden in the mornings, but the afternoons we had free for our play.

Practically every afternoon for eight or ten years father collected his three boys and a dozen others from the neighborhood and accompanied us down thru the meadows and the woods to the river, where we swam, dived, played in the sand, rode down the river on logs, and shot the rapids thru a break in an old dam in the river. After we came back we played baseball, sheep fold, "anti over," or any one of a dozen games known to all boys.

We kept two cows of our own which I milked twice a day for six or seven years, and for some three years, in order to earn a little money, I tended a neighbor's horse and milked his cow. One of the finest of youthful experiences came when one of our farmer neighbors let us three Millikan boys break three of his colts for riding. The thrill of riding bareback on a racing horse is something never to be forgotten.

We often got up at three o'clock in the morning to see the circus come to town or to get down to the river to fish when the biting was best. We always spit on our bait for luck and did all the other things

[2] Annie Laurie Peters, "How Can We Strengthen the American Family?" *Bulletin of America's Town Meeting of the Air*, May 29, 1947, pp. 11–12.

recounted in William Allen White's *Court of Boyville*. Each fall we gathered many sacks of hazel nuts and walnuts for our winter supply. As we grew older we rigged up in our barn a turning pole, parallel bars, and we invested in boxing gloves and dumbbells. I later earned most of my way thru college by acting as student gymnasium director, a job which I got simply because I had acquired some competence and the necessary muscles in our old barn, which was the rendezvous of all the neighborhood boys. I never had an absence in my four-year high-school course because the life we led kept me in good physical condition— this more than once included milking cows at 40 below zero, too. I was urged at one time to make physical education a life work and had the road all opened for it but I chose another field instead.[3]

As an educational agency, the twentieth-century home differs in many respects from its pioneer predecessor. Some of the changes may be traced to the industrialization and urbanization of modern society. Over a period of years many economic functions have been taken from the family. Spinning, weaving, soap making, baking, canning, sewing, and laundering have been transferred from home to factory.

With the shift of occupations from home to factory, the economic importance of women in the home has been lessened. Labor-saving devices further reduce the time required for household tasks so that many women seek outside employment or activities. In 1950 about 28 percent of all women over 14 were employed away from home.

Besides a lightening of household activities, there has also been a change in other functions of the family. Educational activities are provided by other institutions. The school may take a child at two or three years of age and provide many services that once were prerogatives of the home. Establishing smooth working coöperation with the school, rather than giving formal instruction, becomes a major task for the family.

Commercialized amusements and other outside recreational agencies make further inroads into family life. Movies, public playgrounds, swimming pools, and youth centers are but a few of the

[3] Robert A. Millikan, "Midwest Progressive Education in the Seventies," in American Association of School Administrators, *Official Report*, 1942, p. 117.

attractions that lure young people away from home for entertainment.

For many children, home influence is lessened by the instability of the modern family. Divorces are all too common. The divorce rate in 1920 was 1.6 per 1000 population; in 1956 it was 2.3 per 1000 population. Large numbers of maladjusted children bear witness to the deleterious effects of broken homes.

Decrease in size of family also changes the character of the home. In a small family children have limited opportunities to acquire experience in human living together. An only child in particular may suffer from lack of association with other children.

However, not all the changes that have been mentioned necessarily weaken the effectiveness of the home. For example, release from household drudgery and decrease in size of family may mean that mothers can give more time to supervising and guiding their children and may rear them more satisfactorily than did the old-fashioned mothers whom we are wont to praise.

CHURCH

The church is another potent educational force. In 1956 churches of 258 different denominations in the United States included in their membership more than 103 million persons.

Since its origin the church has displayed a keen interest in education. In some of the darkest days of ancient and medieval times it encouraged learning and scholarship. Often, however, its concern was not so much with training children in literacy as with training adults in worship and ritual.

Even after schools were established, religious influence was prominent in them. Early colonial schools taught religion. Schoolmasters were required "to catechise their scholars in the principles of the Christian religion," and it was made "a chief part of the schoolmaster's religious care to commend his scholars and his labors amongst them unto God by prayer morning and evening, taking care that his scholars do reverently attend during the same." In early New England schools, reading of the Bible was essential. Many textbooks had a distinctly religious flavor. The *New England*

Primer, published near the close of the seventeenth century, contained such material as the Lord's Prayer, the Creed, and "An Alphabet of Lessons for Youth." The lesson in the opening couplet

> In Adam's Fall
> We sinned all

set the tone for somber verses that concluded with

> Zaccheus he
> Did climb the Tree
> His Lord to see.

For a century and a half the *Primer* exerted tremendous influence. Truly, "it taught millions to read, and not one to sin."

With the separation of church and state religious teaching was dropped by public schools. However, provisions were often made to permit pupils to receive religious instruction under the supervision of the church at designated hours during the school week. One arrangement was the released-time plan. Pupils were excused from classes at a specified time to receive religious instruction usually given by representatives of their church either in the public school building or in the church. Pupils who did not wish to attend classes in religion remained in their home rooms or in study halls.

Another arrangement was the dismissed-time plan. Under this system all the children were dismissed at a given hour in order that parents, rather than school authorities, might coöperate with the church in maintaining classes in religious education.

Legality of the released-time plan was raised in a suit instituted by Mrs. McCollum of Champaign, Illinois. In an 8-to-1 decision on March 8, 1948, the United States Supreme Court ruled that the Champaign system of released-time religious instruction, conducted within the public school buildings under public school auspices, was a violation of the constitutional principle of separation of church and state declared in the First Amendment and made applicable to the states by the Fourteenth.

The McCollum decision has not ended controversy over the scope of the doctrine of separation of church and state. Certain aspects of the problem, such as legality of released-time instruction conducted outside public school buildings, and the dismissed-time plan, remain to be settled.

Whatever religious instruction is received today, however, comes chiefly from home and church. The amount received at home depends on the parents. Many modern families leave to the church responsibility for formal spiritual training of children. Family worship is less common than in an earlier generation. Children often grow up with little knowledge of religious traditions.

The teaching of religious doctrine, therefore, becomes the responsibility of the church. Usually the church is handicapped by its dependence on voluntary workers who are unfamiliar with up-to-date teaching methods. Little wonder that children find Sunday school uninteresting and that they form distorted concepts. One writer observed that children hear little about Jesus. If they do hear of him, it is "not as an ideal grown-up who helped people, but as a little baby whose mother put him in a straw thing in a barn instead of a crib, and to whom queer-looking men in striped gowns brought presents no baby could use. They learn, too, that there was a bad king, with a ferocious face, of whom the baby's mother was afraid, so that she had to take him a long way from home, riding on an animal that is not seen in the city, nor even in the zoo."

Even singing hymns results in striking misinterpretations. For years one Sunday school pupil sang lustily "Fight in the corner where you are." Another puzzled his parents with

> Jesus knows all about our troubles.
> He will wait till the pies are done.

Churches, aware of the new demands upon them, frequently employ educational directors who organize suitable programs and train volunteers to assist in working with young people. Some have vacation Bible schools with sessions of from one week to four weeks. Others have youth fellowship organizations. Still others incorporate activities, such as recreational programs and counseling clinics, which would once have been considered alien and would have been disapproved.

MEDIA OF MASS COMMUNICATION

Media of mass communication are a potent educational force. For untold numbers of our population they transcend the school in significance. We shall discuss the following agencies: the press, motion pictures, radio, and television.

The Press

Newspapers. The twentieth century has witnessed amazing technological advances that give the press almost incredible range, variety, and speed of service. The steam-driven press of the nineteenth century has been followed by the high-speed rotary press, linotype machine, and photoengraving machinery.

Along with technological changes has come concentration of newspaper ownership in the hands of chains. "The newspaper business," said Mark Ethridge of the Louisville (Kentucky) *Courier-Journal* and *Times*, "has gone beyond the stage where the man with ideas or even brains can start a newspaper. He must have money." In 50 years the number of dailies has decreased 750 from its peak of 2600 in 1909. Concentration is shown even more vividly by the fact that, in 1947, 85 percent of all newsprint used in the United States was purchased by 200 big dailies. Eighty-one, or 40 percent, of these newspapers were operated by six chains. Only larger cities have competing dailies. News gathering is almost exclusively in the hands of three press associations, and features are supplied by syndicates.

The number of weekly newspapers has also decreased. The drop has been from about 16,000 in 1910 to 9854 in 1957.

The fact that many newspapers are owned by powerful individuals and groups makes it possible for them to spread one-sided propaganda. They may present only the point of view of their owners. In some cases they may follow the dictates of advertisers. Such domination is not widespread, however, and is more likely to occur among weak than financially strong units.

One of the most serious results of the disappearance of competing newspapers in many communities is the difficulty of securing local reforms if the only paper supports the local administration. Opportunities for publicizing opposing points of view are markedly decreased when one newspaper dominates an area.

A study of major trends in newspaper content at the beginning of four decade years from 1910 to 1940, reveals marked increase in foreign news, Washington news, and financial news. Comic strips and news illustrations are a new device for arousing reader interest. The New York *Times*, which did not publish news pictures until 1925, is still a standout against comics.

A study of trends in newspaper content is inadequate without consideration of the meaning of the word news. As is pointed out in A *Free and Responsible Press*: "The word 'news' has come to mean something different from important new information. When a journalist says that a certain event is news, he does not mean that it is important in itself. Often it is; but about as often it is not. The journalist means by news something that has happened within the last few hours which will attract the interest of the customers. The criteria of interest are recency or firstness, proximity, combat, human interest, and novelty. Such criteria limit accuracy and significance." Undue attention is given to crime, vice, and sex. In short, "the press emphasizes the exceptional rather than the representative, the sensational rather than the significant."

The amount of news reading increases with age, education, and economic status. Also the type of news read varies with these factors. Public affairs materials are read by 7 percent of boys and girls from 10 to 19, and by 31 percent of men and women age 60 and older. Editorials are read by 5 percent of the 10- to 17-year-olds and by 34 percent of persons 60 and older. Professional and businessmen usually pay more attention to public affairs and similar information than skilled workmen or skilled laborers. Teenagers, persons with grade school education, and people in the lower economic groups are more likely to read crime and disaster news than any other type.

Whether or not more people would be interested in serious news if it were less ponderously written is an open question. Paul Scott Mowrer of the Chicago *Daily News* believes that, despite attempts at popularization, people not interested in the subject remain uninterested and those who are really interested resent oversimplification.

"Let us not deceive ourselves," says Mowrer. "Many experiments have been made, and it is now well established that newspapers devoted mainly to the fair and serious presentation of political, economic, scientific, and artistic events must be content to sell few copies. The big circulations go to the papers which give only a minimum of space to such news, and devote their pages primarily to photographs and brief articles having to do with crime, sex, sport, and cinema actors, with, by way of international interest, frequent chauvinistic attacks on foreign nations. . . ."

Surpassing news in popularity are comic strips. They are read by over half the adults and by two-thirds of all children over six. Daily and Sunday strips are read by 60 or 70 million people. For boys and girls the comics are the favorite section of the newspaper. The peak of comic strip reading occurs from age 10 to 19 years with 74 percent reading the comics. The percent declines to 24 for age 60 and older.

The school has an inescapable responsibility for teaching pupils how to read a newspaper. Their glance at headlines and their perusal of comics and sport news can scarcely be considered reading. By consistent effort among the present school population we could guide their newspaper reading into more worth-while channels and give it breadth and depth. In the long run we could educate discriminating readers who would support newspapers of high caliber.

Comic Magazines. The popularity of comics in newspapers led to making comic strips available in magazine form. Success of the venture from a business standpoint is attested by the sale of 50 million or more comic magazines every month. Of the 70 million purchasers annually, 40 percent are children between the ages of 8 and 18. Since children "swap" or resell their books, it is impossible to know the number of readers for each book. It has been estimated that 98 percent of all children between the ages of 8 and 18 read comics. The peak of comic-book reading appears in grade 6 and declines through junior and senior high school.

Although comics are referred to as "joke books" or "funnies," they are often not humorous. One writer describes the characters as "serious fellows, intent on dangerous adventure and noble deeds." Humor, if present, is likely to be of the slapstick variety.

The appeal of comics lies in their color and action. They are personal, concrete, and real. Action is easy to follow. Plot follows a stereotyped form. In the end "good triumphs over evil, virtue is its own reward, and evil-doers are undone by their own foul deeds."

Ralph Ojemann of the University of Iowa, who reported an analysis of 58 full-length comics, found that the chief plans were as follows:

1. Plots predominantly for control of riches or of people—never for control over self.
2. Physical force almost invariably used to solve problems, with no attempt to reach peaceful agreement with the enemy.
3. Story climaxes that brought the extermination or complete isolation of the enemy showing no resulting character effects on the principals in the struggle.
4. Heroes and heroines without physical blemish, but deformed villains.

In Cincinnati a committee set up by the Council of Churches evaluated 555 comic books. The committee found that their contents could be described as follows:

Adolescent characters such as bobby-soxers with dates—proms and the like—generally wholesome.

Animal characters with their appeal to small children: and these are nearly always harmless.

Adventure comics which include a good deal of wild west excitement —gun-toting and the like.

Classic comics which brief well-known stories with pictures and action.

Crime comics which include a large proportion of the comic books.

Jungle comics which play upon man's battle with beasts and reptiles, often showing women as the principal actors.

True comics which are generally based upon historical fact.

Wonder comics which deal with the mysterious or awe-inspiring.

Superman comics which portray the activities of characters that display superhuman strength or wisdom.

A rather large number of comic magazines too varied to classify.[4]

Opinion is divided as to quality of comics. The Cincinnati committee evaluated each of the 555 comic books in terms of its cultural, moral, and emotional tone and import. It adjudged 57.45 percent of these magazines as suitable for children and youth, and only 12.43 percent as "very objectionable." It felt that "wholesale condemnation of comic books is unwarranted."

The effect of reading comic books is a matter of controversy. Those who regard the books as harmful present an array of reasons. They point out that comics, through their portrayal of crime and cruelty, accustom children to crime and violence. Children identify themselves with questionable characters and strive to imitate them. Even though comics claim to teach that crime does not pay, children are thrilled by the exploits of a hero-criminal and probably overlook a moral contained in the last picture or two.

Critics of comics think that many of the pictures frighten children and affect them unfavorably not only immediately but also years later. Neurotic or unstable children are particularly likely to be harmed by overstimulation.

Critics also deplore the amount of time wasted on comics. Persistent reading interferes with other activities such as household duties, school work, the reading of good books, and active outdoor recreation. It may induce eyestrain because comic magazines are usually printed on cheap paper with poor-quality colors, drawings, and printing.

On the favorable side, several prominent investigators have cited evidence that the effect of comics is not necessarily bad. For example, Witty contrasted 10 percent of the children who read comics most in one school with 10 percent of those who read them least. He found little difference in the two groups in intelligence or in general reading interests.

[4] Jesse L. Murrell, "Cincinnati Rates the Comic Books," *Parents' Magazine*, February, 1950, p. 80.

R. L. Thorndike studied the word content of the four most popular comics—*Superman, Batman, Action Comics,* and *Detective Comics.* He found that the actual average vocabulary count in each of these magazines was about 10,000 words.

Perhaps the cardinal thing is to understand each child's pattern and variety of reading. Then he can be guided not only to select better comics but also to choose good books that satisfy his desire for fast-moving, easy-to-read stories.

Magazines. Reliable data about the number of magazines published in the United States are difficult to obtain. However, 6500 is probably a conservative estimate.

Although a few giants such as *Reader's Digest, Life,* and *Saturday Evening Post,* with circulations exceeding 11 million, 5 million, and 4 million, respectively, appear to dominate the field, many small-circulation, "quality" magazines of untold influence such as *The Atlantic Monthly, Harper's,* and *Saturday Review* reach a circle of like-minded readers.

While individual publishers and their magazines may come and go, there is no downward trend in either the number of publishers or the number of magazines. The relative stability of the number of magazines may be due not only to the fact that publishers can have their printing done for them on contract, thus avoiding heavy investment in plant and equipment, but also to the fact that they can draw their readers from the nation as a whole.

Magazines that boys and girls mention as having the most general appeal are ones that top the field in circulation. Probably their apparent popularity reflects a wide home circulation. It is a case of liking what one knows. Among elementary school pupils some of the popular magazines are *Jack and Jill, Story Parade, Child Life, Children's Digest, Children's Activities, Humpty Dumpty's Magazine,* and *Junior Language and Arts.*

Schools should teach the use of magazines as one of the tools for developing an alert and informed citizenry, as Edgar Dale so well states: "If students while in high school and college do not 'master' the art of reading magazines, their future chances of being enlightened citizens, of getting a liberal education are poor.

Books can tell us what happened in the past. Newspapers can give us the thin slice of the present. But the magazines mediate between the out-of-dateness of the past and the up-to-dateness of the daily newspapers."

Books. A wealth of children's literature is available to appeal to every age and taste. In 1956 juvenile books under one dollar retail sold 118,386,000 copies while those of one dollar and over retail sold 26,546,000 copies. In 1957 of the total new books published, 1557 were for juveniles.

In general, young children like stories about familiar happenings and places, about other children and animals. They like fairy tales and imaginative stories that help them escape from the world of reality. They like adventure, mystery, and action. As they grow older, boys especially show strong scientific interests, with volumes on atomic energy and guided missiles in demand; girls favor romantic stories and books about adolescents with a school background. Biography and books on etiquette are coming to the fore. Girls at an early age are asking for books on beauty care.

For most children books are fairly accessible. Public libraries as well as school libraries place them within easy reach. Remote areas are served by bookmobiles. Both public and school libraries may employ children's librarians. Often they arrange reading programs and story hours for youngsters. Libraries as well as newspapers, schools, and civic groups conduct book fairs to acquaint the public with suitable books.

Since 1955 the Book Manufacturers Institute, a trade association for the manufacturers of hard-bound books, has sponsored the Library Club of America. The club is nonprofit; it neither sells nor recommends books. It encourages children to read by awarding merit badges. There are no dues and no requirements for admission other than that the child be of school age. The club has over 2600 chapters with a total membership of more than a half million. Most of the chapters are organized by principals of schools, teachers, or librarians, with headquarters in school or public libraries.

The amount of time that children spend in reading books depends in part upon the home. Children who have stories told or read to them and who are surrounded by books are likely to turn to reading as one of their favorite leisure-time pursuits.

Like adults, children read fewer books than magazines. Among adolescents the amount of voluntary reading often decreases. Perhaps this is due to a growing desire to participate in the life of the crowd.

Motion Pictures

The twentieth century has witnessed the development of motion pictures as a dominant form of mass communication.[5] Their forerunner was the kinetoscope invented by Edison in 1889. So little was he concerned about this invention that he did not patent it in Europe. Later the projector and screen were perfected, and in 1894 the kinetoscope had its first public commercial showing in New York City. One customer at a time could look into a machine and see the pictures move. Pictures included such things as boxers in parts of rounds and bits of vaudeville acts.

Soon the magic lantern was used in connection with the kinetoscope so that an entire audience could view the screen. At first pictures were used as a part of variety shows which were called "vaudeville." Later penny-arcade owners presented all-movie programs. By 1905 the five-cent movie theater, the "nickelodeon," had arrived with the opening of a theater in Pittsburgh.

In these early years from 1903 to 1908 the foundation of the motion picture industry was laid. Pictures were made hastily to meet the demands of growing audiences. Soon there were about 10,000 exhibitors in the United States alone.

From 1908 to 1914 was a period of struggle for economic control in the industry. Ten leading manufacturers of cameras and projectors and the producers of movies pooled their resources to form the Motion Picture Patents Company. They made rental of their films and use of their projectors mutually contingent. In addition to the rental cost of films, they charged exhibitors two dollars a week for the use of their projectors. By 1914 the power of the

[5] Ruth A. Inglis, *Freedom of the Movies*, University of Chicago Press, 1947.

Patents Company was reduced, and by 1917 the company was out-lawed.

The motion picture industry flourished during World War I. With European studios closed by war, American pictures took over more than three-fourths of the world's screen time. Audiences increased. People were becoming more discriminating in judging pictures and were more willing to pay higher prices for entertainment. The "feature" picture was beginning to replace short pictures. The production of Griffith's *Birth of a Nation* in 1915 gave strong impetus to the feature movement.

The next striking advance was in 1926 with Warner Brothers' release of *Don Juan*, the first feature picture with sound. Within three years the industry was virtually made over by the talking picture.

The rapid expansion of the motion picture industry created many problems. Costs of production were high. Large numbers of pictures had to be filmed. Movie-goers began to identify and to prefer certain actors and actresses, and the star system with its consequent salary increases arose. Advertising became essential to keep up the movie-going habit. Changes in distribution took place. "Block-booking" called for the simultaneous leasing of a group of films in a given block and caused theaters to take many bad pictures in order to secure a good one. Although block-booking has been eliminated, it still influences the basis on which films are rented. Pictures are selected by exhibitors from written descriptions often before they are produced. Such factors as production costs and reputation of stars and directors influence the choice.

Until a Supreme Court decision in 1948 separated theater owning from production, the motion picture industry was virtually in the hands of five companies that not only produced pictures but also owned theaters. The big five, together with three other companies commonly listed with them, constitute the eight major companies. In 1945, 65 percent of the feature films were released by the majors. They produce the most expensive Hollywood films, a large proportion of the short subjects, and nearly all the newsreels. Executives of the major companies inestimably influence the character and policies of the motion picture industry.

Public concern as to the influence of motion pictures has led to both legal and self-censorship. However, the federal government has not enacted general legislation to regulate motion pictures. Censorship is left largely to states and cities. A few states require that all films be previewed by a board of censors. Some cities have their own censorship boards.

More promising than legal censorship are the attempts of the industry to provide self-censorship. A code adopted by the industry stresses three basic principles:

1. No picture shall be produced which will lower the moral standards of those who see it. Hence the sympathy of the audience shall never be thrown to the side of crime, wrongdoing, evil or sin.
2. Correct standards of life, subject only to the requirements of drama and entertainment, shall be presented.
3. Law, natural or human, shall not be ridiculed, nor shall sympathy be created for its violation.

As of July, 1955, there were 14,100 permanent four-wall motion picture theaters in the United States and 4500 drive-in theaters, one-third of which are open the year around. Weekly attendance ranges from 50 million to 55 million persons. The impact of television has cut attendance so drastically that in some areas from 22 to 40 percent of the motion picture theaters have closed. However, in 1954 motion picture theaters took in nearly 75 cents of every dollar spent by the public on spectator amusements. Drive-ins account for about 20 percent of the total box-office gross.

Essentially the motion picture audience is a fairly young one. The 1950 *Film Daily Yearbook* estimates that 10 percent of the persons attending the motion picture theater are between 5 and 11 years of age; 20 percent are between 12 and 17; 35 percent are between 18 and 30; 20 percent are from 31 to 45; and only 15 percent are over 45. Although average attendance for boys and girls is about once or twice a week, some go three or four times a week.

Yet with the millions of young people who go to movies, almost no pictures are made especially for them. Pictures are made for a general, nonspecific mass audience. They try to interest everyone and offend no one. "And the thing which interests everyone, the producer concludes, is action—action about love, crime, and sex, woven into a fantasy which spells escape from reality."[6] Perhaps one picture in five is suitable, whereas one in three is objectionable for children.

Movie interests of children follow much the same line as their reading and radio interests. Children in elementary school like films about cowboys and pilots. They are less interested in pictures of current events, news shorts, biography, and travel. As they reach high school age, boys show a preference for mystery, western, and G-man stories, while girls prefer love stories.

However, in considering reports of movie interests, we must remember that the choices of children hinge upon what they have seen rather than upon what they might like to see. Instead of giving people pictures that they want, the movies accustom people to wanting what they see.

The effects of attending motion pictures is a moot question. In general, the findings as to their influence on physical and emotional health are not altogether favorable. Frequent attendance may result in disturbed sleep, eye fatigue, increased nervousness, fears, and night terrors. Scenes of danger, conflict, and tragedy have the most marked effect on children from 6 to 12, and romantic and erotic scenes have the most noticeable effect on those from 12 to 18. There is a possibility that frequent movie attendance renders maladjusted children unstable and unhappy. They substitute movies for more active, creative recreation and for contact with other children.

Children's conduct is profoundly altered—whether for good or ill—by what they see at the movies. They tend to identify themselves with motion picture stars and to imitate their behavior. They accept stereotypes and attitudes popularized by movies.

[6] National Society for the Study of Education, *Mass Media and Education*, Fifty-Third Yearbook, 1954, Part II, p. 55.

Parents have a responsibility for regulating attendance. The Motion Picture Association advises that children under 8 are too young to attend movies. Even 8-year-olds should be accompanied by an adult, preferably a parent.

Radio

In 1895 when Marconi transmitted a message by wireless across his father's estate, a new field of science and industry was opened. In 1897 he organized a British company for wireless communication. Two years later this company incorporated an American subsidiary.

By the close of World War I three American companies—General Electric, American Telephone and Telegraph, and Westinghouse—had acquired patents vital to the future of wireless. Each firm needed equipment controlled by the others and also by American Marconi. Eventually Owen D. Young, chairman of the board of General Electric, proposed that the three firms combine their resources to buy out American Marconi. In line with this suggestion, the Radio Corporation of America was organized on October 17, 1919. Since then the growth of the broadcasting industry has been astonishing. As of January 1, 1957, there were 2974 AM and 530 FM stations on the air. In 1956 there were 143 million radio sets in use in the United States. Of this number, 53 million were in homes and in automobiles.

The size of the radio audience can scarcely be estimated accurately. Probably it numbers 77,500,000 some time each day.

Radio, like the press, is sponsored by giant financial resources. Fewer than 150 advertisers provide all but 3 or 4 percent of the income of radio networks. As in the case of the press, monopoly is a threat. The titanic consumer industries, notably food, tobacco, drugs, and soap, which give the networks nearly three-quarters of their income, may determine what American people shall hear on the air.

Approximately 25,000 different radio programs are broadcast daily. They are predominantly musical and about half of them present popular and dance music. Dramatic programs occupy sec-

ond place, consuming about 16 percent of radio time. News is in
third place, with about one-eighth of radio time.

Children like radio programs that abound in thrills and adven-
tures. Since it is estimated that radio kills 2400 persons annually
on crime, thrill, and soap-opera programs, blood-curdling episodes
are not lacking. Children also enjoy comedy, especially if it supplies a broad rather than a subtle type of humor. Teen-agers like
dance music, romantic serials, sports, general news, and quiz programs. They display little interest in educational shows.

The discussion of the effects of motion picture attendance can
be almost completely paralleled for radio listening. Unquestionably
radio programs influence behavior. Listeners identify themselves
with their favorite entertainers and often copy their exploits. Immediate effects are frequently clearly observable.

The long-time effects of radio listening cannot be discerned.
Probably standards in many areas such as speech and music are
affected. If "taste is discrimination many times exercised," as
Robert Underwood Johnson, formerly editor of *Century Magazine*, once said, the need for raising critical standards among children and young people is apparent.

Television

"It's hazardous to commit anything to paper about TV these
days. What's news one week is passé the next." Three decades ago
only an insignificant number of people had ever seen television.
Today approximately 75 percent of the nation own TV sets. More
time is spent each day watching TV than on any other activity
except cooking or sleeping—nearly six hours each day. As of January, 1957, there were 511 TV stations on the air.

As *Fortune* has pointed out, television is "the product of thousands of unrelated scientific experiments, the results of which have
been pieced together with the painstaking care of a paleontologist
assembling the brittle calcified shards of a dinosaur's skull." To
mention only a few among the parts, we find: a telegraph operator
in 1873 reporting that selenium could change light energy into

electrical energy; an experimenter trying to transmit pictures by dividing them into sections; Nipkow, a German, in 1884 patenting a scanning disk for transmitting pictures by wireless; Fournier and Rignoux transmitting a moving image over wire in 1906; Lee De Forest inventing in 1906 a vacuum tube amplifier with grid, plate, and filament; Marconi in 1915 predicting a "visible telephone"; and Vladimir Zworykin in 1925 patenting the iconoscope (TV camera tube).

In 1927 at a public demonstration in which Herbert Hoover, then Secretary of Commerce, participated, an experimental TV program was sent by wire between New York and Washington by the Bell Telephone Laboratories. Thereafter the television race was on. The promotional ability of leaders in industry and the investment of untold millions of dollars have brought television to its present amazing efficiency. The initiation of commercial color broadcasting marks one of the triumphs of the 1950's.

In 1952 the Federal Communications Commission made channel assignments to 242 communities exclusively for noncommercial educational purposes. The first noncommercial educational TV grant was made July 23, 1952, to Kansas State College of Agriculture and Applied Science at Manhattan. In April, 1953, the first noncommercial station to operate on an educational license went on the air at the University of Houston, Texas. By 1958, 34 educational stations operated on reserved channels.

Commercial TV stations devote about three-fourths of all the time they are on the air to the entertainment-type program. Within this group the largest class is drama, whether motion pictures or live TV drama. Information programs occupy the second largest segment of TV time, slightly less than one-fifth of the total time. News constitutes the largest class of programs in this group.

Many citizens feel that the amount of violence portrayed on TV is a legitimate cause for concern. The National Association for Better Radio and Television, a nonprofit organization, made its eighth annual survey of crime on television during the week of

May 3 to 9, 1958. Its evaluation committee monitored the crime programs aired before 9 PM by the seven TV stations (three networks, four independents) in Los Angeles.

The tabulation of crimes presented included 161 murders, 60 "justifiable" killings, 2 suicides, 192 attempted murders, 83 robberies, 15 kidnapings, 24 conspiracies to commit murder, 7 attempted lynchings, 21 jailbreaks, 6 dynamitings, 2 cases of arson, and 2 instances of physical torture. These were only the major crimes depicted. This total of 221 killings represented 500 percent more televised killings than were tallied during a similar survey in 1952.

A great deal of this violence and murder took place on programs earmarked for children. Their fare included 15 murders, 52 attempted murders, 7 "justifiable" murders, 3 mass killings by gangland shooting, 2 attempted lynchings, 3 conspiracies to murder, 2 kidnapings, and countless threats to kill, sluggings, scenes of mob violence and lawlessness.

The question of the effects upon viewers of acts and threats of violence arouses heated controversy. Whether or not the increase in volume and violence of nature of juvenile crime can be linked with the saturation of TV programming with sadism and brutality no one knows. But even though youngsters may not be driven to emulate the crimes they view, it is not unreasonable to assume that their sensibilities may be blunted by repeated portrayal of violence.

That children find excitement, adventure, and interest in programs involving no gunplay, murder, or violence is proved by the success of children's programs on educational television stations. For example, "The Children's Corner," an educational program presented five days per week over station WQED in Pittsburgh, has attracted nation-wide attention. The program covers a wide variety of subjects including zoölogy, poetry, foreign languages, hobbies and crafts, music and art. No crime, acts of violence or horror are included in its format to secure and sustain interest. Yet more than 4000 letters per week have been received from enthusiastic fans in the Pittsburgh area. More than 25,000 children in the area are members of the "Tame Tiger Torganization" which is associated with the program.

Since television is still relatively new, numerous attempts are being made to find out how much time is spent before TV screens. Each year since 1950 Paul Witty of Northwestern University has studied the reactions to TV of approximately 2000 elementary and high school pupils, their teachers, and their parents.[7]

The prediction in 1950 that televiewing would be a passing fancy has not been realized. Children spend as much time or more with TV than they did when it offered them a new experience. In 1950, the elementary school pupils spent 21 hours each week with TV, while in 1957 it was 20 hours for Evanston (Illinois) children and 23 for Kenosha County (Wisconsin) children. The average for high school pupils was 14 hours in 1955 and 12 in 1957. In 1950 parents spent 24 hours weekly in televiewing and about 20 hours in 1957. In 1951 teachers spent 9 hours per week televiewing and 12 hours in 1957.

Favorite programs change over the years. In 1957, among the children *Disneyland* held first rank; *Mickey Mouse Club*, second; *I Love Lucy*, third; and *Lassie*, fourth. In the same year the favorite programs of parents included *I Love Lucy, Lawrence Welk, Perry Como*'s variety show, and *Father Knows Best*. In 1957 teachers gave first place to *Lawrence Welk* and second place to *Perry Como. Omnibus* and *Disneyland* also ranked high on their list.

Witty's findings were inconclusive as to the effects of TV in such areas as children's health; amount of time spent in sports, outdoor play, creative activities, hobbies, and reading; emotional adjustment; and school attainment.

Home, School, and Community Responsibility and Mass Media

Some responsibilities of home and school in connection with mass media have already been mentioned. They lie along similar lines for many media—comics, radio, movies, and television.

[7] Paul Witty, "Some Results of Eight Yearly Studies of TV," *School and Society*, Summer Issue, 1958, pp. 287–289.

In trying to judge the effects of mass media we must recognize both desirable and undesirable features. On the one hand, they offer a means of enriching a child's experience, of extending his horizon, and of broadening his views of life. They may have therapeutic value by giving him release from humdrum everyday affairs. According to Murphy: "Reversal of child-adult roles, triumph of childish ingenuity, defeat of rigid or aggressive parental activity, resolution of sibling conflicts, transcendence of reality limitations, are important themes for children along with the melodramatic ones; and all together provide an important world of fantasy to be shared with friends as well as to be enjoyed alone."

On the other hand, mass media often claim time that children should spend in work or active recreation. They may adversely affect both physical and mental health. They may debase standards of taste and behavior, and even lead to crime.

To evaluate their effects we must take into account the individual child. What constitutes an unacceptable program for one may not necessarily be so regarded for another. For example, a normal child with a secure home atmosphere may not be harmed by the portrayal of crime in comics or movies, whereas an unstable child from a broken home may be induced to emulate the villain-hero.

The problem of sensible use of mass media calls for coöperation of home, school, and community.

Parents should sensitize children to high standards of taste. They should call attention to desirable features of certain comics, radio and television programs, and motion pictures. They should share some of their children's experiences with mass media. The habit of doing things together is worthy of cultivation. To paraphrase Ogden Nash, a child would be in much less danger from the evil effects of these media "If one's kin and one's kith were more fun to be with."

Parents should encourage children to budget their time so that reasonable provision is made for the enjoyment of mass media. If a child wants to spend an excessive amount of time in sedentary pursuits like listening to the radio or attending movies, his parents should ascertain the reason. They should teach children to entertain themselves, and they should take their share of responsibility for providing appropriate recreational facilities.

Schools as well as parents should teach children to exercise discrimination in choosing entertainment. Teachers must be familiar with experiences that pupils obtain from mass media. Occasionally class discussions and projects can grow out of their experiences. From time to time school facilities, such as radio and movie projector, may be used to give pupils opportunities for learning to appreciate approved programs.

The best efforts of home and school in dealing with problems related to mass media are hampered, however, unless the entire community coöperates. Local groups can exert influence in such matters as discouraging the sale of trashy comics, protesting objectionable motion pictures and patronizing good ones, and writing to radio and television stations to express their opinions of programs.

Questions like these framed by Edgar Dale might well be asked of all mass media material:

1. Does it do good, not will it be harmful or harmless?
2. Do children need this experience, not do they want it?
3. Is this experience preparing them for something better, more mature? Or will it arrest them at a low stage of emotional development?
4. Does it help build love and affection, the ability to love and be loved?
5. Does it help individuals creatively put themselves into the other fellow's shoes?
6. Does it disclose that helping, not hitting, that reason, not physical force is the decent way of life?
7. Is the way of life seen in the mass media one respected by our great spiritual, moral, religious, civic leaders?
8. What responsible thinking can an individual do about the mass media? What responsible action can be taken in cooperation with others?[8]

[8] Edgar Dale, "What About the Comics?" *The News Letter*, December, 1954, p. 4.

SUMMARY

All groups have processes for inducting the young into their cultural heritage. In our society the school is the special, though not the sole, agency for carrying on education. In this chapter we have discussed the educational role of the school, home, church, and media of mass communication—press, motion pictures, radio, and television.

Schools provide a deliberately created and controlled environment for the purpose of bringing about desirable changes in behavior. They not only perpetuate a culture but they also contribute to its improvement.

The home is the most important educative agency in any culture because of its basic role in shaping the personality and character of the younger generation.

The church, under the American doctrine of separation of church and state, has a major responsibility for the teaching of religious doctrine. Often educational directors are engaged to organize programs especially for young people.

Mass media of communication are powerful educative influences in modern society. The school has an obligation to elevate standards of taste so that young people will choose the best from available fare. It has a further obligation to contribute to the improvement of the quality of the content of mass communications media.

QUESTIONS AND EXERCISES

1. Mrs. Douglas Horton, former president of Wellesley College, said in a radio broadcast: "Expecting schools to be all things to all men has minimized the time available for doing the things that schools are theoretically better able to do than the other institutions. As it is, intellectual discipline has become almost an accident in the life of the ordinary boy and girl." Support or refute her contention.

2. In an editorial in *Life*, October 16, 1950, Henry Steele Commager wrote: "Schools reflect the society they serve. Many of the failures we ascribe to contemporary education are in fact failures of our society as a whole." Cite examples to illustrate Commager's point of view.

3. How may activities of school and community be interrelated in a program of education? How may people be induced to take an intelligent interest in their schools?

4. Read ten or more comic books. Tabulate material which might encourage high ideals and desirable conduct, and that which might lead to any form of delinquency. Propose ways of counteracting the effects of undesirable material. From your analysis of these comic books, do you think that John Mason Brown is justified in labeling comics "the marijuana of the nursery" and "the bane of the bassinet"?

5. Listen to several radio programs or watch television programs intended primarily for children. List their good and bad features.

6. Should schools or commercial firms be responsible for education on television?

7. How can the school teach better use of media of mass communication?

SELECTED REFERENCES

American Association of School Administrators, *Public Relations for American Schools*, Twenty-Eighth Yearbook, 1950.

Commission on Freedom of the Press, Robert M. Hutchins, Chairman, *A Free and Responsible Press*, University of Chicago Press, 1947.

Folsom, Joseph Kirk, *The Family and Democratic Society*, John Wiley & Sons, Inc., 1943.

Frank, Josette, *Comics, Radio, Movies—and Children*, Public Affairs Pamphlet No. 148, Public Affairs Committee, Inc., 1949.

Inglis, Ruth A., *Freedom of the Movies*, University of Chicago Press, 1947.

Mead, Margaret, *The School in American Culture*, Harvard University Press, 1951.

National Society for the Study of Education, *Mass Media and Education*, Fifty-Third Yearbook, 1954, Part II.

Schramm, Wilbur (ed.), *Mass Communications*, University of Illinois Press, 1949.

Shayon, Robert Lewis, *Television and Our Children*, Longmans, Green and Co., 1951.

Waller, Judith C., *Radio, the Fifth Estate*, Houghton Mifflin Company, 1946.

White, Llewellyn, *The American Radio*, University of Chicago Press, 1947.

Wieman, Regina W., *The Modern Family and the Church*, Harper & Brothers, 1937.

AUDIO-VISUAL MATERIALS

Films

Bridges for Ideas (28 minutes, Sound, B & W, University of Southern California). Examines media of communication as bridges for ideas.

Our Changing Family Life (22 minutes, Sound, B & W, McGraw-Hill Book Company, Inc.). Contrasts the life of a closely knit farm family of the year 1880 with that of a modern family.

Recordings

Home Sweet Home—The Ways of Mankind (30 minutes, National Association of Educational Broadcasters). The family is a natural grouping in all societies. Relations in the family influence our behavior. Contrasts attitudes toward the family in China and the United States.

Sticks and Stones—The Ways of Mankind (30 minutes, National Association of Educational Broadcasters). A study in religion. Includes a description of initiation ceremonies among the Arunta.

CHAPTER VII

Safeguard of Democracy

In Chapter VI we pointed out that the school has its origin in the desire of society to transmit the cultural heritage to the younger generation. "The school is," to quote Dewey, "the essential distributing agency for whatever values and purposes any social group cherishes. It is not the only means, but it is the first means, the primary means, and the most deliberate means by which the values that any social group cherishes, the purposes that it wishes to realize, are distributed and brought home to the thought, the observation, judgment, and choice of the individual."

Accordingly, in order to understand the school, we must consider it in relation to its social setting. It reflects the ideology of the group. It directs its energies toward teaching knowledge, skills, and general patterns of conduct approved by the culture of which it is a part. Its success is judged by the degree to which the younger generation acquires these outcomes of learning.

Our schools were established to function in the social-cultural order of America. Some aspects of our culture were mentioned in Chapter V. Varied as these aspects are, one characteristic—general belief in democracy—is dominant. Hence, ideals of democracy color the character of our education. We look to the school to promote understanding and appreciation of the democratic tradition. We expect the school to aid pupils in acquiring skills, knowledge, and desire not only to preserve but also to improve our way of life.

If the school is to prepare pupils to live effectively in a democratic society, educators must seek to understand the meaning of democracy. Upon their interpretation depend the organization and administration of school systems, formulation of objectives, choice of portions of the cultural heritage to be stressed, attitude toward social change, and selection of methods and materials of instruction.

WHAT IS DEMOCRACY?

Democracy is an elusive term. In the original Greek it meant government of the people. How many people should have a part in the government and how they should govern in order to have a democracy have never been definitely decided.

Even in America the idea of who should vote has gradually changed. The framers of the Constitution had no idea of giving all the people the ballot. They feared popular rule. For the common man without property the right to vote was fairly long delayed. New York abolished property qualifications for white men in 1826 after a petition containing 75,000 names was submitted. In Rhode Island property qualifications were abolished in 1842 after a kind of civil war known as Dorr's Rebellion. Votes for colored men were made possible by the Fifteenth Amendment. Votes for women were sanctioned in 1920 by the Nineteenth Amendment.

Since the founding of our country we have been concerned with perfecting political democracy. We have striven for rule by the majority, protection of the rights of the minority, and the coöperative solution of problems. In short, we have sought what Lincoln described as "government of the people, by the people, and for the people."

Perhaps our concern for political democracy has been prompted by the belief that, given political democracy, we could work out our other problems. In the early history of our country there was considerable justification for this point of view. With changes in our society, however, it has become necessary to broaden our concept of democracy to include phases other than political democracy.

Today we often say that democracy is more than institutions and ways of life. "It is a great social faith which, in response to the yearnings and struggles of many races and peoples, has been developing through the centuries." In this sense it includes not only political but also economic and social democracy.

We shall consider briefly some of the implications of economic and social democracy.

Economic Democracy

Economic democracy means security in a mutually interdependent society. Everyone must have an opportunity to obtain through his own efforts the material goods necessary for maintaining a suitable standard of living. The worker should help in determining working conditions and should receive a fair share of the wealth that he helps to produce. Natural resources must be used wisely for the benefit of all. So great is the power bestowed by wealth that without economic democracy social justice can scarcely prevail.

That economic democracy is an unrealized ideal is indicated by the maldistribution of wealth. Many people have inadequate diets, substandard housing, and low incomes.

TABLE 3. Total Income and Employment Income, 1956
(Percentage distribution of spending units)

Amount	Total Money Income Before Taxes	Income from Wages, Salary, and Self-Employment Head	Income from Wages, Salary, and Self-Employment Wife
Zero	—	21	78
Under $1,000	9	8	8
$1,000–$1,999	12	7	5
$2,000–$2,999	12	9	4
$3,000–$3,999	12	—	—
$4,000–$4,999	14	26	4
$5,000–$7,499	24	—	—
$7,500–$9,999	9	24	1
$10,000 and over	8	4	—
Not ascertained	—	1	—
All cases	100	100	100

SOURCE: *Federal Reserve Bulletin*, Board of Governors of the Federal Reserve System, Washington, D.C., August, 1957, p. 879.

Inequality of income is shown by the findings of the 1957 Survey of Consumer Finances conducted by the Board of Governors of the Federal Reserve System in coöperation with the Survey Research Center of the University of Michigan. The results are based on 3041 interviews in the 12 largest metropolitan areas and in 54 additional sampling areas. As will be seen from Table 3, about 41 percent of all spending units reported 1956 incomes of $5000 or more, 26 percent reported $3000 to $5000, and 33 percent reported less than $3000.

When the distribution of total money income before taxes was considered by income tenths, the Survey revealed that the mean income for the highest tenth was $15,760, and the mean income for the lowest tenth, $660. Thus families in the highest tenth have incomes that average more than 23 times as high as the average of the bottom tenth.

In the early history of our country the government was expected to remain aloof in economic matters. As long as frontier life with its self-contained rural civilization prevailed, the government could properly maintain a "hands-off" policy. The American people, says Perry, felt "that they were quite competent to look out for their own happiness if only they were let alone to do it, and that government could best serve their happiness by seeing to it that they *were* let alone. Government was designed to afford the maximum of free-play to those motives and forces by which self-reliant individuals carve out their own fortunes."

The right of the individual to exercise his own initiative to advance his economic interests was taken for granted. Lincoln expressed this point of view in a speech at New Haven in 1860:

I take it that it is best to leave each man to acquire property as fast as he can. Some will get wealthy. I don't believe in a law to prevent a man from getting rich; it would do more harm than good. So while we don't propose any war upon capital, we do wish to allow the humblest man an equal chance to get rich with anybody else. When one starts poor, as most do in the race of life, free society is such that he knows he can better his condition; he knows that there is no fixed condition of labor for his whole life . . . he may look forward and hope to be a hired laborer this year and the next, work for himself afterwards and finally hire men to work for him. That is the true system.

The problems of economic democracy, however, are tremendously complicated in the United States. No longer is each family practically a self-sufficient unit. No longer is production carried on chiefly for the family group. A striking illustration of the change is contained in the following description:

The Vermont farmer, with his small property, his poor, rocky soil, and his very short growing season, has been specializing in dairy farming ever since the refrigerated railroad car made possible long-distance transportation of milk and milk products. But during the past twenty-five years the character of his specialization has been changing profoundly. Where before he specialized in a product, he can now—with little exaggeration—be said to specialize in one process. He no longer grows his own fodder. In many cases he no longer raises his own calves. He feeds fodder grown in the Midwest and South to cows bought from a breeder. He also no longer processes the milk. He delivers the raw milk to a creamery which processes it and delivers it to a distributor. The distribution of this apparently so simple product requires actually one of the most complicated organizations in our entire economy— and one based on such mass-production principles as the breakdown of the operation into simple component operations, the synchronization of the flow of materials and sub-assemblies, and the interchangeability of component parts.

The farmer does not even make his own butter; the butter he buys comes from Wisconsin or Iowa, fifteen hundred miles away. Sometimes it is not even economical for the farmer to keep his own milk for his own consumption but cheaper to buy his supply in the store. Outwardly little seems to have changed, but actually the Vermont dairy farmer—or the Iowa corn-hog farmer, the Minnesota wheat farmer, the citrus grower in California—has become a link in an agricultural assembly line. It would be difficult to say who his "management" is or where it is, but he is surely being managed. His processes, his policies, very largely even his actual operations are laid out for him by the machinery over which he has very little control. The only positive action left for him is to go on a "milk strike"—the very term is significant. The farmer's relationship to the economy and to society has become increasingly remote as well as increasingly complex. Almost as much as the man on the automobile assembly line he needs to understand what he is doing and why, and it is almost as hard for him to obtain a view of the whole as it is for an accountant in Washington.[1]

Not only is the family no longer independent, but even the local community is no longer self-sufficient. The changes brought about by the transformation of our economic system by modern technology baffle the imagination. The invention of hundreds of machines has revolutionized manufacturing. The central factory with its economical and efficient production has replaced or integrated independent industries. Responsibility for production is often in the hands of mammoth enterprises.

Studies of the 200 largest nonfinancial corporations in the United States in fields other than banking and insurance, show that they extend in size from less than $100 million of gross assets to about $4 billion in the case of American Telephone and Telegraph Company. About half of the 200 are railroads or other utilities, and the greater part of the other half are manufacturing companies. Nine of the railroads and three of the manufacturing companies are in the billion-dollar class.

Firms may be measured not only in absolute units but on the basis of their relative size in relation to the industry of which they are a part. Peterson points out that before the war one firm in each field produced:

Most of the aluminum, nickel, molybdenum, magnesium, shoe machinery, and glass-container machinery; two firms most of the bananas, plate glass, electric bulbs, electric accounting machines, and sulphur. The four largest firms in each industry produced more than 90 percent of the chewing gum and cigarettes; more than 80 percent of the motor vehicles, explosives, linoleum, rubber tires, and tin cans; more than 70 percent of the oleomargarine, soap, farm implements, and matches. At the other extreme, the four largest firms produced less than 5 percent of the women's and children's clothing, fur goods, printing and publishing, and lumber products, and less than 10 percent of the men's and boys' clothing, furniture, house furnishings, and jewelry.

[1] Peter F. Drucker, "The New Society," *Harper's Magazine*, September, 1949, p. 29.

This method of measurement is less significant in analyzing the economies of size than in appraising the degree of monopoly and competition in industry.[2]

In such an economy the idea of a laissez-faire system with complete freedom of competition becomes outmoded. Mere absence of restraint no longer suffices. Instead some measure of control is necessary in order that all may have an equal opportunity for freedom. "Hence," concludes Perry, "the increasing tendency of government to intervene in business—to regulate, or even control."

The role that the government should play in our economy is demanding the attention of our best thinkers. Just how much freedom can be given up in the economic realm while retaining freedom in the political realm is a basic question. On the one hand, we have a case for planning in such a book as *The Good Society* by Walter Lippmann. On the other hand, we have the case against planning in such books as *The Road to Serfdom* by Friederich A. von Hayek and *Ordeal by Planning* by John Jewkes.

Eisenhower took cognizance of the changing role of government in his inaugural address at Columbia University:

A paternalistic government can gradually destroy, by suffocation in the immediate advantage of subsidy, the will of a people to maintain a high degree of individual responsibility. And the abdication of individual responsibility is inevitably followed by further concentration of power in the state. Government ownership or control of property is not to be decried principally because of the historic inefficiency of governmental management of productive enterprises; its real threat rests in the fact that, if carried to the logical extreme, the final concentration of ownership in the hands of government gives to it, in all practical effects, absolute power over our lives.

There are internal dangers that require eternal vigilance if they are to be avoided. If we permit extremes of wealth for a few and enduring poverty for many, we shall create social explosiveness and a demand for revolutionary change. If we do not eliminate selfish abuse of power by any one group, we can be certain that equally selfish retaliation by other groups will ensue. Never must we forget that ready cooperation in the solution of human problems is the only way to avoid governmental intervention.

[2] Shorey Peterson, *Economics*, Henry Holt and Company, 1949, pp. 168–169.

All our cherished rights—the rights of free speech, free worship, ownership of property, equality before the law—all these are mutually dependent for their existence. Thus, when shallow critics denounce the profit motive inherent in our system of private enterprise, they ignore the fact that it is an economic support of every human right we possess and that without it, all rights would soon disappear. Demagoguery, unless combatted by truth, can become as great a danger to freedom as exists in any other threat.[3]

Still another warning against the possible loss of freedom that might result from governmental planning is given by Peter Viereck: "If you base society solely on the idea of economic gains, scrapping freedom and justice for the sake of the tyranny needed to organize total planning, then you lose not only the freedom but the economic gains. In place of the economic philosophy of Adam Smith or of Marx, the world through trial and error will come to see the *economic necessity of an anti-economic philosophy*, the material necessity of anti-materialism."[4]

Whether or not a solution to our pressing economic problems can be found may determine whether democracy can survive. Whether we can assure economic opportunity while keeping a suitable balance between responsibility for the welfare of the group and the responsibility of the individual for the results of his own efforts may determine the very existence of our form of government. Almost any form of government will work as long as basic human needs are met. But, as Counts insists, "the experience of our time shows that, if a people is forced to choose between jobs and political liberty, they will choose jobs, or the promise of jobs. The peculiar task of our people in the present age is to demonstrate that economic stability and political liberty are both possible at the same time. Only through the achievement of such a union can our democracy hope to endure."

We now turn from this discussion of economic democracy to a consideration of social democracy.

[3] Dwight D. Eisenhower, "Notes for Inaugural Address," *Educational Forum*, January, 1949, pp. 135–136.

[4] Peter Viereck, "Conservatism Revisited," *Harper's Magazine*, August, 1949, p. 65.

Social Democracy

Social democracy is based upon the ideal of justice and welfare for all. There shall be no class distinction based on inheritance. Everyone shall have the right to make a place for himself by his efforts and ability. There shall be no unfair discrimination and no oppression because of race, class, color, or creed.

Such is the ideal Walt Whitman had in mind when he wrote in *Song of Myself*:

Whoever degrades another degrades me,
And whatever is done or said returns at last to me.

. . . .

I speak the pass-word primeval—I give the sign of democracy,
By God! I will accept nothing which all cannot have their
counterpart of on the same terms.

Such is the ideal set forth in the Report of the President's Committee on Civil Rights. The report declares: "We can tolerate no restrictions upon the individual which depend upon irrelevant factors such as his race, his color, his religion, or the social position to which he is born."

That our ideal of social democracy is far from realized goes without saying. Some of our ethnic groups, especially Orientals, Negroes, and Jews, are objects of discrimination and prejudice. In international councils we are in a vulnerable position when we try to defend the rights of colored and colonial people beyond our borders. Once when Gandhi was asked how we could best help India he replied, "By solving the Negro problem in America."

To what extent democracy can insure equality in the social or in any other realm is a moot question. One point of view is stated in the following excerpt: "Above all, American democracy is not, never was, and never can be a guarantor of equality. On the contrary, it is a guarantor of essential inequality, for its function is to release the talents with which men are endowed; and the moment talents are allowed full play men become unequal. Democracy can guarantee equality before the law, but that is a tiny part of the whole field of human relations; and to a limited extent it may guarantee equality of opportunity, although the founders of American democracy did not believe that that could or should be carried far."[5]

Although we have stressed political, economic, and social aspects of democracy, there are still other phases that might well occupy our attention. By way of summary let us list some "articles of democratic faith."

"First, the individual human being is of surpassing worth.

"Second, the earth and human culture belong to all men.

"Third, men can and should rule themselves.

"Fourth, the human mind can be trusted and should be set free.

"Fifth, the method of peace is superior to that of war.

"Sixth, racial, cultural, and political minorities should be tolerated, respected, and valued."

Even the foregoing statements should not be regarded as final. The concept of democracy is ever changing. As long as people have new needs and as long as they have new thoughts, the last word will not be said on the subject. In the words of Henry W. Holmes: "Democracy is not finished. It is the nature of democracy not to be finished. Democracy is a way of finding out the best thing to do. It is a way of tackling problems, not a set of solutions to problems."

NEED FOR EDUCATION FOR DEMOCRACY

The fact that democracy is never finished implies the paramount importance of education for its perpetuation. It is not won once and for all and passed on automatically. Instead it must be continually won and continually improved by the efforts of each generation.

The founding fathers recognized that being born into a democracy does not give the ability to keep it alive. They saw clearly the need for education.

Washington, in his first annual message to Congress in 1790, de-

[5] Gerald W. Johnson, "Overloaded Democracy," *Harper's Magazine*, September, 1949, p. 84.

clared: "There is nothing which can better deserve your patronage than the promotion of science and literature. Knowledge is in every country the surest basis of public happiness. In one in which the measures of government receive their impressions so immediately from the sense of the community as in ours it is proportionably essential."

In his Farewell Address to the American people, written in 1796, Washington said: "Promote, then, as an object of primary importance, institutions for the general diffusion of knowledge. In proportion as the structure of a government gives force to public opinion, it is essential that public opinion should be enlightened."

John Adams likewise stressed the need for education: "Education is more indispensable, and must be more general under a free government than any other. In a monarchy, the few who are likely to govern must have some education, but the common people must be kept in ignorance; in an aristocracy, the nobles should be educated but here it is even more necessary that the common people should be ignorant, but in a free government knowledge must be general, and ought to be universal."

In 1816 after his retirement from the Presidency, Jefferson asserted: "If a nation expects to be ignorant and free, in a state of civilization, it expects what never was and never will be. . . . There is no safe deposit [for the function of government], but with the people themselves; nor can they be safe with them without information."

These and other early leaders envisioned the public schools as institutions to insure the success of democracy by preparing citizens to discharge their duties intelligently.

As the years passed, some people failed to see as clearly as did our early national leaders the relationship between education and democracy. Some came to regard education as a means of enabling the individual to further his own interests.

Discerning statesmen, however, have continued to stress the significance of education not only for the individual but for the state. For example, Theodore Roosevelt once said: "Each one of us, then, who has an education, school or college, has obtained something free from the community at large for which he or she has not paid, and no self-respecting man or woman is content to rest permanently under such an obligation. Where the State has bestowed education the man who accepts it must be content to accept it merely as a charity unless he returns it to the State in full in the shape of good citizenship."

The idea that schools are primarily for the general welfare of society rather than for the benefit of the individual has always been upheld by the courts. Their decisions have held that schools are established in the interests of all. For example, half a century ago the Supreme Court of Connecticut ruled as follows:

"Free schooling furnished by the state is not so much a right granted to pupils as a duty imposed upon them for the public good. If they do not voluntarily attend the schools provided for them, they may be compelled to do so. While most people regard the public schools as the means of great personal advantage to the pupils, the fact is often overlooked that they are governmental means of protecting the state from the consequences of an ignorant and incompetent citizenship."

Later the Illinois Supreme Court ruled that "the conduct and maintenance of schools by school directors, school trustees, and boards" is in the same class with the performance of many other duties by public officials, which, "however beneficial to individuals, are not undertaken from philanthropic or charitable motives, but for the protection, safety, and welfare of the citizens of the State in the interests of good government."

The significance of organized education in preparing people to carry on their duties in a democratic government is summarized by Beard in this way: "As organized education turns toward the future, then, it discards the theory of automatic democracy. It recognizes the rights to life, liberty, property, work, and the pursuit of happiness are shadows unless those who claim the rights are competent and have the moral power necessary to the creation and maintenance of the social arrangements in which rights may be realized."

ROLE OF THE SCHOOL IN PREPARING
DEMOCRATIC CITIZENS

Since democratic ideals and practices are not inherited biologically, the school has a heavy responsibility for preparing pupils for intelligent citizenship in a democracy. The kind of education necessary to accomplish this needs special consideration.

The American people, with their almost unlimited faith in the power of education, seem to take for granted that any kind of education liberates the mind and advances the cause of human freedom. They assume that it is beneficial for democracies but dangerous for despotisms.

In fact, many people do not yet realize that the idea of education for the masses is now accepted in authoritarian as well as democratic societies. From 1920 to 1940 the Axis powers spent large sums on education. The Soviet Union, too, witnessed a period of educational expansion. Enrollment in schools of all grades in the USSR increased from approximately eight or nine million to more than 30 million.

The vast difference in education in autocracies and in democracies lies in the nature of the education. In the former, education glorifies docility and unquestioned acceptance of the prevailing order. In the latter, education emphasizes "(1) ability to analyze problems involved in group living in order to make intelligent judgments; (2) ability to appraise men and women, in order to be intelligent in the selection of honest and capable representatives; (3) discipline and practice in taking democratic group action."[6] A succinct presentation of contrasts in education in dictatorships and democracies follows:

In Democracies	In Dictatorships
A school for democracy—The school itself is democratically organized with students, teachers, and parents participating in the planning of the group life, the	A school for dictatorship—The school is organized by the headmaster, who takes his orders from the educational dictator in the government. Teachers take orders

[6] John W. Studebaker, "Contrasts in Education," *Journal of the National Education Association*, October, 1948, p. 420.

In Democracies

school program, and class activities. This democratic procedure is begun in the kindergarten and gradually elaborated as the learners grow up.

The open mind—Distinctions are made between demonstrable truth—such as the fact that the world is round—and debatable areas of knowledge—such as economic theories. Learners are exposed to different points of view and interpretations in science, history, sociology, economics, and literature.

Respect for differences of opinion—Learners are trained in best methods of collecting, analyzing, organizing facts, reviewing conflicting opinions and interpretations, discussing alternative proposals; are encouraged to come to their own conclusions and respect others' right to come to different conclusions.

Critical students of propaganda—The tricks of propaganda are studied and students given experience in comparing and analyzing conflicting propagandas. They are taught the rules of evidence and learn to apply them in controversial subjects.

Premium on originality and tolerance—Originality, differences, initiative, fair play, and tolerance are cultivated as desirable attributes of the democratic spirit. Learners are encouraged to respect rules, democratically imposed, and authority, democratically selected.

In Dictatorships

from the master and the learners from the teacher. This habituates everyone to the "*leader-precept*" —power at the top, obedience at the bottom.

The dogmatic decree—The "truth" in all essential questions is predetermined by the dictatorship. The teachers drill the minds of the learners to accept the views of the high command. Nothing significant is debatable. The mind that gets out of step with the mind of the dictator is punished.

Planned hatred of those who doubt—The learners are regarded as receptacles into which approved knowledge is to be poured by the dictatorship via the transmission line—the teacher. Pupils are taught to adopt the dictator's conclusions unquestioningly, and to hate and persecute anyone who does question them.

Blind followers of propaganda —The school is merely an arm of the central ministry of propaganda. The students are expected to become expert proselyters and carriers of the propaganda into the home and community.

Glorification of docility and intolerance — Uniformity, obedience, intolerance are engendered. Differences in thinking and acting are penalized. Youth are taught to win approved objectives by any means, give opponents no quarter, and violate the rules in the inter-

IN DEMOCRACIES

Youth are taught good sportsmanship.

Personal freedom exalted— Youth and adults study the history of the age-old struggle for civil and religious liberty. The schools promote understanding of the meaning of our freedoms, of the rights, privileges, and responsibilities of individuals expressed and implied in the Bill of Rights. The educational system develops a determination to defend these liberties.

Enlightenment thru radio and motion pictures—Modern methods of communication are used to spread enlightenment, increase the reach of great teachers, and make problems and alternative solutions more understandable. Educators guard against use of these instruments as centralized means of spreading propaganda.

Variety of reading encouraged —More attention is paid to books. Classroom libraries and collateral reading are encouraged, to expose learners to the thinking of many writers with different outlooks. Less reliance is put on single books and more time given to the reading of supplementary books, pamphlets, and magazines.

Teachers free to teach the truth —Public-school teachers are not required to belong to a particular party or church or race. They are expected to be good teachers in the sense that they help the learners at all points to understand the

IN DICTATORSHIPS

est of victory. "The end justifies the means."

Personal freedom denounced— The rights of free speech, press and assembly, petition, fair trial, religious freedom, and suffrage are bitterly denounced. Opportunities to study the history of tyranny and the principles of individual liberty are denied. Civil liberty is interpreted to the people as a subversive, traitorous thing.

To secure uniformity of opinion—The motion pictures and radio are major devices for molding all minds to the same pattern of thought and opinion. The most effective devices of propaganda are employed thru these media, which are centrally controlled and carefully censored.

Unapproved books banned— Only the books approved by the dictatorships are offered to the learners. Books which encourage freedom of thought or express philosophies contrary to that of the dictatorship are condemned and burned. People who are caught with them are imprisoned.

Teachers required to propagandize—Teachers are required to impose the conclusions prescribed by the central ministry of education, an arm of the party in power. Teachers whose opinions are in conflict with the approved conclusions are not only dismissed, but

In Democracies	In Dictatorships
subject. Teachers refrain from interfering with the right of the learners to explore significant and honest data and to evaluate different points of view.	are likely to be imprisoned or exiled. Some of the world's greatest teachers and thinkers now live in democracies as refugees from dictatorships.[7]

Helping Pupils Attain Desirable Behavior Responses

If boys and girls are to learn patterns of democratic living and faith, teachers must set up appropriate goals. The goals may be expressed in various ways. A helpful approach is to state them in terms of behavior judged best in a democratic society. For example, pupils should learn to work coöperatively with others in a group; to participate in activities of their group; to share in reaching decisions that affect the group and to assume a fair portion of responsibility for carrying them through; to contribute to solving group problems; to abide by majority decisions; to respect the right of individuals to express minority opinions; to oppose actions detrimental to group welfare; to show concern about ways of improving the conditions of living together in widening social groups —family, play, class, school, community.

To help pupils attain desirable behavior responses, attention must be given to (1) selection of suitable subject matter, (2) provision of experiences in democratic living, (3) maintenance of a democratic atmosphere in the school, and (4) evaluation of school practices and outcomes of learning.

Selection of Suitable Subject Matter.   One of the ways in which the aims of teaching democratic citizenship may be realized is through choice of suitable curriculum content. Material may be drawn from many subject-matter areas, such as literature, painting, music, and social studies.

In the choice of materials we must represent fairly various points of view on controversial issues. As John De Boer reminds us:

American schools have the responsibility of educating for democracy. They do not have the responsibility of indoctrinating in behalf of capitalism, or the FCC, or the FHA, or the Federal Reserve System,

[7] *Ibid.*, pp. 420–421.

or our present foreign policy. These are matters which the school must help young people to understand, but the school owes no fixed allegiance to them. Our democracy must be a changing, growing democracy, and every effort to freeze its institutions through education in behalf of the status quo can eventuate only in the death of democracy.

Education for democracy implies that the school will consciously and systematically cultivate in youth a deep devotion to the fundamental values of the democratic society. The social arrangements and structures by which these values are to be achieved must always remain within the realm of free controversy. The school in a democracy is committed to a belief in the essential worth and dignity of the common man, in the freedoms of thought and speech and assembly and worship and association, in equality of economic and educational opportunity, in security and peace. It is not committed to any system of planning or lack of planning, to any specific kind of legislation or lack of legislation.[8]

While information about democracy alone will not lead to behavior patterns acceptable in a democracy or to appreciation of democracy, it is none the less essential. Bradley points out that during World War II many of our young troops were political illiterates who understood neither the great spiritual possessions to which we are born nor the threat facing free, democratic self-government.

The blame does not lie on education alone. It must be shared with the people as a whole. Their shocking apathy to the sterility of their school curricula is responsible even today for the political immaturity, the economic ignorance, the philosophical indifference and the spiritual insolvency of so many young men. Throughout Europe, wherever our armies were stationed, the people were bewildered by Americans who appeared indifferent to the political and philosophical origins and nature of the most powerful and progressive nation in the world. When driven into a corner intellectually our soldiers were forced to fall back on our wage scales, our automobiles, our refrigerators—and eventually and triumphantly to the American bathroom—for their defense. Here is an indictment not only of American education but of irresponsible citizens who have permitted this vacuum to remain.[9]

[8] John J. De Boer, "Communism and Fascism in the Schools," *School and Society*, October 29, 1949, p. 273.

[9] Omar N. Bradley, "What We Owe Our Country," *Reader's Digest*, August, 1949, p. 3.

Totalitarian states recognize the expediency of choosing material that will teach their doctrines. In *I Want To Be Like Stalin* the program for indoctrination in Russian schools is clearly set forth. The values of school subjects are stated in terms of their contribution to Russian ideology. A few illustrations will make apparent the penetration of Soviet moral doctrine into every phase of education.

The teaching of history, according to the authors, "possesses exceptional significance for the education of the growing generation in communism." Study of the past will give children "pictures of the exploitation, the oppression, the backwardness, and the humiliation of the workers under the czarist autocracy . . . an understanding of the achievements of the socialist revolution and of the heroic battle waged by their fathers and grandfathers for their freedom . . . a desire to continue the work of their fathers in building a communist society in the Soviet Union." The study of the past "cultivates in children high idealism and deep devotion to the interests of the working people, irreconcilability toward all reactionary forces, and resoluteness, courage, and bravery in the struggle for the finest ideals of humanity, for communism." History prepares the young to "realize the great historic role of the Party of Bolsheviks in the struggle for the liberation of the workers of all the peoples of our land of many nationalities from exploitation and oppression, from national and religious persecution." History also inspires children "with deep love for the highly gifted leaders of the proletarian revolution—Lenin and Stalin." These "greatest leaders of history" struggled "supremely, unswervingly, persistently, and stubbornly" against "all enemies of the people" and "brought our country to the victory of socialism."

. . . .

In the selection of the materials to be used in his daily work in any subject the teacher is admonished to make his choices "in full accord with the purposes of communist education." Thus, among subjects for essays "he selects stories about the exploits of the heroes of the Great Patriotic War and the extraordinary deeds of people capable of sacrificing personal interests for the common good." In the field of mathematics the teacher chooses or devises "problems which involve calculations relating to the rural economy, which teach pupils to save state pennies in industry and daily life, or which instruct in the application of mathematical knowledge to military affairs." These problems "must reflect our socialist reality" and make the pupil "realize that mathematics is necessary for technics, for production, and for the strengthen-

ing of the defense of the socialist Motherland." Finally, the teacher is
told that pupils must be trained in auditory discrimination so that
they may be able "to hear the faintest sounds, even to a barely per-
ceptible rustling," because "in modern warfare the future defender
of the Motherland, and particularly the scout, must possess such
powers."[10]

Undoubtedly, with proper education, American youth can be
taught to appreciate their own culture. They can understand the
glory of the democratic system that is based on the principle of
claiming the absolute value of the human individual. They can
take just pride in such a society where a human being is an end
in himself and not merely a means to an end; in a society where
he is not a tool for another's use and cannot be used merely for
another's purpose.

Provision for Practice in Democratic Living. Since pupils learn
what they live, they must have practice in democratic living. The
futility of mere verbalizing is illustrated by the experience Don
Rogers of Chicago had when he set the writing of the salute to the
flag as a penmanship exercise in the public schools of Chicago. He
found that hundreds of children were saying: "I pledge a legion."
"And to the republicans for which I stand." "One nation invisible."
"With liberty and*jesters." Some years later Olander of the University of Pittsburgh found a similar situation in his study of 13
school systems. One fifth-grader wrote: "I pleg the leggens to the
flag of the United States of America. To which it stands on nation
inavibl for liberty justest for all."

Pupils may experience democratic living in a variety of school
situations. We shall mention opportunities in the regular work of
the classroom, in classroom management and control, in extraclass
activities, and in participation in community activities.

In regular work in the classroom where democratic methods are
used, pupils work harmoniously with groups, set up common purposes for group planning, assume responsibility, share ideas, learn
to give others a chance to express opinions, and learn to appreciate

[10] George S. Counts and Nucia P. Lodge (trans.), *I Want To Be Like
Stalin*; from the Russian text on pedagogy by Esipov Boris Petrovich and N. K.
Goncharov, The John Day Company, 1947, pp. 7–9.

abilities of others. A concrete presentation of classroom procedures that implement a democratic way of life is given in *Democratic Education in Practice* by Rose Schneideman.

Through general school management pupils acquire a sense of self-control and responsibility. They take turns at such duties as cafeteria work, hall duty assignments, library assignments, and the care of equipment. They obey rules agreed upon for the common good.

Through extraclass activities pupils have abundant social experiences with democracy in action. Extraclass activities make possible a realistic and concrete approach that is not readily duplicated in regular course work. Through participation in clubs, planning of assemblies, participation in student councils, preparation of school newspapers and yearbooks, production of plays and group musical events, athletic team membership, Junior Red Cross, Girl Scouts, Boy Scouts, pupils have a chance to practice skills and to learn democratic values. Such coöperative endeavors give an appreciation of the worth of others that is not easily obtained in any other way.

A moving example of such appreciation occurred several years ago at the University of Illinois when a brilliant end on the football team, Ike Owens, a tall colored lad, was voted by his teammates as the most valuable player. Upon announcement of the coveted honor, Ike expressed his feelings in words his listeners will always remember:

"Thanks, fellows. This is a great honor; I want to thank you a lot. I've had a great time here at Illinois. These have been the happiest days of my life. In fact, I'm already starting to be homesick. You boys on the team have been like brothers to me."

Like brothers! What a tribute to democracy in action!

Through participation in community affairs pupils have firsthand experience with democracy in action. Participation may take manifold forms. It may include excursions and interviews. It may involve young people as members of boards and planning committees of churches and other community organizations. It should also include service to others. Pupils may participate in such activities as landscaping school grounds, gardening, checking soil erosion, and conducting cleanup campaigns.

A *Democratic Atmosphere in the School.* An intangible but inestimably important factor in encouraging democratic living and engendering democratic ideals is a democratic atmosphere in the school. Many elements combine to contribute to such an atmosphere. One of them is democratic coöperation in administration. Although administrators and teachers usually express belief in the ideals of democracy, they seem to find it difficult to incorporate them in the organization and administration of schools. Paradoxically enough, the very institution that is supposed to teach democracy is often highly autocratic. In a system dominated by undemocratic administrators, teachers can scarcely maintain a democratic classroom. "Autocracy at the top never breeds democracy at the bottom."

Another highly significant factor is the teacher. It is eternally true that "as is the teacher, so is the school." A well-adjusted teacher with truly human qualities and genuine devotion to democratic ideals can create a classroom environment favorable to learning and appreciating the democratic way of life. He will strive for a general atmosphere that reflects mutual respect of pupil for pupil, pupil for teacher, and teacher for pupil. He will act in such a way as to exemplify the ideals and practices of democratic living.

Studies of the comparative effects of authoritarian and democratic forms of control have shown that authoritarian teacher-pupil relationship hinders the growth of the child into an independent and coöperative individual while a democratic relationship fosters confidence, coöperation, and leadership.

The effects of social climates on teacher-pupil relationships is well stated by Lewin: "There have been few experiences for me as impressive as seeing the expression in children's faces change during the first day of autocracy. The friendly, open, and coöperative group, full of life, become within a short half-hour a rather apathetic looking gathering without initiative. The change from autocracy to democracy seemed to take somewhat more time than from democracy to autocracy. Autocracy is imposed upon the individual. Democracy he has to learn."

If we bear in mind that "zeal for democracy" is an indirect outcome of instruction, the importance of a democratic atmosphere can scarcely be overemphasized.

Evaluation of School Practices and Outcomes of Learning. As a means of ascertaining progress toward the realization of goals for preparing democratic citizens, teachers and pupils should evaluate school practices and outcomes of learning. Tests have been devised for measuring information about and attitudes toward democracy. Besides, informal judgments may be made about such points as improvement in putting away materials, in participating in games, and in contributing to committee work.

Evaluation of outcomes of learning should be made by each pupil as well as by the teacher. A child is most likely to improve if he sees clearly what standards are desirable and if he realizes his own responsibility for their attainment. He may be aided by check lists worked out either with or without the help of the teacher, by comments of his classmates, and by conferences with the teacher.

Intergroup Education

One aspect of the problem of education for life in a democracy that deserves special consideration is intergroup education. The term is used here to designate education intended to promote justice and understanding in our relation with people who differ in religion, race, nationality, and income levels.

The goals of intergroup education are well stated by Kilpatrick, as follows:

1. All pupils shall learn to live well together.
2. Parents and the citizens of the community accept these same goals for themselves and encourage their children so to live.
3. Teachers in the schools shall themselves accept and live the finer and better attitudes in group relations.
4. Children shall increasingly understand how those feel who suffer discrimination, and then act accordingly.

5. Each group shall know and respect the cultural contributions of other groups.
6. Each one may, as age increases, learn to reconsider objectively his own prejudices.
7. Older boys and girls shall for themselves study the evidence regarding the psychology of race.
8. Older students—and teachers—shall study and evaluate the various reasons and rationalizations which in the past supported discriminations.

We learn what we live, we learn each response as we accept it for our living purposes, and we learn it in the degree that we live it. And what we thus learn we therein build at once into character.[11]

Understanding people who differ in religion, race, or nationality is important in a country that has many minority groups. Over a period of 124 years America has received 39 million immigrants. According to the 1940 census, among 100 typical Americans we should expect to find 81 native whites, 10 Negroes, and 9 foreign-born. Great as has been our progress in assimilating the many groups, we are by no means free from prejudice. In a nation-wide opinion poll in 1948, 50 percent of those interviewed expressed prejudice against some group in the population. Racial and religious prejudices were the most common.

Difficulties in understanding come from contrasts between cultural groups. Each regards his own group as right. The problem is accentuated when the minority group becomes large enough to constitute a threat to the majority group.

The problem is further complicated by the fact that

Under threat the members of each group tend to respond by an accentuation and idealization of the group characteristics. It is only by placing emphasis on their differences from the other group that they can feel superior to them. The claim to be a master race is the result of a feeling of encirclement and threat from other groups and is an effort to enhance the threatened phenomenal selves of the group members. Propaganda stressing "encirclement" is a common technique of governments wishing to create a greater feeling of unity in their own group.

[11] William H. Kilpatrick, "Modern Education and Better Human Relations," *Freedom Pamphlets*, Anti-Defamation League of B'nai B'rith, 1949, pp. 20–25.

Both Hitler and the Russian communist leadership have used it with conspicuous success, and it is not unknown in America. It is most eagerly accepted by those members of the group who are most in need of self-enhancement. As a general thing, group conflict is at its maximum between the lower levels of the conflicting groups, especially if these levels are the victims of aggression and domination within their own groups.[12]

Interestingly enough, more attention has been given to intergroup education with reference to promoting understanding of minority groups than promoting understanding of different social classes. Possibly the unwillingness of Americans to admit that classes exist in their society may partially account for the problem being ignored.

However, studies such as *Elmtown's Youth* and *Children of Brasstown*, which were mentioned in Chapter V, reveal that children are aware of social class position. Just what can be done to help children of different social classes live together successfully is a knotty problem. At the primary level the teacher's own attitude toward lower-class children influences children's attitudes. She can recognize their accomplishments, help them win friends, and in general build up their status in school. However, we must agree with Stendler when she says:

What works on a primary level may be much too naïve a technique for older groups. On the eighth grade level, the twofold problem of integrating a group made up of social classes and of helping the lower-class child deal with his lower-classness is more difficult. The program described by Lloyd Cook at the high school level, consisting of an individual guidance approach and a group management approach, has much in it that seems praiseworthy. Under the first approach, an attempt was made through a system of individual conferences to effect certain changes in the group sociogram. Under the second and more fruitful approach, three types of projects were instituted: fun parties (hay rides and stunt nights) organized by the class, war service activities, and role practice, or the sociodrama, in which a persistent gripe, "The Youth Problem," was dramatized. Such projects are suggestive of the many activities which could be carried on so that all classes in

[12] Donald Snygg and Arthur W. Combs, *Individual Behavior*, Harper & Brothers, 1949, p. 192.

working together on projects or on common problems might get to view one another in a different light. Individual conferences by a trained counselor might help the lower-class child articulate his feelings and his problems.[13]

Intergroup education must begin early. Children are born without prejudices, but they soon acquire them through exposure to the attitudes of adults. "Learning prejudices seems to be, to a great extent, a matter of learning 'the way things are.' They are part of the folkways which the child 'inherits,' and, as such, are not matters about which he makes independent judgments."[14]

Before the culture firmly molds their prejudices, the school should help children understand people of different backgrounds from their own. They should learn to avoid the false assumption that all members of a group are alike, and to judge each person as a separate individual.

The paucity of suitable ready-made teaching materials that portray the diversity of our American culture is one of many difficulties encountered in carrying on a program of intercultural education.

Primers and pre-primers tend to depict family and neighborhood life in completely static, unreal terms. Every family is named Jones, Smith, or something equally Anglo-Saxon. Everybody lives on a middle-class street, in a neat, white suburban house with shutters. Every family owns a shiny new car. Daddies always work in an office. There are seldom more than two children in any family. There are always a dog named "Spotty" and a cat called "Fluffy." Families visit Grandpa and Grandma, who always have their own farm. Church is always a quaint, white clapboard building with a steeple, perhaps with a diminutive cross, but there is no denomination. The assumption is that there is only one kind of church, that "everybody" goes there, and that everybody is Protestant.

From many school books one could assume that all parents and friends—as well as policemen, storekeepers, firemen, teachers, farmers, and other "neighbors"—are always white people. If there is a story about a train ride, sometimes there is a porter who is Negro, and he

[13] Celia Burns Stendler, *Children of Brasstown*, University of Illinois Press, 1949, p. 100.
[14] Helen G. Trager and Marian Radke Yarrow, *They Learn What They Live*, Harper & Brothers, 1952, p. 347.

always carries white people's bags. Participants in all recreation situations pictured in school books, whether camping, ball playing, picnicking, are always Caucasians. An Oriental person is often in "native" costume and with a "pig-tail." Unless the story is exotic or about far-away places the Oriental is rarely present and, when he is, he has the role of the ubiquitous laundryman.[15]

But whether teaching materials are adequate or inadequate, intergroup education must be more than verbalizing. Deeply rooted prejudices and behavior patterns are usually not changed simply by presentation of facts. Children must practice what they learn. Each community has its own problems to solve. Whether the special interest grows out of tensions resulting from the presence of Negroes, Mexicans, Japanese, Jews, or Catholics, or from conflict along economic lines, a realistic program of education begins with immediate issues within the experience of the pupils. As pupils examine patterns of community living, they should relate them to the larger setting of national and world affairs.

The National Council for the Social Studies suggests a number of helpful activities for making the study of human rights realistic. To quote:

Students need to understand how it feels to know of rights but not to have them. Some identification may be gained by reading fiction or through sociodrama. Here is a situation for a sociodrama:

A Jewish boy, whose application for admission was filed two months ago, is turned down by a college official because "our enrollment is filled." The boy knows that a friend of his, non-Jewish, applied to the same college only two weeks ago and has already been accepted. Include in the setting such details as the facts that the two boys come from the same high school and have similar records.

To deepen insight and broaden understanding of the many sides of the problem, ask these questions: "How do you think the boy who was turned down felt?" "Why do you think he felt that way?" "What could he have done?" "How do you think the man felt who turned him down?" "Why did he do it?"

Similarly, select an incident from fiction, read it to the class, and provide the same discussion opportunities. A good case is presented in

[15] *Ibid.*, pp. 358–359.

Gentlemen's Agreement when one of the characters is refused lodging at a hotel. The same sequence of questions might follow.[16]

The Council suggests seven ways to help students survey the human rights policies and programs in their school:

a. Consult with the school administration for approval and support. The plan might be talked over with "sympathetic leading citizens" to enlist and insure community support.
b. Form committees to investigate various aspects of the problem.
c. Get all school organizations to participate in planning your survey.
d. Study practices of your school community in such areas as class groupings, athletics, activities, social life, etc.
e. Evaluate your findings carefully before releasing them for public use.
f. Present your findings through brief mimeographed summaries, bulletin board displays, assembly programs, etc.
g. Tie your survey to constructive suggestions for improving the situation. Don't let the matter die with the analysis of the problem— act![17]

Students may reach the entire school with ideas and information about human rights through such activities as these:

a. Corridor displays.
b. Assembly programs and presentations given in other classes.
c. News stories on class activities for school paper or local paper.
d. Opinion polls.
e. Guest speakers.[18]

Students may also interest the community through such activities as these:

a. Display cartoons, charts, class projects, useful materials, etc., in public library, courthouse, theater lobby, or other appropriate public place.
b. Arrange for a student speaking team, panel discussion group, or sociodrama group to appear before civic and service clubs, including Lions, Rotary, Kiwanis, church and women's clubs.

---

[16] Ryland W. Crary and John T. Robinson, *America's Stake in Human Rights*, National Council for the Social Studies, Bulletin 24, September, 1949, p. 30.
[17] *Ibid.*, p. 48.
[18] *Ibid.*, p. 49.

c. Offer to cooperate with civic, service, church, labor, or veterans' organizations in activities to develop better human rights patterns.
d. Contact local editors to develop news coverage and editorial outlets for your activities.
e. Survey your community to see what agencies are operating in this field; contact the leaders in these groups. Create confidence in your ability to be of aid to them. Plan effective programs of cooperation wherever you find good allies.[19]

In the area of intergroup education, as in the whole field of teaching democratic values, indirect instruction may be more significant than direct instruction. For example, if all racial and economic groups are permitted and encouraged to participate freely in organized school activities, pupils will receive a lesson in human rights that is more effective than many hours of classroom study of this subject.

The influence of the teacher is especially significant. Rabbi Rosen describes one of his teachers who never lectured on tolerance but who skillfully led her pupils into the paths of brotherhood:

Nancy Gaffney taught us mathematics—and respect for one another.
Protestant, Catholic, Greek Orthodox, and Jewish—we were descended from parents who were Italian, Syrian, Polish, American, Hungarian, Czechoslovakian, German, and Dutch. We were white and Negro.
And the unfounded prejudices we brought with us from our homes and our neighborhoods were revealed thru our petty snobbishness and antagonisms.
It was a few months after we had been brought together from all parts of the city as Cleveland's first Major Work Group, in the middle of the second semester of the seventh grade, that she began her campaign for the formation of a homeroom club to include all 22 of us. So subtle was her propaganda that, on the day the formal proposal was made, each of us was convinced that the idea had originated with him.
We planned skating parties and sledding parties, wiener roasts and outings. At Tony Caruso's, after an exciting two hours of sledding one evening, we feasted on Italian spaghetti and veal cutlets—and we learned that Tony's people were kind and good, warmhearted and hospitable. We learned the same about Effie Lee Morris' folks, who, tho

[19] *Ibid.*, pp. 49–50.

their skin was black, were no different from the Panuskas, the Cechs, the Abookires, or the Mativetskys.

Before many weeks had passed, we were eagerly discussing our differences of religion, family custom, and origin with complete naturalness. We were growing up with the realization that we were part of America's partially realized dream of human sharing and cooperation and understanding.[20]

The problem is not one that the school, working alone, can solve. It must have the coöperation of the community. The best efforts of the school may be rendered ineffective by community conditions. When pupils witness discrimination against minority groups in such matters as employment practices and segregation, they may well wonder whether we render more than lip service to democracy. When pupils observe the social ostracism of people from "the other side of the tracks" they may properly question the sincerity of our pronouncements concerning the dignity and worth of all human beings.

International Education

Another aspect of the problem of education for life in a democracy that deserves special consideration is education for world citizenship. Our responsibilities and rights extend to an ever-widening community. Whether we like it or not, whether we know it or not, we are world citizens. Powerful forces are breaking down ancient barriers between nations. Improved communications and transportation shrink space. Jet planes cross the United States in three and a half hours and circle the globe in 45 hours. New mutual economic interdependence and constant interchange between nations of travelers, goods, information, and ideas increase the growing awareness that all peoples are members of one family with certain basic responsibilities toward each other.

We have discovered through bitter experience that foreign affairs are a matter of life and death for every one of us. We have witnessed the staggering cost of two global conflicts. In World War II the trillions of dollars in goods and services and the loss of 40

[20] Sanford E. Rosen, "Not Out of Books," *Journal of the National Education Association*, May, 1949, p. 344.

or 50 million human lives were part of the sacrifice. How dramatically Norman Corwin portrayed the cost in his stirring book, *On a Note of Triumph*:

How much did it cost?

Well, the gun, the half-track and the fuselage come to a figure resembling mileages between two stars:

Impressive, but not to be grasped by any single imagination.

High octane is high, and K-rations in the aggregate mount up; also mosquito-netting and battleships.

But these costs are calculable, and have no nerve-endings,

And will eventually be taken care of by the federal taxes on antiques, cigarettes, and excess profits.

However, in the matter of the kid who used to deliver folded newspapers to your doorstep, flipping them sideways from his bicycle,

And who died on a jeep in the Ruhr,

There is no fixed price, and no amount of taxes can restore him to his mother.

. . . .

And if you wish to assess the cost of beating the fascists, you must multiply the number of closed files in the departments of war, by the exchange value of sorrow, which is infinite and has no decimals.[21]

Yet almost as soon as "the good news of damnation," as Robert Maynard Hutchins called the news of the dropping of the first atomic bomb, reached us, the world launched upon a program of perfecting new instruments for mass destruction. So determined do men seem to destroy themselves that Bertrand Russell may have been right when he declared: "Ninety percent of the human race would rather be dead than sensible."

So complete could be the devastation wrought by the hydrogen bomb that Einstein believed all life on the globe might be destroyed. Not even the two monkeys that the cartoonist imagined on a deserted island at the close of World War III might be left to inquire, "My God, do we have to start this all over again?"

[21] Norman Corwin, *On a Note of Triumph*, Simon and Schuster, 1945, pp. 39–41.

Little wonder that many thoughtful citizens see a world community as the only hope of survival.

To the typical American reared in a tradition that glorifies national sovereignty, the idea of world citizenship is perplexing. He questions whether loyalty to America is compatible with acceptance of world citizenship. He lacks the point of view so ably expressed by Conant: "We can be both intensely American and yet international-minded, both loyal to the unique manifestations of democracy in the United States and staunch friends of free societies of all types wherever they may be found. Indeed, one is tempted to go further and say not only is such dual loyalty a possibility, it is the essential condition for the freedom of this nation and the continuance of Western civilization."

The goals for international education are suggested by this statement of the ten marks of the world-minded American:

1. The world-minded American realizes that civilization may be imperiled by another world war.
2. The world-minded American wants a world at peace in which liberty and justice are assured for all.
3. The world-minded American knows that nothing in human nature makes war inevitable.
4. The world-minded American believes that education can become a powerful force for achieving international understanding and world peace.
5. The world-minded American knows and understands how people in other lands live and recognizes the common humanity which underlies all differences of culture.
6. The world-minded American knows that unlimited national sovereignty is a threat to world peace and that nations must cooperate to achieve peace and human progress.
7. The world-minded American knows that modern technology holds promise of solving the problem of economic security and that international cooperation can contribute to the increase of wellbeing for all men.
8. The world-minded American has a deep concern for the wellbeing of humanity.
9. The world-minded American has a continuing interest in world affairs and he devotes himself seriously to the analysis of inter-

national problems with all the skill and judgment he can command.

10. The world-minded American acts to help bring about a world at peace in which liberty and justice are assured for all.[22]

Methods and materials for furthering democratic education that were discussed earlier in the chapter may be adapted to promoting world-mindedness. Special attention should be given to organized efforts to secure world coöperation through the United Nations. As Counts so well points out: "The United Nations has been founded and the first steps toward the creation of a world organization have been taken. But all of this is but a delicate plant that will wither and die unless it is carefully and tenderly nurtured. Without the necessary good will, understanding, and discipline on the part of the nations of the earth, the organization launched at San Francisco may actually serve the ends of war. The American people, because of their great power, probably have a heavier responsibility for making their daring venture successful than any other."

Without loss of a sense of pride in our heritage as Americans, we must be free to stretch our loyalties beyond the limits set for us by habit and tradition. Our concern for people cannot be differentiated by race, religion, color, or nationality.

We must look to education to equip the oncoming generation to take its place in an environment that encompasses the whole world. The task is not easy because we must experiment with new methods and materials and curriculums. Pupils need to learn the great languages of the world. They have to learn history—not only the history of the United States and of western Europe but also of more than two-thirds of the people in the world who are non-Europeans. They will have to understand the ideas of people in South America, Asia, and Africa. They should study geography. It is difficult for a man to be a citizen of the world if he does not even know the names of the other nations of men in his world—

[22] The educational implications of these ten marks are discussed in National Education Association, Committee on International Relations, *Education for International Understanding in American Schools*, 1948.

let alone the environments of these nations out of which spring
the local and regional problems which cause them to act and think
as they do.

A possible contribution to teaching an understanding of people
of other countries is the exchange of students and teachers. The
innovation began in 1946–1947 with the exchange of 74 American
and 74 British teachers. In 1958–1959 more than 600 teachers from
the United States and 42 other countries participated in the program. This brought the total of participants in 12 years to nearly
5000 teachers from the United States and 64 other countries.

The exchange programs are administered by the Office of Education. The Office furnishes assistance in the form of guidance,
orientation, program planning, and placement in environments
most conducive to the teachers' educational development. Such
exchange may help to produce a friendly attitude among nations.
While the change may be gradual and mostly intangible, it should
nevertheless be immensely valuable. L. G. Derthick, United States
Commissioner of Education, sees this program as an opportunity
"to extend the frontiers of international understanding and goodwill throughout the world." He views the participants as "true
ambassadors for their countries and their people."

Providing Equality of Educational Opportunity

If our schools are fully to serve their purpose of preparing pupils
for life in a democracy, we must solve the problem of giving youth
equal access to education. In spite of our boast of a free educational system for all the children of all the people, we are far from
realizing this goal.

In 1947 illiteracy in persons 14 years old and over was 2.7 percent. Nearly 2¾ million Americans over 14 years of age could not
read or write any language. The percentage of illiteracy among
the nonwhite population was 11 percent, and for residents of rural
farm areas 5.3 percent. However, eventual success in the campaign
against illiteracy is forecast by the fact that there is less and less
of it at successively younger ages. The rate varied in 1947 from 6.7
percent among persons 65 years of age and over down to 1 percent

for persons 14 to 24 years of age. In 1947 the median of years of school completed was 9.6 as compared with 8.7 in 1940. From 1940 to 1950 the relative decrease in percent of the population in the United States 25 years old and older with less than five years of schooling was 18.5. (For other pertinent statistics, see Chapter XIV, Table 9.)

What, then, are some of the obstacles that prevent millions of our youth from having equal access to education? What are the major sources of educational inequalities? We shall mention four.

1. Our educational programs are often ill adapted to the needs and interests of children of different abilities. On the whole, children who excel in abstract thinking are more likely to achieve success in school than children who show chiefly mechanical aptitude. Our programs tend to be intellectually selective. Either willingly or unwillingly, many children leave school because they cannot do satisfactorily the type of work offered.

Even the intellectually gifted often leave school not because the work is too difficult but because it is too easy to challenge them. Contrary to popular opinion, gifted pupils are the most neglected group in our public schools. In *Education of the Gifted*, a bulletin prepared by the Educational Policies Commission, the fact that half of this group do not go to college is attributed in part to lack of encouragement and recognition from teachers and parents, and to lack of incentive because of our tendency to belittle exceptional ability.

2. Economic status may determine the amount of schooling boys and girls receive. That lack of money accounts for withdrawal from school is not surprising when we note the distribution of family income in the United States, mentioned earlier in this chapter.

If education is to be effectively free at all age levels, provision must be made for free tuition, scholarships, and living expenses. Paid work opportunities should be provided for youth in the upper years of high school and in college.

To be sure, all this costs money. Just how much would be

needed to provide assistance for only the most gifted is unknown. In their book entitled *Who Shall Be Educated?* Warner, Havighurst, and Loeb suggest that such assistance for about 5 percent of the youth of high school age and for 3 percent of the youth of college age would cost only about as much as the NYA spent in 1938 when the load was greatest.

3. Differences in the ability of states to support education affect educational opportunities. The accident of living in a state with little wealth may doom a child to inferior schooling. (See Chapter XIV.)

4. Discrimination against certain minority groups prevents equality of educational opportunity. Segregation is one pattern of discrimination. Negroes have probably suffered most from an "equal but separate" system of segregated schools. Often only about one-half as much money is spent per pupil in schools for Negroes as is spent in schools for whites. As a result, inferior buildings and equipment, crowded classrooms, poorly prepared teachers, and inadequate curriculums are the rule.

In a historic decision on May 17, 1954, the federal Supreme Court ruled that racial segregation in public schools of the several states is unconstitutional. The Court's ruling held that "in the field of public education the doctrine of 'separate but equal' has no place. Separate educational facilities are inherently unequal." Segregation, the Court concluded, "is a denial of the equal protection of the laws." A year later the Court enjoined communities where segregation was practiced to integrate their schools "with all deliberate speed."

The impact of the decision has been tremendous and the response mixed. While some areas have sought to bring about integration in the schools "with all deliberate speed," others have searched for ways to maintain segregation. A few states have set up legal machinery to abolish the public schools and substitute publicly supported, segregated private schools.

The "quota system" is another form of discrimination. The Report by the Commission on Higher Education stated that "many colleges and universities, especially in their professional schools, maintain a selective quota system for admission under which the chance to learn, and thereby to become more useful citizens, is denied to certain minorities, particularly to Negroes and Jews. . . . The quota system cannot be justified on any ground compatible with democratic principles."

Until we can offer educational programs suited to pupils of different abilities and interests, until we can make education effectively free to rich and poor alike, until we can provide good schools for children in poor as well as in wealthy states, and until we provide equal programs for pupils regardless of race, color, or creed, our ideal of giving youth equal access to education will be unattained.

SUMMARY

In the United States the school is expected to prepare pupils to assume intelligently their responsibilities as citizens. They must learn not only to appreciate the democratic way of life but also to preserve and improve it. To help them attain desired behavior responses, the school endeavors to select suitable subject matter, provide experiences in democratic living, maintain a democratic atmosphere, and evaluate school practices and outcomes of learning in the light of democratic living. Special aspects of the problem of the school and democracy involve provision for intergroup and international education and for equality of educational opportunity.

QUESTIONS AND EXERCISES

1. How may daily living in the classroom group contribute to preparation for citizenship?
2. Outline a program for improving attitudes toward minority groups of pupils at the grade level that you prefer to teach.
3. Evaluate the statement: "Dare we educate for democracy? If we are to give it more than lip-service; if we are to practice democracy as a way of life; if we are to believe in the inherent worth of each learner—many school systems and schoolmasters must topple from their thrones. Yet this must come to pass if the education of

free men in a free nation is to be attained. We dare not do otherwise."[23]

4. Prepare a report on the monograph, *The Unique Function of Education in American Democracy* (Educational Policies Commission, 1937).
5. List reasons for preferring democracy to dictatorship.
6. Should schools indoctrinate for democracy?
7. Defend or refute Dewey's statement: "The problem is not whether the schools *should* participate in the production of a future society (since they do so anyway), but whether they should do it blindly and irresponsibly or with the maximum possible of courageous intelligence and responsibility."
8. Should teachers deal with controversial issues in their classes?
9. Show how a teacher's concept of democracy may shape his ideas of discipline. Does treating a child in a democratic fashion mean letting him do as he pleases?
10. Read "I Was a Hobo Kid," by Billie Davis, *Saturday Evening Post*, December 13, 1952.

SELECTED REFERENCES

Bode, Boyd H., *Democracy as a Way of Life*, The Macmillan Company, 1937.

Brameld, T. B. H., *Minority Problems in the Public Schools*, Harper & Brothers, 1946.

Conant, James Bryant, *Education in a Divided World*, Harvard University Press, 1948.

Dewey, John, *Democracy and Education*, The Macmillan Company, 1928.

Edwards, Newton, and Richey, Herman G., *The School in the American Social Order*, Houghton Mifflin Company, 1947.

Everett, Samuel, and Arndt, Christian O. (eds.), *Teaching World Affairs in American Schools*, Harper & Brothers, 1956.

John Dewey Society, *Democracy and the Curriculum*, Third Yearbook, Appleton-Century-Crofts, Inc., 1939.

John Dewey Society, *Educational Freedom and Democracy*, Second Yearbook, Appleton-Century-Crofts, Inc., 1938.

John Dewey Society, *Intercultural Attitudes in the Making*, Ninth Yearbook, Harper & Brothers, 1947.

National Education Association and American Association of School Administrators, Educational Policies Commission:

[23] A. I. Oliver, "Dare We Educate for Democracy?" *Educational Forum*, November, 1950, p. 23.

Education and Economic Well-being in American Democracy, 1940.

Education and the Defense of American Democracy, 1946.

Education for All American Children, 1948.

Education for All American Youth, 1944.

Education for All American Youth—A Further Look, 1952.

Education of Free Men in American Democracy, 1941.

Learning the Ways of Democracy: A Case Book of Civic Education, 1940.

Moral and Spiritual Values in the Public Schools, 1951.

The Purposes of Education in American Democracy, 1938.

The Unique Function of Education in American Democracy, 1937.

President's Commission on Higher Education, *Higher Education for American Democracy,* Harper & Brothers, 1948.

Schneideman, Rose, *Democratic Education in Practice,* Harper & Brothers, 1945.

"The Social Framework of Education," *Review of Educational Research,* February, 1946, and February, 1949 (entire issue).

Trager, Helen G., and Yarrow, Marian Radke, *They Learn What They Live,* Harper & Brothers, 1952.

Vickery, William E., and Cole, Stewart G., *Intercultural Education in American Schools,* Harper & Brothers, 1943.

AUDIO-VISUAL MATERIALS

Films

A Desk for Billie (57 minutes, Sound, B & W, or C, National Education Association). The thrilling true story of a migrant child who found opportunity in the free public schools across America. Today Billie is a successful editor, writer, and lecturer.

Democracy (11 minutes, Sound, B & W, Encyclopaedia Britannica Films). Two unique characteristics of democracy—shared respect and shared power—are defined and described. Then two conditions are examined which have historically promoted the growth of democracy—balanced economic distribution and enlightenment.

Freedom to Learn (27½ minutes, Sound, B & W, or C, National Education Association). A teacher called before an open meeting of the school board to defend herself against the charge of teaching communism in her classes makes it clear that students must be allowed to study and learn about controversial questions in our democracy if it is going to survive. No teacher can be the final judge

of truth, since this judgment remains for the decision and conscience of every free man.

Practicing Democracy in the Classroom (22 minutes, Sound, B & W,
Encyclopaedia Britannica Films). Depicts the coöperative efforts of
teacher, students, and parents in using democratic methods in a
course in American history.

Secure the Blessings (25 minutes, Sound, B & W, National Education
Association). The role of education in the United States as it prepares people to use the democratic method of solving problems.

Recording

Why a Former Hobo Kid Believes in Our Public Schools (30 minutes,
33⅓ rpm, Educational Recording Services). Billie Davis relates her
own story.

PART THREE

THE EDUCATIONAL LADDER

Courtesy, Samuel Myslis

The pride of the American school system and a major contribution to the advance of civilization is the educational ladder. This ladder, composed of the elementary school, the secondary school, and the state university, constitutes a continuous and unbroken program of instruction from early childhood to maturity and from the first beginnings of school education to the most advanced forms of professional training and graduate study. If the influence of family fortune and tradition be disregarded, the individual in his progress up this ladder encounters no barrier beyond the increasing difficulty of the ascent and the limitations set by his own capacities. The entire range of institutions involved is supported by the state, and any individual able to meet the very modest scholastic requirements enforced is free to attend.

George S. Counts, THE AMERICAN ROAD TO CULTURE

Part Three, The Educational Ladder, introduces students to the way in which the dream of universal public education has developed in the United States. It sketches the increasing struggle for an educational ladder stretching from the elementary school through the university, and presents salient features of schools of today.

CHAPTER VIII

From Humble Beginnings—
the Common School

Eric A. Johnston once said: "To my mind, there is a great story in education—a succession of stories. I think education is dramatic. It has everything in it to make it so: struggle, pathos, triumph, competition, good humor and interesting people."

In the brief space of five chapters we can present only a few pages from the history of three centuries of educational progress in the United States—pages that help explain how the schools of today came to be and how the schools of tomorrow may take form. In this chapter and in Chapter IX we shall note some outstanding events in the growth of elementary education and, in Chapters X, XI, and XII, of secondary education and education beyond the high school.

Although it was not the first unit to develop, we shall begin our story with the elementary school. We shall trace its growth as a traditional eight-year institution and show how its structural organization has been modified by the addition of nursery school and kindergarten and by the emergence of the junior high school.

Elementary schools may have had their origin in the vernacular school of the Middle Ages. To understand the character of vernacular schools we must catch a glimpse of the society they served. Until about 1100 two social classes, the nobility and high clergy, dominated European life. Both were supported by the labor of common people known as serfs and villeins who received only a bare subsistence. Near the end of the eleventh century when commerce and trade revived and towns and cities sprang up, persons who engaged in trade came to be recognized as a new social group, the burghers or middle class. With the growth of business, orders, bills, accounts, letters, and many other kinds of papers were required. At first Latin was the language used in business. Since only churchmen could write, they were pressed into service for secretarial duties. As business expanded and the ecclesiastics could not keep up with the demands made upon them, the burghers either learned Latin or sent their sons to Latin schools to acquire skills needed in preparing papers and keeping accounts.

During the thirteenth century, with a shift away from Latin for business documents, the middle class had little preference for a foreign tongue in comparison with the local language. After about 1350, writing schools taught reading and writing in the vernacular, and reckoning schools gave instruction in practical arithmetic for commercial purposes. Not a part of the organization of Latin schools which led to the university, these schools are referred to by Reisner as "an educational pocket, leading nowhere, but serving the needs of many." They were intended only for the common people.

In the fifteenth and sixteenth centuries the invention of printing and the Protestant Reformation gave fresh reasons for education. When they were made by hand, books were so scarce and expensive that their circulation reached hardly beyond university faculties, court circles, literary groups, and ecclesiastics. With the invention of printing came an upturn in the number and accessibility of books and a consequent incentive to learn to read. With the Protestant Reformation came the incentive to learn to read the Bible as a means of personal salvation. Without this strong impetus given by the Reformation and without the multiple pamphlets and books made possible by the printing press it is impossible to say how long the advent of vernacular schools might have been delayed.

ELEMENTARY SCHOOLS IN COLONIAL AMERICA

Before the Revolutionary War colonists were more pressingly occupied with conquering a howling wilderness than with advancing learning. They met the challenges of grim, toilsome days—

building houses, clearing farms, and subduing hostile Indian tribes. They lived in scattered settlements isolated from one another because of crude means of transportation and communication. Cultural affairs played a meager part in their lives. Their learning came not from books but from the activities of everyday life.

We should avoid the facile judgment, however, of attributing the almost imperceptible growth of schools to the austere colonial climate. Not to be overlooked is the influence of Old World ideas. Reared in lands where education was carried on under private auspices, the settlers engaged in no concerted drive for schools financed from public coffers. Instead they relied upon three methods for providing for education: church, charity, and government support.

In western Europe until about 1800 the elementary school, a handmaiden of the church, was maintained to propagate the faith of a particular sect. Familiar with parochial schools in their homeland, the colonists established their counterparts on this side of the Atlantic. For more than a century religion profoundly affected provisions for education in the United States.

In the middle colonies—New Netherland (later New York), New Jersey, Pennsylvania, and Delaware—with their diversities of nationality and religion, church support gained a strong foothold. New Jersey followed the pattern set by New York. Delaware, a small independent colony, had a relatively unimportant educational history. Hence we shall follow happenings only in New Netherland and Pennsylvania.

New Netherland had its beginning early in the seventeenth century when the Dutch West India Company sent over about 30 families. Other settlers followed, until eventually the Dutch had far-flung trading posts on the Hudson, Delaware, and Connecticut Rivers. Expansion of the colony was so gradual that 40 years later not more than 7000 colonists were dwelling chiefly in about a dozen villages along the Hudson. Despite the presence of many national and religious groups, the culture of New Netherland was predominantly Dutch, with the Dutch Reformed Church the state church.

Although obligation to make education available rested upon the Company, the Dutch Reformed Church coöperated closely in promoting a public school in each community in order that the children might acquire a knowledge of religion and the ability to read the Dutch language. In keeping with Holland's high educational standards, the charter of the colony directed that the "colonists shall in particular endeavor as quickly as possible to find some means whereby they may support a minister and schoolmaster, and thus the service of God and zeal for religion may not cool and be neglected among them." The church itself supervised, inspected, and controlled the schools. It chose the schoolmaster who had to subscribe to orthodox views. Although support was in part from secular funds, the school was expected to teach the one true faith. The civil government decreed that the schoolmaster and minister catechize the children on Wednesday and Saturday. The school day opened and closed with prayer. Although the evidence is not indisputable, the school of New Amsterdam, founded probably in 1633, is often hailed as the first permanent one within the thirteen original colonies.

In evaluating the influence of the Dutch on American education, Monroe wrote:

The significant fact in regard to this system of parish schools is the marked contrast which it offers to the villages or towns where English customs prevailed. In all of these Dutch settlements a community school existed as one essential part of the structure of society and of the local system of government. While church and town government co-operated, these were essentially town schools supported as a town charge. To the Dutch a church was essentially a part of the local government scheme. The "church masters" were selected by the town government. So while the school was immediately under the church, it was essentially a town school. In the early national period these schools continued to form the basis or nucleus of a system of public schools. Undoubtedly the traditions represented by these state-church or parish schools, and the actual working system which they presented were a leading factor in the establishment of the first system of public schools created after the Revolution (New York, 1795).[1]

[1] Paul Monroe, *Founding of the American Public School System*, The Macmillan Company, 1940, vol. 1, p. 82.

After England gained possession of New Netherland, English traditions dominated education. Because the Anglican church had no interest in supplying funds for schools founded by another sect, the Dutch had the burden of supporting the schools they had already instituted. As additional communities sprang up, arrangements for schools fell to the lot of religious and charitable organizations. The Society for the Propagation of the Gospel in Foreign Parts, the foreign missionary society of the Church of England, began work in New York City in 1703. For the most part, schools of this society were typical charity schools for the children of the poor. One master reported that he taught "Church of England catechism, as also what other learning he had, to render them able to know their duty to God by reading the Scriptures," and "as much reading and writing and arithmetic as may relieve the common occasions of vulgar people, which is the most these people aspire to."

Parochial schools flourished under the conditions afforded by Pennsylvania. Basking in the religious freedom assured by the Quakers, the colony became a haven for people of many faiths who set up their own schools.

Nowhere else in America, perhaps, was there so little unity in the population as here. Catholics, Quakers, Dutch Reformed, Lutherans, Episcopalians, Baptists and Methodists all had their own church schools and refused to send their children to any other. In addition to the more powerful denominations, an unusual number of tiny sects, such as the Moravians, Mennonites, Amish, Schwenkfelders, Dunkers, and Seventh Day Baptists, founded their settlements within the province.

There was, moreover, as little harmony of race as there was of religion. The Swedes and Dutch along the Delaware still clung desperately to their old language and customs; Germans, often referred to as "Pennsylvania Dutch" by their English neighbors, settled the country in large numbers; and the Scotch-Irish became a vanguard on the edge of the backwoods in the West.

As the most numerous of the alien elements of the population, the Germans early attracted the benevolent interest of the English and to such a degree that in 1754 there was organized in London a "Society for the Promotion of Christian Knowledge Among the Germans in

America." The free schools founded by this missionary agency were unquestionably needed, but the Germans resented the patronizing implication that they were fit objects of charity, and they also feared that if their children went to these schools they might forget their native language and abandon the religion of their fathers. Isolated by distance from the well-educated people of Germany and unwilling to enter heartily into what was to them a foreign culture, the Pennsylvania Germans too frequently grew indifferent to the schooling of their children, though their churches, notably the Moravian, labored to keep alive to some extent the old love of learning. In consequence, though the educated were but few, they never wholly "ceased out of the land."[2]

The Quakers recognized the need for public schools. In his first Frame of Government drawn up for Pennsylvania in 1682, William Penn specified that "the Governor and Provincial Council shall erect and order all public schools. . . ." The second frame contained the stipulation that all 12-year-olds "be instructed in reading and writing" and taught "some useful trade or skill, that the poor may work to live, and the rich if they become poor may not want. . . ." The third frame, the last to mention education, carried a statement similar to that of the first frame. It read:

"That the Governor and Council shall erect and order all public schools and encourage and reward the authors of useful sciences and laudable inventions in the said Province and Territories."

With a population of mixed religious beliefs, however, the Quakers could not enforce their early idea of making the state responsible for education. Rival sects feared that public schools would become instruments for propagation of the Quaker faith. Accordingly, the Quakers granted the right to all "religious societies or assemblies and congregations of Protestants . . . to purchase any lands or tenements for . . . houses of religious worship, schools, and hospitals." Thus the way was open for parochial schools.

Throughout the colonial period there was, as Butts and Cremin

[2] E. E. Slosson, *The American Spirit in Education*, vol. 33 of *The Chronicles of America*, Yale University Press, 1921, pp. 36–38.

remark, "acceptance of the principle that the church and state were legitimate partners in the propagation and maintenance of an established religion," but there was at the same time the equally authentic tradition of separation of church and state. Space does not permit a review of the intricate problems involved in the patterns of church-state relations as they emerged in the United States. Suffice it to say that problems growing out of denominational support of schools still perplex us.

In the southern colonies—Maryland, Virginia, the Carolinas, and Georgia—the policies of the church blended with charity maintenance of schools. Among the Quakers in North Carolina and the Catholics in Maryland, church schools similar to those in the middle colonies developed. Elsewhere most of the settlers were adherents of the Church of England who came to a foreign soil not for religious but economic reasons. The ownership of extensive landholdings that called for a large number of laborers resulted in sharp class distinctions. Children of members of the landed aristocracy had private teachers, while children of the servant class gained their education through charity schools and the apprentice system.

Virginia, more closely than the other colonies, resembled England. Children of well-to-do families received instruction from a tutor or parish clergyman, if not sent to England for their education. A tutor might be engaged by several families, thus setting up a tuition school. Often classes were held in a log cabin in an "old field" no longer suitable for tobacco cultivation. Sometimes the teacher was paid in corn, bacon, or brandy. How closely the Virginia scheme of education followed English traditions is clearly shown in Governor Berkeley's response in 1671 to the question, "What course is taken about the instructing the people within your government in the Christian religion?" The governor replied: "The same that is taken in England out of towns; every man according to his own ability instructing his children. . . . But, I thank God there are no free schools and printing, and I hope we shall not have these hundred years; for learning has brought disobedience, and heresy, and sects into this world, and printing has divulged them and libels against the best government. God keep us from both!"

Learning fell into such neglect that in 1715 Governor Spotswood reproached the colonial assembly for having two standing committees whose chairmen could not "spell English or write common sense."

In accordance with English custom, children of the poverty-haunted were apprenticed to learn a trade. In 1701 Virginia enacted legislation specifying that "the master of every such orphan shall be obliged to teach him to read and write." This was the first stipulation in Virginia of any educational requirement in the training of an apprentice. For nearly two centuries the principle of apprenticeship left its mark on colonial education.

Just as the tradition of church support has persisted to some extent, so too has the plan of private support. Some parents arrange for tutorial or private-school instruction for their children. From time to time organized efforts to reduce appropriations and curtail educational opportunities are made by people who object to educating at public expense "all the children of all the people."

Free, public, government-supported schools were the choice of colonists in the northern colonies—New Hampshire, Massachusetts, Connecticut, and Rhode Island. Determined to build a society in harmony with their ideals, people in many of these regions soon began to formulate school legislation.

The Puritans in Massachusetts represent a group who came to America to find a place where they could worship God in their own way without interference. They did not, however, tolerate religious freedom for others. They excluded from the colony Quakers, Baptists, and all other denominations who differed from them. They kept strict control of affairs by requiring church membership for voting on matters concerned with the general government of the colony, and by barring from membership anyone not in favor of the established order. Leaders in the church were also leaders in civil society. Pastors supervised the schools. The main materials of instruction were the Bible and the tenets of Calvinism.

Massachusetts was the first colony to make ample provision for the education of its people. In his *History of the United States*, Bancroft attributes to the laws establishing public schools the secret of the success of New England. "Every child, as it was born into the world, was lifted from the earth by the genius of the country, and, in the statutes of the land, received, as its birthright, a pledge of public care of its morals and its mind."

In 1642 the General Court of Massachusetts commanded the selectmen of every town "to have a vigilant eye over their brethren and neighbors, to see that none of them shall suffer so much barbarism in any of their families, as not to endeavor to teach, by themselves or others, their children and apprentices, so much learning as may enable them perfectly to read the English tongue and [obtain] a knowledge of the capital laws." If parents failed in that duty they were deemed "unnatural parents" and their children were taken away from them and placed where their right to learn would be safeguarded. Here was the first law to set a precedent for an inquiry into the ability of all children to read.

The law of 1642 did not establish schools or order employment of schoolmasters. So unsatisfactory were the results that five years later it was replaced by the law of 1647, known as "The Old Deluder, Satan, Act," from the preamble which opened with the words, "It being one chief project of that old deluder, Satan, to keep men from the knowledge of the Scriptures. . . ." The law ordained that in every town "of fifty householders" one person within that town should be appointed "to teach all such children as shall resort to him to write and read," and that "where any town shall increase to the number of one hundred families or householders, they shall set up a grammar school, the master thereof being able to instruct youth so far as they shall be fitted for the university," that is, in the Latin and Greek languages.

While the law exacted high qualifications for the master of the grammar school, it specified only "one within their town" to teach young children to write and read. The master was to "be paid either by the parents or masters of such children, or by the inhabitants in general, by way of supply, as the major part of those that order the prudentials of the town shall appoint." Payment of some form of tuition was customary for a least a century.

The laws of 1642 and 1647 are usually regarded as the germ of the common-school system in the United States. However, such distinguished historians as Charles A. and Mary R. Beard do not so classify them. "Unquestionably the first of these acts was conceived partly in the spirit of the English poor law; while the second flowed from a great desire to impose on all children the creed of the Puritan sect. The fact that the education was ordered by 'the state' was of no special significance, for the state and church were one in Massachusetts at the time; indeed, if the Mathers were to be believed, the church was superior to the state."

Despite difference of opinion as to whether or not the laws of 1642 and 1647 represent "foundations upon which our American state public-school systems have been built," we are indebted to the Puritans for two fundamental contributions. First, they discerned that "the good education of children is of singular behoof and benefit to any Commonwealth." Second, they introduced the idea of government-supported schools for every community and child. Although these New England leaders had in mind schools to inculcate acceptance of the prevailing pattern of religious, political, and social affairs of their day, which was a far cry from our modern democratic ideals, they gave us invaluable principles. Fortunately, as Edwards and Richey point out, "fundamental principles of social policy have a way of outliving the particular circumstances in which they develop." So it happened that these guides to action stood us in good stead when democratic commonwealths emerged.

Throughout the colonial period learning was at a low ebb. Responsibility for making education available for the children rested on parents. Dame schools and writing schools afforded rudimentary training. The dame school, kept by a housewife in her home, derived support from small tuition fees and occasionally from public funds. Here pupils studied the alphabet, the Lord's Prayer, and elements of reading, writing, and counting, together with some domestic skills, such as sewing and knitting for girls. For many pupils, especially girls, this was the end of formal instruction. Boys who desired to learn a trade apprenticed themselves to someone skilled in the work of their choice. Only boys destined to become leaders in church or state went to the Latin grammar school.

Writing schools, which generally admitted pupils who had made some progress in reading, offered the rudiments of reading and writing and, in more favored cases, especially in commercial centers, arithmetic. Toward the end of the colonial period spelling was added.

Teachers had no special preparation for their work. They were indentured servants, errant rogues, adventurers, or theological students waiting a call to a pulpit. They were often called on to assist at the church as either janitor or assistant to the pastor, to act as sexton, to run errands, to keep records, and in general to render whatever services the community demanded. Their teaching was dull and inefficient. Rarely did they give any actual instruction. They simply heard recitations. Pupils were called up one by one to recite memorized material that held little meaning for them.

Motivated by belief in the natural depravity of children, teachers administered severe punishments. John Robinson, a Pilgrim preacher, remarked: "Surely there is in all children (tho not alike) a stubbernes and stoutness of minde arising from natural pride which must be broken and beaten down so that the foundation of their education being layd in humilitie, other virtues may in their time be built thereon." "For the good" of the child, liberal use was made of the dunce cap, placards such as "Tell-Tale" and "Idle Boy" that were pinned on offenders, the ferrule, the cowhide whip, and the "whispering-stick"—a small green branch with a split in it to confine the whisperer's tongue.

Salaries for elementary teachers probably did not often exceed $50 per year in addition to board. The first teacher in Northampton in 1664 was a farmer who was paid by the town "six pounds towards the scoole & to tacke the benifet of the scollers provided that he teach Six months in the yeare together." Payments were irregular and often partly in produce or livestock. We are told that in one school a pupil was placed near a window where he

A
In Adam's Fall,
We sinned all.

B
Thy life to mend,
This Book attend.

C
The Cat doth play,
And after slay.

D
A Dog will bite,
A thief at night.

E
An Eagle's flight
Is out of sight.

F
The idle Fool,
Is whipped at school.

An Alphabet of Lessons for Youth.

A WISE son maketh a glad father, but a foolish son is the grief of his mother.

B ETTER is a little, with the fear of the Lord, than great treasure, and trouble therewith.

C OME unto Christ, all ye who labour and are heavy laden, and he will give rest to your souls.

D O not the abominable thing which I hate, saith the Lord.

FIGURE 2.   New England Primer, p. 13.

could hail any passerby for the purpose of selling the surplus truck that had accumulated. Little wonder that teachers had to supplement their incomes by engaging in other occupations.

School buildings were crude, uncomfortable, and meagerly equipped. They were built of logs, floored with puncheon or dirt, and roofed with bark. Greased paper took the place of windowpanes. An open fireplace, perhaps of stone and clay, furnished heat. Some schoolmasters banished from the fireside children whose parents were remiss in supplying wood. The teacher's desk, puncheon seats or benches made from a slab of log rudely carved and probably full of knots and splinters, a table or shelf attached to the wall, and an hourglass comprised the equipment.

Textbooks were few and unattractive. The "hornbook," the child's first "book," consisted of a piece of board with a handle, on which was nailed a sheet of paper or parchment covered with transparent horn to protect it from wear. The paper contained the alphabet, the vowels listed separately, short meaningless syllables, and the Lord's Prayer. The next book was the *New England Primer*, filled with moral lessons. Each letter of the alphabet appeared in connection with rhymed verses of two or three lines, illustrated with crude pictures. (See Figure 2.) There were almost no printed textbooks for arithmetic. Pupils wrote down problems and rules dictated by the teacher.

ELEMENTARY EDUCATION FROM 1776 TO 1900

In the century and a quarter from 1776 to 1900 we note two fairly distinct stages in the development of elementary schools. In the first part of the period occurred an awakening of educational consciousness and a struggle for free schools, while in the second part came reorganization within the system as the result of new theories from abroad.

Elementary Education During the Early National Period

The early national period, which extended from Revolutionary to Civil War days, falls into two subperiods. During the first, which lasted until about 1830, a vision of universal education began to stir public imagination. During the second, from 1830 until the War Between the States, the struggle for state schools was waged.

When the national period began, the country was exhausted from the sacrifices entailed by the struggle for independence. The population was scattered, with approximately one-third of the people far from the settlements along the seacoast. In spite of the magnificent pronouncements of the Declaration of Independence, people had only a vague notion of the real meaning of democracy. Aristocratic ideals still shaped political practice. The right to vote was often conditioned by ownership of property or by other qualifications which met the approval of the governing classes. Standards for education fell below those of the colonial period. Ultimately, unfamiliar economic and social forces began to enter the picture and to make universal education imperative. Many of the factors can be traced to two events that exerted momentous influence toward the close of the eighteenth century: migration of the people westward and the Industrial Revolution.

The westward movement with its accompanying hardships fostered among the frontiersmen economic and social equality which in turn led to political equality. The granting of full manhood suffrage enormously augmented the number of voters. Many of them had little or no schooling. The hazards that threatened the country from abysmal ignorance made education a necessity, not to save souls as was urged after the Reformation, but to save the country. The election of Andrew Jackson, a man of humble origin, to the Presidency in 1828 ushered in a new epoch. In a sense, "the new West and the frontier had taken the whip hand in political management." With the proven fact that any man might be elected to high office, it became obvious that "a people who mean to be their own Governors, must arm themselves with the power which knowledge gives."

The Industrial Revolution, perhaps even more than the westward movement, hastened the awakening of educational consciousness. Invention and science changed the entire system of agriculture, manufacture, and commerce. People flocked to industrial centers that grew as if by magic. Youngsters whose parents could not afford to send them to schools that charged tuition went to work in factories at an early age or roved aimlessly about the streets in idle groups. Dangers inherent in such a situation were so frightening that they constituted a strong argument for free public schools. Even more powerful, though, in the push for universal education was the insistence of the workingman upon equality of opportunity for his children. He sensed the value of education in improving socioeconomic status and coveted for his boys and girls an institution untainted by the stigma attached to pauper schools.

Not yet prepared to tax themselves to carry the entire load of maintaining schools, the people turned to the church and to philanthropic societies to solve this problem. One of the first ventures was the establishment of secular Sunday schools, patterned after similar English schools, to give indigent children instruction one day per week in reading, writing, arithmetic, and religion. The movement spread until by 1820 all leading denominations were operating Sunday schools. Millions of children enrolled. Eventually the churches reduced their teaching to an hour or so of religious instruction on Sunday morning. With such neglect of secular education came a demand for an innovative type of educational venture.

Voluntary school societies financed by contributions from public-spirited citizens started to take over instructing the children of the less fortunate. Foremost among these organizations was the Society for Establishing a Free School in the City of New York, formed in 1805 with De Witt Clinton, then mayor of New York City, as its president. Soon the Association was renamed the Free School Society. When reorganized in 1826 under the name Public School Society, its schools accepted both tuition and charity pupils. The fee plan, intended to allay criticism among parents who sent their children to private schools and derived no benefit from state funds given to the Society, created class consciousness and, after bitter dissension, was abolished. Finally in the middle of the eighteenth century the Society's schools merged with the city schools operated by the Board of Education of New York City.

Through Governor Clinton's urging, the monitorial type of instruction, originated in England by Lancaster early in the nineteenth century, was adopted by the Free School Society. Clinton hailed Lancaster as "the benefactor of the human race," and praised his system as "creating a new era in education, as a blessing sent down from heaven to redeem the poor distressed of this world from the power and dominion of ignorance." Soon the idea spread to other cities throughout the United States.

Under the monitorial plan masters taught "monitors," the older and brighter pupils, who taught other children. Not only were there monitors for instruction but there were also monitors to take attendance, to keep order, to care for equipment, and to take charge of monitors. Thus one teacher could have four or five hundred pupils in his care. Although mechanical methods, stressing drill and memorization prevailed, the Lancasterian schools proved highly popular. By reducing the cost of instruction sufficiently to render education of the masses feasible, they hastened the day of free schools.

Another mechanical system of education introduced about the same time as the Lancasterian was the infant school, which sprang up in England to care for children of factory workers. The first infant school in this country had its inception in the early 1800's in Boston. Like other Massachusetts towns, Boston admitted to its public schools only children who could read, thereby barring many from attending. The infant school took children of two years of age or less, which stimulated interest in extending educational opportunities to young children.

By 1830 a gradual transition from church and pauper schools to public schools had taken place. The groundwork had been laid for free tax-supported schools. The next two or three decades witnessed the "battle for free state schools." Conspicuous leaders in the "battle" were Horace Mann and Henry Barnard.

In 1837 Horace Mann relinquished a promising legal career to accept a position as secretary of the newly created Massachusetts Board of Education. He announced: "Henceforth, so long as I hold this office, I devote myself to the supremest welfare of mankind upon earth." To his friends who questioned the wisdom of his decision, he explained: "The interests of a client are small, compared with the interests of the next generation. Let the next generation, then, be my client." Of his low salary as secretary he said: "I will be revenged on them; I will do them more than $1500 worth of good."

Mann took up his duties at a time when schools had deteriorated until they were worse than in pre-Revolutionary days. His diary and letters present a picture of apathy or opposition on the part of the people, and of ignorance and incompetence in the teachers.

To accomplish his aim of improving the schools Mann employed three methods: first, lectures delivered to conventions of teachers which were held annually in each county in the state; second, twelve annual reports to the Board of Education; third, publication, as his own private venture, of an educational magazine called *Common School Journal*.

When he resigned his secretaryship in 1848 to enter Congress, he had the satisfaction of knowing that the state school system had a sound footing. Many of the improvements that he sought had come to pass. Among them were better teachers and teaching, improved school buildings, school consolidation, improved attendance, larger school appropriations, longer school terms, higher salaries for teachers, new courses of study, better local administration, and the establishment of three state normal schools—Lexington in 1839, Barre in 1839, and Bridgewater in 1840.

Like Horace Mann, Henry Barnard forsook law to campaign for better schools. He took the stand that "the common school should not be regarded as common because it is cheap, inferior, and attended only by the poor and those who are indifferent to the education of their children, but *common* as the light and air because its blessings are open to all and enjoyed by all."

As secretary of the Board of Commissioners for Common Schools in Connecticut, as State Commissioner of Public Schools in Rhode Island, and as first United States Commissioner of Education from 1867 to 1870, Barnard rendered notable service. However, his most memorable project, initiated in 1855 and continued for virtually the rest of his life, was the publication of the *American Journal of Education*. Its 31 volumes of approximately 800 pages each, replete with information about education in both Europe and America, constitute a veritable storehouse of reference material. Fittingly enough, Barnard has gained recognition as our first outstanding educational scholar.

By 1860 the idea of a free school system had been extended to every part of our country. However, while the idea of public schools was generally sanctioned, their establishment was still far from complete. A description by one of the teachers gives us insight into conditions in the Springfield, Illinois, public school system inaugurated on April 14, 1856.

When this school was first opened, the behavior of the children indicated their joy on an occasion so auspicious. They came in numbers so great that the accommodations of the house were insufficient for them. They seemed frantic with curiosity and delight. The sudden gathering together of so many children into one school, subjected their youthful excitability to a trial for which they were wholly unprepared. Children so situated could not be expected to deport themselves in an orderly manner and with moderation. They ran, they jumped, they screamed. The boys brought their bone-rattles, and the girls and boys came with whistles. They leaped over the chairs, from desk to desk rattling, singing, hooting and screaming, in joyous exhilaration, as if the occasion and the house had been gotten up expressly for frolic and fun, and without any design whatever for study, discipline and improvement of mind and morals. They had, indeed, a notion that the school was intended for learning and saying lessons; but their ideas on this point were exceedingly vague. The feeling for pleasure and play was by far the most potent, and heartily did the glad youngsters yield their busy feet and hands and mouth to the promptings of this feeling. Self restraint was out of the question. Morning, noon and the recesses were seasons of noise, merriment and confusion, with scarcely an exception. Threats and flagellations were the chief resorts of the teacher, with any reasonable hope of being able to abate the outrageous fun.

But now, in the fourth session (spring of 1857) we have the pleasure to witness a happy change. The pupils have exhibited a high degree of natural talent. They have learned well, considering the want of discipline, and other disadvantages connected with the first attempt to organize them into a large public school. (The number then in this school was 360.) The excitement produced by the numbers and novelty of the school has manifestly declined, and the scholars have a far clearer appreciation of the order, obedience and application to study for which such an institution is designed.

The parents, also, are becoming more helpful and less inclined to be mere censors, pronouncing hasty and arbitrary judgments and harsh opinions respecting the teachers, the tax principle and the board of inspectors. People who formerly paid but little attention to the real difficulty and delicacy of the teachers' duties and responsibilities, are beginning to feel the generous sympathy which stimulates to cooperation. Among the pupils there is an increasing pride of scholarship— a feeling at first so feeble that, in the large majority of individuals, I could scarcely discern its existence. Patient and accurate study is beginning to assume the force of habit. The degradation of insufficient lessons is becoming more dreaded than the drudgery of laborious attention to the assigned portions for recitation.[3]

Discipline in the mid-nineteenth century was difficult. A Champaign (Illinois) paper, *The News Gazette*, told how obstreperous boys in that vicinity once barred Mr. Bruer, a pioneer teacher, from a schoolhouse at Christmas time in order to make him furnish a treat for the crowd.

Mr. Bruer did not give in easily, however, but climbed up on the roof at the corner of the log house and covered the chimney with an old blanket, and then with a board, thus smoking the boys out. By means of a long pole, poked up the chimney, the boys managed to dislodge the covering, but Mr. Bruer seized the pole and pulled it away from them. Their weapon gone, one of the boys managed to escape through the space between the logs and the roof in the attic and was chased into the woods by Mr. Bruer and caught. The others unbarred the door and captured the teacher. The trouble was finally ended by Mr. Bruer sending for a bushel of apples and a gallon of whiskey. That night the boys all met at the schoolhouse and had a celebration. The frolic was endorsed by patrons of the school and afforded what was considered "innocent fun."

The curriculum boasted of no "fads and frills." One school-

[3] *Third Annual Report of the Superintendent of Public Schools of Springfield, Illinois* (1861), pp. 18–19.

master of the era, from western Illinois, recalled that when he was a boy there was no set curriculum. Boys and girls studied what they wanted. "Grammar," he related, "usually was shunned like the plague. Reading, writing, and arithmetic were the mainstays. Pupils studied Ray's Arithmetic and McGuffey's Readers. They also got a smattering of geography and history."

Throughout the early national period teaching conditions remained unsatisfactory. Teachers' salaries were a mere pittance. The growing practice of employing young unskilled women who could live at home tended to keep the pay at a low level. Samuel Appleton, who later became a wealthy merchant, taught in 1786 for board, lodging, and washing, and 67 cents a week. This was considered liberal pay. In 1841 the average weekly salary of women teachers in rural schools was $2.51 and in urban schools $4.44; the corresponding sums for men were $4.15 and $11.93. By 1861 the salaries for women in rural schools rose to $4.05 and in urban schools to $6.91, and the figures for men reached $6.30 and $18.07.

Records of the School District of Chesterfield, New Hampshire, supply a vivid description of conditions surrounding teaching in the 1850's. The total district expenses in 1851 were $88.09. "But by 1854 the ugly head of inflation had reared itself and the school budget was struck a staggering blow." The total money expended rose to $101.68. The report of the clerk of the district itemizes expenditures:

Pade Mis Ophelia T. Hubbard, teaching for 11 weeks—$16.50; Pade Clark Streeter for horse and waggon to take Mis Hubbard home—25¢; Pade for bording Mis Hubbard 11 weeks—$16.50; Pade Marshall Smith for repairs on privy—$1.75; Pade Mr. T. L. Locke for teaching 10 weeks & 3 days—$42.18; Pade Warrin Farr for bording teacher 10 weeks, 3 days—$18.25; For two cords of wood—$5.00. Total money expended is $101.68.[4]

Elementary Education in the Later National Period

During the latter half of the nineteenth century ideas from abroad profoundly influenced elementary education. Foremost

[4] Charles L. Bowlby, "Let's Go Back to the Good Old Days," *School Executive*, October, 1952, p. 75.

among the men who shaped educational thought were Pestalozzi, Herbart, and Froebel.

Johann Heinrich Pestalozzi (1746–1827), a Swiss, laid the foundation for reforms that revolutionized elementary school practice. His thinking was colored by the theories of Jean Jacques Rousseau (1712–1778), a French philosopher whose opening sentence of his book *Émile* gives a key to his belief: "Everything is good as it comes from the hands of the Author of Nature; but everything degenerates in the hands of man." To Rousseau society was evil and he would have the child take his lessons from nature, not from man. He pleaded for recognition of the child as a child, not as a miniature adult, and for education suited to the level of his ability. Although Pestalozzi did not accept Rousseau's extreme individualism, he welcomed the revolutionary idea of recognizing child nature as the basis of education.

Pestalozzi defined education as the "natural, progressive and harmonious development of all the powers and capacities of the human being." In light of this definition, knowledge of the natural development of the child became essential. Pestalozzi recommended attention to the instincts, interests, capacities, and activities of the learner. A "thinking love" and kindness were to replace harsh and repressive discipline. "A wise liberty induces the child to keep his eyes and ears open and makes him happy and even-tempered." He rejected the teaching of mere words and shifted the emphasis from the book to the child's experiences and immediate environment. He advised introduction of natural objects in place of words. "Send your child out into nature, teach him on the hill-tops and in the valleys. Teach him absolutely nothing by words that you can teach him by the things themselves." Observation and investigation were to replace memorization and class discussion; thinking was to replace reciting. To Pestalozzi's school in Switzerland flocked people from many lands. Visitors publicized their impressions not only through oral reports but through articles in educational periodicals and books.

Under the sponsorship of Edward A. Sheldon, superintendent of schools in Oswego, New York, Pestalozzian practices gained a foothold in the United States. From a Canadian museum Sheldon obtained for use in his schools a collection of "objects" consisting of pictures, color charts, and other visual materials. He revised the course of study to shift the emphasis from knowledge to observation and started a series of lectures to acquaint teachers with the basic principles of the new method. From these beginnings the Oswego Normal School was founded in 1861 with Sheldon as its head. So well advertised were Oswego methods that they soon gained acceptance in normal schools throughout the country. In a few decades they led to improved methods of instruction in language, elementary science, home geography, and primary arithmetic.

In the course of time the "object method" degenerated into a formal type of exercise with the focus on memorizing a vast array of facts. Lessons often had no relation to one another. They abounded with such unfamiliar words as "fetlock," "pastern," "withers," "chalybeate," "imbricated," and "amorphous." Criticism mounted until by the 1880's the method had practically run its course in the United States. It was succeeded eventually by theories and practices initiated by a German professor, Johann Friedrich Herbart.

Johann Friedrich Herbart (1776–1841), a disciple of Pestalozzi, is sometimes called the father of modern psychology and modern methods. He introduced a new psychology and emphasized organization and technique in classroom instruction. He stressed general ideas and principles as outcomes of education and elaborated the mental process by which they are derived. He believed that learning should come from the child's own interests and should proceed from the known to the unknown. He pleaded for a general method based on the way man thinks. The "five formal steps" of the recitation, formulated by his followers, remained in vogue for several decades.

Herbart's ideas reached the United States through teachers who studied at the University of Jena under Dr. William Rein, a student and follower of Herbart. The Illinois State Normal University at Normal became the principal center of Herbartianism in this country, its leading exponents being Charles De Garmo, later president of Swarthmore College, and Charles and Frank McMurry, authors of *The Method of the Recitation*.

Herbart and his followers favored the unification and correlation of all school subjects around a central core. They enriched the curriculum with the addition of historical and literary material. They made the child the center of study.

Ways in which correlation and integration were practiced in the 1890's in the training department at Illinois State Normal University are related by Helen Marshall in the centennial history of the school entitled *Grandest of Enterprises*. The culture epoch was used to correlate work in history, geography, science, arithmetic, and language.

McMurry would teach an epoch only one time and then it would be done thoroughly. For example, in the fifth grade at Normal University the story of Captain John Smith would be read in history. At the same time, in geography the class would investigate the Chesapeake area, its climate, soil and products, such as clams, oysters, fruit, and tobacco. In science the tobacco plant, oyster, and other products would be studied. In arithmetic there would be statistics on amount of tobacco produced, exported, and consumed. The findings in these various areas would be carefully recorded and thus serve the purposes of language composition in narration, description, and exposition. To McMurry and his fellow Herbartians, history was very important in the elementary curriculum.[5]

While Herbartian pedagogy did not become "the angel to roll away the stone from the sepulchre of formalism in which the schools of America have been entombed," its influence extended well into the twentieth century.[6] It served to pave the way for the movement for the scientific study of education.

The founding of the Herbart Club in 1892 marked the beginning of the period of modern education. In 1910, after two changes in name, it became the National Society for the Study of Education.

[5] Helen E. Marshall, *Grandest of Enterprises*, Illinois State Normal University, 1956, p. 188.
[6] *Ibid.*, p. 190. (Quoted.)

Friedrich Froebel (1782–1852), a German educational reformer, was also a disciple of Pestalozzi. Perhaps his own sad childhood made Froebel eager to be an instrument for creating happiness in children. His years as a teacher in Pestalozzi's school altered the course of his life. In 1837 he opened the first kindergarten at Blankenburg, Germany. Until his death he devoted his time to founding kindergartens and training teachers for them.

Froebel was a contributor to the activity school movement. He believed that self-activity leads to feeling and knowing and constitutes the dynamic factor in education. He introduced activities not unlike those in modern schools.

In addition to extolling self-activity, Froebel set forth the principles of education by natural development, motor expression, creativeness, and social participation. He believed in freedom of play because it permitted the natural development of the child's nature. He also stressed participation in organized social life. He saw in the classroom, an immature society, a chance for the child to learn coöperation.

Germans who migrated to the United States when the German Revolution of 1848 proved unsuccessful brought Froebel's ideas with them. Mrs. Carl Schurz, one of Froebel's pupils, founded what is generally regarded as the first kindergarten at Watertown, Wisconsin, in 1855. It was a small, private school in her home, with instruction conducted in the German tongue. Before 1870 nine kindergartens had come into being in the United States.

The best known of the early kindergartens was opened at Boston in 1860 by Elizabeth Peabody, sister of Mrs. Nathaniel Hawthorne and Mrs. Horace Mann. After a trip abroad in 1867 to study Froebelian principles, she dedicated her life to advancing the education of young children. In *The Peabody Sisters of Salem*, Louise Hall Tharp states that whenever Miss Peabody saw a sweet young girl with sufficiently saintly devotion in her eyes she would say, "My dear, you must take up kindergartening."

Thanks to Miss Peabody's efforts, the first kindergarten training school, conducted by Madame Matilde Kriege and her daughter, was founded at Boston in 1868. Four years later another was established in New York. It claimed the distinction of training Susan Blow and Elizabeth Harrison. Miss Blow directed the first kindergarten in the public schools of the United States, in St. Louis, Missouri, in 1873; William T. Harris, superintendent of schools in St. Louis, deserves much credit for encouraging her work. Miss Harrison assisted in establishing the Chicago Kindergarten College at Evanston, Illinois, in 1886; it is now the well-known National College of Education.

By the close of the nineteenth century the elementary school was a free, tax-supported public institution designed to give a type of education valuable for all pupils regardless of sex or social status. It was a graded school, usually made up of eight grades. In a few communities kindergartens were in operation. School terms had increased in length (135 days in 1890). The curriculum had expanded to include shop work, cooking, sewing, music, art, and physical education. Teachers concentrated their efforts on imparting knowledge and disciplining mind and body. They relied on time-honored procedures. The question-and-answer method with stress on rote learning prevailed. They ruled the schoolroom with a rod of iron, often the stovepoker. They had to resort to sheer force or be "run out." Pupils marched in and out of the school building in military fashion. Classrooms were drab with rows of desks screwed down to the floor. Although some progressive communities had begun to introduce educational innovations that paved the way for striking changes in the twentieth century, the majority of schools clung to traditional practices.

ELEMENTARY EDUCATION IN THE TWENTIETH CENTURY

Since the turn of the century the structural organization of the elementary school has been modified in some communities by the loss of the seventh and eighth grades to the junior high school and by the addition of the nursery school. However, the nursery school has never become an integral part of our public school system. Its privileges, instead of being available to all, are almost entirely restricted to children whose parents want and can afford the best opportunities for them, and to children whose parents are impoverished or whose mothers are employed outside the home. Kindergartens have gained acceptance as the introductory unit of the elementary school. By 1947 a survey of 203 school systems in cities of over 30,000 population showed kindergartens operating in 139. In 1950 about 750,000 4- and 5-year-olds were enrolled in public kindergartens.

The concept of its function has changed so that the elementary school is expected to do more than its traditional task of grounding pupils in the three R's. In line with modern ideas the Educational Policies Commission, in a volume entitled *Education for All American Children*, issued in 1948, stated three values to guide and direct the education of all American children. According to the Commission a good elementary school should develop "those basic skills and that sturdy independence and initiative which will enable our citizens to attack the problems that face them and to press forward toward ever-improving solutions"; strive "for the discovery and full development of all the humane and constructive talents of each individual"; and emphasize "social responsibility and the coöperative skills necessary to the progressive improvement of social institutions."

Leading changes that have occurred in practices and methods in elementary education during the twentieth century are discussed in Chapter IX.

SUMMARY

In keeping with ideas brought from their mother countries settlers in the United States employed three methods of financing education: church, charity, and government support. Throughout the colonial period dame and writing schools supplied the rudiments of education. Teachers had little preparation; their methods were ineffective and punishments were severe. School buildings were crude, equipment meager, and books few and unattractive. After the Revolutionary War education sank to a low level. In the first part of the national period occurred an awaken-

ing of educational consciousness stimulated by migration westward and the Industrial Revolution. By 1830 the groundwork had
been laid for public education. The next three decades witnessed
the "battle for free schools" spearheaded by Mann and Barnard.
In the second part of the national period, from 1860 to 1900,
reorganization took place within the school system as a result of
ideas from abroad. Particularly influential were the theories of
Pestalozzi, Herbart, and Froebel. By the turn of the century the
elementary school was a free tax-supported public institution open
to "all the children of all the people." It was a graded school, usually with eight grades and, in a few communities, a kindergarten.
Since 1900 its structure has been modified in some instances by
the loss of the seventh and eighth grades to the junior high school,
and by an expansion downward to include nursery school as well
as kindergarten.

QUESTIONS AND EXERCISES

1. Show that the character of education reflects the political and
   social theories of the times.
2. How and why were conditions for public education different in the
   northern, middle, and southern colonies?
3. Characterize early teachers in the United States.
4. What factors prevented teaching from acquiring professional characteristics?
5. What differences would have resulted if a system of schools based
   upon religion or social class had won out over our present system?
6. Why did the conception of education as a private or religious obligation persist after the establishment of our national government?
7. What were the educational consequences of the "Great Awakening"?
8. Prepare a report on the educational contributions of one of the
   following: Horace Mann, Henry Barnard, Pestalozzi, Froebel,
   Herbart, Rousseau.
9. What are the values of knowing the historical background of the
   development of our schools?
10. Conduct a round-table discussion on the question: Would you
    prefer to send your child to a private, parochial, or public school?

SELECTED REFERENCES

Bagley, William C., A *Century of the Universal School*, The Macmillan Company, 1937.

Butts, R. Freeman, A *Cultural History of Education*, McGraw-Hill Book Company, Inc., 1947.

Butts, R. Freeman, *The American Tradition in Religion and Education*, The Beacon Press, 1950.

Butts, R. Freeman, and Cremin, Lawrence A., A *History of Education in American Culture*, Henry Holt and Company, 1953.

Caldwell, Otis W., and Courtis, Stuart A., *Then and Now in Education, 1845: 1923*, World Book Company, 1923.

Cubberley, Ellwood P., *Public Education in the United States*, Houghton Mifflin Company, rev. ed., 1934.

Cubberley, Ellwood P., *Readings in Public Education in the United States*, Houghton Mifflin Company, 1934.

Eby, Frederick, *The Development of Modern Education*, Prentice-Hall, Inc., 2nd ed., 1952.

Elsbree, Willard S., *The American Teacher*, American Book Company, 1939.

Good, H. G., A *History of American Education*, The Macmillan Company, 1956.

Knight, Edgar W., *Education in the United States*, Ginn & Company, 3rd ed., 1951.

Knight, Edgar W., *Fifty Years of American Education*, The Ronald Press Company, 1952.

Knight, Edgar W., *Twenty Centuries of Education*, Ginn & Company, 1940.

Knight, Edgar W., and Hall, Clifton L., *Readings in American Educational History*, Appleton-Century-Crofts, Inc., 1951.

Meyer, Adolphe E., *An Educational History of the American People*, McGraw-Hill Book Company, Inc., 1957.

Monroe, Paul, *Founding of the American Public School System*, The Macmillan Company, 1940, vol. 1.

Monroe, Paul, *Text-Book in the History of Education*, The Macmillan Company, 1910.

National Education Association, Research Division, *The State and Sectarian Education*, Research Bulletin, December, 1956.

Parker, Samuel Chester, A *Textbook in the History of Modern Elementary Education*, Ginn & Company, 1912.

Reisner, Edward H., *The Evolution of the Common School*, The Macmillan Company, 1930.

Russell, John Dale, and Judd, Charles H., *The American Educational System*, Houghton Mifflin Company, 1940.

AUDIO-VISUAL MATERIALS

Films

Education in America: The Seventeenth and Eighteenth Centuries (16 minutes, Sound, B & W, or C, Coronet Films). From the early New England school laws to the educational provisions of the Northwest Ordinance, the beginnings of American education are reënacted in actual locations of dame schools, Latin grammar schools, church schools, and pauper schools.

Education in America: The Nineteenth Century (16 minutes, Sound, B & W, or C, Coronet Films). The development of free public school systems from the Northwest Ordinance to 1900 includes the westward movement; the change to secular education; the influence of American textbooks; the rise and decline of the district school; the struggle for tax support and state control; the contributions of some early schoolmen; the effect of the Civil War; compulsory attendance laws; and the rise of teacher education institutions.

Education in America: Twentieth Century Developments (16 minutes, Sound, B & W, or C, Coronet Films). Effects of the Industrial Revolution on American education; influence of such men as Herbart, Binet, Dewey, and Thorndike; appearance of the junior high school and graduate education; the building of consolidated schools; federal aid to education; recent Supreme Court decisions.

Horace Mann (19 minutes, Sound, B & W, or C, Encyclopaedia Britannica Films). Important episodes in the life of the "father of the common schools." The story of Mann's work in pointing up the need for good schools, suitable textbooks, democratic methods of learning, schools for teachers, and universal education in the United States.

Section Sixteen (13 minutes, Sound, B & W, National Education Association). Highlights in the history of education in the United States, with implications for today's schools.

Recording

Lift a Mountain (15 minutes, Tape, Minnesota State Department of Education). A dramatized event in the life of Horace Mann.

CHAPTER IX

Living and Learning in Modern Elementary Schools

Does this criticism sound familiar? "The air is full of theories, schemes, frills and fads. Especially do we fear that with so much that is new and old, fundamentals are in danger of being neglected. The children may learn these new things, but they must first learn to read, write, spell, and cipher."[1] (The frills referred to were history, science, drawing, music, and manual training.)

Have you encountered the following verbal brickbats?

When we were mere boys, boys had to do a little work in school. They were not coaxed; they were hammered. Spelling, writing and arithmetic were not electives; you had to learn.

In these more fortunate times, elementary education has become in many places a sort of vaudeville show. The child must be kept amused and learn what he pleases. Many sage teachers scorn the old-fashioned rudiments; and it seems to be regarded as between a misfortune and a crime for a child to learn to read and spell by the old methods. . . . As a result of all the improvements, there is a race of gifted pupils, more or less ignorant of the once prized elements of ordinary education.[2]

The foregoing excerpts, the first dated 1883 and the second dated 1902, have the flavor of current pronouncements. Adults view through rosy-hued and distorted glasses the day of "readin' and

[1] *The Popular Educator*, 1883; reprinted in *The Grade Teacher*, February, 1953, p. 82.

[2] "When Grandfather Was a Boy," editorial, *New York Sun*, October 5, 1902; reprinted in *Education Digest*, September, 1952, p. 12.

'ritin' and 'rithmetic, taught to the tune of a hick'ry stick." They picture teaching as a process of routine drill on the three R's. They long for old-fashioned spelling bees with demons like *syzygy* and *parallelepipedon*. They want arithmetic taught as a highly abstract, formalized subject. They do not know that such instruction results in the use of the method that Sally (in a story perhaps first told by Thorndike) made famous: "If there are lots of numbers, I add. If there are only two numbers with lots of parts, I subtract. If there are just two numbers and one is a little harder than the other, I divide if they come out even. But if they don't, I multiply."

The older generation glorifies practices like those prevalent in Middletown at the close of the first quarter of the twentieth century when the Lynds wrote:

The school, like the factory, is a thoroughly regimented world. Immovable seats in orderly rows fix the sphere of activity of each child. For all, from the timid six-year-old entering for the first time to the most assured high school senior, the general routine is much the same. Bells divide the day into periods. For the six-year-olds the periods are short (fifteen to twenty-five minutes) and varied; in some they leave their seats, play games, and act out make-believe stories, although in "recitation periods" all movement is prohibited. As they grow older the taboo upon physical activity becomes stricter, until by the third or fourth year practically all movement is forbidden except the marching from one set of seats to another between periods, a brief interval of prescribed exercise daily, and periods of manual training or home economics once or twice a week. There are "study-periods" in which children learn "lessons" from "text-books" prescribed by the state, and "recitation-periods" in which they tell an adult teacher what the book has said; one hears children reciting the battles of the Civil War in one recitation period, the rivers of Africa in another, the "parts of speech" in a third; the method is much the same. With high school come some differences; more "vocational" and "laboratory" work varies the periods. But here again the lesson-text-book-recitation method is the chief characteristic of education. For nearly an hour a teacher asks questions and pupils answer, then a bell rings, on the instant books bang, powder and mirrors come out, there is a buzz of talk and laughter as all the urgent business of living resumes momentarily for the children, notes and "dates" are exchanged, five minutes pass, another bell, gradual sliding into seats, a final giggle, a last vanity case snapped shut, "In our last lesson we had just finished"—and another class is begun.[3]

In the mid-twentieth century some schools are reasonable facsimiles of their predecessors in Middletown. Autocratic control, repressive discipline, "teaching by subjects," and "recitations" still hold sway.

Gradually, however, there are appearing on the scene modern schools where genuine living and learning go on. Buildings are designed and equipped so that pupils and teachers may work together under favorable conditions in a stimulating environment. They contain special rooms, such as shops, art rooms, laboratories, auditoriums, libraries, gymnasiums, and lunchrooms. They have tastefully decorated classrooms, often with soundproofed ceilings and gaily tiled floors, large enough for children to move about freely at work and play. Movable tables and chairs permit informal arrangement for group conferences. All sorts of objects invite investigation and creative expression—workbench with tools and materials for construction work; easel with art materials; basic science equipment; piano and instruments used in creative activities; and attractive books and magazines. Bulletin boards display samples of the pupils' work. Charts show progress in skills and drills. Murals depict scenes related to units of study. In short, the schoolroom is a child's world.

In such a setting the children plan and carry out their tasks; they accept responsibility and use their freedom wisely in the self-imposed discipline of a democratic society. Each pupil feels himself an active member of a group that is facing a real situation and meeting it in a wholesome spirit. He is there not only to acquire knowledge and skills but to carry on a way of life. He learns the value of orderly participation and coöperation. Through wise guidance desirable standards of conduct become habitual. Happy and secure in appropriate surroundings and with work suited to his needs and abilities, he plods not "slow to school," but journeys forth eagerly and willingly.

[3] Robert S. and Helen Merrell Lynd, *Middletown*, Harcourt, Brace and Company, 1929, p. 188.

THE INFLUENCE OF DEWEY

Credit for modernizing schools goes to many "frontier thinkers" and investigators. Towering above the educational philosophers is John Dewey (1859–1952), who more than any other single person, to use Max Eastman's words, "saved our children from dying of boredom in schools."

The experimental laboratory school that Dewey founded at the University of Chicago in 1896 and his voluminous writings have had profound influence upon contemporary practice. In 1899 he pointed out that the center of educational gravity was beginning to shift. He recognized that "the child becomes the sun about which the appliances of education revolve; he is the center about which they are organized." He stressed preparing pupils to live not in some future world but here and now. Through living in the fullest sense the life of today, they would be ready for tomorrow. "Education is life; that is, education is a process of living and not a preparation for future living."

Not only did Dewey regard education as life but he looked upon it also as growth. "Since growth is the characteristic of life, education is all one with growing; it has no end beyond itself. The criterion of the value of school education is the extent in which it creates a desire for continued growth and supplies means for making the desire effective in fact."

Dewey conceived of the school as a social institution. "The school cannot be a preparation for social life excepting as it reproduces, within itself, typical conditions of social life. . . . The only way to prepare for social life is to engage in social life. To form habits of usefulness and serviceableness apart from any direct social need and motive, apart from any existing social situation, is, to the letter, teaching the child to swim by going through motions outside the water."

Dewey stressed the importance of self-activity. He believed that a child learns by doing and thinking. "The child is already intensely active, and the question of education is taking hold of his activities, of giving them direction." When he opened his laboratory school at Chicago he sought in vain for desks and chairs that lent themselves to pupil activity. One salesman finally remarked: "I am afraid we do not have what you want. You want something at which the children may work; these are all for listening." Although he emphasized the need for self-activity, Dewey was critical of those who laid "overemphasis upon activity as an end, instead of upon *intelligent* activity." He did not place in opposition learning by doing and learning through the use of word symbols.

CONTRIBUTIONS OF RESEARCH ON CHILD DEVELOPMENT, GROWTH, AND LEARNING

Hand in hand with the theories of Dewey and other philosophers goes the influence of research workers who are contributing to improved understanding of children and the learning process. They are drawing upon many fields—education, psychology, sociology, anthropology, psychiatry, biology, physiology, and pediatrics—to broaden our knowledge of the ways in which growth, development, and learning occur, and of the conditions under which they can best take place.

To these investigators we are indebted for the developmental approach. We see the child at a given moment in relation to both his past and his future. In the light of his past experiences and present status, we explore ways of helping him go on from there to become a more effective learner and a better-adjusted mature person.

We are mindful that time is an inescapable factor in the organization of behavior. Some children mature slowly, others rapidly; the process of growth cannot be hastened. According to Willard Olson, we must "take each child where he is and help him to grow by a process and in a direction personally satisfying to him and socially desirable."

In line with this concept we appreciate the reason for timing educational tasks. "When the body is ripe, and society requires, and the self is ready to achieve a certain task, the teachable moment has come. Efforts at teaching which would have been largely wasted if they had come earlier, give gratifying results when they come at the *teachable moment,* when the task should be learned."[4]

Developmental Tasks

To the successive series of learnings, adjustments, and achievements that a child must master in the process of growing up has been applied the term "developmental tasks." To use Havighurst's explanation: "The tasks the individual must learn—*the developmental tasks* of life—are those things that constitute healthy and satisfactory growth in our society. They are the things a person must learn if he is to be judged and to judge himself to be a reasonably happy and successful person. A *developmental task is a task which arises at or about a certain period in the life of the individual, successful achievement of which leads to his happiness and to success with later tasks, while failure leads to unhappiness in the individual, disapproval by the society, and difficulty with later tasks.*"[5]

Developmental tasks are determined by three factors: (1) physical maturation, (2) experiences and demands of the culture, and (3) self-assigned tasks of the individual. Learning to walk in early childhood and learning acceptable behavior toward the opposite sex in adolescence are tasks necessitated by different stages of organic growth. Tasks arising from impact of the culture include learning to read, learning to control elimination of body wastes, and learning to participate as a responsible member of society. Tasks stemming primarily from motives and aspirations of the individual include choosing and preparing for an occupation and achieving a philosophy of life.

Since the adjustments that a child faces emanate partly from societal demands, lists of developmental tasks vary from one culture to another and reflect the values of those who make them. Havighurst has formulated a list based on a middle-class point of view. He organizes tasks in terms of the period when they are thought

---

[4] Robert J. Havighurst, *Human Development and Education,* Longmans, Green and Co., 1953, p. 5.

[5] *Ibid.,* p. 2.

to have most significance for children. However, some tasks run through all the periods and some are never completely accomplished.

Developmental Tasks of Infancy and Childhood. For infancy and early childhood Havighurst identifies nine tasks:

1. Learning to walk.
2. Learning to take solid foods.
3. Learning to talk.
4. Learning to control the elimination of body wastes.
5. Learning sex differences and sexual modesty.
6. Achieving physiological stability.
7. Forming simple concepts of social and physical reality.
8. Learning to relate oneself emotionally to parents, siblings, and other people.
9. Learning to distinguish right and wrong and developing a conscience.[6]

Developmental Tasks of Middle Childhood. In the next stage, middle childhood, Havighurst believes that developmental tasks grow out of "three great outward pushes. . . . There is the thrust of the child out of the home and into the peer group, the physical thrust into the world of games and work requiring neuromuscular skills, and the mental thrust into the world of adult concepts, logic, symbolism, and communication. By the end of middle childhood the individual has worked out his particular style and his level in all three areas."[7] Nine tasks growing out of the three thrusts of growth are:

1. Learning physical skills necessary for ordinary games.
2. Building wholesome attitudes toward oneself as a growing organism.
3. Learning to get along with one's age mates.
4. Learning an appropriate masculine or feminine social role.
5. Developing fundamental skills in reading, writing, and calculating.
6. Developing concepts necessary for everyday living.
7. Developing conscience, morality, and a scale of values.

[6] *Ibid.*, pp. 9–17.
[7] *Ibid.*, p. 25.

8. Achieving personal independence.
9. Developing attitudes toward social groups and institutions.[8]

FACTORS IN THE TEACHING-LEARNING PROCESS

Another contribution from research on child growth and development is an understanding of the conditions under which learning takes place and a knowledge of the principles that guide in directing learning. Among significant factors in the teaching-learning process that shape curriculum design and teaching methods are the following:

Children are alike in many ways.

Each individual is different in some ways from all other children. Each develops according to his own growth pattern.

Within each individual there are differences: that is, all parts of a child do not grow at the same rate.

Girls develop somewhat faster than boys, especially before the age of 14.

Each stage of growth presents certain basic needs and certain interests.

Everything a child does is caused by something or someone. In other words, all behavior is caused.

No matter what a child does he is learning. Growth and learning are continuous.

Children learn to do by doing.

Each child needs to feel that he is important, is loved, and that he "belongs." Such security helps him toward becoming a healthy individual.

Each individual has many demands and pressures from his cultural environment.

The developmental needs of a child vary with his own stage of development and with the cultural influences bearing on him.[9]

GOALS OF EDUCATION

In setting goals for the modern school we should take into account both the nature of the child and the needs of society. The concept of developmental tasks helps in discovering and stating

[8] *Ibid.*, pp. 25–41.
[9] Mildred Thurston, *Helping Children Live and Learn.* Reprinted by permission of the Association for Childhood Education International, 1200 Fifteenth St., N.W., Washington, D.C. From Bulletin No. 89, 1952, p. 11.

the purposes of education. "Education may be conceived as the effort of the society, through the school, to help the individual achieve certain of his developmental tasks."[10]

While consideration of the nature of children furnishes a starting point as a source of objectives, it supplies only one type of basic information. Coupled with it should be recognition of the culture in which the children are growing up. Since goals of education represent values that society approves and endeavors to preserve and promote, they vary from group to group.

Objectives Formulated by the Educational Policies Commission

Objectives based on a consideration of the nature of the learner and the values which our society cherishes have been formulated by the Educational Policies Commission. They are intended not for any particular educational level but rather for "all educational agencies for all American citizens." They recognize that "the general end of education in America at the present time is the fullest possible development of the individual within the framework of our present industrialized democratic society. The attainment of this end is to be observed in individual behavior or conduct."[11]

The Commission classifies aims into four groups growing out of the areas with which education is concerned. Under each of the four major objectives are specific objectives which clarify the general statement.

THE OBJECTIVES OF SELF-REALIZATION

The Inquiring Mind.   The educated person has an appetite for learning.

Speech.   The educated person can speak the mother tongue clearly.

Reading.   The educated person reads the mother tongue efficiently.

Writing.   The educated person writes the mother tongue effectively.

Number.   The educated person solves his problems of counting and calculating.

[10] Havighurst, *op. cit.*, p. 5.

[11] National Education Association and American Association of School Administrators, Educational Policies Commission, *The Purposes of Education in American Democracy*, 1938, p. 41.

Sight and Hearing. The educated person is skilled in listening and observing.

Health Knowledge. The educated person understands the basic facts concerning health and disease.

Health Habits. The educated person protects his own health and that of his dependents.

Public Health. The educated person works to improve the health of the community.

Recreation. The educated person is participant and spectator in many sports and other pastimes.

Intellectual Interests. The educated person has mental resources for the use of leisure.

Esthetic Interests. The educated person appreciates beauty.

Character. The educated person gives responsible direction to his own life.

The Objectives of Human Relationship

Respect for Humanity. The educated person puts human relationships first.

Friendships. The educated person enjoys a rich, sincere, and varied social life.

Cooperation. The educated person can work and play with others.

Courtesy. The educated person observes the amenities of social behavior.

Appreciation of the Home. The educated person appreciates the family as a social institution.

Conservation of the Home. The educated person conserves family ideals.

Homemaking. The educated person is skilled in homemaking.

Democracy in the Home. The educated person maintains democratic family relationships.

The Objectives of Economic Efficiency

Work. The educated producer knows the satisfaction of good workmanship.

Occupational Information. The educated producer understands the requirements and opportunities for various jobs.

Occupational Choice. The educated producer has *selected* his occupation.

Occupational Efficiency. The educated producer succeeds in his chosen vocation.

Occupational Adjustment. The educated producer maintains and improves his efficiency.

Occupational Appreciation. The educated producer appreciates the social value of his work.

Personal Economics. The educated consumer plans the economics of his own life.

Consumer Judgment. The educated consumer develops standards for guiding his expenditures.

Efficiency in Buying. The educated consumer is an informed and skillful buyer.

Consumer Protection. The educated consumer takes appropriate measures to safeguard his interests.

The Objectives of Civic Responsibility

Social Justice. The educated citizen is sensitive to the disparities of human circumstance.

Social Activity. The educated citizen acts to correct unsatisfactory conditions.

Social Understanding. The educated citizen seeks to understand social structures and social processes.

Critical Judgment. The educated citizen has defenses against propaganda.

Tolerance. The educated citizen respects honest differences of opinion.

Conservation. The educated citizen has a regard for the nation's resources.

Social Applications of Science. The educated citizen measures scientific advance by its contribution to the general welfare.

World Citizenship. The educated citizen is a cooperating member of the world community.

Law Observance. The educated citizen respects the law.

Economic Literacy. The educated citizen is economically literate.

Political Citizenship. The educated citizen accepts his civic duties.

Devotion to Democracy. The educated citizen acts upon an unswerving loyalty to democratic ideals.[12]

LEARNING EXPERIENCES

Growth in the direction indicated by the above objectives is attained through learning experiences of the pupils. The focus of attention has shifted from formally organized subject matter deemed indispensable for a child's future well-being to his present

[12] *Ibid.,* pp. 50, 72, 90, 108.

interests and needs. In *Education for All American Children* the curriculum is defined as ". . . those experiences which the child has at school or under its jurisdiction. Through those experiences, plus those outside the school's program, the child grows and learns."

The preceding statement does not mean, however, that just any type of experience is acceptable. Several decades ago John Dewey asserted: "The fundamental thing is to find types of experiences, that are worth having not merely for the moment, but because of what they lead to, the questions they raise, the problems they create, the demands for new information they suggest, the activities they invoke, the larger and expanding fields into which they continuously open."

Experiences should be selected that have greatest potentials for achieving our goals. As a guide for measuring their suitability the following criteria are appropriate:

1. Children are given opportunities in both individual and group situations for physical, mental, social, emotional, and spiritual development.
2. The child is expected to do that which is in harmony with his ability and growth.
3. Each child has freedom within the limits of a learning situation to move, to investigate, to try out his ideas, to plan projects, to assume responsibilities, to test his skills, and to use materials and equipment.
4. The learning experience has importance for the learner in that it deals with problems of concern to him as a person and as a member of his cultural group.
5. Opportunity is provided for activities varied in type and content, wide in range and challenging in nature.
6. Opportunities are provided for children to recognize that there is more than one way of doing things, to make choices, and to understand and accept the results of their decisions.
7. There is constructive interaction between teacher and children and among children of the same and different maturity levels.
8. The child may practice the behaviors indicated by the objectives of the learning experience.
9. Opportunities are provided for children to appraise their achievements in terms of their own abilities and in terms of the relation-

ship of those achievements to the welfare and the commonly accepted standards of the group.

10. Provision is made for an atmosphere that fosters self-respect, self-reliance, respect for others, and a coöperative attitude.

11. Children are given equal opportunities with adults to plan and carry out many ideas and activities.[13]

Ever so many kinds of learning experiences take place in school. Some, particularly in the lower grades, are too brief to justify organization into units. Their variety is infinite—the first snowfall, a squirrel gathering nuts, a sprig of forsythia, a shiny pebble, a bicycle, a pet dog. These and other interests galore have possibilities for meaningful social learnings and behaviors and the attainment of subject-matter outcomes.

The following account of a real-life situation illustrates a characteristic short learning experience:

Seven-Year-Olds Entertain Parents

"Wouldn't it be fun to have a party and invite our mothers and fathers!" piped up one enthusiastic youngster in the second grade.

"Oh, yes!" said Rocky.

"We could serve something yummy to eat," added Mason.

"Could we have punch?" "Could we have ice cream and cake or cookies? Maybe we could have some sandwiches, too." The suggestions were many and varied, with homemade ice cream and cookies leading all.

"Let's make chocolate chip cookies. They're my favorite," said Margaret.

"I know how to make molasses cookies, because I've helped to make them at home," replied Sally.

Garo said, "Peanut butter cookies would be a good combination with chocolate chip."

We finally decided on two kinds of cookies and thereupon appointed a chocolate chip cookie committee and a peanut butter cookie committee. We also planned to make two gallons of chocolate and vanilla ice cream in freezers obtained from a willing parent.

The day before the party found two very industrious committees in the kitchen giving full vent to their domestic tendencies.

"I'll cream the butter and sugar together," said Sally, "but, oh, boy! that's hard work, and when I get tired you can have a turn, Peggy."

[13] Thurston, *op. cit.*, pp. 12–14.

"How about it if Paul and I beat up the eggs," said Johanna, "and then when it's mixed we can all have a turn to beat it."

"O-oh, this looks wonderful! I wish I could taste it," sighed Pat.

The children timed the cookies in the oven, amid squeals of delight and remarks such as, "Don't they look simply delicious!"

The day of the party twenty-four bright-eyed seven-year-olds arrived at school ready and anxious for a morning of vigorous churning. Lined up ready for a turn at the handle of the ice cream freezer Paul remarked, "Boy, I can really do this! Want to feel my muscles?"

"Aw, I'll bet I'm stronger than you are," said Kenny.

"Come on, give me a turn," called Pat.

As the handle became more difficult to turn the children realized that their mixture was at last beginning to become real ice cream.

The party was a success. Happy, beaming boys and girls served ice cream and cookies to their guests, and it was difficult to tell who enjoyed the party most—adults or children.

. . . .

The experience was a rewarding one. The whole project was planned and carried out by the children—even to the details of figuring costs and going to the store to buy ingredients.[14]

UNITS OF WORK

Beyond the early elementary years learning experiences are commonly organized around a theme or a center of interest known as a unit of work. Such organization is consistent with sound psychological principles. It provides a setting wherein learning is an active process. Children learn more and remember better because they select tasks suited to their level of development and related to their own values and goals. They set up problems for which they wish to find solutions; they plan their activities, execute their plans, and evaluate the results. They have some freedom of choice in exploring the problem area. For example, they may secure their information from numerous sources, such as books, field trips, interviews, and demonstrations. Again and again they are obliged to relate their new and old experiences so that they are motivated to assemble their information and knowledge in a meaningful fashion.

The unit approach makes possible an effective adaptation of

[14] *Ibid.*, pp. 19–20.

learning situations to take into account individual differences. Each child can work on his own level. Since many types of individual contributions may be utilized, each pupil has an opportunity to participate in an area where he can obtain satisfaction and recognition. Under skillful guidance the group may gain respect for the unique contributions of each of its members.

Units may be classified as resource units and teaching units.

Resource units furnish source material, usually worked out by a group of teachers and providing much more material than could be used in any one class. They comprise objectives, suggested approaches, activities, evaluation procedures, and a bibliography of teaching aids. From the resource units teachers gain perspective in formulating problems with children, become acquainted with new subject matter and teaching aids, and secure help in preparing a teaching unit.

Teaching units are built by a teacher in coöperation with his pupils in a specific classroom situation. Although he may profit by the experience of others, he and his pupils decide on the particular aims, content, activities, materials of instruction, and evaluation techniques of their unit.

Selection of a unit may be made in several ways. The following four methods are common:

1. The unit of work can be chosen cooperatively by teacher and children out of the interests and on-going activities of the group and in line with their self-appointed goals for the year.
2. The unit of work can be chosen cooperatively by teacher and children within the framework of a flexible curriculum requirement so that it fits the needs and interests of the children.
3. The unit can be selected from source volumes which list units of work or from collections of units and logs or diaries of units which are available commercially.
4. The unit of work can be developed from and around required textbook material so that it meets the textbook-course-of-study requirement and still incorporates as much as possible of child interest and opportunities for initiative, enrichment, and differentiated work.[15]

[15] Ruth G. Strickland, *How to Build a Unit of Work*, Federal Security Agency, Office of Education, Bulletin 1946, No. 5, 1946, pp. 2-3.

Each teacher must find units which will best serve a particular community and group of pupils. Examination of a list of topics for units suggested by Hildreth for the first six grades gives an idea of the kind of areas often covered.[16]

GRADE I

A Grocery Store
Our Happy Playhouse
Our Very Own Circus
Farm, Plant and Animal Helpers
Dogs
Trains

GRADE II

A Fair and a Study of Milk
A Play City
Cotton
Wheat
Our Bird Friends
Bees
Farm to City and Back
Post Office
Police Protection
Boats and the Harbor

GRADE III

The Story of Wool
Shoes
Indian Life
Cotton
Paper
Aviation
Weather
Transportation
Homes

GRADE IV

The Spanish Trail
A Trip to Hawaii
Indians of the Southwest
Mexico
Trees
Creatures of the Sea
When We Were Nomads
Story of Communication: The Telephone
The History of Lighting
Our Feathered Friends
Round and Round the World

GRADE V

The Spanish Trail
A Trip to Europe and the British Isles
History of Transportation in the United States
Conserving Our Plant Life
How the Fishing Industry Helps Man

GRADE VI

Conserving Our Plant Life
Saving
Travel on Land, on Sea, and in the Air
Bonds of Air (How Aviation Binds the Nations Together)
Rome from Legendary Kings to Great Emperors

[16] Gertrude Hildreth, *Child Growth Through Education*, Ronald Press Company, 1948, pp. 98–99.

Grade V	Grade VI
Egypt	A Medieval Tournament
History of Communication	The Story of Records
Clothing	History of Communication
Young Nutritionists in Action	Budgeting: The Arithmetic of Finance
Marionettes Tell the Story of Robin Hood	Our Trip Abroad
	Farm Life

After a unit has been chosen a teacher thinks through the learning possibilities and sets up teaching objectives. The more thoroughly he works out a flexible preliminary outline, the better prepared he is to assist the children as they make their plans and set up their own goals.

In organizing and carrying out a unit of work the teacher may have recourse to these points as a guide:

1. Survey the needs and interests which justify this unit and make it significant. Are there any general needs and problems of life which make this study important? Are there community needs which might be helped? Do these children have need for the study and are they interested in it?
2. List important objectives or goals which might be achieved through this study.
3. Make an overview of the subject matter which might enter into the study, the kinds of experiences which would be good, and any ways in which different subjects could be drawn in or integrated with this unit.
4. List books and other materials for the children to use as well as some for teacher reference.
5. Plan possible ways of introducing the study and getting children interested in it.
6. Plan the working period, keeping in mind the fact that only part of the working plan can be arranged in advance because the children are to help plan it.
    (a) Carrying on discussion and other activities which help the teacher find out what children know about the subject, their attitudes toward it, and what they are interested in.
    (b) Planning the unit with the children and getting the work underway by listing questions on which information is wanted; making charts showing what to do; planning excursions, construction, and other activities; finding and listing sources of in-

formation, tools, and materials; and arranging committees to work on some of the questions or problems.

(c) Gathering information and ideas from books and other sources and sharing through discussions, reports, and other means. Carrying out the plans for excursions and other projects.

(d) Organizing the ideas gathered, checking the list of questions to see whether adequate answers have been found, and to see that the children really understand the material they have been studying.

(e) Summarizing the total learnings in some way. It could be done through giving a program for parents or another group of children, writing an original play, painting a mural, or making a record for the class yearbook. Evaluating would be necessary to give the children an opportunity to consider the worth of the work they have been doing. There might be a group-made test on important points to be mastered.

7. Plan the evaluation of the total unit of work. Final evaluation would be concerned with two main points:

(a) Growth and changes which have taken place in the children.

(b) Individual strengths, weaknesses, and problems which need further attention.[17]

SAMPLE UNIT

This sample unit, Community Living in Switzerland, was used in the fourth grade in Ithaca, New York.[18]

GRADE 4, UNIT IV
COMMUNITY LIVING IN SWITZERLAND

Suggested time allotment: 7 weeks

I. *Suggested Specific Objectives*

A. An understanding of the ways in which the people of Switzerland have adapted themselves to the physical features of their environment

B. A knowledge of the effects of geographic factors on the climate of Switzerland
   Altitude

C. An understanding and appreciation of the character of the Swiss people

[17] Strickland, *op. cit.*, pp. 5–6.
[18] Loretta E. Klee, *et al.*, *Curriculum Guide in Social Studies Grades Three and Four*, Ithaca Public Schools, Ithaca, New York, 1949, pp. 54–59.

D. An understanding of how the Swiss provide for their needs during the winters

E. An increased willingness on the part of the pupils to work together for the common good of the class

F. A growth in map reading skills

II. *Suggested Approaches*
   A. Travel motif
   B. Story of William Tell
   C. Pictures and other visual aids

III. *Content*
   A. What type of people are the Swiss?
      1. Strong
      2. Courageous
      3. Liberty-loving
      4. Well educated
      5. Independent
      6. Resourceful
      7. Energetic
      8. Thrifty
      9. White race
      10. People dress as we do
      11. Government much like ours
          Country divided into states called cantons
   B. Location and topography
      1. Distance from the equator
         Compare with Ithaca
      2. Southern Europe
         a. Bordered by France, Germany, Italy
         b. Land of three languages
            1) French
            2) German
            3) Italian
         c. Many speak English
      3. Absence of large bodies of water
      4. Northern Hemisphere
      5. Eastern Hemisphere
      6. The Alps
   C. In what type of homes do these people live?
      1. Wood
         a. Many trees on mountainsides
         b. Easy to obtain
         c. Cheap

      2. Lower part covered with plaster
           Keeps out cold winds
      3. Burn wood for heating and cooking
        a. Abundance of trees
        b. No coal, gas or oil
      4. Steep roofs in some parts of country
      5. Flat roofs in regions of high winds
        a. Winds blow snow off
        b. Roofs held down by heavy stones
  D. What things help many people earn their livings in this mountainous land?
      1. Herds
        a. Cows
          1) Taken to mountain pastures in early May
          2) Stop at May pasture
            a) Hut built of wood
               Many trees
          3) Move on to alp pasture in early June
            a) Hut built of stone
              (1) No trees
              (2) Above tree line
          4) Milk made into cheese
          5) Begin journey homeward in early September
            a) Stop again at May pasture
            b) Arrive home in October
        b. Goats
          1) Taken to mountain pasture each morning during summer
          2) Will eat coarser and shorter grass than cows
          3) Can graze on slopes too steep for any other use
      2. Factories
        a. Watches and clocks
        b. Music boxes
        c. Laces and embroideries
        d. Milk chocolate
        e. Cheese
        f. Condensing and canning milk
        g. Cloth—"dotted Swiss"
        h. Furniture
      3. Tourist trade
        a. Switzerland—"the playground of Europe"
          1) Beautiful scenery

          a) Snow-capped mountains
          b) Waterfalls
          c) Lakes
      2) Sports
          a) Skiing
          b) Mountain climbing
          c) Skating
          d) Coasting
          e) Tobogganing
          f) Ice-boating
      3) Some go for health
   b. Swiss furnish hotels
   c. Farmers supply hotels with dairy products
   d. Men serve as guides
   e. Men operate trains and automobiles
E. What is summer like on the farms?
   1. Season of preparation for long, cold winter
      a. Most land is used for raising hay
         1) Country is rough and mountainous
         2) No large areas of level land
         3) Small farms
      b. Animals graze out of doors
      c. Make cheese from goat's milk
      d. Raise vegetable garden
      e. Make woolen clothes for winter
F. What is winter life like on the farms?
   1. Barn attached to house
      a. Makes farm work easier
      b. Need not wade through snowdrifts
      c. Animals remain in barns
   2. Men carve wooden toys and make watches and clocks
   3. Women make lace and embroidery
   4. Dangers—peculiar to mountainous regions
      a. Avalanches
         1) Building sheds over highways in path of avalanches
         2) Planting forests in path of avalanches
         3) Building walls in the path of avalanches
      b. Deep snows
         1) Monks
         2) Hospices
         3) St. Bernard dogs
      c. Glaciers
        Method of crossing

G. Why are the mountains of Switzerland a source of wealth to her people?
   1. Many waterfalls
      a. Produce electricity
         1) Runs machinery in factories
         2) Furnishes cities and towns with electric light
         3) Furnishes power for trains and street cars
   2. Beautiful scenery
H. Why are the Swiss not great world traders?
   1. No seacoast
   2. No harbors
   3. No ships
   4. Do carry on foreign trade
      a. By road
      b. By railroad
      c. By river boat
I. What important rivers have their sources in the Alps?
   1. Rhine flows into North Sea
   2. Rhone flows into Mediterranean Sea
   3. Po flows into Adriatic Sea
   4. Danube flows into Black Sea
   5. Trace all from source to mouth
   6. Roads and railroads often follow the rivers
J. What are the leading Swiss cities?
   1. Located in the valleys or on the plateaus
      a. Geneva
         1) Largest and best known
         2) Manufacturing and business center
      b. Basel
      c. Zurich
      d. Bern—capital
      e. Locate each on the map
K. Schools in Switzerland
IV. *Activities*
   A. Globe and map study—Training in Basic Skills
      1. Find Switzerland on the globe and on a map of the world.
      2. Compare the distance of Geneva and Ithaca from the equator.
      3. On a physical map locate: highlands, lowlands, mountains, lakes, tunnels.
      4. In what direction would you travel in going up the Rhine? Rhone? Po? Danube? Going down each of these rivers?

5. Locate the body of water into which each of these rivers flows.
6. Find the source and mouth of each of these four rivers.
7. Locate on the globe and maps: France, Germany, Italy—the countries that border Switzerland.
8. Locate the Alps Mountains on a globe and on a map.

B. Problems to talk over—Critical Thinking, Interpretation and Judgment
   1. Why do the Swiss dress and live much as we do?
   2. What do the Swiss eat?
   3. Compare the dinner you had yesterday with a Swiss dinner.
   4. Why are the summers in Switzerland seasons of preparation for the winters?
   5. How do the Swiss prepare for the winter seasons?
   6. Why are the cows taken to the mountain pastures for the summer?
   7. How have the mountains been a source of wealth for the Swiss people?
   8. Why do many rivers have their sources in Switzerland?
   9. Compare the length of daylight in Switzerland with that in Ithaca.
   10. How are the Swiss homes heated and lighted? Why?
   11. Compare your home with one in Geneva.
   12. Show how the climate of Switzerland becomes different as you travel from lowlands to highlands.
   13. In what parts of Switzerland is the climate most like that found in Ithaca?

C. Floor talks—Finding Information and Sharing Learning with Others
   1. An Airplane Trip Across Switzerland
   2. A Glacier
   3. A Skiing Party in the Swiss Alps
   4. A Climb to the Top of a Mountain
   5. A Day in a Swiss Village
   6. A Visit to a Mountain Pasture
   7. A Tour of Swiss Cities
   8. William Tell

D. Writing activities—Opportunity for Working Together in Groups
   1. Collect and mount pictures of the people, homes, occupations, sports, etc. Label for the use of future classes.
   2. Write original stories and poems.
   3. Write a class book on "Living in Switzerland."

4. Divide the class into groups to write each chapter. Illustrate with original sketches.

5. Write letters for tourist information.

E. Construction—Provision for Individual Differences and Interests

1. Model of a chalet

2. Model of an Alpine peak, colored green at the base and white at the top

3. Pictorial map of Switzerland with small drawings or pictures of cows and goats, chalets and villages. Show the special products of the cities, too.

4. Sand or project table: May pasture, alp pasture, mountain climbing, a skiing party, etc.

F. Dramatization

1. Mountain Climbing Trip

2. Story of William Tell

3. A Day in the May Pasture

4. A Day in the Alp Pasture

5. A Year with a Swiss Family

   a. Summer—a season of preparation for winter

   b. Winter

      1) Work

      2) Sports

G. Art

1. Sketch a map of Switzerland, showing also France, Germany and Italy.

2. Prepare a map of Europe with Switzerland in solid black.

3. Sketch a map showing the main rivers.

4. Draw pictures of Swiss scenery and sports.

5. Draw pictures of a Swiss boy; a Swiss girl.

6. Illustrate by posters or frieze any of the phases of Swiss life which particularly interest the class.

H. Games

1. Make up guessing games: "What Am I?" based on the flowers, animals, leading manufactured products, cities, rivers, etc., of Switzerland.

2. Make up games to find the meaning of these words:

valley	falls	tree line
pass	avalanche	altitude
source	mountaineers	snow line
tunnel	upstream	chalet
mouth	downstream	
glacier	summit	

PLACE OF SUBJECT MATTER IN UNITS

Although the unit approach centers attention on the desires and needs of pupils, it does not abruptly jettison subject matter. Instead it achieves a balance between formal instruction in skills and a program of worth-while learning activities. Tools of learning are taught in a functional and useful manner. Whenever feasible, information is acquired through study of actual problems. Practice in mastery of skills is provided when readiness and need exist.

An analysis of units of work reveals how the tools of learning become an integral part of learning experiences. Although the daily program does not list the three R's as separate subjects, they are better taught and are often given more time than was formerly the case. Instead of conning a single reading book over and over again, pupils read from dozens of books for real purposes—to solve problems, to locate information, to understand a process, to check or verify a point, to share a bit of prose or poetry with classmates. They use arithmetic in connection with many phases of units—to measure material in constructing an exhibit case, to draw maps of a community to scale, to figure the weekly and yearly wages of laborers, to count money, to make change, to keep accounts in connection with class projects, to keep temperature recordings, to read decimal fractions in interpreting statistics. They turn to spelling, handwriting, and oral and written language as genuine needs arise. They keep individual and class records of class projects, discuss plans of work, outline material for stories, organize talks, write letters, make booklets of their experiences, compose verses and songs, write labels for maps, diagrams, and charts. We could take other subjects and show how they too are incorporated into an integrated program. Actually, all learning experiences involved in units can be identified as parts of traditional subject-matter fields.

Although units constitute a large part of the curriculum, they are not the whole of it. Some topics, like weather and seasonal changes, are taken up occasionally throughout the year. Other interests, such as news items, holidays, unexpected contributions from children or guests, and books not related to the unit, are short-lived and for a time turn attention from the unit. Often time is set aside for systematic practice of skills in addition to the drill afforded in units. Fields like music and art offer contributions that are worth-while ends in themselves. To make these areas hand-maidens that further the interests of a unit is to miss some of their most potent possibilities. At all times the teacher keeps the organization of the work flexible enough to make use of unexpected learning opportunities.

DAILY PROGRAM

In the traditional school the program was cut up into short periods ten to 30 minutes long. Typical of its day was the accompanying program, prepared in 1926 by the Supervisor of Rural Schools in the State Department of Education in Illinois, and recommended for use in one-teacher schools.[19]

In a modern school with a curriculum built not around subjects but around units of work we find a new type of daily program. The schedule changes somewhat from day to day to fit the children's needs and purposes as well as the local situation. Variable factors make it impractical to set up an unalterable program for every school or for every teacher. However, each teacher should prepare a tentative schedule to insure progress with economy of time and effort.

A few guiding principles may assist a teacher in formulating a daily program. First, a program should be flexible. Often different amounts of time are shifted to meet emergencies, to allow for continuity of work, and to take advantage of temporary interests and occasional learning opportunities. Excursions and auditorium programs demand this shifting. Second, a program should be consistent. Flexibility does not mean lack of plan. Some aspects of the day adjust readily to a routine. Thus provision can be made for

[19] U. J. Hoffman, A *Program for Study and Instruction in One-Teacher Schools*, Circular No. 210, Issued by the Superintendent of Public Instruction, Illinois, 1926, p. 15.

Program for Study and Class and Individual Instruction

Begin	Time	Subject	Grades	Kind of Instruction	Pages in Course
9:00	10	Gen. Exercise	All	Music, Current Events, etc.	327–329.
9:10	20	Reading	(5, 6)(7, 8)	Individual, to classes that will not recite.	127–153–187–213–260.
9:30	30	Reading	1, 2, (3, 4)	Class Daily.	57–83–104.
10:00	15	Reading	(5, 6)(7, 8)	Class to those that did not have individual.	127–153–187–213–260.
10:15	15	Writ. & Spell.	All	Class on Alternate Days.	78–123–168–234–45–169–199–235–282.
10:30	15	Rest		Directed Play.	
10:45	20	Arithmetic	4, 5, 6, (7, 8)	Individual to classes that will not recite.	139–155–190–215–262.
11:05	20	Read & Num.	1, 2, 3	Class Daily.	57–83–104–67–88–110.
11:25	35	Arithmetic	4, 5, 6, (7, 8)	Class to those that did not have individual.	139–155–190–215–262.
12:00	60	Noon		Lunch and Games	
1:00	20	Grammar	5, 6, 7, 8	Individual to those that will not recite.	162–194–219–268.
1:20	15	Read & Language	1, 2	Class Daily.	57–83–71–95.
1:35	10	Language	(3, 4)	Class Daily.	117–132.
1:45	30	Language & Gram.	5, 6, 7, 8	Class to those that did not have individual.	162–194–219–268.
2:15	15	Phys. & Civics	(5, 6)(7, 8)	Class or individual as desired.	174–202–253–301–242–288.
2:30	15	Rest		Directed Play.	
2:45	15	Const.& Nat. Study	(1, 2)(3, 4)	Class Daily.	70–94–79–101–123–142.
3:00	20	Hist. & Geog.	(5, 6)(7, 8)	Individual to those that will not recite.	171–199–236–282–182–209–257–305.
3:20	20	History	(5, 6)(7, 8)	Class to those that did not have individual.	171–199–236–282.
3:40	20	Geography	(5, 6)(7, 8)	Class to those that did not have individual.	182–209–257–305.
4:00	10	Dismissal			

This program makes possible a better division of time. Sufficient is assigned for individual instruction and more is allowed for class periods of those that receive class instruction. If grades are absent, longer class periods are possible. Every grade should have either individual or class instruction every day in every subject, except in writing and spelling.

regularly recurring events such as rest and lunch periods, recess, health inspection, and dismissal. Third, the school day should be divided into relatively large blocks of time. Children require time to work uninterruptedly at well-chosen tasks. Fourth, a program should insure balance and variety of activities. Both daily and long-range planning call for consideration of the breadth of the school program and relative emphasis on different areas in terms of the needs of a given class.

Sample Programs

The following suggested time allotments from Pennsylvania and New York, respectively, illustrate possible ways of employing time to the best advantage:

SUGGESTED APPROXIMATE TIME ALLOTMENTS
(Pennsylvania)[20]

(These were based on the total day, including lunch hours and recesses. The order in which the items are given is not significant.)

	General Percentage of Time by Weeks	
Areas of Experience	Primary	Intermediate
Opening Routines Attendance, reading the Bible,[a] flag salute, music, exchange of news and interesting experiences, care of the room and equipment, checking individual health, social and emotional needs, etc.	4%	4%
Language Arts—Reading Activities Systematic development of basic reading skills and abilities—mechanics of reading, vocabulary, understandings and meanings, independent word recognition, essential study habits; library reading; and reading activities which grow out of the experience unit in progress.	25%	14%

[a] Sections 3901, 3902 of the Pennsylvania School Laws.

[20] *The Elementary Course of Study*, Bulletin 233-B, The Interim Report, 1949, Department of Public Instruction, Harrisburg, Pennsylvania, pp. 42–43.

Areas of Experience	General Percentage of Time by Weeks	
	Primary	Intermediate
Free Play Activities (Recesses, A.M. and P.M.)	8%	8%
Experiences in the Social Living Areas	14%	17%
Development of experience units—planning and discussing activities, executing planned activities, using elementary industrial arts materials, using community resources, doing research and reporting, evaluating work done, pooling experiences of committees and individuals, listening, reading, writing, and creative expression.		
Lunch Period Activities	15%	15%
Lunch, development of correct eating habits, and social courtesies. Rest or quiet games, recreational listening and recreational reading. Free play.		
Arithmetic Experiences	7%	11%
Developing number concepts, development and drill in fundamental operations, and development of skills in reasoning. Application to real experiences —social uses.		
Aesthetic and Creative Experiences	10%	10%
Teaching art and music; free reading, literature, crafts, assemblies, dramatization, dramatic play, club meetings; and activities of a creative or aesthetic nature which grow out of the experience unit in progress.		
Health Activities	8%	8%
Health and safety instruction, physical education, recreation and rest.		
Language Arts Activities	9%	13%
(Phases other than reading) Listening, usage in both oral and written expression, spelling, handwriting, use of dictionary and library techniques. Supplemented by language activities which grow out of the experience unit in progress.		

(This is how one teacher of the intermediate division worked out
her schedule from the general time allotments.)

Hour	Number of Minutes	Area of Work
9:00 A.M.	15	Opening routines.
9:15	60	Language arts, particularly reading activities of all kinds.
10:15	15	Health, Physical Education, etc. Free play activities (recess)
10:30	15	Rest, safety instruction, etc.
10:45	15	(Planned as a whole, exact times differ daily.)
11:00	40	Arithmetic.
11:40	20	Language arts—Spelling and/or Handwriting.
12:00 Noon	60	
1:00 P.M.	75	Social Living Area.
2:15	15	Afternoon recess.
2:30	45	Language arts (wide variety to suit situation).
3:15	45	Aesthetic and Creative Experiences.
4:00		Dismissal.

Total 420 minutes

SUGGESTED TIME ALLOTMENTS (New York)[21]

Morning Session, 8:45—11:45 a.m.

8:45—10:20 a.m.

Health inspection will take place as discussed on pages 152–53.
Probably group discussion, work period, trips and assemblies will take
place during this hour depending on the needs and plans of the group.
Sometimes more than this time will be necessary for trips; at other
times the whole hour and a quarter will be given over to the work
period with a discussion at either the beginning or the end. The assembly may be held every week or even less often, except in a small
school where there may be daily or triweekly assemblies. Assemblies
which are held frequently would not take more than 15 or 20 minutes.

[21] The State Education Department, *Child Development Guides for Teachers of Six, Seven and Eight-Year-Old Children,* University of the State of New
York Press, 1949, pp. 151–152.

A short period for rest or relaxation is necessary for the younger children in these age groups. This should be followed by a lunch such as milk or a drink of water and a graham cracker or fruit.

10:20—11:45 a.m.

An outdoor period of at least one-half hour should begin this second block of time. The teacher and children may plan to use the rest of this time for language arts, singing and/or rhythms.

11:45 a.m.—1 p.m. Lunch hour

Afternoon Session 1—3 p.m.

Part of this time will be used by the teacher of the younger children as a work period during which toward the end of the year the teacher may give individual or group help in reading while other children are following their own interests. In such a scheme special teachers would have a splendid opportunity to help children who are working on a special interest. Some may want help in science, others in art or music. Part of the time may be used for original stories or the teacher may read to the group.

This time will be used by teachers and children of older age levels for group instruction in mathematics, word study, writing; for individual work to eradicate particular difficulties; and for workbooks or the use of similar practice materials. During this time these older children may also need to use the services of the special teachers.

NEW PROCEDURES AND INSTRUCTIONAL MATERIALS

The modern approach to teaching involves new methods and instructional materials. The assignment-study-recitation-test method has been superseded by an array of procedures. Among them are oral report; discussion; dramatization; committee work; demonstration; experiment; collection and classification of exhibits; and manipulative and creative activities as in dancing, art, and music.

Changed methods call for multiple materials of instruction. A single book has been replaced by unnumbered books, magazines, pamphlets, and newspapers. Audio-visual aids such as radio, television, motion pictures, slides, filmstrips, models, specimens, flat pictures, maps, globes, and charts are available. Community resources are exploited by excursions, real experiences, interviews, camping, and service projects.

MEASUREMENT AND EVALUATION

Intimately bound up with the process of learning are measurement and evaluation. Teachers employ instruments of evaluation not merely to discover whether pupils have mastered bits of subject matter but to find out whether they are making progress toward desired objectives of the school program. Education, being concerned with the total development of the child, requires that appraisal of his attainments take into account all the factors that contribute to his becoming an efficient, useful, and emotionally stable person.

Evaluation is often a coöperative process in which pupils and teachers join forces. It is not restricted to any special time. Almost daily the pupils summarize and appraise their learning, plans, and procedures, and weigh evidences of growth.

Teachers have a host of ways of finding out about a pupil's progress. They avail themselves of teacher-made tests, standardized tests, collections of the pupil's work, discussions, conferences, transcriptions, anecdotal records, diaries, case studies, and sociograms.

RECORDS AND REPORTS

Information about each child is kept as part of a cumulative record of his school history. Some is preserved for only a year; some becomes part of his permanent record. Among the data are information concerning attendance, grade placement, and family background; reports on health examinations; scores on psychological and achievement tests; anecdotal records; samples of his work; comments by teachers; summaries of questionnaires and interviews; and reports on parent-teacher conferences.

In the traditional school, report cards containing marks in attendance, deportment, and each school subject were sent to the parents at regular intervals. Sometimes percentage terms were used; sometimes the letters E, G, F, P, for "excellent," "good," "fair," "poor," or S and U for "satisfactory" and "unsatisfactory," respectively. The marking system usually involved comparison of a pupil with his classmates or with standards set up for his grade. Parents and pupils alike found the system baffling and disturbing.

To give parents a meaningful picture of a child's progress, schools have experimented with diverse plans. Some have used improved forms of report cards to provide comprehensive information concerning the child's attitudes, study skills, character and personality traits, achievement, and reasons for progress or lack of progress. Others have used individual descriptive letters addressed to parents and parent-teacher conferences.

Two ways of presenting reports are illustrated by the following excerpts:

HOME REPORT OF SECOND GRADE PUPIL[22]

June report.   Two such reports are made each year.

R.'s school attendance has been much more regular this year, and this has had a definite effect upon his progress. It is so necessary for his feeling of security and his general stability that he have as few deviations from schedule as possible. He becomes upset and shows much insecurity if he has only partial information on a subject.

He has shown a strong interest in the science work with Miss B. He is very eager for facts and to be better informed regarding things about him. This work furnishes him this opportunity. He has found it difficult to be patient enough to stick to one problem until it is thoroughly answered. His tendency has been to get a little information, then go off to something quite irrelevant. Miss B. has been trying to help him stay long enough with a question to answer it as completely as he can at his age. He seems to show quite a bit of improvement in this respect. Your cooperation in helping him to get material relative to the subject under discussion, in helping him formulate his questions and make his list to bring to school, and in giving him facts in answer to his questions helps him to get his materials better organized and in more usable form.

Recently R. has shown a decided interest in his reading. He is acquiring enough independence so that he is enjoying the content more. He is a little less analytical in his approach. This means he attends more closely to the content, and is less concerned about making mistakes. He has a tendency to attend so much to the word whether or not it is right that he loses the story. Then he goes back and rereads it saying, "That doesn't make sense." All this tends to make him read slowly. He did as good a piece of work in reading his birthday book, "The House at Pooh Corner," as I have ever seen him do. Even though the material was very difficult, the content was so interesting

[22] *Ibid.*, pp. 171–172.

to him that it carried him along. I was hoping he would continue to read some of this book himself, with your help, of course.

He is expressing his ideas a little more freely in writing. He is able to write very well.

He enjoys the arithmetic work and is accurate in it. He is working in his second arithmetic book.

Miss W. says R. always has many good ideas to express in art. She is encouraging him to take time to finish his pictures more carefully. His eagerness to hurry on to something else undoubtedly expresses his wealth of ideas.

Miss S. says R. shows more control in his rhythm work. He is less scattered in his ideas, less tense in his interpretations and more reasonable. He is not so easily upset when he does not understand things.

R. is less disturbed by others than he was. Their seemingly unsocial actions do not seem to upset him so much. Several times I have noticed him taking a definite stand for something he feels to be right and not giving up too easily. If we can help him to be reasonable along with this determination, I think it will be to his advantage.

It seems, too, R. has a little better perspective on things than he had last year. We shall continue in our efforts to help him to recognize nonessentials more readily, and to worry less about unimportant details. It seems extremely important that we do all we can to help him overcome this habit since it so limits his effectiveness.

Have you suggestions about R. or our work with him that would help us to work more intelligently with him?

Report to Parents of Third Grade Pupil

Name of Child: M.   *Date:* June
                                                                Grade: III

M.'s academic record is about average for a child her age. In reading, accuracy of vocabulary recognition is good. She reads rather slowly. She has a bad habit of asking words she already knows, just to get attention. (Do you know the reason for her great desire for attention? Do her older brother and sister take time to listen to her ideas?)

M. has a fairly good knowledge of the fundamental arithmetic processes with which she has had experience. Speed and accuracy in simple addition and subtraction combinations are good. She can do simple column addition and borrowing in subtraction. She has a tendency to lose interest in any piece of work which becomes a little irksome.

M. has recently shown excellent ability in written English. We considered her story of "The Coronation on the Radio" unusually good. She has excellent ability to select and organize important facts in writing the account of an event. She recently has shown real interest in improving her handwriting.

Miss W. says about M.'s art work: "Drawing has improved. Composition of pictures also much better. Handles crayons very well. Needs much more practice in painting."

Miss S. feels that M. is much more cooperative in outdoor play activities. She is more "sure of herself and not so much on the defensive" as she was in the fall.

She has again shown great interest in the Bird Club. Miss W. says she has excellent ability in finding and organizing materials. She reads all types of books to gather the information she wants.

M. has gained six pounds since June of last year. Her weight in May was 51¾ pounds.

She is a fine, cooperative member of this group. She is alert and interested in so many things. She contributes much in introducing new interests to the group. She should do good fourth grade work next year.

School days covered by report: 87   Days absent: 2½
Times tardy: 1

Periodic parent-teacher interviews have proved one of the most revealing ways of reporting to parents. Such conferences present a teacher with an opportunity to interpret the school to parents, and to help them view their child's achievements in relation to the school's purposes. He singles out such points as physical and emotional status, social adjustment, capacities, attitudes, interests, and progress in subject-matter areas. He draws on samples of work, lists of library books the child has read, and anecdotal records of behavior in social situations whether in the classroom or on the playground, and also, occasionally, on the child's self-appraisal. He tries to give the parents a true picture of their child's attainments and to furnish information that may aid them in guiding the child and coöperating with the teacher.

The following two records of contacts with parents illustrate different reasons for such conferences and methods of carrying on effective home-school relations.

RECORD OF SIX-YEAR-OLD (FIRST GRADE) J. M.

Date: November.   *Teacher:* Miss X.
Notes: Mrs. M. has been worried about J.'s lack of interest in reading.

T. said she was glad J. had not buried himself in a book at this stage of his development because he has so many other fine contributions which would be sacrificed if he narrowed his interests. He will learn to read without difficulty when he once begins. An outstanding characteristic of J. is his imaginative ability. He tells most original and consistent stories which are full of choice phrases and dramatic appeal.

J. is very direct and straightforward—admits his mistakes with sincerity and apparently profits almost immediately from the error.

Date: February

Mrs. M. came to inquire about J.'s reading.

T. reported that J.'s wide range of interests kept him from driving ahead in reading. There was value of preserving those interests. However, J. is beginning to want to read.

Date: June

T. reported to Mr. and Mrs. M. that J. has passed his reading tests. His writing has improved—general ability is very good, and his interests are appreciated by the group.

This brief record tells the high points of the parents' contacts during the year, indicates how the teacher reassured the parents, gave them confidence in J.'s ability and helped them to give J. time to develop.

RECORD OF SEVEN-YEAR-OLD (SECOND GRADE) B. L.

Date: April. Nature of conference: At request of mother
Teacher: Miss N.
Notes: Mother wanted to know how B. was getting along. At home she is irritable and does not get to sleep as early as she should.

Teacher reported no such difficulty at school. Only sign of nervousness this year is the usual biting of nails. She talks a great deal, but that is due to her keen eagerness to be in everything, to know everything and to have friends. On the whole she is much more calm and stable this year—less excitable—interrupts much less.

B. has more friends this year.

Takes responsibility quite seriously. Is easily distracted by almost anything even when engaged in something that is important or serious to her, because of her interest in everything and desire to know about everything.

B. continues to be very capable in thinking and doing. Thinks quickly, independently, with originality. Works accurately, precisely, neatly.

Loves music—quite responsive to it. Has done creative work in rhythms. Is reading more independently, with better understanding and more pleasure.

Nearly passed second grade test in March. Has finished arithmetic expected in second grade and has been doing supplementary work to get some problem work. Is working more accurately than when she was trying to get ahead of someone.

Mother thought camp was very good for B. last summer and hopes to send her again.

Mother said that the relation between B. and her older brother is better. Brother is more tolerant—more appreciative of her and beginning to be helpful to her.

B. has been collecting stamps.

This is a record of a single interview between the mother and teacher, both interested in doing their best to guide B. L.'s development. By comparing notes and exchanging information both teacher and mother gained in understanding and ability to help B. L.[23]

CLASSIFICATION AND PROMOTION

Classification in a conventional school follows rigid lines. A child is placed in a given grade because of his achievement in traditional subjects. Sometimes homogeneous grouping, usually on the basis of scholastic ability, prevails.

A modern school uses flexible methods of classification. Pupils shift freely from one group to another within the class according to the nature of the activity. Temporary grouping on the basis of the child's needs, interests, and abilities replaces inflexible sectioning. Children may be with one group for music, another for dramatic play, and still another for reading or arithmetic.

A marked departure in effect in a few schools is interage grouping. Howard A. Lane makes the following proposal:

Let us have two grades in the elementary school; *upper* and *lower* might suffice as names for them although I should like to get away from implications of greater worth for either. Children would remain in the lower grade until the ninth birthday. . . .

We shall have four lower grade teachers working as a team with one hundred children, and we can handle more if we must. These teachers will have neighboring rooms and some common facilities and equipment. They will teach with their doors and hearts open to all of the

[23] *Ibid.*, pp. 165–166.

children in that grade. When we first organize this grade the teachers will deal out the children into groups of approximately equal size. They will then make shifts in grouping in terms of individual children and each teacher's suitability for working with certain individuals. They will manipulate the grouping so that the groups will differ in average age, some predominantly older, some younger, but each will include children from the entire age range. This will permit children to be with children predominantly younger or older as his peculiar needs will require. This need is seldom related to mental age or academic skill.

This team of teachers, knowing the children as people, will in consultation make such shifts in grouping as individual and group needs indicate. In these mixed groups children will actually and clearly be different in all aspects of growth and adjustment. In the mixed group no one could expect everyone to achieve even similar goals, do the same lessons, learn from the same books. Yet, most of us discuss each day the United Nations, the blessings and perils of soap and water, the merits of radio programs, the price of butter, the antics of Congress, and other significant topics in social groups that range thirty years or more in age. In this new grade, teachers cannot escape the responsibility for providing opportunities for activities which engage the common interests and permit the participation of individuals with differing interests, resources, and abilities without attendant differences in value and respect.[24]

Closely akin to classification policies are promotion policies. In light of our present knowledge about child growth and development, the trend is to permit children to progress continuously through all the grades with practically no failure and nonpromotion. Flexible standards replace fixed standards and identical subject matter. Work is adjusted to individual abilities so that pupils can progress regularly.

More than a quarter of a century ago Strayer endorsed the practice of adjusting standards to the abilities of pupils. "Every pupil in the ideal school system is judged by the best which he can do and not by the median performance of a nonselected group." Studies of repeaters show that the average repeater does little if any better than he did the first time he undertook the particular work.

[24] Howard A. Lane, "Moratorium on Grade Grouping," *Educational Leadership*, March, 1947, pp. 394–395.

From the point of view of mental hygiene the no-failure plan yields high dividends. Pupils are spared discouragement and the feeling of hating society that contribute to personal and social maladjustment.

Dr. Val B. Satterfield, psychiatric consultant to the Police Department of St. Louis, discerns a possible relationship between failure and juvenile delinquency. He believes that children should not be graded on their school work. According to him:

"Some children are naturally slow to learn. If a youngster seems a little dull he becomes a target for ridicule. He becomes ashamed. He stops studying.

"He becomes a tough guy and holds 'sissies who study' in contempt. He stays away from school where he has not honor and resorts to breaking the law to gain what he believes is admiration."

THE TEACHER

In the last analysis the quality of modern education depends upon the character and personality of the teacher and upon his knowledge and teaching skill. No longer is he a taskmaster, an assigner of tasks, and a hearer of lessons; instead he is a wise guide who furnishes sympathetic understanding, intelligent direction, and encouragement. As the best-prepared member of the group his influence is constantly felt, but it does not deprive pupils of initiative or activity. To him we could apply Lao-tse's words:

> But of a good leader, who talks little,
> When his work is done, his aim fulfilled,
> They will all say, "We did this ourselves."

SUMMARY

In this chapter we have pointed out some of the differences between elementary schools of yesterday and today. As a result of the philosophy of John Dewey and other "frontier thinkers" and of the contributions of research in the areas of child development, growth, and learning, fundamental changes have taken place in aims and procedures.

The four general aims for elementary education enunciated by the Educational Policies Commission are concerned with self-realization, human relationship, economic efficiency, and civic responsibility.

Growth in the direction of these goals is attained through suitable learning experiences. To provide a setting for learning consistent with sound psychological principles, experiences are commonly organized around a center of interest known as a unit of work. Since children need time to work without interruption at many activities growing out of a unit, the school day is divided into relatively large blocks of time.

The modern approach to teaching involves use of a diversity of methods and a wealth of materials of instruction. Evaluation is often a coöperative process in which pupils and teachers try to find out what progress is being made toward desired objectives. Information about each child is kept as part of his school history. Reports to parents are made through report cards, letters, and personal interviews. Methods of promotion and classification are often flexible. In the final analysis, the quality of modern education depends upon the effectiveness of the teacher. He is not a mere hearer of lessons, but he is a guide who by intelligent direction stimulates pupils to realize their own potentialities.

QUESTIONS AND EXERCISES

1. How can we determine the needs that the elementary school should satisfy? Compare and contrast several statements of the aims of elementary education. Does the modern elementary school meet the basic needs of childhood better than the old-fashioned school did?
2. Why did progressive education start in the elementary rather than in the secondary school?
3. Collect evidence to evaluate the charges that modern education neglects the fundamentals.
4. Distinguish between resource and teaching units.
5. Invite the director of audio-visual aids in your college to show your class some types of audio-visual materials that can be used in classroom teaching.
6. Secure and evaluate a pupil report card.
7. What should be the basis for promoting pupils in the elementary

school? Evaluate the practice of assigning passing marks to almost all the pupils.

8. Visit an elementary classroom. Observe the children at work. Invite the teacher to visit your class and discuss the work that you observed.

9. Prepare a paper on the educational contributions of Francis Parker; of John Dewey.

10. Prepare a report on Marion Nesbitt's A *Public School for Tomorrow* (Harper & Brothers, 1953).

11. Conduct a panel on the question: What are the characteristics of a good elementary school?

SELECTED REFERENCES

Association for Supervision and Curriculum Development:
   Action for Curriculum Improvement, Yearbook, 1951.
   Growing Up in an Anxious Age, Yearbook, 1952.
   Organizing the Elementary School for Living and Learning, Yearbook, 1947.
   Toward Better Teaching, Yearbook, 1949.

Bereday, George Z. F., and Volpicelli, Luigi (eds.), *Public Education in America*, Harper & Brothers, 1958.

Caswell, Hollis L., and Foshay, A. W., *Education in the Elementary School*, American Book Company, 1950.

Clapp, Elsie Ripley, *The Use of Resources in Education*, Harper & Brothers, 1952.

Havighurst, Robert J., *Human Development and Education*, Longmans, Green and Co., 1953.

Kandel, I. L., *American Education in the Twentieth Century*, Harvard University Press, 1957.

Kearney, Nolan C., *Elementary School Objectives*, Russell Sage Foundation, 1953.

Klausmeier, Herbert J., *et al.*, *Teaching in the Elementary School*, Harper & Brothers, 1956.

Langdon, Grace, and Stout, Irving W., *Teacher-Parent Interviews*, Prentice-Hall, Inc., 1954.

Lee, J. Murray and Lee, Dorris May, *The Child and His Curriculum*, Appleton-Century-Crofts, Inc., 2nd ed., 1950.

Mehl, Marie A., Mills, Hubert H., and Douglass, Harl R., *Teaching in Elementary School*, The Ronald Press Company, 1950.

National Education Association, Research Division, *Ten Criticisms of Public Education*, Research Bulletin, December, 1957.

National Education Association and American Association of School Administrators, Educational Policies Commission, *Education for All American Children*, 1948.

Otto, Henry John, *Principles of Elementary Education*, Rinehart & Company, Inc., 1949.

Ragan, William B., *Modern Elementary Curriculum*, The Dryden Press, Inc., 1953.

Stratemeyer, Florence B., *et al.*, *Guides to a Curriculum for Modern Living*, Bureau of Publications, Teachers College, Columbia University, 1952.

Washburne, Carleton, *What Is Progressive Education?* The John Day Company, 1952.

Wiles, Kimball, *Teaching for Better Schools*, Prentice-Hall, Inc., 1952.

AUDIO-VISUAL MATERIALS

Films

Curriculum Based on Child Development (12 minutes, Sound, B & W, McGraw-Hill Book Company, Inc.). Projects undertaken by typical fourth-grade pupils illustrate methods employed by an elementary school teacher to adapt the curriculum to pupil needs.

Effective Learning in the Elementary School (20 minutes, Sound, B & W, McGraw-Hill Book Company, Inc.). A fifth-grade teacher tells of her experiences in making learning more effective. Teacher and pupils work together on such basic skills as the 3 R's, but motivation for their work is strengthened through unit study projects.

Skippy and the 3 R's (29 minutes, Sound, B & W, or C, National Education Association). A competent teacher translates a boy's yearning for a bicycle into an urge to learn the 3 R's. An accurate account of how children learn the basic tools naturally and easily.

Recording

Trends in Elementary Education (30 minutes, 33⅓ rpm, Educational Recording Services). Discussion by Clarence W. Hunnicutt of Syracuse University.

CHAPTER X

Development of Secondary Education

At the opening of the present century Brown defined secondary education roughly "as education of a higher stage than that of the elementary school and lower than that of institutions authorized to give academic degrees." Now as then, we discern not "clean-cut boundaries" but "shadowy and variable" limits.

In the United States, the history of secondary education centers around three institutions: the Latin grammar school, the academy, and the high school. During the twentieth century secondary education has reached downward to include the junior high school, and upward to embrace the junior or community college.

THE LATIN GRAMMAR SCHOOL

On the thirteenth day of the second month of 1635 the citizens of Boston voted "that our brother Philemon Pormont, shalbe intreated to become scholemaster, for the teaching and nourtering of children with us." With this modest statement was launched the Boston Publick Latin School, forerunner of the modern high school. When the school, which has been in continuous existence, celebrated its tercentenary in 1935, observance of the event was nation-wide.

Latin grammar schools in the United States were transplanted from Europe and England. They were college preparatory schools, to train young men "for the service of God, in church and commonwealth." The Boston Latin grammar school took boys of seven or eight years of age, after they had mastered the elementary art of reading in the dame school. Originally the course was seven years in length, but later the entrance age was raised to ten years and the course shortened to four.

The curriculum of the Latin grammar school was restricted to the classics—at first only Latin, which took up about three-fourths of the time, and Greek. It was determined by the standards of colleges. Entrance requirements to Harvard show what was expected:

"When any Schollar is able to understand *Tully*, or such like classicall Latine Author *extempore*, and make and speake true Latine in Verse and Prose, *suo ut aiunt Marte*; and decline perfectly the Paradigm's of *Nounes* and *Verbes* in the *Greek* tongue: Let him then and not before be capable of admission into the Colledge."

Additional information about the studies of the Latin school follows:

In the Latin school itself, the boys studied Latin from eight o'clock to eleven in the forenoon, and from one in the afternoon till dark. They began with Cheever's Latin Accidence, which was followed by Ward's Lilly's Latin grammar. The reading consisted of Aesop, with a translation; Eutropius, also with a translation; Corderius, Ovid's *Metamorphoses*, Vergil's *Georgics* and *Aeneid*, Caesar, and Cicero. Of these, Caesar and the *Georgics* seem to have been less commonly used in grammar schools than the other works mentioned. In the sixth year of the course, the boy was half through Vergil. The master permitted the reading of such translations of Vergil as Trappe's and Dryden's. Composition was begun, apparently, at about the same time with the reading of Aesop or of Eutropius, and Clarke's *Introduction to writing Latin*, was the first textbook used. Near the end of the course, Horace was read, and Latin verses were composed with the help of the *Gradus ad Parnassum*.[1]

Although under public control and financed in part by land grants and general taxes, the Latin grammar school drew most of its support from gifts of money and fees collected for the pupils'

[1] Elmer Ellsworth Brown, *The Making of Our Middle Schools*, Longmans, Green and Co., 1903, pp. 131–132.

tuition. This meant that attendance was practically limited to boys from the more prosperous and aristocratic families. However, some poor parents, who could not send all their sons, sacrificed in order to send one chosen son as a representative of all. Brown relates that in New England, as in Scotland, when a master winnowed out a gifted scholar, "his brothers and sisters would give their wages, and the family would live on skim milk and oat cake [or their colonial equivalents] to let him have his chance."

By 1700 the Latin grammar school had reached its peak, and rumblings of popular disfavor were heard. The sturdy frontiersmen preferred to abandon the classics and to substitute studies that would prepare youth for the practical affairs of everyday living. A century later, practically every Latin school had been abandoned.

Whatever its shortcomings, the Latin grammar school kept alive interest in education above the primary level. Its traditions are probably reflected in classical college preparatory courses in the modern high school.

THE ACADEMY

The academy took form in answer to agitation from the middle-class settlers for a school with a curriculum focused to help them cope with their everyday problems. To Benjamin Franklin goes credit for chartering the first academy at Philadelphia in 1751. In 1749, six years after his initial suggestion, he outlined his ideas in "Proposals Relating to the Education of Youth in Pensilvania- Philadelphia: Printed in the Year MDCCXLIX." He noted that "the good Education of Youth has been esteemed by wise Men in all Ages, as the surest Foundation of the Happiness both of private Families and of Commonwealths," and proposed "that some Persons of Leisure and publick Spirit apply for a Charter, by which they may be incorporated, with Power to erect an ACADEMY for the Education of Youth. . . ." He prefaced his suggestions for the curriculum with this observation: "As to their STUDIES, it would be well if they could be taught *every*Thing that is useful, and *every*Thing that is ornamental: But Art is long, and their Time is short. It is therefore propos'd that they learn those Things that are likely to be *most useful* and *most ornamental*. Regard being had to the several Professions for which they are intended."

Franklin's academy had three schools—Latin, English, and mathematical—each with a separate master. Although he expected practical studies to prove most popular, Franklin found to his disappointment that they were accorded a less favorable place than classical subjects. Near the close of his life he proposed that the English school be set apart as a separate institution, but no action was taken in the matter.

Soon the new type of secondary school appeared in other states. The first academy in Massachusetts, Dummer, was established in South Byfield in 1763. Inspiration for later schools in the northern states came from the founding of the two Phillips academies, one at Andover, Massachusetts, in 1778, and the other at Exeter, New Hampshire, in 1781. Their emphasis on practical aims is shown by a statement of the donors of the Andover school, who sought "to lay the foundation of a public free School or Academy for the purpose of instructing Youth, not only in English and Latin Grammar, Writing, Arithmetic, and those Sciences wherein they are commonly taught; but more especially to learn them the Great End and Real Business Of Living."

The extent of the academy system is not known accurately. However, by 1820 academies almost exclusively supplied the opportunities for instruction at the secondary level. By 1850 there were some 6000 academies with over a quarter of a million students.

Although academies often had grants of state aid, they were mainly tuition schools under private control, usually denominational. Only in New York were they incorporated into the state school system.

One of the contributions of the academy was its admission of girls. This policy led directly to higher education for women. Seminaries for girls were established by Emma Willard at Troy, New York, in 1821; by Catherine Beecher at Hartford, Connecticut, in 1828; and by Mary Lyon at Mount Holyoke, Massachusetts, in 1838.

Rules of the South Hadley Seminary, which later became Mount Holyoke College for Women, give a clue to the atmosphere in which women students lived.

1. Admission.   No young lady shall become a member of this school who cannot kindle a fire, wash potatoes, and repeat the multiplication table.
2. Outfit.   No cosmetics, perfumeries, or fancy soap will be allowed on the premises.
3. Exercise.   Every member of this school shall walk at least a mile every day unless a freshet, earthquake, or some other calamity prevent.
4. Reading.   No member of this school shall devote more than one hour each week to miscellaneous reading. The Atlantic Monthly, Shakespeare, Scott's novels, Robinson Crusoe, and immoral works are strictly forbidden. The Boston Recorder, Missionary Herald, and Washington's Farewell Address are earnestly recommended for light reading.
5. Company.   No member of this school is expected to have any male acquaintances unless they are retired missionaries or agents of some benevolent society.
6. Time at the Mirror.   No member of this institution shall tarry before the mirror more than three consecutive minutes.

Some of the Female Seminaries had a Normal Department where girls prepared for teaching in the elementary school. Thus the academy was a predecessor of the normal school. One can only surmise how many students destined for teaching were "of the poorer Sort" that Franklin thought might be recommended "as Schoolmasters in the Country, to teach Children Reading, Writing, Arithmetic, and the Grammar of their Mother Tongue."

By the middle of the century the academy had drifted away from its original concern with practical studies and had taken on the character of a college preparatory school. Critics pounced upon such weaknesses as expense, distance from students' homes, and lack of democracy. Eventually the academy gave way to a unique school for the masses.

The academy with its hundred years or more of service left an enduring impression. It gave girls their first opportunity for more than a rudimentary education. It expanded the curriculum to embrace practical and vocational subjects as well as cultural. English grammar, composition and rhetoric, the modern languages, the sciences, the social studies, mathematics, and the arts and music— all found a place among its offerings. Here was proof that a secondary school could adapt its program to fit the changing social scene. Perhaps eclipsing all else was the fact that the academy built upon the elementary school instead of running parallel to it, thus forming a link between elementary school and college and contributing to the development of a one-track school system.

THE HIGH SCHOOL

Early in the nineteenth century several circumstances combined to bring into being an institution to replace the academy. Foremost among them was the popular demand for a free institution available alike to rich and poor. Added to this were arguments in favor of keeping young people at home rather than sending them away to boarding school, for removing older pupils from the common schools in order to permit better instruction for younger children, and for training teachers for the common schools.

In response to these pressures a fledgling institution, the high school, emerged. In 1821 the English Classical School, the first high school in the United States, opened in Boston. It was a three-year school "with the design of furnishing the young men of the city who are not intended for a collegiate course of study, and who have enjoyed the usual advantages of the other public schools, with the means of completing a good English education to fit them for active life or qualify them for eminence in private or public station." Three years later it took the name English High School to make clear that its purpose was not that of preparation for college, but, rather, education for life outside the traditional professions.

In 1826 Boston provided the first high school for girls, with 130 pupils chosen from 286 candidates. By the end of the second year the school had become so popular that it had to turn away applicants for admission. The clamor for larger accommodations that would involve more bountiful expenditure led to closing the school and extending the course of study for girls in the elementary schools.

Massachusetts has the distinction not only of having the first high school but, through the influence of James G. Carter, of passing in 1827 the first state-wide law providing for common secondary schools. The law did not contain the words "high school," but it specified that "every city, town, or district containing five hundred families or householders" should maintain a school for at least ten months of each year, in which should be taught, in addition to the subjects of the elementary schools, "the history of the United States, bookkeeping by single entry, geometry, surveying, and algebra." Every city or town of four thousand inhabitants was required to add to the foregoing branches "the Latin and Greek languages, history, rhetoric, and logic." These schools were to be open to all and supported by taxation.

Undoubtedly, according to present-day standards, life was bleak in the early high schools. The rules of the Scribner High School of New Albany, Indiana, in 1854 were typical of the times. One section dealing with teachers' duties stated: "Teachers are to exercise a firm and vigilant discipline, punishing as sparingly as may be consistent with securing obedience; to see that fires are made in cold weather in their respective rooms at a season to render them comfortable by school time, and to take care that their rooms are carefully swept, dusted, and ventilated, daily, and that a due regard to neatness and order is observed, both in and around the schoolhouses."[2]

For the pupils at New Albany 26 rules were drawn up. These were to be read on the first Monday of each month to the pupils in each schoolroom. For example, pupils were required to be punctual at school. If not present when the roll was called they were not admitted. They were required to bow respectfully on entering or leaving a schoolroom when a teacher was present. They were strictly forbidden to exchange with each other, by buying, selling, borrowing, or lending, and to give away anything except fruit or other eatables, without the teacher's permission. They were

[2] "Has Teaching Changed Much?" *Indiana Teacher*, October, 1954, p. 69.

forbidden to use profane language; to smoke or chew tobacco; to have at school any book, picture, or writing without the teacher's knowledge; to bring bats, shinny sticks, bows and arrows or other dangerous playthings upon the school premises; and to quarrel, fight, or use angry or boisterous language about the schoolhouse or grounds; or to strike, kick, push, or otherwise annoy their fellow pupils or others.

An idea of the curriculum of the early high schools may be gained from noting the subjects proposed in 1870 for the York, Pennsylvania, High School "after a careful review of the course of study adopted for many of the best High Schools in the state." The course of study was to embrace "Etymology, Elocution and Reading, Higher Grammar and Rhetoric with Composition and Declamation, Bookkeeping, Physical Geography, History, Algebra, Geometry, Natural Philosophy, Chemistry, Physiology, Zoology, Botany, Latin, Greek, French, German, Political Economy, Drawing, Painting and Vocal Music, to complete which would require a period of three years."[3]

It was recommended "that the study of the classics, mathematics and natural sciences, should be sufficiently thorough to enable those graduating in the school to enter the Junior Class in the best colleges in the country." This original intent of the York High School anticipated the modern idea of junior colleges.

It was also recommended "that the male pupils might very properly be excused from the study of French and Painting, and the females from the study of Greek, German, Political Economy, Bookkeeping by double entry and Declamation."

At first, the high school movement progressed at a snail's pace. The opposition of friends of the academy who did not wish to see it displaced by a "people's college," and of citizens who felt the burden of taxation and did not understand the purpose of the school combined to make progress difficult. Repeatedly they challenged the right of school boards to use tax funds to support high schools. Finally a test case reached the Supreme Court of Michi-

[3] *How Have Our Schools Developed?* National Citizens Commission for the Public Schools, 1954, p. 14.

gan. In 1872 the city of Kalamazoo had voted to establish a common secondary school and to levy additional taxes for its support. Skepticism of the state superintendent of public instruction as to the legality of directing public funds to this purpose led a local citizen to instigate a friendly test case. The decision, written by Chief Justice Thomas M. Cooley, held that it had always been the obvious intent of Michigan to provide not only the rudiments of education but also education beyond the elementary level. He closed with this statement:

If these facts do not demonstrate clearly and conclusively a general state policy, beginning in 1817 and continuing until after the adoption of the present constitution, in the direction of free schools in which education, and at their option the elements of classical education, might be brought within the reach of all the children of the state, then, as it seems to us, nothing can demonstrate it. We might follow the subject further and show that the subsequent legislation has all concurred with this policy, but it would be a waste of time and labor. We content ourselves with the statement that neither in our state policy, in our constitution, or in our laws, do we find the primary-school districts restricted in the branches of knowledge which their officers may cause to be taught, or the grade of instruction that may be given, if their voters consent in regular form to bear the expense and raise the taxes for the purpose.

The Kalamazoo case was a social victory for public high schools. With their legality finally clarified, they increased tremendously in number and enrollment. In 1870 records show only 160 high schools. By 1900 the count rose to 6005; by 1930, 22,237; and by 1958, 28,000. High-school enrollment has approximately doubled every decade since 1890. From 200,000 students in 1890 it reached nearly 9,700,000 in 1958.

By the close of the nineteenth century the high school was firmly established as a typical American institution. It admitted girls on an equal footing with boys. It professed to serve the needs of all youth rather than of the college preparatory group only. It subscribed to the doctrine of formal discipline. Students were steeped in facts regardless of whether or not the facts were meaningful. Here is a vivid description of the situation by one who knew it from first-hand experience:

We went to school for facts and got them. Facts about Latin, facts about history, facts about algebra, which gave us a valuable experience in taking intellectual punishment without a quaver. But of education there was very little because, with one exception, none of the teachers were educated. They had knowledge but, not knowing what to do with it, passed it on to us in its raw condition of fact. They knew facts, but could neither relate nor co-ordinate them. They believed in their subjects with the absolute conviction of the baker that his bread is the staff of life, but there was no passion in their belief, and, to tell truth, not much reason. If you learned history, you knew history—whether you became thus historically minded I never heard anyone either in school (or college) inquire.[4]

REORGANIZING THE HIGH SCHOOL

Until the early 1900's the high school was traditionally a four-year institution based on an eight-grade elementary school. Then almost simultaneously came a reorganization that extended the secondary program downward and upward. The program extended downward to include the junior high school and upward to embrace the junior college. Although the junior college is ordinarily thought of as constituting part of the secondary school, it is sometimes regarded as part of the system of higher education. We shall discuss the junior college in Chapter XII, Education Beyond the High School.

Junior High School

The downward extension of secondary education began with the appearance of junior high schools about 1910 in Los Angeles and Berkeley, California, and Columbus, Ohio. For the traditional 8-4 plan was substituted the 6-3-3 plan, or some other combination such as 6-6, 7-5, or 6-2-4. A few schools have included the sixth grade in the junior high school, and the ninth grade in the senior high school, thus creating a 5-3-4 pattern.

[4] Henry S. Canby, *The Age of Confidence; Life in the Nineties*, Rinehart & Company, Inc., 1934, pp. 104–105.

For two decades junior high schools developed fairly rapidly and by 1930 they numbered 1842. Then the movement moved forward slowly during the 1930's and 1940's but again showed an upward spurt in the 1950's. By 1957 more than 60 percent of all secondary schools were reorganized and more than two-thirds of all secondary school students were enrolled in reorganized schools.

The spurt in growth both in the 1920's after World War I and in the 1950's may be explained in part by the fact that the junior high school is a handy device to provide flexibility of building space. Many communities have organized junior high schools, not so much because of concern about serving well the specific needs of young adolescents, as because of concern about relieving over-crowded buildings. Often junior high schools are housed in antiquated structures originally designed for four-year high schools.

Many reasons have been given for reorganizing secondary education. At first, advocates of the junior high school thought that, by easing the transition from elementary to secondary school, the reorganization would strengthen the holding power of the school. A pupil would proceed gradually instead of abruptly from instruction by one teacher to instruction by several teachers; he would move slowly from a system where he studied under close supervision to one where he was largely on his own responsibility. He would have the advantage of improved provision for individual differences in guidance programs, enrichment of the curriculum, and vocational exploratory work. A slow pupil might profit from a departmentalized program with promotion by subjects since failure in one subject would not doom him to repeating an entire grade. A gifted pupil might have a chance for acceleration with a consequent saving of time.

In light of contemporary conditions and practices, some of the claims made by early proponents of the junior high school no longer carry much weight. Vocational exploratory work is not so necessary as in the days when the ninth grade rather than the twelfth marked the end of education for the majority of pupils. Enrichment of the curriculum rather than acceleration is generally approved for gifted pupils. Most striking of all is the swing away from strict departmentalization with highly specialized teachers toward integration of learning experiences under the supervision of one teacher.

The soundest purposes for establishing junior high schools are those having to do with meeting the special needs of early adolescent youth. This is an in-between age—a time of leaving late childhood and entering adolescence, but not being really in advanced puberty yet.

The junior high school teacher must recognize and try to satisfy the pressing needs of adolescents. Every early adolescent needs:

1. To continue to acquire and maintain fundamental knowledge, attitudes, appreciations, and skills.
2. To attain the social skills required for living in a democratic society.
3. To adjust to physical, emotional, and social changes and growth.
4. To establish satisfying relationships with boys and girls of his own age.
5. To grow in understanding of self.
6. To establish new relationships with family and other adults.
7. To plan and prepare for a career.
8. To build a personal system of standards and values.[5]

One of the problems of the junior high school is provision of an appropriate curriculum. A retarding influence has been the tendency to mimic the senior high school rather than to pioneer in new areas. Junior high school programs vary from subject-based programs to those concerned primarily with a core of common learnings. Block scheduling of time is often employed so that a given group of students and one teacher remain in the same room for two or more consecutive periods to study two or more general areas.

Another problem is securing a well-qualified school staff. Schoolmen differ in their opinions as to whether the junior high school should be staffed by those who hold the high school teaching certificate, the elementary school certificate, by some of each, or by those who have a special junior high school certificate.

Most states issue secondary school certificates valid for teaching

[5] *Our Junior High Schools—What Are They Like?* Curriculum Office, Philadelphia Public Schools, 1956, p. 2.

in grades 7-12. Only Vermont and the District of Columbia do not authorize the holder of a secondary certificate to teach in grades 7 and 8 of the junior high school. They require special preparation for junior high school teaching as do also Arkansas, California, Maine, Maryland, and Texas. Several states do not authorize holders of the elementary certificate to teach in grades 7 and 8 of the reorganized school nor prohibit them from doing so.

SUMMARY

The secondary school in the United States had its inception in the Latin grammar school, which was followed by the academy and the high school. The Latin grammar school with its classical curriculum was intended to prepare young men for college. The academy came into being in response to demands for a school to educate students for the practical affairs of everyday living. It offered a broader curriculum than the Latin grammar school and opened its doors to girls as well as boys. Some of the academies had a Normal Department, a forerunner of the normal school. Although the recipient of some public aid, the academy was really a tuition school under private control. Early in the nineteenth century the high school evolved as a result of clamor for a democratic institution to serve the needs of young people desirous of continuing their education beyond the common school but not of attending college. During the twentieth century the structure of the high school has been modified by extension downward with the organization of the junior high school and by extension upward in the junior or community college.

QUESTIONS AND EXERCISES

1. Compare or contrast the Latin grammar school with the academy; with a modern public high school.
2. Trace the development of the academy movement and show its importance in the evolution of our school system.
3. Point out the significance of the Kalamazoo decision.
4. What basic social philosophy, peculiar to America, led to the creation of the free public high school?

5. Account for the increase in enrollment in the high school between 1890 and the present.
6. To what extent is the private secondary school a survival of the European dual system of education?
7. Justify the paradoxical statement that the traditional academic curriculum is essentially vocational.
8. Give reasons for the changes that have taken place in the interpretation of the functions of the junior high school.

SELECTED REFERENCES

Brown, Elmer Ellsworth, *The Making of Our Middle Schools*, Longmans, Green and Co., 1903.

Butts, R. Freeman, and Cremin, Lawrence A., *A History of Education in American Culture*, Henry Holt and Company, 1953.

Cubberley, Ellwood P., *Public Education in the United States*, Houghton Mifflin Company, rev. ed., 1934.

Cubberley, Ellwood P., *Readings in Public Education in the United States*, Houghton Mifflin Company, 1934.

Edwards, Newton, and Richey, Herman G., *The School in the American Social Order*, Houghton Mifflin Company, 1947.

Good, H. G., *A History of American Education*, The Macmillan Company, 1956.

Knight, Edgar W., *Education in the United States*, Ginn & Company, 3rd ed., 1951.

Knight, Edgar W., *Fifty Years of American Education*, The Ronald Press Company, 1952.

Knight, Edgar W., *Twenty Centuries of Education*, Ginn & Company, 1940.

Meyer, Adolphe E., *An Educational History of the American People*, McGraw-Hill Book Company, Inc., 1957.

Monroe, Paul, *Founding of the American Public School System*, The Macmillan Company, 1940, vol. 1.

Monroe, Paul, *Text-Book in the History of Education*, The Macmillan Company, 1910.

Seybolt, Robert F., *The Evening School in Colonial America*, University of Illinois, 1925.

AUDIO-VISUAL MATERIALS

Films

Education in America: The Seventeenth and Eighteenth Centuries (16 minutes, Sound, B & W, or C, Coronet Films).

Education in America: The Nineteenth Century (16 minutes, Sound, B & W, or C, Coronet Films).

Education in America: Twentieth Century Developments (16 minutes, Sound, B & W, or C, Coronet Films).

Recording

The Effective Junior High School (30 minutes, 33⅓ rpm, Educational Recording Services). Description by Myron S. Olson of the University of Southern California.

CHAPTER XI

Secondary Schools for Today's Youth

Modern secondary schools have a task of greater complexity and magnitude than our forefathers could have imagined. Theirs is the problem of fitting unprecedented numbers of young people for life in a world transformed by science and technology. Circumstances combine to retain many children who in an earlier period would have dropped out before reaching the secondary level. Technological advances, a crowded labor market, changes in compulsory attendance laws, and public sentiment for a longer period of education have strengthened the holding power of the school. In 1906 a child in the fifth grade had only 14 chances in 100 of being graduated from high school. Today he has 60 chances in 100 of finishing the twelfth grade and receiving a diploma.

Although still catering to a somewhat select group both intellectually and socially, the secondary school tends more and more to give every boy and girl an equal chance regardless of home, racial, community, economic, or social barriers. *Education for All American Youth—A Further Look* underscores this idea:

These youth are created male or female, black or white, halt or hale. Birth and environment have tended to make some of them more alert or more shrewd or more bold than others. Environment and education have made them rich or poor, law abiding or delinquent, employed or idle.

Their names are Dumbrowski, Oleson, Cabot, MacGregor, Veschinni, Adamatoulous, Okada, Chin, Valdez, Descartes, Kerchevsky, Schmidt, Smith, and Smythe.

They reside in farmhouses, cabins, trailers, packing boxes, skyscrapers, tenements, hotels, housing projects, houseboats, dormitories, mansions, prison cells, and just plain houses.[1]

The trend toward making secondary education available to *all* American youth has resulted in a change in the character of secondary education as that term was originally interpreted. The college preparatory school with an academic curriculum has been largely replaced by the comprehensive high school with several curriculums. While there are special high schools, such as technical, commercial, trade, and vocational, still the comprehensive high school enrolls the greatest proportion of students.

The diversified offerings of the modern high school represent an attempt to meet the vast differences among students. As the Harvard Committee asserted, "Unlike the old high school in which no one was compelled to stay if he could not or did not wish to do the work, the modern high school must find a place for every kind of student whatever his hopes and talents. It cannot justly fail to adapt itself, within reason, to any."

In the wake of changes in goals and trends have come myriad issues still unresolved. Lack of a common understanding of the situation has resulted in uninformed and harsh criticism of programs of modern secondary education.

NEEDS OF YOUTH

In order better to devise a program for all youth with their similarities and differences we seek to know their nature and needs. In the past three or four decades scientific studies have sharpened our knowledge about how young people mature through learning, and have fashioned our concepts of their abilities and requirements.

Youth have both common and special needs. The former apply to all students growing up in our culture, but the latter apply only to certain students.

[1] National Education Association and American Association of School Administrators, Educational Policies Commission, *Education for All American Youth—A Further Look*, 1952, p. 29.

Common Needs

Common needs may be phrased in numerous ways. Two well-known statements are those by Havighurst and the Educational Policies Commission.

Developmental Tasks. Havighurst labels common needs "developmental tasks." He outlines ten developmental tasks of adolescence:

1. Achieving new and more mature relations with one's age-mates of both sexes.
2. Achieving a masculine or feminine social role.
3. Accepting one's physique and using the body effectively.
4. Achieving emotional independence of parents and other adults.
5. Achieving assurance of economic independence.
6. Selecting and preparing for an occupation.
7. Preparing for marriage and family life.
8. Developing intellectual skills and concepts necessary for civic competence.
9. Desiring and achieving socially responsible behavior.
10. Acquiring a set of values and an ethical system as a guide to behavior.[2]

Developmental tasks are real. They are not to be viewed as "preparation for life." They stress present concerns of the student. They are goals toward which he should move. Working toward them consumes much of the adolescent's time and energy. The way he feels that he is performing these tasks seriously affects his self-respect.

Imperative Needs of Youth. The Educational Policies Commission identifies ten "imperative needs" of youth:

1. All youth need to develop salable skills and those understandings and attitudes that make the worker an intelligent and productive participant in economic life. To this end, most youth need supervised work experience as well as education in the skills and knowledge of their occupations.

[2] Robert J. Havighurst, *Human Development and Education*, Longmans, Green and Co., 1953, pp. 111–158.

2. All youth need to develop and maintain good health and physical fitness.

3. All youth need to understand the rights and duties of the citizen of a democratic society, and to be diligent and competent in the performance of their obligations as members of the community and citizens of the state and nation.

4. All youth need to understand the significance of the family for the individual and society and the conditions conducive to successful family life.

5. All youth need to know how to purchase and use goods and services intelligently, understanding both the values received by the consumer and the economic consequences of their acts.

6. All youth need to understand the methods of science, the influence of science on human life, and the main scientific facts concerning the nature of the world and of man.

7. All youth need opportunities to develop their capacities to appreciate beauty in literature, art, music, and nature.

8. All youth need to be able to use their leisure time well and to budget it wisely, balancing activities that yield satisfactions to the individual with those that are socially useful.

9. All youth need to develop respect for other persons, to grow in their insight into ethical values and principles, and to be able to live and work cooperatively with others.

10. All youth need to grow in their ability to think rationally, to express their thoughts clearly, and to read and listen with understanding.[3]

Special Needs

Besides common needs, students also have special needs, interests, and desires which arise from differences in intelligence and aptitudes, occupational outlook, and avocational preferences. No sharp line can be drawn between ways in which the secondary school meets special and common needs. A given curricular offering or specialized service may satisfy a common concern for some students and a special one for others.

GOALS OF SECONDARY EDUCATION

Analysis of the needs of youth furnishes a starting point for formulating the goals of secondary education. A pronouncement

[3] *Education for All American Youth—A Further Look, op. cit.,* p. 216.

such as the ten "imperative needs" is often taken as an adequate statement of aims.

However, as in the case of the elementary school, the demands of society as well as concerns of the learner must be recognized. Several decades ago Thomas H. Briggs observed that education should be conceived of as "a long term investment by the state, to make itself a better place in which to live and in which to make a living, to perpetuate itself, and promote its own interests." The secondary school has a responsibility for preserving our culture by transmitting skills, knowledge, ideals, attitudes, and values which supply the capital of human experience. It has a further obligation of helping to modify the culture by preparing young people to be capable of passing sound judgment and working out desirable improvements. Any acceptable statement of aims should take these responsibilities into account.

The Commission responsible for the 1958 Yearbook of the American Association of School Administrators recognized that *"the public secondary school,* open to all and available to all, and representing the public, as it is supported and controlled by all, has the responsibility for guaranteeing to each American youth the opportunity for achieving *self-realization* and *social* effectiveness."

In line with these concepts, the Commission stated two "legitimate and critically important" goals of secondary schools:

The maximum development of all the mental, moral, emotional, and physical powers of the individual, to the end that he may enjoy a rich life thru the realization of worthy and desirable personal goals, and

The maximum development of the ability and desire in each individual to make the greatest possible contribution to all humanity thru responsible participation in, and benefit from, the great privileges of American citizenship.[4]

THE CURRICULUM

Once the goals of secondary education are formulated, they must find expression through activities which make up the total curricu-

---

[4] American Association of School Administrators, *The High School in a Changing World,* Thirty-Sixth Yearbook, 1958, p. 28.

lum. At least a dozen or more curriculum patterns are found in American schools. For our purposes we shall mention two central patterns: the subject-centered curriculum and the core curriculum.

Subject-Centered Curriculum

Traditionally the curriculum has been subject-centered, planned in terms of knowledge set up in advance, with stress on the subjects that would satisfy admission to college. The report of the Committee of Ten of the National Education Association helped retain emphasis on college preparatory subjects. In spite of its statement that secondary schools "do not exist for the purpose of preparing boys and girls for colleges," the Committee nevertheless gave its hearty endorsement of subjects that met long established college entrance requirements. Its list included Latin, Greek, English, German, French, algebra, geometry, trigonometry, physics, chemistry, astronomy, natural history, and general history.

Furthermore, use of the Carnegie unit as a device for counting credits has discouraged tampering with traditional school practices. According to this plan, credit is given on the basis of hours of class work successfully completed. One credit requires 120 hours of class work in subjects calling for outside preparation. Additional classes or lengthened periods are arranged for material demanding little or no preparation. Although the Carnegie unit proved satisfactory when high schools were almost exclusively college preparatory institutions, its use today calls for reëvaluation.

The Eight-Year Study of the Progressive Education Association, inaugurated in 1933 and completed in 1941, attempted to ascertain if secondary schools can adapt the curriculum to students' present and future lives, and their differing personal requirements, without handicapping those who continue their study in college.

The experiment involved 1475 pairs of matched students, half of whom had attended experimental schools; the other half had gone to conventional schools. Graduates of the 30 experimental schools went to coöperating colleges on recommendation of high school principals, regardless of the pattern of subjects they had pursued.

Those in charge of the experiment concluded that students from the experimental schools attained greater success in college than the students from standard schools. There was no discoverable relationship between patterns of high school subjects and success in college.

Graduates of the 30 experimental schools had the following record:

1. earned a slightly higher total grade average;
2. earned higher grade averages in all subject fields except foreign language;
3. specialized in the same academic fields as did the comparison students;
4. did not differ from the comparison group in the number of times they were placed on probation;
5. received slightly more academic honors in each year;
6. were more often judged to possess a high degree of intellectual curiosity and drive;
7. were more often judged to be precise, systematic, and objective in their thinking;
8. were more often judged to have developed clear or well-formulated ideas concerning the meaning of education—especially in the first two years in college;
9. more often demonstrated a high degree of resourcefulness in meeting new situations;
10. did not differ from the comparison group in ability to plan their time effectively;
11. had about the same problems of adjustment as the comparison group, but approached their solution with greater effectiveness;
12. participated somewhat more frequently, and more often enjoyed appreciative experiences, in the arts;
13. participated more in all organized student groups except religious and "service" activities;
14. earned in each college year a higher percentage of non-academic honors (officership in organizations, election to managerial societies, athletic insignia, leading roles in dramatic and musical presentations);
15. did not differ from the comparison group in the quality of adjustment to their contemporaries;
16. differed only slightly from the comparison group in the kinds of judgments about their schooling;

17. had a somewhat better orientation toward the choice of a vocation;
18. demonstrated a more active concern for what was going on in the world.[5]

Although critics of the study point out flaws in the techniques employed and consider the evidence inconclusive, the experiment, together with subsequent ones, has caused some colleges to modify their entrance requirements. Secondary schools are given increased freedom to depart from conventional patterns of content and organization and to offer whatever experiences are most valuable for their students.

In spite of enthusiasm in many quarters in the past two decades for curriculum reorganization, the majority of secondary schools have clung tenaciously to "tried and true" patterns. Only a few have abandoned conventional subject-centered programs.

A study of trends in enrollment in high school subjects from 1934 to 1949 showed some tendency toward fusion.[6] In science, biology gained ground at the expense of zoölogy and botany, as did also general science at the expense of more specific divisions of science. General mathematics expanded at the expense of algebra and geometry.

In general, though, the changing trends were evident mainly in the enrollment in subject-matter fields and the introduction of new subjects. Changes took the direction of more "functional" education to serve a heterogeneous group of pupils. Enrollments in mathematics and foreign languages decreased. Art and business education subjects held their own. Percentage enrollments in all other broad subject fields increased. The largest enrollments were in health, safety, physical education, English, and social studies— subjects required in most states. Of the broad subject fields home economics and industrial arts had the largest percentage increases in enrollment.

Among individual subjects physical education, typing, general

[5] Wilford M. Aikin, *The Story of the Eight-Year Study*, Harper & Brothers, 1942, pp. 111–112.

[6] Federal Security Agency, Office of Education, *Biennial Survey of Education in the United States, 1948–50*, 1951, pp. 26–29.

mathematics (including arithmetic), and United States history had the highest percentage increase in enrollments, and Latin and French had the greatest percentage decreases. In 1949 for the first time more students studied Spanish than Latin. A few subjects— English history, industrial history, nature study, the novel, and the short story—were disappearing.

Some subjects, reported for the first time in 1949, were taught in as many as 15 states. They included conservation, consumer buying, safety education, driver education, home management, fundamentals of electricity, remedial English, mathematics review, radio speaking and broadcasting, vocational radio, diversified occupations, and coöperative office training.

The gain in popularity of new subjects at the expense of academic studies is a matter of public moment. The fact that the actual numbers of students enrolled in academic branches are not declining fails to allay concern over the drop in the proportions interested in these areas.

Core Curriculum

Here and there secondary schools are trying to bridge the gap between isolated subjects and help students see the relationship among the several fields of knowledge. The core curriculum represents one attempt to break down subject-matter barriers and to furnish a meaningful general education. It includes learning experiences that are fundamental for all learners because they are derived from problems of personal and social development common to all youth, and from civic and social problems of all citizens in a democratic society.

The appellation, core curriculum, has a bewildering variety of meanings. Alberty explains it in this way: "The term is applied in some fashion to *all* or *part* of the total curriculum which is required of all students at a given level. In other words, the core is used to designate all or part of the program of general education."[7]

[7] National Society for the Study of Education, *Adapting the Secondary School Program to the Needs of Youth*, Fifty-Second Yearbook, 1953, Part I, p. 119.

Obviously, then, some core programs represent no break with tradition, whereas others show striking departures.

Alberty presents six designs for the core in order of their deviation from conventional curriculum organization:

1. The core consists of a number of logically organized subjects or fields of knowledge each of which is taught independently.

    Example: English, world history, and general science are required at the ninth-grade level. They are taught without any systematic attempt to show relationships.

2. The core consists of a number of logically organized subjects or fields of knowledge, some or all of which are correlated.

    Example: American history and American literature are required of all twelfth-grade students. When the history teacher is dealing with the Civil War, the English teacher introduces the literature of that period.

3. The core consists of broad problems, units of work, or unifying themes which are chosen because they afford the means of teaching effectively the basic content of certain subjects or fields of knowledge. These subjects or fields retain their identity, but the content is selected and taught with special reference to the unit, theme, or problem.

    Example: "Living in the Community" is selected as a unit of work for the tenth grade. The unit is then organized in terms of such subjects as science, art, and social studies and may be taught by specialists or by one teacher.

4. The core consists of a number of subjects or fields of knowledge which are unified or fused. Usually one subject or field (e.g., history) serves as the unifying center.

    Example: American history and American literature in the eleventh grade are unified through a series of epochs, such as "The Colonial Period," "The Westward Movement," "The Industrial Revolution." The unification may be extended to include other fields, such as the arts, science, and mathematics.

5. The core consists of broad, preplanned problem areas, from which are selected learning experiences in terms of the psychobiological and societal needs, problems, and interests of students.

    Example: A unit on "Healthful Living," in the twelfth grade, stresses the health problems of the group and how they are related to the immediate and wider community. The unit is teacher-student planned, but in terms of a basic curriculum structure.

6. The core consists of broad units of work, or activities, planned by

the teacher and the students in terms of needs as perceived by the group. No basic curriculum structure is set up.

Example: An eighth-grade group, under guidance of the teacher, decides to landscape the school grounds. The activity meets criteria decided upon by the group.[8]

Even a fairly conservative type of reorganization, represented by No. 4, has won a place in scarcely a handful of schools. In a study conducted by the Office of Education in 1949, high school principals were asked to report as core those courses which "involve the combination of two or more class periods for subjects that would ordinarily be taught separately."[9] Only 3.5 percent, or an estimated 833 of the approximately 24,000 high schools covered, followed this practice. It was used more frequently in junior and undivided high schools than in regular and senior high schools. Eighty-six percent of all core programs were in the three junior high school grades, and usually in not more than one or two of these grades. In junior high schools about 12 percent of the pupils were in core classes, whereas in public secondary schools the figure was less than 4 percent.

More than nine-tenths of the programs merely combined English and social studies in a double period. Sometimes science or mathematics was added. Instruction in health, music, art, and group guidance was often correlated with problems studied in the core.

The persistence with which secondary schools have retained subject-centered education programs and rejected general programs may be attributed to several forces. In the first place, teachers and administrators tend to feel secure with the traditional curriculum. Undoubtedly, many of them still have faith in the theory of formal discipline and concur with Mr. Dooley's remark: "But I believe 'tis as Father Kelly says: 'Childher shuddn't be sint to school to larn, but to larn how to larn. I don't care what ye larn thim so long as 'tis onpleasant to thim.'" Second, teacher-education institutions have not made much progress in preparing teachers for core pro-

[8] *Ibid.*, pp. 119–120.
[9] Grace S. Wright, *Core Curriculum in Public High Schools*, Federal Security Agency, Office of Education, Bulletin 1950, No. 5, 1950, p. 32.

grams. Students are required to build up majors and minors in specialized courses. State certification requirements stated in terms of credits in subjects and fields of knowledge perpetuate the practice of compartmentalizing knowledge. Third, college entrance requirements continue to be defined in terms of Carnegie units. However, many colleges are shifting the emphasis from subject pattern to the predicted ability and success of the student. Fourth, many school officials are afraid to embark on new ventures when schools are so frequently victims of unwarranted attacks by pressure groups. They know full well that charges of subversion spring not from teaching the binomial theorem and Chaucer's *Canterbury Tales* but from dealing with controversial socioeconomic issues.

There are, however, observable trends which augur well for progress in curriculum reorganization. First, institutions of higher learning are reorganizing their programs of general education. Eventually the modifications will affect procedures in high schools. Second, some teacher-education institutions are exploring ways of preparing teachers to capitalize on the needs of students. Third, results of curriculum experimentation in a few key schools are beginning to bear fruit. Fourth, laymen are taking part in curriculum planning. Their understanding and approval of innovations will remove obstacles that often impede progress.

Conflicts between friends and foes of core programs will not soon be resolved. Lack of reliable evidence as to the value of the new pattern presents a stumbling block. Continued exploration and experimentation are essential.

Education in American City

Two publications prepared by the Educational Policies Commission publicize types of core curriculums that represent marked departures from traditional practice. *Education for All American Youth* and *Education for All American Youth—A Further Look* describe a pattern of education from junior high school through junior college. Activities in schools in hypothetical Farmville and American City may be modified to serve as a basis for the reorganization of schools possible in the third quarter of the twentieth century.

In American City the educational program from the seventh to the fourteenth grade is planned and operated as a whole. The curriculum of each school embraces four divisions of learning: Individual Interests; Vocational Preparation; Common Learnings; and Health and Physical Education. In addition, in the tenth grade there is a science course closely related to the course in common learnings. The last two divisions are known as the "area of common studies," since all students follow the same general program.

Figure 3, which represents major areas of the curriculum in American City, shows how a student divides his time from the tenth to the fourteenth year. Vocational preparation claims one-sixth of his time in grade 10, one-third in grades 11 and 12, and one-half in community college. Common learnings occupy one-third of his time in each year of high school and one-sixth in community college. Science takes one-sixth of his time in grade 10, and health and physical education and individual interests each receive one-sixth.

The common learnings course, continuous from grades 10 to 14 inclusive, is "designed to provide most of the learning experiences which, it is believed, all young people should have *in common* in order to live happily and usefully during the years of youth and grow into the full responsibilities of adult life." The distinctive purposes are to help all young people grow in six areas:

1. Civic responsibility and competence.
2. Understanding of the operation of the economic system and of the human relations involved therein.
3. Family relationships.
4. Intelligent action as consumers.
5. Appreciation of beauty.
6. Proficiency in the use of language.[10]

To these should be added other purposes which are looked upon

[10] *Education for All American Youth—A Further Look, op. cit.*, p. 238.

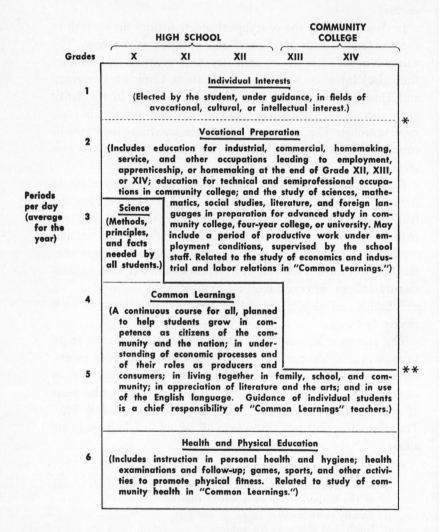

FIGURE 3. Major Areas of the Curriculum in American City. Broken line indicates flexibility of scheduling. Heavy line marks the division between "different studies" (above) and "common studies" (below). (National Education Association and American Association of School Administrators, Educational Policies Commission, *Education for All American Youth—A Further Look*, 1952, p. 233.)

as aims for every course and teacher in American City schools. These aims are to help youth grow in the following ways:

1. In ability to think rationally and in respect for truth arrived at by rational processes.
2. In respect for other persons and ability to work cooperatively with others.
3. In insight into ethical values and principles.
4. In ability to use their time efficiently and to budget it wisely.
5. In ability to plan their own affairs, as individuals and as groups, and to carry out their plans efficiently.[11]

To organize a high school curriculum along the lines envisaged for American City is a task of no mean proportions. Such innovations involve changes in school plants, in the extent and quality of teaching aids, and in instructional methods. However, a few key schools have undertaken promising core programs that presage progress in curriculum reorganization. If the results of their ventures are convincing, other schools may explore the possibilities of such curricular revision.

EXTRACLASS ACTIVITIES

For years secondary schools have had under their jurisdiction both class and extraclass programs. The term extraclass is used here to denote activities organized outside the regular schedule of courses and variously known as extracurricular, co-curricular, allied, and class-related. Now that the curriculum is defined as including all experiences under the direction of the school there can, strictly speaking, be no extracurricular undertakings.

When they originated, however, extraclass activities were separate from the regular work of the school. They were discouraged and even suppressed. At first interscholastic athletics held the center of the stage. Nonathletic organizations included dramatics, debate, and music. After 1910 outside projects gained momentum and won acceptance as a necessary evil. A decade later they were recognized, at least theoretically, as an integral part of the school program.

[11] *Ibid.*, p. 239.

Scores of activities have been organized so that students may have considerable freedom of choice. *Evaluative Criteria,* the manual prepared by the Cooperative Study of Secondary-School Standards, lists ten categories, each of which covers a multiplicity of forms of activity.

1. Pupil participation in school government.
2. Homerooms.
3. The school assembly.
4. School publications.
5. Music activities.
6. Dramatic and speech activities.
7. Social life and activities.
8. Physical activities for boys.
9. Physical activities for girls.
10. School clubs.[12]

Extraclass activities have a wealth of potential values. As seen through the eyes of 3525 students, the values rated highest were as follows: These activities developed new friendships, created added interest in school, taught how to win and lose in a sportsmanlike manner, engendered greater loyalty to the school, furnished worthwhile leisure-time pursuits, resulted in more friendly relations with teachers, increased willingness to accept criticism, and gave valuable information that would not have been obtained in a regular course.[13]

If they are to fulfill their purposes, extraclass activities must be properly supervised and soundly administered. Although final responsibility for their conduct and success devolves upon the principal, both the staff and the student body should coöperate in determining major policies. Details of administration must be delegated to various persons. Each activity should be sponsored by a well-qualified teacher.

Of the numberless problems related to directing activities we shall mention only two: participation and cost.

[12] "Cooperative Study of Secondary-School Standards," *Evaluative Criteria,* The George Banta Publishing Company, 1950, p. 191.
[13] J. Lloyd Trump, *High School Extra-curriculum Activities,* University of Chicago Press, 1944, pp. 111–123.

"The principle of extraclass activities for *all* pupils does not necessarily imply that all pupils participate, but rather that all pupils have the opportunity to participate and are encouraged to do so."[14] Participation of 85 percent or more of the student body is excellent, but 70 percent or less is a hazard to the entire program of such activities.

In order for a high school to have adequate information about student participation, answers to the following questions and the questions on page 334[15] are essential:

DATA REGARDING SCHOOL POLICY

1. Have pupils been surveyed for preferences regarding extraclass activities during the last full school year? If they have, how do their preferences compare with the present offering of extraclass activities?
2. What is the policy regarding released teaching time for teachers sponsoring "heavy" pupil activities?
3. What is the policy regarding extra pay for teachers serving as sponsors, coaches, or faculty advisers of "heavy" pupil activities?
4. How much average time per week does the staff member (principal, coordinator, director) responsible for the coordination of pupil activities devote to his duties?

Some schools try to control minimum and maximum participation by requiring all their students to take part in at least one activity and by limiting the number of activities which a student may enter. Most schools, however, prefer to depend upon counseling rather than regulations to take care of the matter.

Tied up with the problem of participation in activities is the question of costs. Students from economically underprivileged families can ill afford to have any share in extraclass undertakings. The 1947–1948 Participation in Extra-Class Activities Study sponsored by the Illinois Secondary School Curriculum Program revealed that in 79 representative Illinois secondary schools the cost of participating in activities was often high.[16] More than one-tenth

[14] Ellsworth Tompkins, *Extraclass Activities for All Pupils*, Federal Security Agency, Office of Education, Bulletin 1950, No. 4, p. 24.

[15] *Ibid.*, pp. 25–27.

[16] Harold C. Hand, *Principal Findings of the 1947–1948 Basic Studies of the Illinois Secondary School Curriculum Program*, Office of the State Superintendent of Public Instruction, Bulletin No. 2, May, 1949, pp. 23–64.

Data Needed Regarding Pupil Participation

Questions	Nonathletic		Intramural		Athletic	
	Number	Percent	Number	Percent	Number	Percent
1. How many pupils participate in one extraclass activity?						
2. How many participate in two activities?						
3. How many participate in more than two?						
4. How many do not participate in any extraclass activity?						
5. How does participation by grade compare? 12th 11th 10th 9th 8th 7th						
6. How does participation by sex compare? Boys Girls						

Data Regarding Faculty Participation

Questions	Nonathletic		Intramural		Athletic	
	Number	Percent	Number	Percent	Number	Percent
1. How many staff members sponsor one activity?						
2. How many staff members sponsor two activities?						
3. How many staff members sponsor more than two?						
4. How many staff members do not sponsor an activity?						

of the schools required a membership fee that ranged from a low of 40 cents to a high of $16.70 per student. In one-fourth of these schools the fee was in excess of $10 per student. About two-fifths of the schools studied charged class dues in grade 9 and above. Dues ranged up to $5, with a median of $1 per school year in grades 11 and 12. Students who represented their schools in athletics were burdened with "hidden tuition" charges. Median costs at the senior high school level were: baseball—$12.25; basketball—$2.80; football—$2.10; golf—$50; swimming—$1.50; tennis—$15; track—$2.70; wrestling—$1.

Some other median costs at the senior high school level follow: band—$3.50; orchestra—$2.25; pep or cheer clubs—$3.50; attendance at home basketball and football games—$2.50 and $1.40, respectively; yearbook—$2.25; and newspaper—$1. The median cost of all school dances for which a student was eligible amounted to $2.45 for juniors and seniors. Other school parties added $1.10 for juniors and $1.20 for seniors. Picnics and banquets added $2.35 and $2.85 for juniors and seniors, respectively.

In the light of these findings we can readily understand why the family purse often determines who participates in activities. In a democracy such a situation is indefensible. Hand's conclusion is a challenge to action: "If the activities permitted or sponsored are educative in nature, no public school in a democracy can justify making the accident of birth in an economic (or any other) sense determine who shall and who shall not benefit from said educative activities."[17]

A few schools are defraying costs of activities from tax funds. For example, in the Bloomington (Illinois) High School the board of education has abolished admission charges to all home athletic, dramatic, and music events, and gives each student a free copy of the school paper and yearbook. Funds are also available for certain other activities such as school parties and dances. As a result, the holding power of the Bloomington High School seems to have been strengthened.

How much longer schools will draw a distinction between class

[17] *Ibid.*, p. 64.

and extraclass activities cannot be foreseen. However, there are five signs that the gap is narrowing: the practice of giving credit, sometimes toward graduation, for extraclass undertakings; the inclusion in the regular program of subjects once regarded as extraclass, such as physical education, music, art, journalism, speech, and drama; innovations in teaching methods, such as student-planning activity and evaluation that had their origin in extraclass pursuits; the introduction of an activity period in the regular time schedule given over to extraclass affairs; financial support not from student fees but from tax money.

SPECIAL SERVICES OF THE SECONDARY SCHOOL

In addition to curricular and extracurricular experiences, most secondary schools supply numerous special services. The range is extensive—transportation, hot lunch, health, psychiatric, psychological, testing and appraisal, job placement and follow-up, recreation, summer sessions, adult classes, guidance, provision for exceptional students, and work experience. We have selected the last three of these services for brief discussion.

Guidance Services

As long as the secondary school remained a highly selective institution with a rigidly prescribed curriculum, guidance scarcely presented a problem. Students who did not adjust successfully soon dropped out. Once they severed their connection with school, they looked to other sources for direction.

Today when society favors "education for *all* American youth," the secondary school is trying to adapt its services to a growing clientele. It stands ready to advise young people both in and out of school about personal and social as well as academic and occupational problems. Its expanding functions force the introduction of planned guidance programs, now sometimes called student personnel services.

Guidance services, as applied to the secondary school, should be thought of as organized activities designed to give systematic aid to pupils in solving their problems and in making adjustments to various situations which they must meet. These activities should assist each pupil in knowing himself as an individual and as a member of society; in making the most of his strengths and in correcting or compensating for weaknesses that interfere with his progress; in learning about occupations so that he may intelligently plan and prepare, in whole or in part, for a career; in learning about educational opportunities available to him; and in discovering and developing creative and leisure interests.[18]

In most small schools the teachers act unofficially as counselors, working informally as occasions arise in class and extraclass activities. Because of their close association with students, they are in a position to know individual needs and problems. Core or common learnings courses, which occupy one-third to one-half of the school day, present unparalleled opportunities for individual and group guidance.

Large schools often have guidance departments with staffs consisting of such specialists as counselors, psychologists, psychiatrists, physicians, and remedial teachers. Theirs is the task of coördinating the program and giving it leadership. Since these specialists rarely have time to become intimately acquainted with the entire student body, they usually enlist the aid of teachers. Only when guidance is an all-faculty function embodying coöperation between specialists and classroom teachers can the welfare of youth best be served.

In connection with guidance services a sizable amount of information is collected for each student's cumulative record. Some sources of information are:

1. Records from pupil's former school.
2. Appropriate tests given near the time of admission and periodically thereafter.
3. Personal data blanks.
4. Individual interviews with pupils.
5. Periodic physical examinations.
6. Periodic ratings by teachers.
7. Teachers' comments and observations.
8. Conferences with the pupils' teachers.
9. Interviews with parents, other family members, and interested friends of the pupil.

[18] "Cooperative Study of Secondary-School Standards," *op. cit.*, p. 221.

10. Appropriate tests administered to individual pupils as need for data arises.
11. Anecdotal records.
12. Autobiographies.
13. Visits to pupils' homes.
14. Case studies of pupils.
15. Sociometric studies.
16. Socioeconomic rating devices.[19]

Guidance Services in Downers Grove, Illinois. To illustrate a functioning guidance program, let us turn to an account of the practices in Downers Grove, Illinois.

Downers Grove Community High School is very proud of its guidance program that has grown rapidly in stature and scope. Starting on a report room basis for checking attendance, it grew to a home room program and now has expanded to a system which incorporates five counsellors who conduct a program that meets the potential freshman as an eighth grader, helps him before he reaches high school, and as he continues through and beyond high school.

For the prospective students of Downers Grove Community High School this guidance program starts early in the spring of their eighth grade when they are brought to the high school in relatively small groups on specified days. The purposes of such a visit are many. In the first place, each student becomes familiar with the building and how the classes operate, and eats his lunch in the cafeteria. In the second place it provides an ideal time to give the following battery of tests: (1) Iowa Algebra Aptitude Tests, (2) Henmon-Nelson Tests of Mental Ability, (3) SRA Reading Tests. Last of all this visit gives each student a chance to discuss his course plans for his first year in high school with one of the counsellors. After consideration is given to his own respective needs, and the results on the battery of tests, each student makes out his tentative freshman program to take home for his parents' approval.

In order to assist each student before he officially enters high school as a freshman, the Wednesday before school opens is designated as Freshman Day. On this day the entire freshman class meets as a group and is greeted and instructed by the superintendent, the principal, and the deans. Each student then receives his program card, is given his locker assignment, has the opportunity to secure his books and class materials, and pay necessary fees.

[19] *Ibid.*, p. 225.

Just as regular classes get started with the assignment of a particular teacher, hour of meeting, and work, so does the high school guidance program, as each freshman is assigned to a particular counsellor. By this assignment each student has a particular person who will act as his advisor and helper for any problems that confront him while he is in school. It will be possible for such problems to be handled in two ways: (1) Personal ones may be discussed with the counsellor alone in a private interview. (2) More general ones may be brought up for discussion in the counselling groups. For as each student is assigned to a particular counsellor he automatically becomes a member of a group that meets as a regular class once a week. This counsellor assignment made in the freshman year will continue during the sophomore and junior years; however, the personnel of the counselling groups and the activities for each year will show variance.

Emphasis of the freshman counselling groups is placed on acquainting the students with everything about the high school through the use of the Handbook. As a freshman, each student starts his personal record folder that includes family background material, curricular and extracurricular activities, work experiences, interests, hobbies, and vocational desires. This he will add to and revise each year he is in school, so that it may be filed as a valuable reference after he leaves school. Besides this cumulative record, each counsellor keeps an up to date record on test scores, attendance, make-up sheets, excuses, diagnostic reports, interviews, and information supplied by teachers.

During the sophomore year, stress is placed on personality development and the problems of school, family and social adjustment. In accordance with this program each sophomore student is given the Kuder Personal Preference Test and the Otis Test of Mental Ability. As the sophomore year progresses attention is directed to vocational thoughts through discussions and the administration of Cleeton's Vocational Interest Inventory. The matter of vocational and educational needs is particularly important at this time, as each sophomore who is registering for his junior year must select three elective subjects.

Greater stress on particular vocational choices and schools is the pattern of attention for the junior counselling groups. Two tests are also given: (1) Kuder Vocational Preference Test and (2) the test provided by the Illinois High School Testing Service. The latter test measures ability in mathematics, science, English, and general knowledge. Results on the various phases of this test help the individual, the high school, a college or university to know just where this student stands in reference to other students of the state.

Besides these activities in the freshman, sophomore, and junior counselling groups the students elect a representative to School Council. Each week each group hears its representative's report of School Council activities. Time is taken to discuss these reports, and many groups sends questions and suggestions back with their representatives for School Council consideration.

The guidance program for the senior year deviates somewhat from the pattern followed during the first three years. The girls have as their counsellor the dean of girls; the boys, the dean of boys. Through the use of the English IV classes each senior is offered a short course in life problems conducted by the principal and the deans. The course is three weeks in length. Attention is directed to the immediate interests of seniors, namely: college requirements, general information on vocations, boy and girl relationships, marriage and family problems, and social and business etiquette. During the second semester girls are assigned to counselling classes which meet once a week to discuss marriage problems and those of current interests.

The guidance program of Downers Grove Community High School does not end with senior graduation. The personal record folder is kept up after the student leaves school. The workings of a sound guidance program incorporate an orientation program for the student before he enters high school, a well directed program for each year of high school, and a follow-up study after graduation for the purpose of evaluating the effectiveness of the school program.[20]

Provisions for Exceptional Students

Secondary schools try to give each student an education in harmony with his innate abilities. Most schools have some young people who deviate so markedly from the so-called "normal" student that they require special educational services. Into this group fall the physically handicapped, the mentally retarded and the slow learners, the socially and the emotionally maladjusted, and the gifted. The services may include special methods of instruction, special equipment, modification of the curriculum, or an adjusted school schedule. Sometimes these services are offered through a special school or class; often they are provided for individual students in a regular class. Illustrative of services that may be available are reading, speech, and hearing clinics; sight-saving and Braille

[20] Betty Lee Chessman (ed.), A *Handbook of Information for Students, Parents, and Teachers*, Downers Grove Community High School, 1952, pp. 20–21.

classes; facilities for crippled youth; and services for the home-bound.

At this point we merely mention the importance of providing for students at all intellectual levels. As measured by intelligence tests, the abstract intellectual ability of students is lower now than formerly. This fact, coupled with changes in vocational expectations, has often led to the work being geared to average or slow students while superior ones suffer from inattention, boredom, and lack of intellectual stimulation.

Insufficient attention to the gifted has fostered charges of "anti-intellectualism." In our valiant efforts to educate all comers, it is little wonder that we have felt pressures toward uniformity and mediocrity. Preoccupation with quantity has at times endangered quality. The pendulum has on occasion swung far toward setting up programs that fail to challenge the more able individuals to their maximum achievement and quality of work.

The launching of Sputnik I in 1957 jarred the public into wrestling anew with the problem of identifying and educating the academically talented high school students. The loudest shouts arose immediately for ferreting out superior students in mathematics and science and training them swiftly. Concern for progress in science and technology has seemed to blind us temporarily to the significance of other fields. Our talent search for potential scientists and mathematicians should not deter us from carrying on a quest for the gifted in other areas such as social science and the creative arts.

The danger inherent in accepting preparation for the greatest possible service to society as a valid criterion for what education for the gifted should accomplish was appropriately stressed by Lewis M. Terman:

The current *Zeitgeist*, under the influence of the cold war, is pointing up the need for many more scientists and engineers than we have, with the result that a desperate effort is being made to increase their number. Granted the great need for such increase, that fact should **not** lead to the neglect of other kinds of talent. What I propose is **that** education of the gifted should be planned not merely to satisfy the **felt** needs of a given time but also to prepare the way for future appreciation of needs not yet recognized. By encouraging the development of all kinds of special talent and of aptitude for every kind of leadership and scholarly achievement, the *Zeitgeist* itself would, in time, be molded along more liberal lines and to the appreciation of whatever enlarges the spirit of men.[21]

Of the many suggestions for dealing with the problem of educating the academically talented, one of the most widely publicized reports is that of James B. Conant, president emeritus of Harvard. He is concerned about identifying the gifted early, preferably in the higher elementary grades, and persuading them to enroll in those subjects which correspond to their ambitions and abilities. He advises that the academically talented, who constitute about 15 percent of the high school population, take 4 years of mathematics, 4 years of one foreign language, 3 years of science, in addition to the required 4 years of English and 3 years of social studies. This program will require at least 15 hours of homework each week. To this recommended minimum program, many students may wish to add a second foreign language or an additional course in social studies.

For the 2 or 3 percent of the high school population who are exceptionally gifted Conant recommends, if their numbers warrant, special classes so that by the senior year they will be ready to anticipate some part of a freshman year in college. If such a formal program is not possible, then the gifted should be challenged by advanced work in the academic courses of the senior year.

For the other 85 percent of the student body Conant proposes that general education occupy one-half to two-thirds of the time, and that an elective program directed toward development of a specialized talent or vocation take up the remainder. He thinks that students should be oriented toward a vocation when they choose their studies in the eleventh and twelfth grades, even though they may change their minds before the high school course is over, or later. He outlines these requirements for graduation for all

[21] National Society for the Study of Education, *Education for the Gifted*, Fifty-Seventh Yearbook, 1958, Part II, p. 17.

students: 4 years of English, 3 or 4 years of social studies, 1 year of mathematics, and 1 year of science.

Recognition of the urgency of upgrading provisions for the academically gifted should not imply making schooling any less satisfactory to below-average and average youth. As a democracy we cannot with impunity adopt procedures which will hinder the school in its basic task of educating *all* youth for satisfying and productive living. As Hollinshead, former president of Coe College, reminds us: "Such faults as our system may have result from the generous grandeur of an idea unique in the world. Our future does not lie in retreat to lesser ideals. It lies in the enrichment and invigoration of what is already ours."

Work Experience

The term work experience has a number of meanings. According to one definition, "Work experience is that experience which students obtain through participating in production of needed goods or services in a normal situation in industry, business, community at large, or school, under the direction of the schools."[22]

The idea of work experience by no means belongs to this century. However, the lean years of the depression with their widespread unemployment brought into sharp focus the problem of making a living. Studies of young people in the 1930's, such as Homer P. Rainey's *How Fare American Youth?* and Howard M. Bell's *Youth Tell Their Story*, indicated that young people were concerned about adjusting to the world of work. Their paramount problem was to find employment and economic security. Acquisition of vocational skills and of knowledge of personal and social relationships on the job became matters of prime urgency.

Various plans are used to enable students to combine school and work experiences. Under one plan they engage in part-time work after school. Under another they work in teams of two and alternate their activities during a period of time (usually two weeks to one month) so that while one is in school the other is on the job.

---

[22] *Adapting the Secondary School Program to the Needs of Youth, op. cit.,* p. 183.

Under still another they spend half the day on the job and the remainder in school. The last plan, which normally involves only juniors or seniors, is the most prevalent.

Whether or not students should receive pay for work that they do in a school program gives rise to sharp controversy. Ivins and Runge suggest the following principle: *"Schools maintaining or establishing work programs shall see to it that students, generally, are paid for their work, except when that work is of a type which is ordinarily contributed freely by the worker for reasons of group welfare or service to other individuals."*[23]

At least eight factors should be considered in applying this principle:

1. Most productive work is paid for in the normal work world.
2. Students get much satisfaction from personal earnings.
3. Students learn to use money wisely through earning at work.
4. Training has money value as well as other values.
5. Many students need financial aid in order to continue in school.
6. Many laws require that students be paid for certain kinds of work.
7. Most community and group welfare work is unpaid.
8. In some situations, pay for student work may arouse opposition from organized labor.[24]

Work Experience in East Hampton, Connecticut. Through work experience a school may fully utilize community resources. The East Hampton (Connecticut) High School furnishes a case in point. East Hampton is an industrial town of 4000 population. Most of its people are employed in its bell and bell-toy factories and its plants that make fish lines and wire products. The people own unpretentious houses, drive average automobiles, and live conservative lives. Insistent upon sound education, they have co-operated in initiating a diversified curriculum.

Regularly planned work experience has now been made an important aspect of the educational program of East Hampton High School. The

[23] Wilson H. Ivins and William B. Runge, *Work Experience in High School*, The Ronald Press Company, 1951, p. 132.

[24] *Ibid.*, p. 133.

plan provides that for 4 days each week all seniors of the industrial arts and commercial curriculums will spend the first two periods in local offices, factories, stores, and garages. They do the same jobs as the regular employees, but less is expected of them especially as to quantity production. One industrial arts teacher and one commercial teacher are scheduled to supervise this work during those two periods, to go through the community and into the industries to arrange for work opportunities, and to help iron out any difficulties which may arise in connection with pupil employment. The pupils are marked on their work experience jointly by these school faculty members and by their employers.

During the past 2 years the industrial arts pupils have elected the following types of work experience: radio repair, machine shop, carpentry, printing, silkscreen work, auto mechanics, and power shovel operation. These have all been in local industries and with local contractors.

This work experience program has given the pupils an opportunity to acquire a great deal of knowledge about the type of work in which they think they would like to engage as adults. Sometimes they discover that the work they have selected is not to their liking and that they would be better off in some other line of work. Many of last year's pupils who benefited from this program are now employed in the industries in which they had their guided work experience. Employers state that because of this arrangement these students are far better trained and have a greater understanding of their jobs than other high-school graduates. In some cases the work experience has also inspired graduates to further their education in trade or technical schools.

Commercial pupils find work experience in typing, shorthand, bookkeeping, and general office work in the various offices in the community. In addition, a group of such pupils has formed a school-centered corporation, known as "Office Services, Inc.," for the purpose of supplying commercial services to the community. This corporation does typing, duplicating, simple bookkeeping, and filing for local business firms. Members are on call from 3 to 5 P.M. on school days and all day Saturday. Facilities of the school's commerce department are available for their use. The project is organized as an informal corporation with 100 shares of stock authorized. Eighty percent of the remuneration for work done goes to pay the pupil, and 20 percent goes to the corporation. Funds accumulated by it are used for the purchase of supplies, equipment, and other operating expenses. If there is a surplus, dividends are declared. The payroll clerk keeps a record of hours worked by all members of the organization. Salaries are paid once a month on the basis of these records. Wages are calculated on an hourly basis, but if it takes a pupil longer than an hour to do an hour's work, he gets paid for only 1 hour.[25]

SUMMARY

Because of social and technological changes, the modern secondary school must serve a growing clientele with diverse needs, abilities, and interests. The needs of youth and of society have to be considered in formulating the objectives of secondary education. These objectives find expression in the activities which comprise the curriculum. The traditional subject-centered curriculum persists in the majority of high schools. Sometimes the term core curriculum is used to designate all or part of the program of general education. The core may vary from a group of logically organized subjects required of all students to an experience-centered curriculum consisting of activities planned by teacher and students in terms of perceived needs. Extraclass activities are sponsored by most high schools and are coming more and more to be recognized as an integral part of the curriculum. Most secondary schools also furnish many special services, including guidance, provision for exceptional students, and opportunity for work experience.

QUESTIONS AND EXERCISES

1. How have social and technological changes affected the responsibility of the secondary school?
2. Why do youth drop out of school? How has the changing character of its students necessitated modifications in the secondary school? Can the secondary school provide a superior education for the intellectually gifted and still provide appropriate education for the average student?
3. Show the relation between the goals of education and the curriculum. Compare and contrast several statements of the aims of secondary education.
4. What experiences do secondary schools offer to assist young people in meeting their developmental tasks?

[25] Grace S. Wright, et al., Education Unlimited: A Community High School in Action, Federal Security Agency, Office of Education, Bulletin 1951, No. 5, 1951, pp. 27–28.

5. What has been the effect of college entrance requirements on the secondary-school curriculum?

6. Compare the curriculum of a rural high school with 50 or 100 students with that of a city high school with more than 1000 students.

7. What responsibility, if any, does the public school system have for providing an adult education program that will serve the needs and interests of persons past compulsory school age?

8. Formulate a series of principles to govern the administration of extraclass activities in a high school.

9. If possible, visit a high school that has a good guidance program. Ask the guidance counselor to describe it.

10. Summarize one of the reports of the American Youth Commission.

11. State arguments for and against ability grouping.

12. Point out the advantages and disadvantages of acceleration for gifted students. Is an accelerated or an enriched program preferable?

SELECTED REFERENCES

Aikin, Wilford M., *The Story of the Eight-Year Study*, Harper & Brothers, 1942.

Alberty, Harold, *Reorganizing the High School Curriculum*, The Macmillan Company, 1948.

American Association of School Administrators, *The High School in a Changing World*, Thirty-Sixth Yearbook, 1958.

Association for Supervision and Curriculum Development, *What Shall the High Schools Teach?* Yearbook, 1956.

Chase, Francis S., and Anderson, Harold A. (eds.), *The High School in a New Era*, The University of Chicago Press, 1958.

Conant, James Bryant, *The American High School Today*, McGraw-Hill Book Company, Inc., 1959.

"Controversies in Education, The American High School," *Phi Delta Kappan*, November, 1958 (entire issue).

Faunce, Roland C., and Bossing, Nelson L., *Developing the Core Curriculum*, Prentice-Hall, Inc., 1951.

Featherstone, William B., A *Functional Curriculum for Youth*, American Book Company, 1950.

French, Will, and Associates, *Behavioral Goals of General Education in High School*, Russell Sage Foundation, 1957.

Haig, George C. (Dan Stiles, pseud.), *High Schools for Tomorrow*, Harper & Brothers, 1946.

Jacobson, Paul B. (ed.), *The American Secondary School*, Prentice-Hall, Inc., 1952.

John Dewey Society, *The American High School*, Eighth Yearbook, Harper & Brothers, 1946.

Johnston, Edgar G., and Faunce, Roland C., *Student Activities in Secondary Schools*, The Ronald Press Company, 1952.

Keller, Franklin J., *The Double-Purpose High School*, Harper & Brothers, 1953.

Klausmeier, Herbert J., *Principles and Practices of Secondary School Teaching*, rev. ed., Harper & Brothers, 1958.

National Association of Secondary-School Principals, *Planning for American Youth: An Educational Program for Youth of Secondary-School Age*, rev. ed., 1951.

National Education Association, *The Identification and Education of the Academically Talented Student in the American Secondary School*, (The Conference Report), February, 1958.

National Education Association and American Association of School Administrators, Educational Policies Commission, *Education for All American Youth*, 1944.

National Education Association and American Association of School Administrators, Educational Policies Commission, *Education for All American Youth—A Further Look*, 1952.

National Society for the Study of Education, *Adapting the Secondary School Program to the Needs of Youth*, Fifty-Second Yearbook, 1953, Part I.

"The Superior and the Gifted," *School and Society* (A Special Section), May 10, 1958.

Watkins, Ralph K., *Techniques of Secondary School Teaching*, The Ronald Press Company, 1958.

Wright, Grace S., *Block-Time Classes and the Core Program in the Junior High School*, Federal Security Agency, Office of Education, Bulletin 1958, No. 6, 1958.

Wright, Grace S., *Core Curriculum Development; Problems and Practices*, Federal Security Agency, Office of Education, Bulletin 1952, No. 5, 1952.

Wright, Grace S., *Core Curriculum in Public High Schools*, Federal Security Agency, Office of Education, Bulletin 1950, No. 5, 1950.

AUDIO-VISUAL MATERIALS

Films

Broader Concepts of Curriculum (21 minutes, Sound, B & W, McGraw-Hill Book Company, Inc.). Surveying the curriculum of the modern secondary school, this film shows ways the needs of youth may be served through a variety of learning experiences.

High School: Your Challenge (13 minutes, Sound B & W, or C, Coronet Films). Deals with the future importance of a good high school education and the advantages of taking part in extraclass activities. Designed to help handle the drop-out problem.

Mike Makes His Mark (29 minutes, Sound, B & W, or C, National Education Association). An understanding junior high school counselor learns what is troubling a resentful boy headed for serious difficulty and finds ways to interest him in school through help in reading, the electric shop, and the school orchestra.

Recordings

(The) *Core Program in the High School* (30 minutes, 33⅓ rpm, Educational Recording Services). Harold Alberty of Ohio State University explains types of core programs, with special attention to the "problems-of-living" core and its advantages.

Guidance in Modern Schools (30 minutes, 33⅓ rpm, Educational Recording Services). Presentation by Shirley Hamrin, late professor of education at Northwestern University. Guidance is an attempt to help youngsters get the greatest amount of benefit from schooling and prepare them for the next step, whatever it may be. Every teacher has a part in guidance.

(The) *High School Curriculum for Life Adjustment* (30 minutes, 33⅓ rpm, Educational Recording Services). Harl R. Douglass of the University of Colorado traces the history of the curriculum of the secondary school and proposes curriculum changes to fit modern conditions.

Improving the Services of Extra Class Activities (30 minutes, 33⅓ rpm, Educational Recording Services). J. Lloyd Trump of the University of Illinois suggests ways of improving extraclass activities.

CHAPTER XII

Education Beyond the High School

Three centuries ago education beyond the high school was confined to a few colleges simple in organization. Today opportunities have been expanded and diversified to meet the needs of modern society. An almost unlimited number of types of post-high-school education are available to young people of different aptitudes, interests, and abilities from all walks of life who are preparing for a broad range of occupations.

The principal means of satisfying post-high-school educational needs are liberal arts colleges and universities, professional and technical colleges, junior or community colleges, adult education programs, education and training in industry and business, and programs of the armed services.

In this chapter we shall review highlights in the development of institutions of higher learning and point out some of the current problems that beset higher education. We shall give passing mention to three other areas of post-high-school education: adult education, education in industry, and programs of the armed services.

COLONIAL COLLEGES

Religious motives prompted the founding of the colonial colleges. Virtually all of them were denominational and church-controlled, their primary purpose being the training of ministers. On the west gate in Harvard Yard is this inscription: "After God had carried us safe to *New England*, and wee had builded our houses, provided nececaries for our livli-hood, rear'd convenient places for Gods worship, and setled the Civill Government: One of the next things we longed for, and looked after was to advance *Learning* and perpetuate it to Posterity; dreading to leave illiterate Ministery to the Churches, When our present Ministers shall lie in the Dust."

In 1636 the Massachusetts assembly agreed "to give Four Hundred Pounds toward a School or College. . . ." Newtown, later named Cambridge in memory of the English university town, was selected as the site of the new college. When John Harvard, a minister who died soon after its founding, bequeathed to the college his library of 260 volumes and one-half of his estate (a sum about double what the legislation appropriated), the school took his name. Harvard followed English college precedents, particularly those of Cambridge University, and, in turn, set a pattern for later colleges of English America.

For more than half a century Harvard remained the only college in the original colonies. Then William and Mary, named after the English sovereigns, was established in 1693, in the language of the charter, "to the end that the Church of Virginia may be furnished with a seminary of ministers of the Gospel, and that the youth may be piously educated in good letters and manners, and that Christian faith may be propagated among the Western Indians to the glory of God." Phi Beta Kappa, the first intercollegiate fraternity, was established at William and Mary on December 5, 1776. Among the distinguished graduates of the college were Thomas Jefferson, John Marshall, and James Monroe.

In New England, Harvard remained without a rival until 1701 when a third college, Yale, was chartered. One of the compelling motives of Yale's founders was to counteract the liberal religious outlook that had begun to gain ground at Harvard. They required the "Westminster Confession to be diligently read in the Latin tongue and well studyed (*sic*) by all the Schollars, . . . for the upholding of the Christian protestant Religion by a succession of Learned and Orthodox men." Later in 1754, President Clap declared that "The great design of founding this School (Yale), was to Educate Ministers in our *own Way*."

Six other colleges were founded during the colonial period. In all, then, nine colleges date back to colonial times. These, with their location, the date of their founding, and the religious denomination they represented are given in Table 4.

In this group only the University of Pennsylvania, which evolved from Franklin's academy, was nonsectarian. A foreshadowing of less insistence upon religious conformity, however, is noted in an advertisement of King's College in 1754. Although the chief purpose of the college was "to teach and engage the Children to know God in Jesus Christ," in the matter of "particular tenets" everyone was "left to judge freely for himself, and to be required to attend only such Places of Worship on the Lord's Day as their Parents or Guardians shall think fit to order or permit."

Colonial colleges were small and their curriculums classical. Harvard had 20 students in 1642 and 60 in 1660. After that the number

TABLE 4. Colonial Colleges

Name	Location	Year	Religious Character
Harvard	Cambridge, Massachusetts	1636	Congregational
William and Mary	Williamsburg, Virginia	1693	Anglican
Yale	New Haven, Connecticut	1701	Congregational
Princeton	Princeton, New Jersey	1746	Presbyterian
Pennsylvania	Philadelphia, Pennsylvania	1753–1755	Nondenominational
King's College (Columbia)	New York, New York	1754	Anglican
Brown	Providence, Rhode Island	1764	Baptist
Queen's College (Rutgers)	New Brunswick, New Jersey	1766	Dutch Reformed
Dartmouth	Hanover, New Hampshire	1769	Congregational

decreased and remained small until the close of the century. The first 60 graduating classes had an average of only eight members.

The support of colonial colleges came from both private and public sources. Most colleges conducted lotteries to supplement the income received from donations, bequests, and fees.

In the early colleges class consciousness manifested itself in several ways. The relative status of their families determined the official listing of the students' names. At the top of the list was likely to be the son of an eminent clergyman with high social and official connections; he could be outranked only by the son of a colonial governor. Leaders on the lists occupied the best rooms in dormitories and the front places in academic processions. Students seemed indifferent about the rankings, but their families often harassed college presidents after announcement of freshman lists.

BEGINNINGS OF NATIONAL INTEREST IN EDUCATION

Prior to 1800 colleges grew slowly. The 24 in existence by that date had about one hundred professors, between one and two thousand students, and about one million dollars' worth of property. None of them admitted women. They were typically under denominational control, concerned at least theoretically with educating the clergy in the true faith.

A growing spirit of democracy spurred interest in public support and subsidy of a system of higher education free and open to all. Three significant events—one shortly after the close of the Revolutionary War, another during the early part of the nineteenth century, and still another during the Civil War—contributed to the growth of colleges.

First, a provision in 1787 in the bill of sale giving the Ohio Company the right to settle lands west of the Appalachians set aside two townships (72 sections or 46,080 acres) "for the purposes of a university." Upon its admission to the Union in 1803, Ohio became the first state to benefit from this provision. The grant of two or more townships for state universities continued on the admission of each state thereafter, with the result that state universities were created in all the new western and southern states.

Second, the Dartmouth case was instrumental in promoting the growth of colleges. In the early national period people sought a different kind of education and state control over colleges. The newborn spirit manifested itself in attempts by several states to gain control of the colleges within their borders. Eventually New Hampshire tried to convert Dartmouth College, a privately endowed institution controlled by a self-perpetuating board of trustees, into a state university. The case reached the Supreme

Court of the United States, where Daniel Webster, distinguished alumnus of Dartmouth, represented his alma mater. The decision, handed down in 1819, held that the charter of a college constituted a contract that the legislature could not impair. The decision had two important consequences. On one hand, because it guaranteed perpetuity of endowments it encouraged the growth of private colleges. As a result, about five hundred were opened between 1820 and 1860. On the other hand, since the states could not take over private colleges, they established their own state universities.

Third, the Morrill Act gave an impetus to the establishment of institutions of higher learning. In the middle of the nineteenth century agitation grew up against the classical type of college because it neglected the agricultural classes. Since the existing colleges ignored the swelling dissatisfaction, Justin Morrill, senator from Vermont, proposed federal aid to meet the situation. The first Morrill Act was passed by Congress in 1859, but President Buchanan vetoed it on the ground that it violated the traditional policy of leaving control of education to the states. However, the bill was passed again in 1862 and signed by President Lincoln. Under this act, income from public lands (30,000 acres for each Representative and Senator in Congress) became available to each state for land-grant colleges to foster education in agriculture and mechanic arts. Each state was left free to decide whether the college should be made part of an already established institution or whether it should be an entirely separate institution. Today there are 69 land-grant colleges—one in each of the 50 states and in Puerto Rico, a second institution in Massachusetts, and 17 separate colleges for Negroes. These have shared in grants aggregating almost 11½ million acres of public land.

FROM THESE BEGINNINGS

Space does not permit a review of all the steps in the growth of higher education. Suffice it to say that as more and more Americans have wanted to go to college, public and private institutions have been established so that today we have over 1800 institutions of higher education. Tax dollars, as well as dollars contributed by philanthropists like Rockefeller and Stanford, have vied to support these diverse educational enterprises.

The liberal arts colleges are the most numerous as well as the oldest of the institutions of higher learning. They number well over 700 and educate one-fourth of the college population. As a separate college, not affiliated with a university, the liberal arts college is peculiar to this country. Ordinarily it offers a Bachelor's degree on the basis of a four-year program beyond the completion of the secondary school. It has a proud tradition of being a stronghold of cultural education. However, beset with demands for inclusion of "practical" subjects, many a liberal arts college has yielded to expediency and offered a heavy sprinkling of vocational courses. Few have clung solely to the classic thesis.

Universities enroll about one-half of the students in higher education. They are complex institutions that typically incorporate within one organization a liberal arts college as well as a number of other undergraduate and professional colleges. They also maintain a graduate school, offering Master's and Doctor's degrees.

"A university is, or should be, a place dedicated to the adult pursuit of learning." Thus wrote Howard Mumford Jones of Harvard. It does not confine itself to the activities of teaching. It is concerned with carrying on research, with advancing human knowledge. The spirit of inquiry pervades its atmosphere.

In response to public demands the university does not limit itself to the campus. It has assumed active community service. So heavy are its commitments in this area that Jones believes universities may be overplaying their hands in this matter of service. "Extreme busyness in the name of service, of teaching, of committee work, of laudable outside activities first threatens, then curtails, and finally overwhelms many conscientious and able specialists who might in other circumstances have devoted themselves to thought." Although the university should not abandon its admirable relation to the state, it must remain "the capital and fortress of thought." "Our noisy and pleasant activities on the campus," Jones warns, "fill the ear with sound, but at the heart of the university there should always be a zone of silence, a quiet and protected place away from the market and the Rotary Club, where our best men can discover truth, preserve it, and diffuse it, not as service but as an idea. This is the core of the university concept, and if we lose it, we lose everything."

Many professional, technical, and specialized colleges have come into being in the United States. Among them are colleges for the preparation of teachers. Since many of the readers to whom this book is addressed may become teachers, it is appropriate to note briefly the history of these institutions.

The first normal school in the United States was a tuition school founded in 1823 by Samuel Read Hall. In the absence of professional books on teaching printed in English, Hall taught his classes by means of lectures based on his own knowledge of teaching. Later he collected his lectures into a volume entitled *Lectures on School-Keeping*, the first book for the professional education of teachers printed in English in the United States.

The first public normal school was opened in Lexington, Massachusetts, in 1839, with three pupils and one teacher, Cyrus Pierce, who also served as principal and janitor. Later in the year another school appeared at Barre, and the following year still another at Bridgewater. These schools trained teachers for the elementary level only. In this way the European double-track system of teacher education came to the United States. Says William F. Russell, president of Teachers College, Columbia University:

Thus, the American normal school always, from the start, was on a lower pay level, lower grade, less respected than the college or university; and this fact contributed greatly to the lack of development of these institutions. America has always treated the normal school as the chorus of peers in Iolanthe did when they commanded in song, "Bow down, ye lower middle classes." Under the circumstances, it was difficult for these schools to attract the quality of student body and faculty characteristic of the college and university, and legislatures customarily made smaller grants per student. It was a vicious circle; low public regard, low expenditure, less attractive, less good work, lower regard, and so on *ad infinitum*.[1]

[1] William F. Russell, "The Truce That Failed," *Improving Standards for the Teaching Profession*, National Commission of Teacher Education and Professional Standards, 1953, p. 23.

Russell suggests that another factor in the bad start that teacher education got in the United States may have been the French origin of the normal school (*école normale*). Many things French were suspect among Americans, for they were under the ideological influence of countries that had been ranged against the French during the Napoleonic Wars.

However, as Russell says, "The European idea that the normal school is a sort of an on-the-other-side-of-the-tracks institution and the francophobe suspicions of any agency of Napoleonic origin, imported into the United States, are inadequate to explain the depth and strength of anti-teacher education. The basic cause is a general underestimation of the work of the teacher and the school."[2]

Undeniably teacher education has waged an uphill fight. Gradually the old two-year normal schools moved in the direction of four-year curriculums. The first normal school to become a teachers' college was the Michigan State Normal College at Ypsilanti which granted its first AB degree in 1905. By 1913 there were nine teachers' colleges and by 1920 there were 46. Thereafter the number increased rapidly. Today many of the teachers' colleges have five years of work, usually leading to a Master's degree. Several also offer six years of work.

Despite lowly beginnings and inadequate financial support, teachers' colleges have succeeded in raising their standards, until most of them are fully accredited institutions. Although not yet accorded the prestige of the best liberal arts institutions, they are gaining in stature and favor. Impartial observers concede that an appreciable number of teachers' colleges have equipment, staff, and standards equal to, or better than, those of many liberal arts colleges.

HIGHER EDUCATION FOR WOMEN

Any account of the development of higher education would be incomplete without mention of higher education for women. Before the establishment of the academy, women had a dearth of

[2] *Ibid.*, p. 23.

educational opportunities. Late in the eighteenth century the Female Seminary, Finishing School, and Female Institute appeared on the American scene and paved the way for women's colleges. Indeed, some of the seminaries later became colleges.

Although not originally of collegiate rank, Mount Holyoke, chartered by the Massachusetts legislature in 1836, and opened in the fall of 1837, with Mary Lyon as principal, was the first college for women.[3] From 1834 to 1837 Miss Lyon traveled over New England by horse and buggy and sometimes by train, expressing her views on higher education for women and trying to raise funds for establishing a college. Donations during that period ranged from six cents to one thousand dollars. Businessmen said that she was "unsexing women" and that trying to teach women was "as silly as trying to teach cows." But Miss Lyon struggled on and finally won out. She is quoted as saying, "Oh, how immensely important is this work of preparing the daughters of the land to be good mothers. If they are prepared for this situation, they will have the most important preparation they can have for any other: they can soon and easily become good teachers and then will become in all events, good members of society." The first year 80 students were accepted; the next year 400 were refused because of lack of room.

Vassar Female College was incorporated in 1861, and opened to students in 1865. To quote from the Vassar catalogue: "The founder gave practically his entire fortune to support his idea that women were entitled to the same educational opportunities as men." Bryn Mawr was incorporated in 1880, and began its first academic year in 1885. Randolph-Macon Woman's College was founded in Virginia in 1891, and opened in 1893. Its president stated his belief that there was a place in the South for a college that should give to young women the same educational advantages that were offered to men.

In 1833 Oberlin College, Ohio, admitted women on an equal footing with men, and coeducation, as it is now understood, had its beginnings there. According to its catalogue, "young ladies

[3] The Georgia Female College, chartered at Macon in 1836, is sometimes regarded as the first college for women.

attended recitations with young gentlemen in all the departments."
Oberlin awarded the AB degree to three women in 1841. In the
1850's Antioch College, under the presidency of Horace Mann, also
became coeducational. Nearly all state universities established
after 1850 admitted both men and women. The older private institutions, however, did not readily relax their rules to admit women.
Today nearly two-thirds of the institutions of higher learning in
the United States are coeducational.

The tremendous growth of higher education for women is under-
scored by the fact that they comprise nearly one-third of the enrollment in colleges and universities. Approximately one-sixth of the
institutions of higher learning are women's colleges.

The mounting enrollment has turned the spotlight on current
and long-range needs of women resulting from the impact of
changing social conditions. Women college graduates today face
two major choices: the choice of a family or a career. But even
though she may work a while after graduation, the average young
woman eventually chooses marriage and a family. She probably
agrees with William James that "The aim of a college education
is to teach you to know a good man when you see him." Upon
marriage, a woman may continue her career or abandon it either
temporarily or permanently. Thus the women's college has the
responsibility of preparing its students for what really adds up to
two careers.

Some women's colleges advocate a thorough-going revision of
their curriculums so as to offer a combination of liberal and technical arts. President Lynn White, Jr., of Mills College (California)
points out that women's colleges were modeled after men's colleges
and that with few exceptions their courses have paralleled the
curriculums of men's colleges ever since. The result is that "women
are educated to be successful men. Then they must start all over
again and learn to be successful women."

Other women's colleges cling to the traditional pattern. President Margaret Clapp of Wellesley sees no reason why education
should be different for men and women. "They have the same
functions as members of a community, the same functions as voters

and volunteers." President Clapp believes that college students' minds, male or female, are broadened by the same studies.

JUNIOR OR COMMUNITY COLLEGE

About the middle of the nineteenth century several university presidents proposed transferring the first two years of college work to secondary schools. These leaders felt that the end of the sophomore year marked a dividing point in advanced work. Only students who could map their courses without close supervision should proceed into the upper division. Thus universities would be freed of the burden of freshman and sophomore instruction. Such was the idea of President William Rainey Harper when toward the close of the nineteenth century the University of Chicago was reorganized into two units. The lower unit, including the freshman and sophomore years, was first called academic college and later junior college. Through Harper's influence the first public junior college to survive was established at Joliet, Illinois, in 1902.

Like the high school the junior college for many years had a doubtful status as a public institution. The legality of using public school funds for maintaining junior colleges was questioned. Finally in 1930 the Supreme Court of North Carolina in the case of Zimmerman versus the Board of Education in Buncombe County held that the city of Asheville had the power "to establish, maintain, and operate the junior college as a part of an adequate system of public schools." This verdict was as memorable for publicly supported junior colleges as the Kalamazoo decision was for high schools. Currently more than half of the states have enacted legislation providing for junior colleges.

The growth of the junior college has been spectacular. It was accelerated after World War II to furnish accommodations for returning veterans and it has continued in order to take care of the ever-growing college population. In 1957–1958, 548 junior colleges enrolled over one-fifth of the total first-time college students in the United States.

Some junior colleges, as for example in Iowa and Kansas, are organized, controlled, and largely supported by high school districts. Others, as Eastern Arizona College at Thatcher, Montgomery Junior College in Maryland, and Mesa County Junior College in Colorado, are organized on a county basis. Still others are organized as districts, embracing two or more high school districts or various combinations of sponsoring political subdivisions on a flexible pattern. Tyler Junior College District in Texas is composed of the city of Tyler and 16 independent school districts. In Mississippi public junior colleges have been organized by zones, varying in size from one county to seven. There are also state junior colleges as in Utah, for example.

Most chief state school officers think that the ideal method of financing junior colleges is by combinations of state and local effort. Development of junior college programs has tended to be greatest in those states which furnish rather generous state aid. Among them are California, Texas, Washington, Mississippi, and New York.

At its inception the junior college was a two-year institution that followed the twelfth grade of high school. In some communities it evolved into a four-year unit, grades 11–14, closely articulated with the secondary school. The 6-4-4 plan has enjoyed considerable popularity, especially in cities where a large enrollment in high school justifies support of a junior college.

At first junior colleges gave courses little or no different from those of the first two years of the four-year college, their concern being the preparation of students for transfer to senior colleges. Later, terminal courses were featured to serve the interests of students with a wide range of abilities and ages. Wherever available, these courses have proved the choice of more than half of those enrolled, many of whom are part-time students and adults.

The broadening purpose of the junior college has brought into our vocabulary the term community college. Currently the terms junior college and community college are often used interchangeably. However, the term community college tends to emphasize the fact that the institution studies the needs of the community it serves and builds its program on the basis of such needs. Joint faculty-citizen committees assist in devising appropriate courses and curriculums that reflect community life.

The community college normally enrolls many adults and part-time students. Some seek a type of educational service that might be termed remedial. They may have had substandard education or they may have dropped out of school before completing their high school education. Others seek to broaden their range of cultural appreciations. Courses in the appreciation of literature and of the fine arts usually prove popular. Still other adults seek wholesome avocational pursuits. The increase in the amount of leisure time enjoyed by the average citizen encourages him to cultivate avocational pursuits which will yield a maximum of enjoyment.

Programs are flexible enough to meet the varying goals, interests, and abilities of adults and part-time students. Some courses may carry no credit. Some may be only a few weeks in length.

The community college is experimenting with programs to prepare students for a level of occupational training between the professions, which require a university education, and trades and vocations which require only high school preparation. Inquiries in New York revealed that a professional engineer could utilize about six technologists who had only part of the training he had had. Often a tailor-made training adapted to a certain industry is desired for a particular area. Where community colleges have curriculums in harmony with such requirements, they have had gratifying success.

The community college has the advantage of low cost to the student. Since he can usually live at home, costs are reduced and thus the opportunity for education, especially for young people from families in the lower income brackets, is broadened.

Usually junior or community colleges are operated in the same buildings as high schools. Sometimes they have a special wing but often they use the same rooms as the high school students. The problem is to maintain a feeling of separateness while securing the educational and economic advantages of one overall operation and plant.

Teachers in junior or community colleges ordinarily do not have preservice education designed specifically to prepare them for their position. They are recruited from high schools or colleges, especially the former. About two-thirds hold Master's degrees. For the teacher in vocational fields actual employment service is deemed essential. Courses in education should include material relating directly to the junior college, and student teaching should be done in a junior college rather than in a high school or college.

SOME CURRENT PROBLEMS

Who Should Go to College?

The twentieth century has witnessed a remarkable expansion in all areas of higher education. Enrollment has gone up at an unprecedented rate. In 1900, the college enrollment in the United States was only 237,592, approximately 4 percent of those of college age. By 1920, it had increased to 8.1 percent of the college-age group. By 1940, the figure had reached 15.6 percent, and by 1950, 20 percent. In other words, during the first half of this century, the ratio of actual to potential college enrollment had increased fivefold. By 1957–1958, 3,068,000 young men and women were on the rolls of colleges and universities—45 percent more than six years earlier, although the number of young people in the 18-to-21 age bracket had increased only 2 percent in the same period.

If the present trend continues, institutions of higher learning will be called upon to serve ever-increasing numbers. If our proportional attendance of college-age youth were to increase by 1 percent up to 50 percent by 1970, enrollment would reach nearly six and two-thirds million. Many consider this figure entirely too conservative.

The upsurge in attendance that will tax the capacity of colleges to the utmost is causing people to raise the question, Who should go to college? We are being reminded that living in a democracy does not in and of itself confer the right to a college degree. Ability to do college work and not desire alone to attend college must be given more weight than ever before as a criterion for admission to college.

Since individuals differ in their native capacities and motivations, we should recognize that providing equality of educational opportunity does not mean providing identity of opportunity. A college education is not the only avenue to human dignity and social worth. As John W. Gardner, president of the Carnegie Foundation for the Advancement of Teaching has put it:

> Properly understood, the college or university is the instrument for *one kind of education beyond the high school for those whose capacities fit them for that kind of further education*. It should not be regarded as the only passport to a meaningful life or the sole means of establishing one's human worth. And we have come perilously close to that.
>
> . . . .
>
> The more we allow the impression to get abroad that only the college man or woman is worthy of respect in our society, the more we contribute to the fatal confusion, which works to the injury of all concerned. If we permit the faulty assumption that college is the sole cradle of human dignity, need we be surprised that every citizen demands to be rocked in that cradle?

Similarly I. L. Kandel believes that "To admit all students who wish to enter college may be a perfect expression of the democratic ideal, but it is not socially or financially justified, particularly when other avenues for education beyond the high school are now available."

There is another side to the argument, however. Many competent authorities warn against restricting college and university enrollment to the academically elite. President Virgil M. Hancher of the State University of Iowa holds that in a democracy we must believe in the individual's right to an opportunity for the development of his powers to their highest potential. "To deny him this opportunity is as much an assault upon his individual worth and dignity as are poverty and degradation and slavery."

The Problem of Securing and Educating College Teachers

"Our nation," according to the Second Report of the President's Committee on Education Beyond the High School, "like the prodigal farmer, is consuming the seed corn needed for future harvests. The ultimate result could be disaster." Thus does the Committee approach the discussion of the impending shortage of college teachers.

The Committee recommends that top priority be given to raising salaries as a means of remedying the shortage of good teachers. Noting the serious decline in the purchasing power of faculty salaries since 1940, the report points out that an increase of 100 to 125 percent would probably be required to restore it by 1970. At present rates, only one in eight college teachers can expect ever to earn more than $7500 a year. The Committee further recommends provision for moderate-cost faculty housing, health and life insurance, and other benefits for the teaching staff.

"The plain fact is," the Committee says, "that the college teachers of the United States, through their inadequate salaries, are subsidizing the education of students, and in some cases the luxuries of their families, by an amount which is more than double the grand total of alumni gifts, corporate gifts, and endowment income of all colleges and universities combined. This is tantamount to the largest scholarship program in world history, but certainly not one calculated to advance education." The Committee figures that college teachers, by working for the low salaries they have long accepted, are contributing more than $800 million a year to the students of their schools—more than $3500 per teacher.

Financing Higher Education

The flood of students in institutions of higher learning poses a problem of financial support. Funds are not available to keep pace with needs. To secure additional money calls for tapping many sources.

One of the major sources is the voluntary private contributions. In 1956, these exceeded $500 million. An average of $500 million each year for the next ten years is still needed. Business and industry are heavy contributors. In 1956, their estimated contribution was $100 million, a gain of $60 million since 1950.

Foundations are directing an increasing amount of their resources to higher education. For example, in 1956 the Ford Foundation granted $260 million to private educational institutions to increase teachers' salaries and $90 million to private medical schools. Total foundation grants in 1957 amounted to $600 million from philanthropic sources. The danger of external control arising from the acceptance of philanthropic grants should be recognized. In recent years there have been several instances of powerful foundations awarding grants upon the condition that the recipients carry out plans prescribed by the donors.

Alumni are increasing the level of their financial support through annual giving, individual special gifts, and bequests.

Hikes in student fees have been common in recent years. However, they cannot absorb a substantially greater proportion of the cost of higher education. An average of 60 percent of the full cost of attending privately controlled institutions is paid by the student, although the proportion varies from 10 to 90 percent at different institutions. Students in public institutions pay an average of 20 percent of the total cost of a college education with the proportion varying from practically nothing to 50 percent in different institutions. The mean expenditure for tuition in public institutions in 1952–1953 was approximately $150, while that in private institutions was $550. Since then tuition fees have increased sharply. If students were obliged to pay the full cost of education, the result would be a drastic restriction in educational opportunity or a clamor for the federal government to bear major responsibility for financing higher education.

More and more colleges and universities have turned to the federal government for funds. Some authorities predict that by 1970 the federal government will meet at least one-third and perhaps more of the total bill for higher education of youth. However, many institutions distrust federal aid because they fear jeopardizing their independence.

Traditionally colleges have sought gifts primarily to build up endowment funds. Alfred P. Sloan sums up a changing point of view in this advice: "Let's cut out gifts to endowment. . . . I do not believe that relying on endowments is making the most effective use of your money. You need capital—not only more money for expansion and development but money to take care of the deficits that you are facing."

The Curriculum

A prominent issue in higher education centers around the question of what should be taught. The place of liberal and specialized education continues a matter of debate. The traditional belief that there is a necessary antithesis between the two has not disappeared. However, there is growing recognition that they are complementary parts of complete education. The well-educated person must be both a generalist and a specialist. If he is to avoid being lopsided, he needs more than the subject matter of his particular field. The Commission on Higher Education for American Democracy took cognizance of this fact in its 1947 report when it observed: "The present college programs are not contributing adequately to the quality of students' adult lives either as workers or as citizens." This lamentable state of affairs had come about, the Committee believed, "because the unity of liberal education has been splintered by overspecialization."

Joseph R. Passonneau, dean of the School of Architecture at Washington University, has made a strong plea for a well-rounded education. "An education that teaches you to design a crankshaft, solve a particular equation or conduct a particular business deal is not only trivial but, more important, it is useless. The one thing of which we can be certain is that any technical facts we teach you will be out of date before you graduate. The only useful education is that education which prepares you for the art of living."

The state of near panic about our apparent lag in scientific achievement after the launching of the first Sputnik, led to cries for more emphasis on science at the expense of the humanities. Among the level-headed educators who raised voices in protest was John T. Rettaliata, president of the Illinois Institute of Technology (Chicago), which has the largest undergraduate enrollment among engineering schools in the United States. Said Rettaliata:

There is as much national danger in too much science at the expense of liberal arts as there is of too much liberal arts at the expense of science. Let us not allow the Sputnik scare to cause an over-emphasis of science, or turn in panic to hasty expedients of crash programs which, while promising immediate advantage, weaken our long-range endeavor. Higher education should strive to develop individuals of the kind described by the mathematician and philosopher, Alfred North Whitehead—"men who possess both culture and expert knowledge."

ADULT EDUCATION

With swiftly changing social, technological, and political conditions, citizens often find it desirable and necessary to continue their education throughout their adult life. Growth of adult education programs has been dramatic. They have taken such diverse forms as evening classes; continuation schools; part-time vocational classes in job-related subjects; and short unit courses, especially in agriculture and homemaking. One out of every three adults in the United States is engaged in some kind of continuing education annually. The reasons for seeking such educational opportunities vary. Some mature people must have special training for occupational advancement. Others wish to fill gaps in their formal education, while still others desire to enrich and to improve daily living and citizenship. For the growing segment of our population nearing the age of retirement or who have already retired, programs to help make the later years meaningful have special value.

Sir Richard Livingstone set forth the idea that the primary task of adult education is to continue that education for citizenship which the formal schools can do little more than begin. He argues that there is neither time nor space in the curriculum of the elementary and the secondary school to teach all that the citizen needs to know. Besides, the immature cannot penetrate to any depth in the realms of citizenship and social and personal values. Accordingly, society should provide education for adults.

In 1953 the Bell Telephone Company of Pennsylvania sent with full salary 17 of their young executives from middle levels of management to a specifically organized institute of humanistic studies for executives on the University of Pennsylvania campus for a ten months' study. They were sent not for more courses in management, finance, or contracts but for courses in systematic logic, Oriental philosophy, American history, modern poetry, and fiction.

EDUCATION IN INDUSTRY

According to the report of the President's Committee on Education Beyond the High School, as many people are enrolled in education and training programs in industrial plants and business offices as are now enrolled in all colleges and universities. Eighty-eight percent of the five largest corporations have programs in this field. Some are brief training periods for inducting new employees. Others involve fairly lengthy periods of vocational education, usually to prepare skilled workmen. Often academic education is combined with the vocational. Some "company colleges" have broad curriculums for the instruction of managerial and top clerical personnel.

Labor, as well as management, has engaged in educational efforts. Labor unions, in addition to teaching about trade unionism, have developed staffs to provide education about such things as American foreign policy, social implications of the development of atomic energy, economics, arts and crafts, and foreign languages.

PROGRAMS OF THE ARMED SERVICES

The armed services are making a significant contribution to the training and development of civilian technical skills. The skills with civilian application are principally in the classifications of electronics technicians and of aircraft and engine mechanics. In 1955 over 400,000 service personnel received specialized training in civilian-type specialties of all sorts.

SUMMARY

The chief means of providing for post-high-school educational needs are liberal arts colleges and universities, professional and technical colleges, junior or community colleges, adult education programs, education and training in industry and business, and programs of the armed services.

The founding of the early colleges in the United States was prompted by religious motives. Throughout the colonial period colleges remained small, and their curriculums classical. In the nineteenth century the growth of institutions of higher learning was fostered by grants of land for state universities, the Dartmouth case, and the Morrill Act.

Today we have over 1800 institutions of higher education. The liberal arts colleges are the most numerous as well as the oldest. They number over 700 and educate one-fourth of the college population. Universities enroll about one-half of the students in higher education. They incorporate within one organization a liberal arts college as well as a number of other undergraduate and professional colleges, plus a graduate school. There are also many professional, technical, and specialized colleges.

The first public teacher-education institution was the normal school at Lexington, Massachusetts. Originally normal schools had two-year curriculums for the preparation of elementary teachers. During the twentieth century they have become four-year teachers' colleges. Today many of these colleges have expanded their courses to five years, usually leading to a Master's degree. Several also offer six years of work.

Higher education for women had its beginnings with the founding of Mount Holyoke College in 1837. Earlier, in 1833, Oberlin College had opened its doors to women on an equal basis with men. Today, women comprise one-third of the enrollment in colleges and universities. The mounting enrollment has focused attention on current and long-range needs of women stemming from the impact of changing social conditions. In addition to provisions for post-high-school education in institutions of higher learning, other opportunities are available in the areas of adult education, education in industry, and programs of the armed services.

The junior college, which came into being near the opening of the twentieth century, now enrolls nearly one-fifth of the total first-time college students in the United States. The broadening purpose of the junior college has brought into our vocabulary the term community college. Programs are flexible in order to meet the varied needs of students.

The skyrocketing enrollment in institutions of higher learning poses many problems, among which are determining who should go to college, securing college teachers, financing higher education, and planning the curriculum.

QUESTIONS AND EXERCISES

1. How did the founding of colleges and universities influence the public school movement?
2. Why did education for women develop so slowly in the United States?
3. Trace the development of teacher education in the United States.
4. Summarize arguments for establishing community colleges.
5. Distinguish between the parallel and the ladder type of schools.
6. Why was the Dartmouth case significant? Should the state exercise any control over private colleges?
7. What accrediting agencies have approved the college in which you are enrolled?
8. State arguments for and against limiting college attendance to the academically gifted.
9. Should tuition fees be raised to cover the full cost of higher education?
10. What requirements does your college have to provide students with a liberal education?
11. Familiarize yourself with the organization and control of higher education in your state. Are the state-supported colleges and universities under one board?

SELECTED REFERENCES

Bogue, Jesse Parker, *The Community College*, McGraw-Hill Book Company, Inc., 1950.

Brubacher, John S. and Rudy, Willis, *Higher Education in Transition*, Harper & Brothers, 1958.

Carmichael, Oliver C., *Changing Role of Higher Education*, The Macmillan Company, 1949.

Committee for the White House Conference on Education, A

Report to the President, Superintendent of Documents, U.S. Government Printing Office, April, 1956.

Diekhoff, John S., *Democracy's College,* Harper & Brothers, 1950.

Harper, Charles A., *Development of the Teachers College in the United States,* McKnight & McKnight, 1935.

Hilliway, Tyrus, *The American Two-Year College,* Harper & Brothers, 1958.

Justman, Joseph and Mais, Walter H., *College Teaching: Its Practice and Its Potential,* Harper & Brothers, 1956.

Marshall, Helen, *Grandest of Enterprises,* Illinois State Normal University, 1956.

National Society for the Study of Education, *The Public Junior College,* Fifty-Fifth Yearbook, 1956, Part I.

Pollard, John A., Fund-Raising for Higher Education, Harper & Brothers, 1958.

President's Commission on Higher Education, *Higher Education for American Democracy,* Harper & Brothers, 1949.

Tead, Ordway, *The Climate of Learning: A Constructive Attack on Complacency in Higher Education,* Harper & Brothers, 1958.

White, Lynn, Jr., *Educating Our Daughters; A Challenge to the Colleges,* Harper & Brothers, 1950.

Woody, Thomas, *A History of Women's Education in the United States,* Science Press, 1929.

AUDIO-VISUAL MATERIALS

Films

A Decade of Achievement (20 minutes, Sound, C, University of Michigan). A report from the president of the University of Michigan on progress from 1946 to 1956 in the expansion of plant, enrollment, and campus.

A Longer Shadow (15 minutes, Sound, C, Southern Regional Education Board). Narrated by Senator Lister Hill of Alabama, this film is about the SREB and its program of regional coöperation among 16 southern states in the field of higher education. "Education helps a man to stand taller, to cast a longer shadow in the world around him."

Accent on Learning (30 minutes, Sound, B & W, Ohio State University). Shows teaching techniques used by some teachers at the Ohio State University.

Bennington (21 minutes, Sound, B & W, U.S. Information Agency). Produced by the U.S.I.A. to depict this type of college in our overseas information program. Emphasis on students as individuals is illustrated. Bennington's "widened out campus" is shown as we see students during their nonresident term.

Campus Comes to the Steelworker (18 minutes, Sound, B & W, Pennsylvania State University). An overview of the coöperative plan for workers' education sponsored by the Pennsylvania State College and the United Steelworkers of America.

Colby College (30 minutes, Sound, C, Sloan Foundation). Made by the Foundation to show the influence of a small college on a community. Colby was selected as "the prime example of the kind of small college which must be preserved since it demonstrates in essence what is valuable about such an educational institution."

College: Your Challenge (11 minutes, Sound, B & W, Coronet Films). Tells benefits of college which high school students may expect.

Community College (30 minutes, Sound, C, Mount San Antonio College). Depicts typical community college program of vocational and transfer student activities, community relationships, and district organization.

Day of the Tartan (17 minutes, Sound, C, Carnegie Institute of Technology). Alumnus Charles E. Wilson introduces and narrates much of the film to launch a fund-raising campaign for a building program.

Endowing Our Future (27 minutes, Sound, B & W, Sears-Roebuck Foundation). Explains the critical problems confronting higher education in America and what can be done about them.

Frontier (25 minutes, Sound, C, University of Buffalo). Opening with a broad view of the Buffalo-Niagara area, this film soon focuses on the University of Buffalo, "an urban university close to the people," and emphasizes the important role of this type of institution in present-day society.

Notre Dame (29 minutes, Sound, C, University of Notre Dame). This motion picture shows something of the student body, academic life, and the role of the church at Notre Dame. Distinguished faculty are shown at their research, and information is presented on the operating costs of this university.

Oxford Student (12 minutes, Sound, C, McGraw-Hill Book Company, Inc.). Shows something of life today in the more than 30 colleges at the University of Oxford, including small classes, tutorial supervision, and reliance on individual initiative. "Here dates and facts are only the footnotes of an education."

Princeton (20 minutes, Sound, B & W, Princeton University). Interesting portrayal of the history and traditions of Princeton and of its current offerings.

Take Time for Tomorrow (15 minutes, Sound, B & W, U.S. Army, United World Government Films). Educational opportunities available to all military personnel while in service.

The Five Worlds (25 minutes, Sound, C, University of Miami). This film gives direction to students in selecting a career from among the "five worlds," and it shows in some detail how each of these worlds is explored at Miami.

To Go to College (23 minutes, Sound, C, New Jersey Education Association). The film visualizes a report on present and future needs of higher education in New Jersey. Present crowded conditions in the various state institutions are shown as each president tells us of the problems particular to his college.

To the Age That Is Waiting (43 minutes, Sound, B & W, or C, Harvard University). Much of this film is narrated by President Pusey who tells us something of Harvard's history while rare, early newsreels illustrate memorable events. Harvard today and its plans for the future are also presented.

Waves of Green (38 minutes, Sound, C, Dearborn Motors, produced by Jam Handy). Contributions made to agriculture by the landgrant colleges and their extension services.

Recording

The Community College and Its Function (30 minutes, 33⅓ rpm, Educational Recording Services). Discussion by Jesse P. Bogue, Executive Secretary of the American Association of Junior Colleges, Washington, D.C.

PART FOUR

ADMINISTRATION AND FINANCE

Courtesy, St. Charles (Missouri) Public Schools

Courtesy, Champaign (Illinois) Community Schools

The concept that education in a legal sense is a state function may easily be proved. Its roots had been firmly embedded in the past by colonial law that foreshadowed state law, its pattern was developed through ordinances governing the territories that were to become states. When the United States became a reality the structural pattern of education as a state function began to grow through general reservation of power in the federal constitution, through positive expressions in state constitutions, and through state statutory practice and judicial review.

. . . .

Finance is a universal tool of social and institutional control. In the establishment of a state educational system and maintenance of local schools, finance is always a shaping and often the governing factor. This follows from the fact that in contemporary education, as, indeed, in all forms of enterprise, nearly everything in the way of goods and services must be bought and paid for. It is a simple matter to discontinue a line of educational activity by denying it financial support, or cause it to flourish by increasing its revenue. From this circumstance has arisen the saying that the purse is power.

Lee M. Thurston and William H. Roe,
STATE SCHOOL ADMINISTRATION

Part Four, Administration and Finance, gives an overview of how schools in the United States are administered and financed. It shows that the degree to which schools are operated and controlled under local self-government makes them responsive to the people. To maintain the kind of schools a great country deserves, requires generous financial support.

CHAPTER XIII

Public School Administration

In no other country in the world do people exercise so much direct control over their schools as in the United States. In most foreign countries control is from above; policies are handed down from a central authority to the local units. So much control is exercised over every phase of education that local autonomy and initiative as they prevail in the United States are unknown. The Minister of National Education in France who confidently claimed that he could look at his watch at nine o'clock in the morning and tell what was being taught in every classroom in France did not speak idly. The United States Commissioner of Education would have no basis in fact for such a boast.

Although we commonly refer to the "American educational system" there is not a national system in the strict sense. There is instead a highly complex organization composed of many unique units.

With the growing complexity of school systems, a complicated administrative machinery has become necessary. We recognize it as a means to an end, not as an end in itself. In the last analysis it exists to create conditions under which learning can best take place. Upon its structure and operation hinge the kind and quality of education we offer. Dewey once observed:

"It is easy to fall into the habit of regarding the mechanics of school organization and administration as something comparatively external and indifferent to educational purposes and ideals. . . . We forget that it is precisely such things [as grouping in classes, grading, machinery of curriculum making, selecting, assigning, paying, and promoting teachers] that really control the whole system, even on its distinctively educational side."

In the administration of schools in the United States local, state, county, and federal governments play significant roles. Over the years their functions have been delineated by tradition and statute. This chapter sets forth in broad outline some major features of administration.

LOCAL ADMINISTRATION

The tradition of local control of schools in the United States dates back to eighteenth century New England. Originally each town consisted of one small community within an area of 20 to 40 square miles. Settlers lived within a half mile of a meeting house. The town meeting ran school affairs, often delegating them to special committees. As newcomers arrived land became increasingly scarce and they penetrated farther into the surrounding wilderness. New communities grew up within the town, often several miles from the seat of government. Before long people in the more remote areas were paying taxes to the town but were too far away to send their children to town schools. Education was indeed sketchy. A wandering teacher went from community to community conducting classes on the spot for a few days each year.

Eventually the town was divided into districts, one for each settlement. In a wilderness practically devoid of means of travel, schools had to be within walking distance of the pupils. Thus the size of a district was almost literally determined "by the length of the children's legs." Each district was responsible for its own school. The people elected a local board of laymen or a school committee to spend tax money and to supervise the local school.

Through its board, the community kept control of its schools. The "little red schoolhouse" with its single teacher for pupils of every age became a tradition that has by no means disappeared from the American scene.

Despite its shortcomings, the district organization gave citizens a sense of responsibility for the welfare and support of their schools. The early settlers contributed time, money, or materials to construct school buildings, the first of which were log cabins. Districts vied with one another in raising their schoolhouse. The occasion was a gala affair. An account of one of these raisings indicates that everything was donated except some special "spirits" which were purchased out of the district treasury. The initial purchase was one gallon of "spirits" for 45 cents. When the stock became depleted at a crucial point in the work, the school committee called an emergency meeting and spent 25 cents on a half gallon of "spirits" to finish the job.

A quarter to a half acre of land on which the school building was erected was either donated or purchased, usually at a crossroads. The location of the school building was regarded as a matter of such moment that one historian has said: "Questions involving the fate of nations have been decided with less expenditure of time, less stirring of passions, less vociferation of declamation and denunciation, than the location of a fifteen-by-twenty district schoolhouse. I have known such a question to call for ten district meetings, scattered over two years, bringing down from mountain farms three miles away men who had no children to be schooled, and who had not taken the trouble to vote in a presidential election during the period."[1]

Although originally intended for a rural United States of more than a century ago, the district system still flourishes.[2] Some progress has been made in improving the organization. The number of local districts declined from 127,244 in 1931–1932 to about 45,000 in 1958–1959.

That there are still too many districts is indicated by the fact that only about one district out of every eight is large enough to employ as many as 40 teachers. More than three out of every four

---

[1] George H. Martin, *The Evolution of the Massachusetts Public School System*, D. Appleton & Company, 1904, pp. 93–94.

[2] There are at least 60 different titles and 17 classifications of school districts. Howard A. Dawson, Director of Rural Service of the National Education Association, states that school districts or administrative units can for all practical purposes be classified as follows: (1) common school district, (2) community school district, (3) city or "independent" school district, (4) town or township school district, (5) county school district (county unit), (6) separate high school district.

employ ten teachers or less. More than half of all the districts in the country operate elementary schools only. Thousands operate no schools at all.

Students of school administration recommend that a district should be large enough to employ at least 40 teachers and to enroll 1200 pupils in grades 1 through 12. California laws set 10,000 pupils as the desirable minimum enrollment for newly formed districts, and only in unusual situations permit the formation of new districts with less than 2000 pupils. Pennsylvania school laws recommend a minimum of 1600 pupils per district.

The School Board

The immediate governing body of a district is a board, variously known as a school committee, board of school trustees, board of education, or board of directors. By court decision such a board has been held to be a state agency rather than an adjunct of local government. It operates under state sanction and is the legal educational authority for a district. It may delegate authority, but responsibility for the conduct of schools is under its jurisdiction. It may even be held personally responsible for money not spent according to law.

The board is a policy-making body with broad prerogatives, but with its powers and duties limited by state law. Its chief responsibilities are:

1. To develop and constantly improve the educational program.
2. To provide personnel for staffing the school program.
3. To provide and maintain an educationally efficient physical plant.
4. To secure adequate financial resources.
5. To maintain a two-way contact with the adult community and the schools.
6. To choose the chief executive and work harmoniously with him.[3]

Some features of school boards should be pointed out. Boards are chosen in different ways. About 85 percent are elected by popu-

[3] American Association of School Administrators, *School Board-Superintendent Relationships*, Thirty-Fourth Yearbook, 1956, p. 35.

lar vote, the rest being appointed, usually by the mayor, city council, city manager, judges, or some other city, county, or state
agency. In communities where board members are elected, they are
usually chosen on a nonpartisan basis and at large rather than by
wards or districts. Election by wards has proved unsatisfactory
because members feel that their first duty is to their ward rather
than to the entire city.Whatever the method of choice, members
must have lived in the school district for a specified time.

Most boards have from five to nine members with terms of
three to five years. To assure continuity and to avoid upheavals
based on strong feelings or political considerations, the terms are
staggered or overlapping. Ordinarily members serve without pay.
On the average one in ten members is a woman.

Although special qualities have not been determined for board
members, it is generally agreed that they should be sensible, fair,
tolerant, coöperative, civic-minded, honest, and courageous. They
should represent all the people of the community, not any one
interest or group. They should have a sincere desire to minister
to the educational needs of all the children in their district. Added
to all these qualities should be an ability to direct the business
affairs of the school.

The board elects its officers at the first meeting after an election.
The usual officers are a president, who presides at the meetings,
and a secretary, who records the meetings and sometimes also
serves as treasurer.

Superintendent of Schools

According to accepted educational theory, the lay board determines matters of overall policy and the superintendent and his
staff carry them out. Until the nineteenth century the board tried
to supervise all phases of school operation. Finally, the task became
so vast that schoolmen were employed to execute policies. In the
1830's Buffalo (New York), Louisville, Providence, St. Louis, and
Springfield (Massachusetts) appointed superintendents for their
districts. By 1870, 29 other cities scattered throughout the United
States had followed suit. Thereafter other cities rapidly joined the

movement and the office of superintendent was firmly entrenched.

At first the superintendent was little more than a head teacher with supervisory duties. He looked after the purchase and distribution of supplies and the operation and maintenance of buildings, and he collected data about the school system. Eventually, he rose from a lowly to a leading place. Selected and employed by the board of education, he is its chief executive officer charged with carrying out its program. He is looked upon as a professional adviser of the board. He is usually responsible for every aspect of administration, both business and educational. He is in charge of the selection and improvement of teachers and of what is taught and how it is taught. His influence extends beyond the confines of the school to the entire community. His is a key position of leadership.

In a smooth-running school organization only the chief executive is legally responsible to the board. However, in all but the smallest systems he has administrative and supervisory assistants to whom he turns over responsibility and authority.

The organization shown in Figure 4 is used in Lincoln, Nebraska. It is a modification of the plan proposed by Hill and Brownell, directors of the Cooperative Study of the Lincoln Schools.[4] It will be noted that a single executive is responsible for all the activities of the schools.

Many school systems recognize the need for setting up machinery so as to assure democratic administration. For years the superintendent was considered to be more sympathetic with the board than with the teachers. He handed down orders and directives to persons under his authority. Today he is regarded not only as the agent of the board but as the representative of the teaching staff. He keeps the machinery of administration running smoothly, but he avoids using his authority to make arbitrary decisions. He affords teachers an opportunity to participate in enterprises that concern them, and he encourages them to exercise leadership in accordance with their interests and abilities. Superintendent and

[4] Clyde M. Hill and S. M. Brownell, *Lincoln Looks Ahead*, Board of Education, Lincoln, Nebraska, 1947, p. 92.

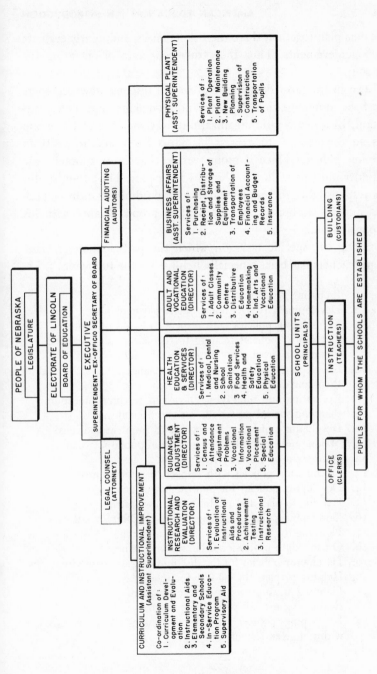

FIGURE 4. Administrative Organization of Lincoln, Nebraska, Schools.

teachers plan together, share their experiences, and jointly evaluate their achievements. Thus they truly coöperate in operating the schools.

Even in the most democratic of school systems, however, there must be differentiation between policy-making and policy-execution. In a democratic organization every member of the group has an opportunity to express his ideas freely and to assist in shaping policies. Once a group verdict has been adopted, the minority must be willing to abide by the policy. The administrator has responsibility for implementation and administration of policies, and his authority must be kept in proper balance with his responsibilities.

Among the specific tasks on which the participation of classroom teachers has been especially helpful are the following:

1. Preparing a salary schedule.
2. Developing a twelve-month salary payment plan.
3. Formulating policies with respect to leaves of absence.
4. Developing policies relating to the selection of teachers.
5. Planning a program of inservice education.
6. Developing a plan for teachers exchanges.
7. Preparing curriculum plans and materials.
8. Evaluating and modifying classroom teaching procedures.
9. Planning special provisions for exceptional pupils.
10. Developing policies with respect to pupil promotions.
11. Making policies and plans for school public relations.
12. Planning a community survey.
13. Formulating policies with respect to pupil transportation.
14. Developing policies for pupil management and discipline.
15. Helping to plan and readjust teaching loads.
16. Developing policies relating to the eligibility of athletes.
17. Planning the schedules of individual schools.
18. Organizing a professional library for teachers.
19. Developing policies for the distribution and use of visual aids.
20. Helping to plan the budget for schools.
21. Planning an improved guidance program.
22. Developing over-all policies for homeroom periods.
23. Developing policies on various phases of administration within a given school.

24. Helping to determine the standard items of equipment and supplies and the standards to be used in their selection.
25. Helping to select textbooks and reference materials.
26. Planning a new system of pupil records and reports.
27. Helping to plan new school buildings.
28. Developing policies with respect to pupil awards.
29. Formulating policies for the extracurricular program.
30. Preparing a local code of ethics for the staff.[5]

Not only is the entire school staff drawn into shaping school policies, but the board of education, nonteaching personnel—such as clerks, custodians, nurses, and cafeteria workers—lay representatives, other than school board members, and pupils are asked to share the responsibility.

Particular attention has been given in recent times to making the general public true partners in educational planning. No longer need the people's natural interest in their schools be displayed as in Lichty's cartoon that has the legend, "Who says I don't take an interest in his education? . . . don't I complain about taxes, find fault with the system, criticize the teachers? . . ." Through coöperative educational planning, interest is turned into constructive channels. In 1949, to help people work for better schools in their own communities, a group of laymen with Roy E. Larsen, president of Time, Inc., as chairman, formed a National Citizens' Commission for the Public Schools with headquarters in New York City. The Commission set for itself two immediate goals: first, to help Americans realize how important our public schools are to our expanding democracy; and second, to arouse in each community the intelligence and will to improve our public schools.

Inspired by the Commission, nearly two thousand local groups organized themselves into special committees to involve laymen in planning for the schools. In 1955, the Commission was succeeded by a grass roots organization, the National Citizens Council for Better Schools, dedicated to arousing citizen interest and

[5] Department of Classroom Teachers and Research Division, National Education Association, *Democracy in School Administration*, 1953, pp. 9–11.

increasing broad understanding essential for proper school support.

In 1955, some 500,000 citizens had an opportunity to express their views on education through a series of conferences at local, county, and state levels. Culminating these meetings was the White House Conference on Education attended by more than 1800 delegates selected at the state level. Two-thirds of the participants were lay representatives; one-third were school people. Their discussions centered around six topics:

1. What should our schools accomplish?
2. In what ways can we organize our school systems more efficiently and economically?
3. What are our school building needs?
4. How can we get enough good teachers—and keep them?
5. How can we finance our schools—build and operate them?
6. How can we obtain a continuing public interest in education?

Intermediate Units

Operating between the state department of education on one hand and the local district on the other is the intermediate unit. As defined by the National Commission on School District Reorganization, it is "an area comprising the territory of two or more basic administrative units and having a board, or officer, or both, responsible for performing stipulated services for the basic administrative units or for supervising their fiscal, administrative, or educational functions."[6] Its officer or board exercises only supervisory or service functions in relationship to basic units.

With the exception of Delaware, Nevada, and 12 county-unit states, all the states have intermediate units. They are of three types: supervisory union, township, and county. (Data do not include Alaska and Hawaii.)

In New England and New York, school districts are grouped into supervisory unions composed of two or more basic local units. Their superintendents or supervisors, usually professionally qualified men, are appointed, often for indeterminate terms. Tenure

[6] *Your School District*, National Commission on School District Reorganization, Department of Rural Education, National Education Association, 1948, p. 52.

is long and salaries are above the national median for rural super-intendents. Duties are limited in scope and effectiveness.

The superintendent of a supervisory union administers the schools of two or more towns, not necessarily adjoining. He is neither a city nor a county superintendent, although his position has some features of both.

In a few states the township performs the functions of an intermediate unit. Usually, however, it is not comparable to a county unit or to a supervisory union.

In 27 states the county is the intermediate unit.[7] Only 16 of these states have county boards of education. All 27 have county superintendents. In seven these officers are appointed, but in 20 they are elected by popular vote, often on a party ballot. They are often considered county officers whose status is defined by law, rather than educational personnel officers.

The intermediate superintendent should know what constitutes good education, so that he can guide toward improvement. He should understand thoroughly the communities and the people he serves so that he can work with them in planning appropriate programs. Above all, he needs to know how to win their support for improved education.

Many factors tend to hinder the effective functioning of the intermediate-unit superintendent. He usually secures his office by popular vote, often on the regular party ticket. He is a member of the civil government of the county, with "many of the trappings of political office" which tend to deter educational leadership. His duties are handed down by the state and by tradition and often are delegated directly to local school boards. Since he must work with numerous local boards, he has difficulty in unifying educational services. The reorganization of school districts means that he must devote more school funds and more thought to problems involving school transportation. Always he is hampered by the

---

[7] The county as an intermediate unit should not be confused with the county as a basic unit in the 12 county-unit states. In these 12 states independent city districts in the county units are administered directly by their local city superintendent and other schools are administered directly by a county superintendent of schools.

lack of funds to provide educational services that will supplement and enrich local programs.

Reorganization of local school units on a natural community basis, as contrasted with a township or district basis, has altered the nature of the county superintendent's work. With this type of reorganization he is not so much a supervisor and business manager as a consultant on professional matters. Excerpts from a report by McClure compare his old and new duties:

Hiring of teachers: Before reorganization—direct recommendation to local boards. After reorganization—advising local superintendents on employment policies.

Supervision of teaching: Before—direct and personal contact with teachers; visits to classrooms. After—indirect supervision only; works through local superintendents.

In-service training: Before—arranging an annual teachers' institute. After—coordinating county-wide institutes, workshops, curriculum studies. (Here, county superintendents are providing valuable services.)

Special subject-matter areas: Before—trend for art, music, industrial arts supervisors to operate through county school office. After—trend for local districts to hire their own. (But many local districts are still too small to employ special instructors.)

Health, guidance, special education: Before—when supplied, usually operated at county level. After—more are operated by local districts. (Many schools don't have them; in many others, services are poor.)

Public relations, finances, recordkeeping, school business affairs: Changes are similar. Local schools are taking over jobs formerly done in the county office. "As schools reorganize, there's a tendency for functions of the county superintendent's office to become ritualistic."[8]

Illustrative of the expanding services and activities of the county superintendent's office is a list reported for Los Angeles County, California.

1. A visual-aids library consisting of 8000 films and a proportionate number of film strips, slides, recordings, and study prints. These instructional aids are purchased by an annual contribution from the local

---

[8] William P. McClure, *Role of the Intermediate Type of County Superintendency*, in *Education Summary*, October 5, 1952, p. 2.

districts of 50 cents per child in average daily attendance. The county superintendent's office provides the supervisory assistance and transportation necessary for making these teaching aids readily available for constructive use in every district.

2. Two special schools maintained in sanitariums and hospitals to meet the special needs of physically handicapped children.

3. Eight special school programs, maintained under the cooperative supervision of the office of the county schools and the county probation department, for boys and girls of elementary and junior high-school age who for some reason are not able to adjust to the normal program.

4. A special director of trade and industrial education to assist with the development and operation of trade and industrial education programs in the local districts.

5. A number of psychologists who assist the local districts in setting up their guidance and counseling programs and give individual help in cases of serious maladjustment.

6. A cooperative school library service.

7. A coordinator of speech education who gives speech diagnostic services to children in the local districts.

8. An audiometer-telebinocularist who tests the hearing and vision of children, organizes otological clinics, and gives guidance and counsel to local districts in developing testing and remedial programs.

9. School nurse service.

10. A training program for school custodians.

11. A four-week summer workshop for teachers developed thru the cooperation of the county school office, the state department of education, and the colleges and universities located in the county.

12. An extensive program of instructional supervisory services and curriculum development.[9]

That organizational and functional changes must occur if the intermediate office is to justify its existence, seems apparent from studies recently initiated in many states. Several investigations stress the importance of providing leadership, educational services, reporting services, and special instruction. Some envision the role of the intermediate unit as shifting from one of instructional improvement service to one of general administration, and business and finance service.

[9] American Association of School Administrators, *The American School Superintendency*, Thirtieth Yearbook, 1952, p. 372.

STATE GOVERNMENT AND EDUCATION

The founding fathers were wary of any central authority. As is explained later in the chapter, they wrote the Constitution without mentioning the word education. Under the blanket powers of the Tenth Amendment, education is committed to the several states. With 50 separate units responsible for education, rather than a single unit, the threat of the use of education by a would-be national dictator is reduced to a minimum. Furthermore, each state is free to experiment with systems of education best suited to local needs. The late Justice Brandeis maintained: "It is one of the happy incidents of the Federal system that a single courageous State may, if its citizens choose, serve as a laboratory to try novel social and economic experiments without risk to the rest of the country." Under this freedom of experiment our present state systems of education evolved.

In recognition of their obligation to provide education, most state constitutions direct their respective legislatures to make provision for the establishment and maintenance of schools. Usually they give only this general charge. Some, however, designate structure and organization and define powers and duties of school officials.

Except insofar as restraints are placed upon it by the state constitution, the legislature is a free agent in educational matters. It sets up public schools and specifies any organization it chooses for administering them. If one method of administration and maintenance fails, it may try another. It has power to tax and to distribute taxes to local agencies. It licenses teachers and prescribes general conditions affecting their work. It sets up compulsory school laws. It may create districts, delegate authority to local communities, and require the agencies to whom authority is granted to exercise it.

As laws multiply, their interpretation and application to specific cases raise questions that are finally settled in the supreme court of the state or of the United States. Complete understanding of the legal basis of a state school system calls for knowledge of the constitution of the state, its statute law, and the interpretation of both of these by the courts.

In furnishing education the state does not act from charitable or philanthropic motives. Instead, it acts on the principle that the school is a service to the community for the benefit of the state. This point is clarified in a decision of an Illinois court:

The public school system of the State was not established and has not been maintained as a charity or from philanthropic motives. The first legislative expression in regard to schools in Illinois was in the Ordinance of 1787, which declares that: "religion, morality and knowledge being necessary to good government and the happiness of mankind, schools and the means of education shall forever be encouraged."

This declaration grew, not out of philanthropic motives, but out of a consideration of the essentials of good government. The conduct and maintenance of schools by school directors, school trustees, and boards . . . is no less an "exercise of the functions vested in those charged with the conduct of government," is no less a part of "the science and art of government," and deals no less with the "organization, regulation and administration of a state" in its internal affairs, than the construction and maintenance of roads by the commissioners of highways; the conduct and maintenance of charitable institutions of the State by the board of administration; the inspection of factories, and the enforcement of the laws for the protection of workmen and in regard to the employment of women and children, by the factory inspectors; the performance by the industrial board of the duties imposed upon it by law, and the performance of many duties by public officials, which, however beneficial to individuals, are not undertaken from philanthropic or charitable motives, but for the protection, safety, and welfare of the citizens of the State in the interest of good government.[10]

The execution of school laws is usually entrusted to state boards and educational officers. Three agencies likely to have the most direct relation with local districts are state boards of education, chief state school officers, and state departments of education.

State Board of Education

The Board of Regents of New York, organized in 1784, has the distinction of becoming the first state board of education. Origi-

[10] Scown v. Czarnecki et al., 264 Illinois 305, 106 N.E. 276.

nally formed to administer the colleges and academies which had been authorized for New York by the king of England, it was given control in 1904 of all public schools in the state. In the 1820's North Carolina and Vermont created state boards. They were joined in the 1830's by Connecticut, Kentucky, Massachusetts, Missouri, and Tennessee. Through its far-visioned secretary, Horace Mann, the Massachusetts State Board exerted such profound influence that other states began to set up similar bodies. The movement spread until today 48 states have general boards of education which exercise some control over elementary and secondary schools and, in some instances, over other types of schools.[11]

In addition, every state has one or more boards to perform certain special educational functions. These include boards of trustees or regents for state universities, state colleges, and state teachers' colleges; boards of vocational education and vocational rehabilitation; and boards to choose textbooks, certify teachers, and manage pensions and retirement funds.

The state board of education is a policy-forming legislative body that should furnish the research service and leadership essential to the formulation of sound educational policies. Its powers and duties vary from a few in some states to many in others. Studies by survey commissions and educational authorities indicate 19 powers and duties that should be assigned by law to a state board:

1. To exercise general control over all public schools.
2. To formulate and adopt educational policies.
3. To appoint a chief State school officer, and to prescribe his duties in conformity with State law.
4. To appoint, upon the nomination of the chief State school officer, such assistants to him as are deemed necessary.
5. To adopt such rules and regulations in conformity with State law as may be necessary for its own government and for the government of all its employees.
6. To organize the State department of education upon recommendation of the chief State school officer.
7. To present to the Governor a budget covering the necessary ex-

[11] Illinois and Wisconsin do not have general state boards of education.

penses of the education department and a budget setting forth the amount of State funds that should be appropriated to the school districts of the State and to such institutions as are under the control of the State board.

8. To decide appeals from decisions of the chief executive officer.

9. To recommend to the Governor and the State Legislature such legislation as the board deems necessary for the improvement of the schools under its jurisdiction.

10. To prescribe subjects to be taught in the elementary and secondary schools of the State.

11. To promote equalization of educational opportunities among all youth of the State.

12. To adopt, in conformity with State law, rules and regulations governing the distribution of State school funds.

13. To be responsible for rules and regulations governing the use of Federal funds for educational purposes.

14. To adopt rules and regulations for the construction of school buildings.

15. To adopt rules and regulations for the certification of teachers.

16. To establish rules for the accrediting of all schools of the State.

17. To determine the number and location of State teachers' colleges.

18. To have final approval of the consolidation of schools and of school districts.

19. To see that all the laws relating to the schools under the board's jurisdiction are complied with.[12]

Sometimes, but not usually, the composition of the state board is detailed in the constitution. It falls into four major patterns: ex-officio members, appointed members, elected members, and partly ex-officio and partly elected or appointed members. The trend is away from ex-officio and toward elected or appointed members. In 1954, only three state boards were composed wholly of ex-officio members.

The number of members per state school board in 1954 ranged from 3 in Mississippi to 21 in Texas, with 29 states having 5 to 9 members. Opinions vary as to the ideal size for a state board of education. While it should be large enough to represent adequately the people's interests, it should not be so large as to hinder

[12] Ward W. Keesecker, *State Board of Education and Chief State School Officers*, Federal Security Agency, Office of Education, Bulletin 1950, No. 12, 1951, p. 107.

efficient conduct of business. The Council of Chief State School Officers recommends 7 to 12 members.

The term of office of elected or appointed members ranges from three years in two states to 13 years in one state. The term of ex-officio members is sometimes two but mostly four years. Ordinarily terms overlap to avoid complete change of personnel at any one time.

Most states have certain qualifications or restrictions for state board members. Among those imposed in the various states are: "One member from each congressional district; one or more members must be engaged in educational work; not more than a certain number shall belong to the same political party; no member may be connected with any textbook publishing concern; no person shall be appointed to the board who is in any way subject to its authority; no board member shall hold any other elective or appointive office in the State."[13] Although educational qualifications are not prescribed by law in any state, most state board members have attended college.

Appointed or elected members usually receive no compensation other than for expenses incurred in attending board meetings. In one-third of the states all except ex-officio members receive a *per diem* or small honorarium.

The Chief State School Officer

Not only was New York the first state to have a state board of education but it was also first to create the position of chief state school officer. Early conceptions of the functions of the office are shown in the New York Act of June 19, 1812.

I. Be it enacted by the people of the State of New York, represented in Senate and Assembly, that there shall be constituted an office within the State, known and distinguished as the superintendent of common schools, which superintendent shall be appointed by the council of appointment, and shall be allowed an annual salary of $300, but not to be under pay until he shall give notice of the first distribution of school money, payable in the same way as is provided for other offices, by the act entitled "an act for the support of government."

[13] *Ibid.*, p. 16.

II. And be it further enacted, that it shall be the duty of the superintendent aforesaid, to digest and prepare plans for the improvement and management of the common school fund, and for the better organization of common schools; to prepare and report estimates and expenditures of the school moneys, to superintend the collection thereof, to execute services relative to the sale of lands, which now are or hereafter may be appropriated, as a permanent fund for the support of common schools, as may be by law required of him; to give information to the legislature respecting all matters referred to him by either branch thereof, or which will appertain to his office; and generally to perform all such services relative to the welfare of the schools as he shall be directed to perform and shall prior to his entering upon the duties of his office, take an oath or affirmation for the diligent and faithful execution of his trust.

In 1813, Gideon Hawley became the first state superintendent of schools in the United States. In his zeal to further the cause of public education he offended so many influential politicians that he was fired from his job eight years later and the office was abolished. Not until 1854 was the post recreated.

Like New York, the other states needed someone to represent them in the work of maintaining schools. Furthermore, someone had to represent the state in dealing with local boards. Someone had to disburse state funds, part of which came from permanent funds that had been accumulating for a number of years. Someone had to receive reports, compile statistics, and see that funds were granted and used according to law. The growing awareness of state responsibility for education and the increasing volume of legislation called for an officer to acquaint lawmakers with the wishes of voters and to help arouse public sentiment for schools. To meet these needs, the states began to provide for state school officers.

Today each state has a chief state education officer, most frequently called superintendent of public instruction or commissioner of education. In 33 states authority for his office is derived from the state constitution, and in 15 from statutory enactments.

In 1954, 26 state school officers were elected by the people at popular elections, four were appointed by the governor, and 18 were appointed by the state board of education. The trend is toward the latter method which is considered the most satisfactory because the office can be divorced from politics which means that the officer can devote his time and energy to professional duties rather than to political activities. Moreover, his tenure depends not upon the uncertain turn of the wheel of political fortune but upon merit. Since residence in the state is not a prerequisite for appointment, the board is free to seek the best-qualified person in the country.

The term of office for chief school officers elected by popular vote is two or four years, corresponding to the terms of other elected state officials. The terms of those appointed by the governor usually coincide with the term of the appointing governor. Of those appointed by state boards, approximately half serve definite terms while the other half continue in office at the pleasure of the board. Educational authorities generally prefer a plan that permits the chief state school officer to remain in office as long as his services are satisfactory.

State Department of Education

The chief state school officer should be the administrative head of the state department of education. Subordinate to him in each state are professional employees who make up the staff of the state department of education. The 50 state departments of education employ more than 4000 full-time professional staff members. Most of the larger state departments have divisions in charge of specialists in certain areas such as vocational education and rehabilitation, instruction, school lunch, administration, secondary education, elementary education, Negro education, and special education.

To carry out its functions effectively, the internal organization of the state department of education must be conducive to genuine teamwork. No prevailing pattern is discernible in the departmental organization in the 50 states. In states where sound principles have been observed, services are closely coördinated, with departments having few major divisions and each division having to do with related areas of service.

Figure 5 shows the functional organization in the State Department of Education of Massachusetts.

Originally the duties of state departments of education were mostly clerical and statistical. Today Beach classifies them into three major categories: leadership, regulatory, and operational.[14]

Leadership functions include making long-range plans for state educational enterprises; carrying on research and assisting in the research activities of other groups and agencies; providing consultative and advisory service to the governor, legislature, school systems, and the public in general; coördinating educational programs in the state; and maintaining a vigorous public-relations program in behalf of education.

Regulatory functions serve to protect the lives and health of children and youth; to guarantee economy in the use of educational funds; to promote efficiency in the management of school affairs; to fix minimum standards that apply uniformly throughout the state; and to set up regulations, carry on inspection, and determine compliance with requirements, and where necessary instigate compliance procedures.

Operational functions, unlike leadership and regulatory functions, are not universally recognized as appropriate obligations of a state department of education. They take the department into activities similar to those engaged in by local school authorities. They may include: (1) operation of schools which provide instruction on the elementary, high school, and college levels, including teachers' colleges, trade schools, correspondence schools, and schools for exceptional children; (2) classes, particularly in citizenship, adult education, and trades, for instruction below college grade; (3) programs of service directed to the public at large, such as state libraries, state museums, state archive and history units, film production units, and film libraries; (4) programs of service to individuals, such as vocational rehabilitation programs for persons over the age of 16, teacher-placement services, and teacher-retirement services.

[14] Fred F. Beach, *The Functions of State Departments of Education*, Federal Security Agency, Office of Education, Miscellaneous No. 12, 1950, p. 3.

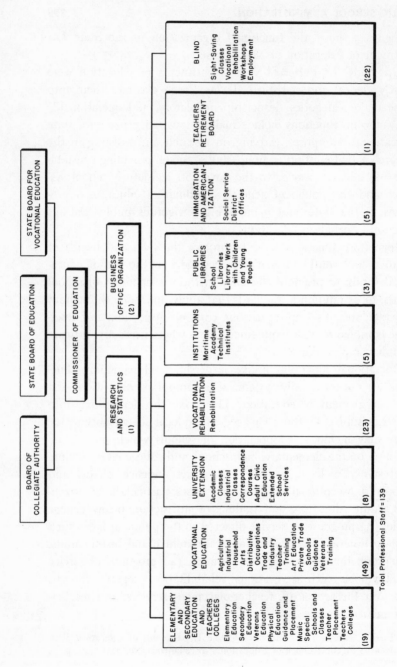

FIGURE 5. Functional Organization Chart for State Department of Education in Massachusetts. (Fred F. Beach and Andrew H. Gibbs. *The Structure of State Departments of Education,* Federal Security Agency, Office of Education Miscellaneous No. 10, 1949, p. 19.)

Improving Organization at the State Level

If state educational machinery is to operate to the best advantage it must be modernized to permit efficient performance of basic services and functions. A composite picture of good practices with respect to the state board of education, the chief state school officer, and the state department of education, which now prevail in some states is given in the following summary:

Lay control of the State education program.—The people of the State are represented in education matters by a lay State board of education. Authority and responsibility for the State elementary and secondary education programs are vested in the State board of education. Such responsibility, of course, includes vocational education and all other phases of elementary and secondary education. The State board is composed solely of able laymen who serve long overlapping terms and are not subject to reappointment or reelection. Members are selected at large in the State in a manner which frees them from partisan political control and makes them truly representative of the will of the people. Members represent no special interest as such and do not receive salary but do receive actual expenses for attending board meetings or a per diem in lieu of subsistence.

The State board of education serves as the single policy-making body for the State elementary and secondary education program.

Professional administration of the State education enterprise.—The administration of the State education enterprise is delegated by the State board to a highly qualified professional chief State school officer. The most important task of the State board of education is the selection of the person to serve as its sole executive officer and head of the State department of education. He is charged with responsibility for carrying out all policies adopted by the State board. His powers and duties and tenure of office are determined by the State board.

Board authority for internal organization.—The State board of education, upon the recommendation of its professional executive, determines divisioning and staffing of the department. The chief State school officer continually studies the education needs of the State. In light of these needs, he makes recommendations from time to time to the State board regarding the staffing and internal organization of the department. He proposes plans for organizing the staff so that the personnel works as a unit in furthering the improvement of education in the State. These plans provide for few major divisions composed of related services, with subdivisions as necessary, similarly composed. The internal organization machinery is simple and flexible and provides for thorough coordination of work.[15]

THE FEDERAL GOVERNMENT AND EDUCATION

The federal Constitution makes no explicit reference to education or schools. We can only conjecture the reasons for the omission. Members of the Constitutional Convention, confronted with an almost superhuman task of reconciling differences, effecting compromises, and establishing a stable government, may have been too busy to take up some problems whose solution could be deferred. If they gave any thought to education, these members, descended as they were from aristocratic ancestors, may have sincerely believed that it should be under private rather than public auspices. Possibly more than anything else they feared a strong central government, and hence preferred to leave education in the hands of the states. Since, as colonies, many states had exhibited concern for educating their children, the framers of the Constitution may have assumed that no action was required. At any rate, not only did they make no mention of a federal school system but they took no action that required the states to set up schools.

With ratification of the Tenth Amendment in 1791, which stipulates that "the powers not delegated to the United States by the Constitution, nor prohibited by it to the States, are reserved to the States respectively, or to the people," the way was cleared for state school systems. Since education is not specifically allocated to the federal government or prohibited to the states, it falls within the jurisdiction of the latter.

However, the relation of the federal government to education still remains somewhat nebulous. The "general welfare clause" in the preamble to the Constitution may be interpreted as conferring authority to engage in educational activity. The preamble reads: "We, the people of the United States, in order to form a more perfect Union, establish justice, insure domestic tranquility, pro-

[15] Fred F. Beach and Andrew H. Gibbs, *The Structure of State Departments of Education*, Federal Security Agency, Office of Education, Miscellaneous No. 10, 1949, p. 18.

vide for the common defense, promote the general welfare, and secure the blessings of liberty to ourselves and our posterity, do ordain and establish this Constitution for the United States of America."

Article I, Section 8 of the Constitution, gives Congress power "to lay and collect taxes, duties, imposts and excises, to pay the debts and provide for the common defense and general welfare of the United States; but all duties, imposts, and excises shall be uniform throughout the United States." Under these two provisions the right of Congress to render financial assistance to education is generally recognized.

Certainly the federal government has always taken steps to encourage education. Its stake in the matter is inescapable in view of the fact that education constitutes the cornerstone of the democratic order.

Office of Education

As early as 1837 Henry Barnard tried to persuade authorities in Washington to create an agency that would collect and diffuse educational statistics and information. After considerable opposition a measure was passed and signed by President Johnson in 1867 authorizing a Department of Education "for the purpose of collecting such statistics and facts as shall show the conditions and progress of education in the several States and Territories, and of diffusing such information respecting the organization and management of schools and school systems, and methods of teaching as shall aid the people of the United States in the establishment and maintenance of efficient school systems, and otherwise promote the cause of education throughout the country."

Two years later the Department was reduced to a Bureau of Education within the Department of the Interior, with resultant loss of prestige and cut in budget. There it remained, its name eventually being changed to Office of Education, until 1939, when it was located administratively in the Federal Security Agency. On April 11, 1953, the Federal Security Agency became the Department of Health, Education, and Welfare, and its Secretary was elevated to Cabinet rank. The status of the Office of Education remains relatively the same even though it is now part of a Cabinet department rather than of an independent agency.

Responsible for the general direction of the Office is the United States Commissioner of Education, who is appointed for a four-year term by the President, subject to confirmation by the Senate.

The activities of the Office are directed through five main channels:

> Division of School Assistance in Federally Affected Areas
> Division of Higher Education
> Division of International Education
> Division of State and Local School Systems
> Division of Vocational Education

Each division is headed by an Assistant Commissioner, and, in collaboration with the other divisions, undertakes all programming and operation within the area of its responsibility.

The Office operates on a modest budget. For the fiscal year 1958, it had a total appropriation for salaries and expenses of seven million dollars. Approximately 645 employees were on the payroll.

To the average person the Office of Education probably seems very remote. Aside from sending out requests for statistical information or for information about educational programs, it ordinarily has no direct relation with the local school system. However, laymen and educators alike should acquaint themselves with the services available through the Office. Reports and publications are obtainable either free from the Office or at nominal cost from the Superintendent of Documents, Government Printing Office. *School Life*, official journal of the Office, published each month of the school year October through June, contains timely information concerning Office planning and action, statistical information of national interest, and federal and state educational legislation. The Office also publishes *Higher Education* each month September through May, with information on federal activities related to higher education.

In addition to keeping abreast of its various publications, local school staffs should know about the assistance offered by the Office through such avenues as conferences, exhibits, radio broadcasts, loans of audio-visual aids, some service to libraries, and occasional advice through correspondence.

SUMMARY

All three branches of government—local, state, and federal—have some functions and responsibilities in the conduct of education. Local administrative units have delegated to them by the state the power and the responsibility for maintaining schools. The immediate governing body of a district is usually a local school board. The executive officer of the board is a local superintendent of schools who may have supervisory and administrative personnel to assist him. Operating between the local district and the state department is ordinarily an intermediate unit which may be supervisory union, township, or county. The officer or board of the intermediate unit has only supervisory or service functions in relationship to basic units. The state has the actual obligation of providing for education. The execution of school laws is usually in charge of a state board of education, a chief state school officer, and a state department of education. Although the federal government exercises no direct control over education, it has a national advisory and research agency, the Office of Education, which promotes the cause of education and discharges some administrative functions. At the head of the Office is the United States Commissioner of Education.

QUESTIONS AND EXERCISES

1. If there is a state department of education in your state, what are its duties and powers? How are its members chosen?
2. How is the chief state school officer in your state chosen? What are his duties and powers?
3. What conditions in American life account for a high degree of local control of education? Point out the strengths and weaknesses of such control.
4. How did the need for increased state control of education arise?

5. What types of school districts are there in your state? Have their number and type changed in the last decade? If so, give reasons for the changes.

6. How are members of the school board chosen in your local district? What is the educational and occupational background of the present members? Consult the school law of your state to find out the powers and duties of the local board. If possible, invite a school board member to visit your class and discuss the functions of the board.

7. Enumerate the principal duties of a city superintendent of schools. If possible, invite a city superintendent to visit your class and discuss his duties.

8. Study a school system in order to ascertain the extent to which teachers participate in formulating school policies.

9. How can lay participation in school affairs be encouraged? What provision is made for lay participation in your home community?

10. Prepare a report on one of these Yearbooks of the American Association of School Administrators:
    The American School Superintendency
    Public Relations in American Schools
    School Boards in Action
    School Board-Superintendent Relationships
    Staff Relations in School Administration

11. Present arguments for and against having the U.S. Office of Education supervised by a national board of lay members empowered to select the Commissioner of Education.

12. Devise a sociodrama to explain to a visiting teacher from England the characteristic features of public school administration in the United States.

SELECTED REFERENCES

American Association of School Administrators, *The American School Superintendency*, Thirtieth Yearbook, 1952.

American Association of School Administrators, *School Board-Superintendent Relationships*, Thirty-Fourth Yearbook, 1956.

American Association of School Administrators, *School Boards in Action*, Twenty-Fourth Yearbook, 1946.

American Association of School Administrators, *Staff Relations in School Administration*, Thirty-Third Yearbook, 1955.

American Association of School Administrators, *The Superintendent as Instructional Leader*, Thirty-Fifth Yearbook, 1957.

Beach, Fred F., *The Functions of State Departments of Education*,

Miscellaneous No. 12, Federal Security Agency, Office of Education, 1950.

Beach, Fred F., and Gibbs, Andrew H., *The Structure of State Departments of Education*, Miscellaneous No. 10, Federal Security Agency, Office of Education, 1949.

Beach, Fred F., and Will, Robert F., *The State and Education*, Miscellaneous No. 23, U.S. Department of Health, Education, and Welfare, Office of Education, 1955.

Knight, Edgar W., *Readings in Educational Administration*, Henry Holt and Company, 1953.

Koopman, George R., Miel, Alice, and Misner, Paul J., *Democracy in School Administration*, Appleton-Century-Crofts, Inc., 1943.

Miller, Van, and Spalding, Willard B., *The Public Administration of American Schools*, World Book Company, rev. ed., 1958.

Moehlman, Arthur B., *School Administration*, Houghton Mifflin Company, 2nd ed., 1951.

National Council of Chief State School Officers, *Our System of Education*, 1950.

National Education Association, Department of Rural Education, *The County Superintendent of Schools in the United States*, Yearbook, 1950.

Pittenger, Benjamin Floyd, *Local Public School Administration*, McGraw-Hill Book Company, Inc., 1951.

Sears, Jesse B., *The Nature of the Administrative Process*, McGraw-Hill Book Company, Inc., 1950.

Shoring Up Legal and Policy Provisions for the Superintendent, American Association of School Administrators, 1957.

Stapley, Maurice E., *School Board Studies*, Midwest Administration Center, University of Chicago, 1958.

Thurston, Lee M., and Roe, William H., *State School Administration*, Harper & Brothers, 1957.

Wahlquist, John T. (ed.), *The Administration of Public Education*, The Ronald Press Company, 1952.

AUDIO-VISUAL MATERIALS

Films

Design of American Public Education (16 minutes, Sound, B & W, McGraw-Hill Book Company, Inc.). Explains organization of the American democratic school system as opposed to an autocratic system.

School and the Community (14 minutes, Sound, B & W, or C,

McGraw-Hill Book Company, Inc.). Problem of separation between the school and the community. Teachers, parents, school officials, and the citizenry share responsibility for bringing them together.

Schoolhouse in the Red (42 minutes, Sound, B & W, or C, Encyclopaedia Britannica Films). Debate in a typical rural community about changing from a system of small rural schools to a larger school district system. Deals with sociological and psychological factors involved.

Recording

A *Superintendent Speaks* (30 minutes, Tape, Minnesota State Department of Education). Describes the joint obligations of teachers and school administrators in carrying forward a sound program.

CHAPTER XIV

Good Schools Cost Money

During T. V. Smith's term as state representative in Illinois an editor of a small-town newspaper opposed a bill to raise teachers' salaries. Mr. Smith relates the story in this fashion:

I went to him one day and I said: "Jim, this is a very anomalous situation. You are one of the most intelligent men I have ever known; and here you are against this bill. I am really afraid you do not know what education is all about." He said: "That is really going too far, that I don't know what education is about. I know all it is about." I said: "What, for instance?" Confronted with the specific question, he said: "Education is—it is to keep the kids out of their parents' hair a sufficient number of hours every day so that the parents can lead their own lives." Then he said: "I think it is worth all its costs. Maybe after all I will vote for the bill. . . ."[1]

To more than one harassed parent the baby-sitting value of education, a value that Mr. Smith dubs "middle-sized," might justify maintenance of public schools. However, there are other more significant reasons for our huge outlay for schools. Social, cultural, aesthetic, and economic values all accrue from education. To Americans who wish to view the problem in a material way, a convincing case can be made for education as an investment in people. In the dark days of the depression in the 1930's Bruce Barton said: "In times like these, invest in boys and girls. Men talk about buying stocks at the bottom. When you invest in a boy or girl, you are always buying at the bottom. You are sure that the youngster

[1] T. V. Smith, "Middle-Sized Values for Higher Education," *Current Issues in Higher Education*, 1952, National Education Association, 1952, p. 54.

is going up and there is no telling how far. I invite every man and woman in America to take a flyer in Children Preferred. I predict a great future for this security. It has an investment merit combined with the most exciting speculative possibilities. You are sure to get a man or woman. You may get a great man or great woman."

Expenditures for education have proved economically productive, as the following makes clear:

The schools are not economic parasites, draining off national income into some nonproductive enterprise. On the contrary, education (a) provides the intelligence and skill essential to modern industry; (b) contributes to health and safety; (c) results in better conservation of natural resources; (d) leads to personal thrift and the development of capital resources; (e) is the basis of efficiency in business management; (f) increases the volume and lifts the level of consumer demands; (g) improves the earning power and spending power of the people; and (h) thru the purchase of buildings, equipment, materials, and thru the salaries of its employees, turns its expenditures quite directly back into the economic life-stream of the nation.[2]

That a positive relationship exists between economic status and educational level has been confirmed by a number of studies. In Table 5 seven countries are compared as to natural resources, educational development, and per capita income. The comparison shows that with high levels of education high standards of living are possible even though natural resources are scant. Where low standards of education prevail, standards of living are low even though natural resources are abundant. For example, Denmark and Colombia present a vivid contrast. Denmark, with poor soil, no natural power sources, and no mineral resources, but with a high level of education, has a favorable economic status and a high standard of living. But Colombia, with millions of acres of rich land, enormous reserves of oil and timber, and a vast range of mineral resources, has a low educational level and low per capita wealth. A country overflowing with natural resources but with a

[2] American Association of School Administrators, *The Expanding Role of Education,* Twenty-Sixth Yearbook, 1948, pp. 281–282.

school system unable to teach the skills to use the resources has one of the lowest standards of living in the world.

TABLE 5.   Natural Resources, Education, and Income

Nation	Natural Resources	Educational Development	Per Capita Income 1952–1954
Brazil	High	Low	230
United States	High	High	1,870
Denmark	Low	High	750
Mexico	High	Low	220
New Zealand	High	High	1,000
Colombia	High	Low	250
Switzerland	Low	High	1,010

SOURCE: John K. Norton, "Education Pays Compound Interest," *Journal of the National Education Association*, November, 1958, p. 557.

Within the borders of the United States we also find striking evidence of the relation of education to productivity. States with a tradition of providing good schools, costing well above the national average, have high per capita incomes. Conversely, states with schools financed at relatively low levels rank low in productivity per person. For example, Connecticut, endowed with limited natural resources, has always given special attention to education, while Mississippi, rich in natural wealth, has always made meager provision for education. In 1956, Connecticut ranked second among the states in per capita income and 9.5 in current school costs per pupil in average daily attendance, while Mississippi ranked forty-eighth in income and forty-seventh in current school costs per pupil in average daily attendance.

For all lands and all ages we reiterate Walter Hines Page's credo uttered at Athens, Georgia, in 1901, "I believe that by the right training of men we add to the wealth of the world. All wealth is the creation of man, and he creates it only in proportion to the trained uses of the community; and, the more men we train, the more wealth everyone may create."

To provide a dynamic system of education to help boys and girls become economically productive citizens requires money—money in ever increasing amounts. With the exception of a few years, the trend in school costs has been almost continuously upward. From $63 million in 1870, total expenditures for public elementary and secondary education rose to more than $14 billion in 1958–1959.

CAUSES OF INCREASED SCHOOL COSTS

Rising school costs may be ascribed to three causes: decrease in the purchasing power of the dollar, increase in attendance, and improved educational standards and services.

One reason for higher school costs is the decline in purchasing power of the dollar. One dollar today is worth about 30 percent of what it was at the turn of the century. Although expenditure per pupil in average daily attendance in current dollars has advanced from $20 in 1900 to $340 in 1958–1959, the increase dwindles in significance when the rise in cost of living is taken into account.

A second reason for growing costs is the growth in school attendance. The school population is more than half again as large as it was in 1900. The mounting birth rate in recent years has beset us with unexpected problems. In 1958–1959, the estimated enrollment in public elementary and secondary schools was over 34.5 million. This figure was 41.5 percent larger than a decade earlier. Each year the typical school district provides for about four additional pupils for every 100 who were in school the preceding year.

Not only has enrollment gone up by leaps and bounds, but with longer school terms and better law enforcement the number of days that children are in attendance has increased. In 1900, schools were in session for an average of 144 days per year. Today they are open roughly 180 days per year. At the turn of the century the average pupil attended school only 69 percent of the time whereas today his counterpart attends 89 percent of the time. Thus the pupils of 1900 attended only 99 days while today's pupils average 160 days in school.

Then, too, the number of children attending the relatively expensive higher grades has reached astonishing proportions. At the turn of the century only 63 percent of the nation's children finished the eighth grade. In 1952 the comparable figure was 88 percent. The growth of high schools has been relatively more rapid than the growth of elementary schools. From less than 5 percent of the total enrollment at the turn of the century, high school enrollment grew until it comprised more than one-fifth of the total enrollment in 1950. In percentages the secondary school enrollments continue to mount faster than elementary school enrollments. In 1958–1959, the increase over the preceding year was 4.4 percent in secondary grades and 3.6 percent in elementary grades.

A third reason for increasing costs is higher educational standards and improvements in school services. Not without their price are our modern artistically constructed and well-equipped buildings located on spacious sites; better-prepared teachers; methods of teaching that call for laboratories, shops, audio-visual aids, and libraries; expansion of curriculum at both elementary and secondary levels; and added services such as pupil transportation, guidance departments, hot-lunch programs, health departments, work-experience programs, summer sessions and camps, and special education for exceptional children.

CAN WE AFFORD THE COST OF EDUCATION?

With spiraling expenditures comes the question, Can we afford the cost of education? Among the factors that we may take into account in trying to answer this query are these: size of the national income; amount of the national income spent for education; amount of the national income spent for other goods and services.

A study of trends in national income shows that we are a prosperous people. From 1939 to 1953 the national income increased more than four-fold—from nearly $73 million to more than $300 billion—and personal income went up a little more than three and a half times. Even with inflation and soaring taxes, Americans have enjoyed increased income. Between 1950 and 1953 taxes rose $15 billion but disposable income, after taxes, rose $46 billion. That we may expect an increase of $160 billion in gross national product between 1953 and 1965 is the conclusion of the National Citizens Commission for the Public Schools.

The amount spent for public education in comparison with the national income is small. In 1930, Americans spent only about 3 percent of the national income on education, and this figure remained about the same in 1956. The projection of school enrollments and future school costs to the year 1965, according to estimates of the National Citizens Commission for the Public Schools, indicates that school expenditures may take only from 3 to 6 percent of the gross national product. Such a modest increase would not interfere with other types of expenditures for goods and services required by our expanded population nor with public expenditures for other services such as hospitals and highways.

The amount spent on public education in relationship to the amount spent on other goods and services is small. In 1956, when Americans spent $10.7 billion for education, they spent $40.6 billion for defense, $15.0 billion for liquor and tobacco, $14.6 billion for automobiles, and $13.8 billion for recreation.

Apparently there is ample margin for the expanding costs of education. As Kaulfers points out, we are not

. . . scraping the bottom of the financial barrel. The amount of money spent each year on gambling alone is over twenty thousand million dollars—or four times the amount of money spent on all forms of education combined. To date the boom has been for gamblers and the bust has been for schools. As Mark Hanna has indicated, even in the highest tax years of the war the American people spent up to six thousand million dollars "just to sit in cocktail bars and get numb" and another eight thousand million dollars "just to watch the rear end of a horse and their money disappear around the race track." Even if the common good should ever require the nation to reduce its chewing-gum bill from a yearly average of more than a dollar per man, woman, and child to a sacrificial low of fifty cents, the strain on the pocketbook would only relieve the strain on the jaw. Who, therefore, can honestly say that we cannot afford to do all an adequate program of education requires?[3]

[3] Walter Vincent Kaulfers, "Our Schools' Vanishing Margin for Disaster," *Progressive Education*, February, 1952, p. 131.

However, the fact that we can afford to finance schools generously does not necessarily mean that we will. "The psychological
point of resistance to taxation is reached long before we actually
reach any danger point in terms of the welfare of the American
people."[4] The element of choice is involved in our spending. Our
folly of niggardly support will continue until we choose to give
education top priority.

If people understood clearly how much they receive for the education dollar they would be unlikely to regard schools as tax eaters.
At a cost of little more than one dollar per day per child, the
education dollar pays for such diverse essentials as instruction,
custodians' services, maintenance and operation of plants, supplies,
equipment, textbooks, health supervision, and sometimes bus transportation. The lion's share of the dollar, approximately two-thirds,
goes for instruction.

WHAT IS THE SOURCE OF THE EDUCATION DOLLAR?

Thorny problems in connection with school finance arise from
the ways in which school revenues are obtained. They come from
three levels of government—local, state, and national. The percentages of all public-school revenue receipts derived from these
levels during 1958–1959 were as follows:

Federal	3.5%
State	39.7%
Local	56.8%

Local Districts

Although the state imposes upon local units the obligation to
provide schools, it usually furnishes them with slight financial
assistance. Over 56 percent of all public school revenue comes from
county and local units. Most of the local revenue (86 percent in
1956) for public schools comes from the property tax. Although
the property tax has the advantage of being easy to collect and of
remaining stable under most economic conditions, it has the dis-

---

[4] National Education Association, Committee on Tax Education and School
Finance, *The Economic Outlook for Public Education*, June, 1952, p. 4.

advantage of not adjusting well to rising prices and population movements. Even more serious, however, is the fact that the tax paying ability of people is poorly reflected today by ownership of property. When we were an agricultural people a general property tax was a natural source of taxation. Property ownership was a fair indication of ability to pay. But now that industry and manufacturing have changed our mode of life, real property represents only a small portion of our wealth.

That sources of income have been changing during recent years is clearly indicated in Table 6, which presents an analysis of the national income in 1929 and 1956. While compensation of employees in the form of salaries and wages increased from 58.2 per cent of the national income in 1929 to 70.2 percent in 1956, farm income declined from 6.8 percent of the total in 1929 to only 3.4 percent in 1956. Clearly, additional revenues must come from intangible sources of wealth where the real wealth is.

TABLE 6.   Sources of National Income 1929 and 1956
(in millions)

	1929		1956	
Source	Amount	Percent	Amount	Percent
Compensation of employees	$51,085	58.2	$241,372	70.2
Corporate profits	10,100	11.5	40,449	11.8
Unincorporated business and professional income	8,791	10.0	28,017	8.1
Farm income	5,968	6.8	11,600	3.4
Rental income of persons	5,425	6.2	10,322	3.0
Net interest	6,445	7.3	11,860	3.5
Total	$87,814	100.0	$343,620	100.0

SOURCE: R. L. Johns, "The Property Tax and Public School Financing," NEA *Legislative Commission*, National Education Association, 1958, p. 4.

Quite aside from the objections already mentioned, glaring inequalities result from property taxes levied on small local units. One district may have manufacturing plants, railroads, coal, iron, copper, and mineral lands, while another has no promising sources of revenue. In Illinois some districts are more than eighty times as able as others to support schools. Contrast Stickney in Cook County, Illinois, which has an assessed valuation per pupil of $288,682, with three towns in Massac County in southern Illinois —Doris Ville with an assessed valuation per pupil of $3539, Johnson City with $4945, and Brookport with $3130. For the nation as a whole the ability of school districts to pay property taxes varies in a ratio of approximately ten to one in states having large districts or county units, and several hundred to one in states with small districts.

States

In recent years the trend has been toward increased state support of schools. In 1958–1959 the states contributed nearly 40 percent of the funds to maintain schools. However, individual states vary in the proportion of school revenue thus obtained. In 1958–1959 in Nebraska only 6.9 percent of all school revenues was derived from state sources, whereas in Delaware the figure was as high as 88.2 percent.

As a source of public school revenue at the state level, the property tax has been waning for a third of a century. At the close of World War I, over one-half of all state revenue was derived from this source. Now it constitutes about 3 percent of the total.

During the same period, the states have found rich sources of revenue in a number of nonproperty taxes. The income tax, first introduced in Wisconsin in 1911, is used in 34 states. The gasoline tax, first used in Oregon in 1919, is collected in all states. The general sales tax, now levied in 27 states, is their most important source of state school money. Most states derive taxes from alcoholic beverages, licenses, motor vehicles, and tobacco. In contrast to the property tax, many of the most productive state taxes react quickly to changes in economic conditions.

Like the local districts, the states vary radically in their ability and effort to support education. Differences among states which reach the ratio of four to one stem from disparities in wealth and educational responsibilities.

TABLE 7. Variations Among the States in Ability and Effort to Support Education

	Per Capita Personal Income, 1957[a]	Number of School-Age Children per 1,000 Adults Aged 21–64, 1957[b]	Personal Income Payments (1957) per Pupil Enrolled in Public Elementary and Secondary Schools in 1957–1958[c]	Public School Revenue from State and Local Sources as a Percent of Personal Income Payments, 1957–1958[a]	Estimated Current Expenditure per Pupil in ADA, 1958–1959[e]
Alabama	$1,324	569	$ 5,501	3.3%	$164.00
Alaska		592			520.00
Arizona	1,750	557	7,581	3.9	331.65
Arkansas	1,151	572	4,811	3.8	201.00
California	2,523	422	12,437	4.1	390.00
Colorado	1,996	482	9,821	3.8	355.00
Connecticut	2,821	397	15,038	3.4	380.00
Delaware	2,740	426	17,306	2.4	420.00
Florida	1,836	434	8,367	3.8	295.00
Georgia	1,431	562	5,603	3.5	208.00
Idaho	1,630	562	6,768	3.9	270.00
Illinois	2,447	406	14,334	2.2	410.00
Indiana	2,010	460	9,744	3.5	325.00
Iowa	1,806	466	9,337	3.5	346.00
Kansas	1,787	470	8,389	4.3	330.00
Kentucky	1,372	546	6,700	3.0	205.00
Louisiana	1,566	559	7,404	4.5	330.00

Maine	1,663	482	8,476	2.8	255.00
Maryland	2,156	451	11,728	3.0	366.00
Massachusetts	2,335	390	13,991	2.1	375.00
Michigan	2,141	462	10,998	3.5	375.99
Minnesota	1,850	481	9,686	4.1	358.00
Mississippi	958	618	3,806	3.8	181.00
Missouri	1,940	420	10,691	2.8	335.00
Montana	1,896	511	9,449	4.1	373.00
Nebraska	1,818	453	9,724	2.6	290.00
Nevada	2,423	428	11,113	3.2	410.00
New Hampshire	1,862	441	11,265	3.0	326.00
New Jersey	2,504	384	15,231	2.9	463.00
New Mexico	1,686	656	7,402	4.0	390.00
New York	2,578	367	16,149	3.2	535.00
N. Carolina	1,317	549	5,588	4.3	220.00
N. Dakota	1,435	538	7,191	3.5	310.00
Ohio	2,255	441	11,938	3.0	330.00
Oklahoma	1,619	484	7,180	3.7	279.00
Oregon	1,914	453	9,403	4.5	413.00
Pennsylvania	2,112	409	12,470	2.9	370.00
Rhode Island	1,990	397	13,611	2.4	380.00
S. Carolina	1,180	635	4,785	3.9	215.00
S. Dakota	1,531	515	7,519	3.9	333.00
Tennessee	1,383	507	6,088	3.0	205.00
Texas	1,791	511	8,627	3.5	308.00
Utah	1,694	591	6,713	5.2	280.00

TABLE 7. Variations Among the States in Ability and Effort to Support Education (Continued)

	Per Capita Personal Income, 1957[a]	Number of School-Age Children per 1,000 Adults Aged 21–64, 1957[b]	Personal Income Payments (1957) per Pupil Enrolled in Public Elementary and Secondary Schools in 1957–1958[c]	Public School Revenue from State and Local Sources as a Percent of Personal Income Payments, 1957–1958[d]	Estimated Current Expenditure per Pupil in ADA 1958–1959[e]
Vermont	1,665	497	8,552	4.2	305.00
Virginia	1,660	505	7,873	3.3	245.00
Washington	2,128	472	10,323	5.4	375.00
West Virginia	1,554	539	6,613	3.3	225.00
Wisconsin	1,920	461	11,392	3.4	360.00
Wyoming	2,038	526	8,624	4.0	435.00
United States*	2,027	455	10,350	3.3	340.00

SOURCES: [a] National Education Association, Research Division, *Rankings of the States*, Research Report 1959–R4, April, 1959, p. 29.
[b] *Ibid.*, p. 13.
[c] *Ibid.*, p. 31.
[d] *Ibid.*, p. 24.
[e] *Ibid.*, p. 20.

* Averages for the United States are based on the following figures: Column *a*. 48 states and D.C.; Column *b*. 50 states and D.C.; Column *c*. 49 states and D.C.; Column *d*. 48 states and D.C.; Column *e*. 49 states and D.C.

The amount of wealth states have with which to maintain schools varies tremendously. Per capita personal income payments constitute one measure of a state's ability to finance education. In 1957 the range was from $2821 in Connecticut to $958 in Mississippi, with the average for 48 states and the District of Columbia, $2027. (See Table 7.)

When income is considered in direct relation to school-age population only, similar disparities exist. Some states have disproportionally large numbers of children of school age and less than their share of the nation's income. Others have fewer children in proportion to adults but abundant economic resources. In 1957, 50 states and the District of Columbia had 455 children of school age per 1000 adults aged 21–64. New Mexico with 656 per 1000 wage-earning adults had the largest number of children, whereas New York, at the opposite extreme, had only 367. (See Table 7.) Income payments in New York, with its few children, amounted to $16,149 per pupil enrolled in public schools in 1957–1958, and in New Mexico, with its many children, to only $7402. Mississippi with 618 school-age children per 1000 adults had personal income payments per child of school age of only $3806. (See Table 7.) In other words, some states with low relative ability to support education were responsible for educating nearly twice as many children as other states with more than average financial ability.

The states with the largest number of children in proportion to adults are in rural areas, particularly in the South, and their average financial ability to support schools is low. That this large proportion may be expected to continue in low-income states is indicated by a comparison of the birth rate for high-income and low-income states. In 1948 the birth rate for the nation as a whole was 24.2 per 1000 inhabitants. Among the high-income states, only Montana had a birth rate that was significantly higher than the national average. In all but two of the low-income states the birth rate was higher than the national average.

No blame attaches to the poorer states for their meager school support. They make a greater effort to pay taxes than wealthy states, but they can raise less money. The effort of the states to support education is indicated by the percentage of personal in-

TABLE 8. Estimated Average Salary of Classroom Teachers
in Public Schools, 1958–1959

1. Alaska	$6,400	26. Wisconsin	$4,525
2. New York	6,200	27. Oklahoma	4,500
3. California	6,050	28. Texas	4,410
4. Delaware	5,650	29. Montana	4,400
5. New Jersey	5,530	30. Wyoming	4,300
6. Connecticut	5,350	31. Missouri	4,280
7. Arizona	5,328	32. New Hampshire	4,142
8. Maryland	5,300	33. Kansas	4,138
9. Nevada	5,250	34. Iowa	4,131
10. Washington	5,250	35. Idaho	4,098
11. Michigan	5,150	36. Vermont	3,975
12. Illinois	5,125	37. Virginia	3,900
13. New Mexico	5,085	38. Maine	3,825
14. Oregon	5,000	39. North Carolina	3,770
15. Pennsylvania	5,000	40. Georgia	3,625
16. Florida	4,980	41. West Virginia	3,610
17. Indiana	4,980	42. Nebraska	3,525
18. Massachusetts	4,950	43. Tennessee	3,475
19. Rhode Island	4,925	44. North Dakota	3,450
20. Minnesota	4,850	45. South Dakota	3,400
21. Ohio	4,800	46. Alabama	3,350
49 states	4,775	47. South Carolina	3,305
22. Hawaii	4,700	48. Arkansas	3,270
23. Utah	4,650	49. Kentucky	3,250
24. Louisiana	4,560	50. Mississippi	3,070
25. Colorado	4,525	Puerto Rico	2,050

SOURCE: National Education Association, Research Division, *Rankings of the States*, Research Report 1959–R4, April, 1959, p. 18.

come payments spent for this purpose. In 1957–1958, for 48 states and the District of Columbia the figure was 3.3 percent, with a range from 2.1 percent in Massachusetts to 5.4 percent in Washington. (See Table 7.) Yet in spite of this difference in effort, in 1958–1959 Massachusetts and Washington each raised the same amount ($375) per pupil in average daily attendance. In Mississippi where 3.8 percent of personal income payments was spent for education in 1957–1958 only $181 was raised for average current expenditures per pupil. Even if Mississippi adopted a model tax system and spent all the resulting tax revenues for education, the amount would still fall short of what it takes to finance an average public school program.

Inequalities among states as revealed by current expenditures for schools in 1958–1959 are revealed in Table 7. Expenditure per pupil in average daily attendance ranged from $164 in Alabama to $535 in New York.

Differences in the ability of states to support education show up in differences in educational opportunity. In education, as in other things, we are likely to get what we pay for. Paul R. Mort of Teachers College, Columbia University, points out that, although not the only factor, "money is the best single index on the quality of education."

In tangible factors that lend themselves readily to quantitative measurements, the differences resulting from amount of expenditures are discernible in such items as value of school property, teachers' salaries, and preparation of teachers. In 1949–1950 the average value of public school property per pupil in average daily attendance was nearly six times as great in New York as in Alabama. Low salaries and poor preparation generally go hand in hand. In 1958–1959 the average salaries for classroom teachers were nearly twice as high in California as in Mississippi. (See Table 8.) Among the elementary teachers in California in 1958–1959, 90.9 percent had four years or more of college preparation, while in Mississippi this was true of only 67.1 percent.

Differences among the states also show up in educational achievement. Table 9 shows how the states rank on five points. In general, the states with low per capita income and a high proportion of children to educate have a relatively low educational level among their adult populations. Furthermore, these states are the ones with high rates of military rejections attributable to educational deficiencies.

Not only does a low level of expenditure result in quantitative differences, it also results in qualitative differences in education. Studies to ascertain qualitative differences are still in their infancy. They are complicated by the fact that money alone does not wholly determine the quality of schooling. Superior education

TABLE 9. Differences in Educational Achievement Among the States

	Median School Years Completed by Persons 25 Years of Age and Older, 1950ᵃ	Percent of Population 25 Years Old and Older with Less than Five Years of Schooling, 1950ᵇ	Percent of Population 25 Years Old and Older with at Least Four Years of High School, 1950ᶜ	Percent of Population 25 Years Old and Older with Four or more Years of College, 1950ᵈ	Percent of Selective Service Registrants Disqualified by the Mental Test, Including Those who Failed the Physical as Well as the Mental Test, 1957ᵉ
Alabama	7.9	22.6%	21.0%	3.6%	42.6%
Arizona	10.0	14.2	37.7	7.4	21.4
Arkansas	8.3	19.8	21.2	3.1	32.1
California	11.6	6.8	46.1	8.1	15.9
Colorado	10.9	7.1	42.5	8.1	8.5
Connecticut	9.8	8.9	36.2	7.0	12.1
Delaware	9.8	9.7	33.8	7.3	15.7
Florida	9.6	13.8	34.8	6.3	31.3
Georgia	7.8	24.2	20.4	4.5	37.0
Idaho	10.6	4.5	40.0	5.5	4.7
Illinois	9.3	7.8	34.0	5.9	16.1
Indiana	9.6	6.6	35.1	5.2	11.8
Iowa	9.8	3.9	37.4	5.0	3.6
Kansas	10.2	5.0	39.5	6.0	4.5

Kentucky	8.4	16.8	21.9	3.8	28.7
Louisiana	7.6	28.7	21.6	4.7	38.9
Maine	10.2	6.7	36.9	4.8	11.1
Maryland	8.9	10.9	30.9	7.0	18.3
Massachusetts	10.9	7.9	41.6	7.2	8.9
Michigan	9.9	7.5	34.1	5.3	10.6
Minnesota	9.0	5.8	34.6	5.6	4.2
Mississippi	8.1	25.2	21.5	3.8	49.9
Missouri	8.8	8.4	29.8	5.0	12.0
Montana	10.1	6.3	39.0	6.1	3.5
Nebraska	10.1	4.9	38.5	5.1	5.8
Nevada	11.5	6.8	44.9	7.3	10.9
New Hampshire	9.8	6.3	36.3	6.0	8.4
New Jersey	9.3	9.2	33.9	6.8	19.1
New Mexico	9.3	18.0	34.2	6.9	20.6
New York	9.6	9.5	34.7	7.4	15.4
N. Carolina	7.9	21.1	20.5	5.0	32.4
N. Dakota	8.7	8.8	30.3	4.5	7.1
Ohio	9.9	6.9	35.6	5.7	10.7
Oklahoma	9.1	10.9	33.0	6.2	9.9
Oregon	10.9	4.3	42.0	6.6	4.6
Pennsylvania	9.0	9.4	31.2	5.4	9.5
Rhode Island	9.3	9.7	30.7	5.8	10.9
S. Carolina	7.6	27.4	18.6	5.4	49.8
S. Dakota	8.9	5.8	34.0	4.9	5.3

TABLE 9. Differences in Educational Achievement Among the States (Continued)

	Median School Years Completed by Persons 25 Years of Age and Older, 1950[a]	Percent of Population 25 Years Old and Older with Less than Five Years of Schooling, 1950[b]	Percent of Population 25 Years Old and Older with at Least Four Years of High School, 1950[c]	Percent of Population 25 Years Old and Older with Four or more Years of College, 1950[d]	Percent of Selective Service Registrants Disqualified by the Mental Test, Including Those who Failed the Physical as Well as the Mental Test, 1957[e]
Tennessee	8.4	18.3	24.3	4.1	28.9
Texas	9.3	15.8	29.9	6.0	23.1
Utah	12.0	4.3	48.9	7.6	5.9
Vermont	10.0	5.5	36.6	5.9	10.5
Virginia	8.5	17.5	28.2	6.3	31.9
Washington	11.2	4.7	43.7	7.2	4.8
West Virginia	8.5	13.7	24.5	4.3	23.0
Wisconsin	8.9	7.2	33.1	5.4	6.9
Wyoming	11.1	5.7	43.2	7.1	5.4
United States	9.3	11.0	33.3	6.0	18.9

SOURCES: [a] National Education Association, Research Division, December, 1957, p. 3 (planographed).
[a] Ibid., p. 4.
[b] Ibid. p. 3.
[c] Ibid., p. 4.
[e] Ibid., p. 5.

426

may be had in a classroom financed at a poverty level but presided over by a master teacher, while inferior education may be provided in a magnificent setting dominated by an incompetent teacher.

However, three significant studies designed to ferret out information about the effects of high-level expenditures have shown that the better financed schools are superior to ordinary schools in five different ways.

1. They do a better job with the individual pupil.
2. They provide a better setting for intellectual and character growth.
3. They employ greater realism in the methods of teaching.
4. They offer greater variety in their courses.
5. They show broader evidence of highly skilled teaching.[5]

The Federal Government

In view of inequalities resulting from disparity in the ability of states to maintain schools, a question arises as to the proper role of the federal government in relation to school support. In 1958–1959 the federal government contributed only 3.5 percent to public elementary and secondary schools. Yet, undeniably, some states and communities cannot from their own resources raise enough money to provide a suitable educational program for their children.

The federal government, by providing for a just sharing of the burden, can obtain adequate money for schools. It has already tapped the most lucrative sources of revenue, particularly the tax on personal income. For the nation to tax wealth where it exists and to distribute funds where they are needed is in harmony with sound principles of taxation.

Not only has the federal government taken over some of the most promising sources of revenue, but it has also, through its system of financing certain other governmental functions, reduced the capability of states to support schools. Federal subsidies for such projects as financing of highways and welfare programs re-

[5] "Relation between Cost and Quality in Public Education," *Education Digest*, November, 1958, pp. 29–31. (Reported from *Does Money Make a Difference?* published by Associated Public School Systems, 525 W. 120 St., New York.)

quire matching state funds. Thus these ventures, by their prior claim on state money, drain off dollars that might otherwise be available for public schools.

That the character of education in any segment of the United States affects the entire country becomes evident when we note the high mobility of our population. Thirteen percent of the people in South Carolina and 68 percent in Nevada were not born within those states. During the period 1947–1956 roughly 6.4 percent of the total civilian population moved each year from one county to another within their respective states and 3.2 percent moved from one state to another. From 1950 to 1956 about five million people moved annually from one state to another. These figures bear eloquent testimony to the truth that educational levels in each state are the concern of all the states.

Even before ratification of the Constitution, the federal government adopted the policy of giving financial support to education in the form of land grants. In the Ordinance of 1785 the sixteenth section of every township in the Northwest Territory, then a national possession, was set aside "for the maintenance of public schools within said townships." Two years later the Ordinance of 1787 emphasized that "religion, morality and knowledge being necessary to good government and the happiness of mankind, schools and the means of education shall forever be encouraged."

When Ohio was admitted to the Union the enabling act of 1802 set aside the sixteenth section of land in each township for the support of schools.

From 1802 until 1848 the policy of reserving the sixteenth section of each new township for school support continued. In 1848, when Oregon was organized as a territory, the thirty-sixth section, in addition to the sixteenth, was set aside as land reserved for school use. As other states were admitted they received grants for schools, sometimes as many as four sections in each township. Eventually more than 175 million acres of land from the national domain, an area larger than Indiana, Ohio, and West Virginia combined, were given to the states for education. Some of the land was sold at prices varying from $1.25 an acre to thousands of dollars an acre. Much of the money was wasted through inefficient administration. However, the gifts helped at a time when financial assistance was needed. In 1940 one-third of the land granted was still owned by the states. Other federal grants to aid education included salt and swamp lands.

In these early grants Congress sought to lay the groundwork for a sound public school system available to all the people. It placed no restriction on the states regarding management of the funds.

The Morrill Act of 1862 instituted a definite change in policy. Under the terms of the act, the money was earmarked for a specific purpose—namely, instruction in agriculture and mechanical arts—and was to be spent under certain conditions. Instead of grants in aid to general education, with no federal control over how the money was to be spent by the states, there began to be grants in aid of specified areas of education, with legal stipulations covering the use of the money by the states.

Another shift in policy came with the Smith-Lever Act in 1914, which allotted continued annual appropriations to the states for extension work in agriculture and home-economics. None of the funds went to public schools. For the first time a federal act required each state to match federal funds. The same provision for matching funds was embodied in the Smith-Hughes Act of 1917, which promoted vocational education in public schools and encouraged special education for teachers of vocational education. Exacting requirements as to how the states could use the funds marked another turn in federal policy.

During the depression of the 1930's and in World War II the principle of matching funds was virtually abandoned. Funds were allocated for specific purposes, often without an objective formula and without regard to the relative needs of the states. The Washington bureaus commonly by-passed state departments of education in administering relief programs and sometimes established their own schools which duplicated local schools. Legislation set forth conditions under which funds could be used. For example, federal funds to aid in providing normal terms for schools were available only on condition that the teachers be paid relief wages and not standard salaries. Similar tendencies were shown in the 1930's in the use of WPA funds for nursery school and adult education; in NYA assistance for needy students; and in 1941 in the use of funds under the Lanham Act to provide, among other projects, school buildings for communities adversely affected by federal activities.

Alarmed by the growing federal control of education, Congress strove to have activities in education administered not by the United States Office of Education but by dozens of federal agencies. Of the more than $3.5 billion expended for education in 1949, only 1 percent was under the jurisdiction of the Office of Education. The programs were concerned less with their general effect upon public education than with implementing activities of certain federal agencies.

The present confusion in the administration of federal aid demonstrates that the basic issues are still unresolved. The whole question of the desirability of federal aid touches off a heated debate. At least three distinct points of view persist. Some people oppose federal aid on the ground that it would inevitably spell federal control. They hold steadfastly to the belief that the agencies supplying money would impose the conditions under which it could be spent. With their aversion to such domination, they would forgo assistance, no matter how critically needed. They admit that federal support may seem all right in theory, but they are wary of the loss of local freedom and fear the possibility of controlling the ideology of millions of school children.

Other people recognize a need for federal aid and concede that federal regulation would accompany it. However, they view some control as a judicious safeguard to protect the funds and insure their proper use. They argue that just as the one-time dire predictions by opponents of state aid regarding loss of local initiative and interest failed to materialize, so too will the worst fears of the objectors to federal aid prove groundless.

Still other people admit the need for federal funds but believe that they can be supplied without federal control. They urge that their administration be put in the hands of one federal agency that would deal with all activities involving public education in the states. They believe that the legislation should be carefully drawn to prohibit federal interference. They would have the funds granted for broad general purposes in order to insure a minimum foundation program of elementary and secondary education, the amount received by a state being determined on an objective basis. Furthermore, they would have the federal government require an audit to make certain that statutory standards were complied with and that the money was used for the purpose specified in the act. They believe that these standards would tend to protect the interests of the children but would not subject the schools to any kind of stifling control.

Some but not all of the group who favor federal aid without federal interference would lodge the administration of the funds in the hands of state and local officials, to be used in accordance with the same regulations as govern other school funds. For years this proposal has been resisted by opponents with two divergent points of view. One faction, deeply concerned with upholding the constitutional doctrine of the separation of church and state, insists that the law prohibit the use of federal funds in support of denominational education. The other faction, sincerely concerned with equalizing education, demands that the law require allocation of federal money to private and denominational schools regardless of state policy. For at least three decades division on the issue of making money available to nonpublic schools has been one of the principal blocks in the passage of an expanded federal aid to education bill.

In 1954 another block to the passage of bills for federal aid to education appeared. Since the decisions of the United States Supreme Court ruled that segregated schools are unconstitutional, amendments requiring the states to provide school facilities open to all children regardless of race have been added to federal aid to education bills. The alignment of opponents of desegration against these amendments has doomed the bills to failure.

SUMMARY

Expenditures for education are economically productive. A positive relationship exists between the economic status of countries and educational level. To supply adequate educational opportunities requires ever increasing amounts of money. Three causes for rising school costs are decrease in the purchasing power of the dollar, increase in pupil attendance, and improved educational services and standards. Although the United States can afford generous expenditures for schools, resistance to soaring tax burdens may lead to cuts in funds. Money for school support comes from three levels of government—local, state, and national. The major share is derived from the local unit, usually through a property tax. Glaring inequalities in the ability of local and state governments to support education have led to attempts to secure federal aid. Opponents of federal aid fear that federal control and other hazards might outweigh possible advantages.

QUESTIONS AND EXERCISES

1. Ascertain the sources of school support in your community. How much money does your community spend for its schools in one year?
2. Summarize the arguments for and against federal aid to education. Does the need for federal aid outweigh the possible dangers of federal control?
3. Should public funds be used to support private or religious schools?
4. How should the obligation for school support be divided among local, state, and federal governments?
5. Compare your state with other states and with the national average as far as expenditures for education and effort to support education are concerned.
6. What effect has the downward and upward extension of secondary education had upon school costs?
7. Are all states, regardless of their wealth, entitled to some federal aid?
8. Should federal aid be given to the states entirely, or partly, on an equalization basis?

9. What are the advantages and disadvantages of property taxes as sources of revenue for public schools?
10. How can the local property tax be improved?

SELECTED REFERENCES

Allen, Hollis P., *The Federal Government and Education*, McGraw-Hill Book Company, Inc., 1950.

Fine, Benjamin, *Our Children Are Cheated*, Henry Holt and Company, 1947.

Harris, Seymour E., *How Shall We Pay for Education?* Harper & Brothers, 1948.

Mort, Paul R., and Reusser, Walter C., *Public School Finance*, McGraw-Hill Book Company, Inc., 2nd ed., 1951.

National Education Association and American Association of School Administrators, Educational Policies Commission, *Education and Economic Well-Being in American Democracy*, 1940.

Norton, John K., and Cocking, Walter, *Still Unfinished Business*, National Education Association, 1948.

Rosenstengel, William Everett, and Eastmond, Jefferson N., *School Finance*, The Ronald Press Company, 1957.

AUDIO-VISUAL MATERIALS

Films

Crowded Out (29 minutes, Sound, B & W, or C, National Education Association). The story of what happens to children and teachers when schools are overcrowded.

Education Is Good Business (10 minutes, Sound, B & W, or C, General Picture Productions, Inc.). Shows the relationship between a community's prosperity and the quality of its educational system. Sponsored by Iowa State Education Association.

Pop Rings the Bell (23 minutes, Sound, B & W, National School Service Institute). Stresses the benefits a community derives from its schools.

Right Angle (29 minutes, Sound, B & W, or C, National Education Association). A newspaper reporter discovers that the taxpayers of Groveton are getting full value for their money.

The Sixth Chair (18 minutes, Sound, B & W, National School Service Institute, produced by Jam Handy). Underscores the importance of adequate financial support of schools in a time of a rapidly expanding population. Points up such problems in education as building construction, class size, teacher shortage, and provision of audio-visual materials. Indicates the dangers of public apathy toward education.

Recording

Education, the Foundation of Business (30 minutes, 33⅓ rpm, Educational Recording Services). Willis A. Sutton, Atlanta, Georgia, past president of the National Education Association, appeals for adequate support for education as a means of stimulating business. Points out the relation between the level of education and circulation of newspapers, life insurance, savings accounts, grocery and department store sales.

APPENDIXES

APPENDIXES

Appendix I

MILESTONES IN AMERICAN EDUCATIONAL HISTORY[1]

1617–1622—First educational efforts in English North America: Henrico College and East India School.

1634—First educational endowment in English North America: the will of Benjamin Syms.

1635—Founding of the Boston Latin grammar school, first college preparatory school.

1636—Founding of Harvard, first permanent college in English North America.

1640—Dismissal of Henry Dunster from Harvard presidency because of his views on infant baptism, apparently first academic-freedom case.

1647—Massachusetts act ["Old Deluder Act," which followed the 1642 law ordering that children be taught to read]—First general school law in America.

1693—Founding of College of William and Mary, first permanent college in the South.

1735—Trial of John Peter Zenger, which helped establish principle of freedom of the press.

1750—Publication of Christopher Dock's *Schulordnung*, first book on teaching published in this country. It was in German.

1753—Chartering of Benjamin Franklin's academy, representing the transition between Latin schools and more practical curriculum.

1779—Thomas Jefferson's bill for religious freedom.

1779—Thomas Jefferson's school bill for Virginia, believed to be first plan for a state-wide school system in the Western world.

1785—Chartering of first state university, Georgia.

[1] From 1617–1952: *Journal of the National Education Association*, February, 1953, p. 97. From 1953–1958: *School and Society* publishes a list of the year's outstanding events in American education in each December issue.

1785, 1787—Northwest Ordinances, which marked beginnings of national aid for education.

1795—Opening of first state university, North Carolina.

1795—New York State's act for the encouragement of schools, first state aid to schools.

1812—New York provision for first state superintendent of schools, Gideon Hawley.

1819—Famous Dartmouth College Decision of U.S. Supreme Court, which established inviolability of a college's charter.

1821—Opening of Troy [New York] Seminary by Emma Willard, which along with opening of Georgia Female College in 1835 and Mt. Holyoke [Massachusetts] Seminary in 1837, pioneered in secondary and higher education for women.

1821—First high school in the U.S., Boston.

1826—First collegiate degree to Negro in U.S.—John Russwurm at Bowdoin College.

1827—First state high school law, Massachusetts.

1829—Publication of Samuel R. Hall's *Lectures on School-Keeping*, first book in English on subject of teaching in this country.

1835—Thaddeus Stevens' speech for public-school support in Pennsylvania, perhaps most powerful plea on this subject in nineteenth century.

1837—Provision for first real state board of education, Massachusetts.

1839—Founding of first state normal school, Massachusetts.

1843—Horace Mann's analysis of public-school conditions in his famous Seventh Report.

1845—First state education associations organized in Rhode Island and New York.

1852—Enactment of first compulsory school law, Massachusetts.

1857—Founding of National Teachers' Association, now the National Education Association.

1862—Passage by Congress of Morrill Act, which became the basis of land-grant colleges.

1867—Federal agency now known as the U.S. Office of Education created by Congress.

1867—Establishment by George Peabody of first big philanthropic foundation in U.S.

1873—First public kindergarten in U.S., St. Louis.

1874—Kalamazoo decision by Michigan Supreme Court, which established state's legal right to public funds for high schools.

1876—Opening of Johns Hopkins University, first graduate school in U.S.

1893—Significant report of NEA Committee of Ten, first of a series of NEA reports with far-reaching effects on curriculum and standards.

1897—Founding of organization now known as National Congress of Parents and Teachers.

1923—Formation of World Federation of Education Associations, forerunner of present World Confederation of Organizations of the Teaching Profession.

1925—Oregon decision of U.S. Supreme Court—children of compulsory school age cannot be required to attend *public* schools.

1938—Gaines decision of U.S. Supreme Court—state must offer Negroes educational opportunity within the state equal to that offered white students.

1944, 1952—GI Bill of Rights.

1945—Creation of United Nations Educational, Scientific and Cultural Organization [UNESCO].

1948, 1949—McCollum and Zorach decisions of U.S. Supreme Court on public schools and religious instruction.

1949—Organization of National Citizens' Commission for the Public Schools.

1952—Decisions of the U.S. Supreme Court on Feinberg and Oklahoma loyalty legislation.

1953—Establishment of the Department of Health, Education, and Welfare with a Secretary in the President's Cabinet.

1954—Racial segregation in public schools ruled unconstitutional by a unanimous decision of the U.S. Supreme Court.

1955—White House Conference on Education called by President Eisenhower.

1956—GI Bill of Rights for veterans of World War II terminated in July.

1957—Conference on the American High School sponsored by the University of Chicago in collaboration with the National Citizens Council for Better Schools.

1958—For the fourteenth consecutive year, enrollment in elementary and secondary schools continued to rise. College and university enrollment increased. The National Defense Education Act made possible student loans; graduate fellowships for future college professors; better identification of gifted students; and improved equipment for science, mathematics, and linguistic instruction.

Appendix II

SOURCES OF AUDIO-VISUAL MATERIALS LISTED

Films

Coronet Instructional Films, 65 East Water Street, Chicago 1, Illinois

Encyclopaedia Britannica Films, Inc., 1150 Wilmette Avenue, Wilmette, Illinois

General Picture Productions, Inc., 621 Sixth Avenue, Des Moines 9, Iowa

Indiana University, Audio-Visual Center, Bloomington, Indiana

Jam Handy Organization, 2821 East Grand Boulevard, Detroit 11, Michigan

Mahnke (Carl F.) Productions, 215 East Third Street, Des Moines 9, Iowa

McGraw-Hill Book Company, Inc., Text-Film Department, 330 West 42nd Street, New York 36, New York.

National Education Association, 1201 Sixteenth Street, N.W., Washington 6, D.C.

National School Service Institute, Shop 307, Palmer House, Chicago 3, Illinois

New York University, Film Library, 26 Washington Square, New York 3, New York.

Ohio State University, Department of Photography, Columbus, Ohio

Pennsylvania State University, University Park, Pennsylvania

Princeton University, Department of Public Relations, Box 284, Princeton, New Jersey

United World Films, Inc., 1445 Park Avenue, New York 29, New York

University of Southern California, Audio-Visual Services, Department of Cinema, 3518 University Avenue, Los Angeles 7, California

Filmstrips

National Film Board of Canada, 630 Fifth Avenue, New York 20, New York

Wayne State University, Audio-Visual Materials Consultation Bureau, 438 West Ferry Street, Detroit 2, Michigan

Recordings

Educational Recording Services, 5922 Abernathy Drive, Los Angeles 45, California

Indiana University, Audio-Visual Center, Bloomington, Indiana

Minnesota State Department of Education, St. Paul, Minnesota

National Association of Educational Broadcasters, 630 Fifth Avenue, New York 20, New York

INDEXES

Index of Names

445

Index of Subjects

States—*Continued*
governments of, and education, 392–402
improved organization at level of, 401–402
intermediate units of administration of, 388–389
lay control of education of, 401
legal basis of school system of, 393
professional administration of enterprise of, 401
requirements of, for junior high school teachers, 313–314
retirement laws of, 47–48
support of education by, 392–393
teachers organizations of, 91, 93
Story Parade, 171
Student National Education Association, 64
Student teaching, 80–83
Subject matter, knowledge of, 14
place of, in units, 284–285
in secondary school, 324–325
selection of, 202–205
in Soviet schools, 204–205
Sunday schools, 29, 165, 245
Superintendent of schools, 383–388
intermediate unit and, 389–390
old and new duties of, 390–391
Superman, 171
Supreme Court, antisegregation decision of, 221
Switzerland, unit on community living in, 277–283

Teacher in America, 13
Teachers, aptitudes, personal abilities, and interests of, 28–33
bias in treatment of children by, 144
certification of, 33–35
college, problem of securing, 364–368
in colonial schools, 241, 243
core, 74
demand for, 36
development of social competences of, 83–85
in early high schools, 308
elementary and high school professional courses for, 78
elementary school, replacement requirements for, 37

Teachers—*Continued*
engenderment of professional attitudes in, 86
general health of, 38–39
good, characteristics of, 5–7, 9–10, 11–12, 13, 23–24
graduate program for, 85
high school, 73
hours of work of, 39–40
in-service education of, 111–113
individuality of, 13
in junior or community colleges, 362–363
in junior high school, 313
leaves of absence for, 48
location of positions for, 98–100
location of positions through own efforts, 99
new, induction of, 110–111
organizations for, 90–93
participation of, in extraclass activities, 334
participation of, in policy-making, with superintendent of schools, 386–387
pensions and retirement allowances for, 47–48
personal influence of, 9
personal and social traits of, 8–14
personality of, 298
physical surroundings and health conditions for, 38–39
placement of, 98–114
preservice preparation of, 69–93
preservice selection and guidance of, 66–70
professional ethics of, 86–90
professional preparation of, 14–15
recruitment, 62–66, 94
relationship to pupils, 207–208
restrictions on personal freedom of, 41–43
rural, 29
self-survey for, 20–24
social and professional associates of, 40–41
source of supply of, 62
successful, 15–20
teaching load of, 39–40
tenure of, 48–50
urban, 29
vacations for, 39–40